LEARN TO READ GREEK

LEARN TO READ
GREEK
WORKBOOK
PART 1

Andrew Keller
Collegiate School

Stephanie Russell
Collegiate School

Yale
UNIVERSITY PRESS
New Haven & London

Yale University Press books may be purchased in quantity for educational, business, or promotional use. For information, please e-mail sales. press@yale.edu (U.S. office) or sales@yaleup.co.uk (U.K. office).

PUBLISHER: Mary Jane Peluso
EDITORIAL ASSISTANT: Elise Panza
PROJECT EDITOR: Timothy Shea
PRODUCTION CONTROLLER: Aldo Cupo

Designed by James J. Johnson.
Set in Arno Roman type by Integrated Composition Systems.
Printed in the United States of America.

ISBN: 978-0-300-11591-8 (part 1)   ISBN: 978-0-300-11592-5 (part 2)

This paper meets the requirements of ANSI/NISO Z39.48-1992 (Permanence of Paper).

10 9 8 7 6 5 4 3 2 1

Cover illustration: Rembrandt van Rijn, *Aristotle with a Bust of Homer*, 1653. The Metropolitan Museum of Art, New York. Purchase, special contributions and funds given or bequeathed by friends of the Museum, 1961 (61.198). Image copyright © The Metropolitan Museum of Art.

CONTENTS

PREFACE

This workbook contains drills written to accompany the Introduction and Chapters 1 through 9 of the textbook *Learn to Read Greek* (Part 1). The drill numbers correspond to numbers of sections (§) in the textbook in which morphology and syntax are presented. After almost every section, students are referred to the appropriate drill in the workbook for reinforcement of the forms and syntax just presented. In addition, this workbook contains exercises for each chapter, synthetic Greek sentences for translation that offer substantial practice in the new vocabulary, morphology, and syntax while also reviewing material presented in earlier chapters. The last exercise sentences are in English, and writing them in Greek provides additional reinforcement of forms and syntax and allows students to practice writing clear, correct Greek in plausible Greek word order.

The workbook pages are perforated in order that the drills and exercises may be detached and used for homework assignments. Following the drills and exercises are summaries for each chapter, the first of which is a duplicate of the vocabulary page of the textbook chapter. There are also compact summaries of all the new morphology and syntax. Students should tear out these summaries and use them for study as each chapter is being learned. After the summaries for all nine chapters there are sample synopsis blanks needed for verb synopsis drills that appear throughout the workbook. Students and teachers can tear out and copy these as necessary. The workbook also contains a morphology appendix and Greek to English and English to Greek vocabularies for ready reference.

ABBREVIATIONS

*	indicates that a form is hypothetical
<	(derived) from
>	becomes
§	section
a, p, u	antepenult, penult, ultima
acc.	accusative
act.	active
adj.	adjective
adv.	adverb
aor.	aorist
conj.	conjunction
d.a.	direct address
d.o.	direct object
dat.	dative
demonstr.	demonstrative
e.g.	exempli gratia, for example
etc.	et cetera, and the remaining things
exclam.	exclamatory
f.	feminine
fem.	feminine
fut.	future
gen.	genitive
i.e.	id est, that is
i.o.	indirect object
imperf.	imperfect
indef.	indefinite
indic.	indicative

infin.	infinitive
interj.	interjection
interrog.	interrogative
intrans.	intransitive
m.	masculine
masc.	masculine
mid.	middle
n.	neuter
neut.	neuter
nom.	nominative
part.	participle
pass.	passive
perf.	perfect
pl.	plural
pluperf.	pluperfect
poss.	possessive
pred.	predicate
prep.	preposition
pres.	present
prin.	principal
pron.	pronoun
rel.	relative
sing.	singular
subj.	subject
suppl.	supplementary
subst.	substantive
trans.	transitive
voc.	vocative

Drill 2: The Alphabet and Pronunciation; Consonants, Vowels, Diphthongs, Iota Subscripts and Adscripts; Rough and Smooth Breathings; Punctuation; Syllabification

A. Next to the given model write each capital letter several times.

A _____

B _____

Γ _____

Δ _____

E _____

Z _____

H _____

Θ _____

I _____

K _____

Λ _____

M _____

N _____

Ξ _____

O _____

Π _____

Ρ _____

Σ _____

C _____

Τ _____

Υ _____

Φ _____

Χ _____

Ψ _____

Ω _____

B. Next to the given model write each lowercase letter several times. Try to make as many of the letters as possible with only one stroke of the pen—to make a **β** with one stroke, for example, start at the tail at the bottom.

α _____

β _____

γ _____

δ _____

ε _____

ζ _____

η _____

θ _____

ι _____

κ _____

λ _____

μ _____

ν _____

ξ _____

ο _____

π _____

ρ _____

σ _____

ς _____

c _____

τ _____

υ _____

φ _____

χ _____

ψ _____

ω _____

C. Recite the Greek alphabet from memory.

D. Pronounce the following words. Where an accent mark (´, `, or ^) appears above a letter, stress that syllable slightly.

1. βάρβαρος	βάπτω	βάς	βίᾱ
2. Βαβυλωνίᾱ	Βάρκη	Βάκχος	Βυζάντιον
3. γε	γέρων	γῆρας	γλίσχρος
4. Γέλων	Γῆ	Γοργίᾱς	Γοργώ
5. τέγγω	πάγκαλος	λόγχη	σφίγξ
6. συγκομίζω	λύγξ	συγγενής	τυγχάνω
7. διά	δῆμος	διαγιγνώσκω	δόξα
8. Δημήτηρ	Δῆλος	Διομήδης	Δρακοντίδης
9. ζέω	ζημίᾱ	ζηλόω	ζωγράφος
10. Ζάκυνθος	Ζάν	Ζέφυρος	Ζωστήρ
11. θάλαττα	θάνατος	θεός	θνητός
12. Θέμις	Θεμιστοκλῆς	Θρασύμαχος	Θρασυμηλίδᾱς
13. κατά	κάθαρσις	κρίνω	κόπτω
14. Κάδμος	Καλλίμαχος	Κλωθώ	Κνωσός
15. λέγω	λήθη	λιγυηχής	λῑμός
16. Λαέρτης	Λᾱομεδοντιάδης	Λοξίᾱς	Λῡσιστράτη
17. μετά	μήτηρ	μνῆμα	μοναρχίᾱ
18. Μέγαρα	Μενέλᾱος	Μνημοσύνη	Μυτιλήνη
19. νεκρόπολις	νέκταρ	νόμος	νυμφόληπτος
20. Νεοπτόλεμος	Νέστωρ	Νῑκίᾱς	Νότος
21. ξανθός	ξενίᾱ	ξεστός	ξίφος
22. Ξανθίππη	Ξάνθος	Ξενοφῶν	Ξέρξης
23. παρά	πατήρ	πίστις	πρόβλημα
24. Πάρις	Περσεφόνη	Πρίαμος	Πῡθώ
25. σανδάλιον	σκέλος	σοφός	σύστημα
26. Σαπφώ	Σικελίᾱ	Σκάμανδρος	Σπάρτη
27. σύν	σκεπτικός	σπονδή	συλλήβδην
28. Σαλαμίς	Σίβυλλα	Σοφοκλῆς	Σωκρατίδιον
29. πρεσβύτης	μίσγω	δυσγενής	μίασμα
30. σμάραγδος	σβέννῡμι	Πελασγικός	Λέσβος
31. τάφος	τέλος	τετράγωνον	τῑμάω
32. Τάνταλος	Τάρταρος	Τισσαφέρνης	Τρώικος
33. φημί	φιλανθρωπίᾱ	φῑτύω	φῡσάω
34. Φερσέφασσα	Φθίᾱ	Φιλοκτήτης	Φρυγίᾱ
35. χάρισμα	χθών	χορός	χρῡσεοσάνδαλος
36. Χάος	Χίος	Χρέμων	Χρῡσόπολις
37. ψηφίζω	ψῑλός	ψοφομήδης	ψῡχρός
38. Ψαμμήτιχος	Ψάρος	Ψῆττα	Ψῡχή

E. Divide the following words into syllables.

Example: συν/τυ/χόν/τας

1. Κάδμος
2. πάλαι
3. Ἅιδης
4. μοῖρα
5. γέμει
6. ὁμοῦ
7. παρά
8. πόλις
9. οἰκίᾱ
10. ἑταῖρος
11. παιάνων
12. θάνατος
13. θοάζετε
14. στενάγματα
15. δυσάλγητος
16. κρατύνων
17. Λακεδαιμόνιος
18. Ἀθηναῖος
19. δείσαντες
20. σθένοντες
21. Θουκυδίδης
22. ἀτερπέστερον
23. Πελοποννησίων
24. εἰσκαταβαίνω
25. εἰρωνείᾱ
26. εὐδαιμονίᾱ

F. Fill in the blanks.

1. A Greek word has as many syllables as it has _____.

2. Only the last _____ syllables of a Greek word may be accented.

3. The names of the last three syllables are:

last _____

second to last _____

third to last _____

G. Pronounce the following words. Slightly stress any syllable where an accent mark (´, `, or ^) appears.

1. ἀγαθός	ἄγκῡρα	ἀδελφός	ἀθλητής
2. ἁβρός	ἅγιος	ἄζομαι	ἅλλομαι
3. ἀδολέσχης	ἆθλον	ἀήρ	ἄκων
4. ἁλίζω	ἁμός	ἄνδρες	ἆσσον
5. Ἄδωνις	Ἀθῆναι	Ἀκαδήμεια	Ἀλέξανδρος
6. Ἁλιαῖος	Ἁλῶα	Ἁρμόδιος	Ἄγις
7. αἰαῖ	αἰγίς	αἶνος	αἴρω
8. αἷμα	αἱμύλος	αἵρεσις	αἱρετικός
9. Αἴᾱς	Αἴγυπτος	Αἰνείᾱς	Αἶα
10. Αἵμων	Αἱμονίδης	Αἴσωπος	Αἰσχύλος
11. ᾄδω	ἀγορᾷ	Θρᾴκη	λάθρᾳ
12. Ἅιδης	ᾀδοφοῖται	βίᾳ	ῥᾴδιος
13. ἐγώ	ἐθίζω	ἔλεγχος	ἔρως
14. ἕδρᾱ	ἑκατόν	ἑρμηνείᾱ	ἕτερος
15. Ἐπιμηθεύς	Ἐπίδαυρος	Ἔρις	Ἔφεσος
16. Ἑκάβη	Ἕκτωρ	Ἑλένη	Ἑρμῆς
17. εἴδωλον	εἶεν	εἰρωνείᾱ	εἰσκαταβαίνω
18. εἷς	εἱμαρμένος	εἷλον	εἷμα
19. Εἵλώτης	Εἰλείθυια	Εἰρέτρια	Εἰρήνη
20. εὐδαιμονίᾱ	εὕδω	εὖγε	εὔνοια
21. βασιλεύς	ψεῦδος	παιδεύω	σκευάζω
22. Εὔβοια	Εὐκλείδης	Εὔμαχος	Εὐμενίδες
23. ἤδη	ἧκα	ἤπειρος	ἠώς
24. ἥδομαι	ἧλιξ	ἥλιος	ἡμέρᾱ
25. Ἡετίων	Ἧλις	Ἠρίδανος	Ἠχώ
26. Ἥβη	Ἡρακλέης	Ἡσίοδος	Ἥφαιστος
27. ἥκαζον	ἧσαν	ἥρημαι	ἥρηκεν
28. ηὔδᾱ	ηὐξήθη	ηὗρον	ηὑρέθην
29. ἰᾱτρός	ἴκταρ	ἴον	ἰσοσκελής
30. ἶβις	ἰός	ἵς	ἷδος
31. ἱδρύω	ἱερεύς	ἵππος	ἱστορίᾱ
32. ἵκω	ἵμερος	ἷζον	ἱκετεύω
33. Ἰνδοί	Ἰθάκη	Ἴσθμια	Ἴακχος
34. Ἴλιον	Ἰνώ	Ἶρις	Ἶδᾱ
35. Ἱέρων	Ἱμέρᾱ	Ἵμερος	Ἴφιτος
36. ὀδούς	ὀδύνη	ὀφθαλμός	ὄφις
37. ὅδε	ὁμολογῶ	ὁρῶ	ὅρκους
38. Ὀδυσσεύς	Ὀρέστης	Ὀτάνης	Ὀρτυγί
39. οἰκίᾱ	οἶκος	οἴμοι	οἶνος
40. Οἰδίπους	Οἰνεύς	Οἰνόμαος	Οἰταῖοι
41. οὖδας	οὐδέποτε	οὐλόμενον	οὐσίᾱ

42. οὕνεκα	οὗτος	οὑμός	οὐκ
43. οἷος	Ὅμηρος	Οὐρανός	Οὐκαλέγων
44. ῥάβδος	ῥέγκω	ῥῑπή	ῥυθμός
45. Ῥαδάμανθυς	Ῥαμνοῦς	Ῥέᾱ	Ῥόδος
46. ὕμνος	ὑπέρ	ὑμεῖς	ὗς
47. Ὕλλος	Ὑρκάνιοι	Ὑστάσπης	Ὑψήνωρ
48. ὠδίνω	ὦπται	ὠφέλιμος	ὤψ
49. ὠθέω	ὠκυδρόμος	ὥρᾱ	ὥσπερ
50. Ὠκεανός	Ὠρείθυια	Ὠρίων	Ὦτος
51. ᾠδή	νήσῳ	Ὠιδεῖον	δῴη

H. Pronounce the following words. Slightly stress any syllable where an accent mark (´, `, or ˆ) appears.

1. βρεκεκεκὲξ κοὰξ κοάξ   2. ὀτοτοτοτοῖ

3. ἰοὺ ἰού   4. βαβαιάξ

5. ξυνταλαιπωρήσομεν   6. καταψευδομαρτυρηθείη

7. γλισχραντιλογεξεπίτριπτος   8. Νεφελοκοκκῡγίᾱ

9. περικονδυλοπωροφίλα   10. ψαμμακοσιογάργαρα

I. Pronounce the following short sentences.

1. γνῶθι σαυτόν. (Plato, *Protagoras* 343b3)

2. δὶς παῖδες οἱ γέροντες. (Aristophanes, *Clouds* 1417)

3. μηδὲν ἄγᾱν. (Euripides, *Hippolytus* 265)

4. ψῡχὴ πᾶσα ἀθάνατος. (Plato, *Phaedrus* 245c5)

5. νόμος ὁ πάντων βασιλεύς
   θνᾱτῶν τε καὶ ἀθανάτων . . . (Pindar, frag. 169, 1–2)

J. Read the following passages out loud.

1. Θουκυδίδης Ἀθηναῖος ξυνέγραψε τὸν πόλεμον τῶν Πελοποννησίων καὶ Ἀθηναίων, ὡς ἐπολέμησαν πρὸς ἀλλήλους, ἀρξάμενος εὐθὺς καθισταμένου καὶ ἐλπίσᾱς μέγαν τε ἔσεσθαι καὶ ἀξιολογώτατον τῶν προγεγενημένων, τεκμαιρόμενος ὅτι ἀκμάζοντές τε ἦσαν ἐς αὐτὸν ἀμφότεροι παρασκευῇ τῇ πάσῃ καὶ τὸ ἄλλο Ἑλληνικὸν ὁρῶν ξυνιστάμενον πρὸς ἑκατέρους, τὸ μὲν εὐθύς, τὸ δὲ καὶ διανοούμενον. κίνησις γὰρ αὕτη μεγίστη δὴ τοῖς Ἕλλησιν ἐγένετο καὶ μέρει τινὶ τῶν βαρβάρων, ὡς δὲ εἰπεῖν καὶ ἐπὶ πλεῖστον ἀνθρώπων. (Thucydides, *Histories* I.1)

2. καὶ ἐς μὲν ἀκρόᾱσιν ἴσως τὸ μὴ μυθῶδες αὐτῶν ἀτερπέστερον φανεῖται· ὅσοι δὲ βουλήσονται τῶν τε γενομένων τὸ σαφὲς σκοπεῖν καὶ τῶν μελλόντων ποτὲ αὖθις κατὰ τὸ ἀνθρώπινον τοιούτων καὶ παραπλησίων ἔσεσθαι, ὠφέλιμα κρίνειν αὐτὰ ἀρκούντως ἕξει. κτῆμά τε ἐς αἰεὶ μᾶλλον ἢ ἀγώνισμα ἐς τὸ παραχρῆμα ἀκούειν ξύγκειται. (Thucydides, *Histories* I.22)

K. On a separate sheet of lined paper, copy the following passages, writing on every other line. Be sure to copy all long marks, accents, breathings, and subscripts. After copying each passage, read it out loud.

1. Πολλάκις ἐθαύμασα τίσι ποτὲ λόγοις Ἀθηναίους ἔπεισαν οἱ γραψάμενοι Σωκράτην ὡς ἄξιος εἴη θανάτου τῇ πόλει. ἡ μὲν γὰρ γραφὴ κατ' αὐτοῦ τοιάδε τις ἦν· Ἀδικεῖ Σωκράτης οὓς μὲν ἡ πόλις νομίζει θεοὺς οὐ νομίζων, ἕτερα δὲ καινὰ δαιμόνια εἰσφέρων· ἀδικεῖ δὲ καὶ τοὺς νέους διαφθείρων. (Xenophon, *Memorabilia* I.1.1)

2. ὦ χαῖρε λαμπτὴρ νυκτός, ἡμερήσιον
   φάος πιφαύσκων καὶ χορῶν κατάστασιν
   πολλῶν ἐν Ἄργει τῆσδε συμφορᾶς χάριν.
   ἰοὺ ἰού·
   Ἀγαμέμνονος γυναικὶ σημαίνω τορῶς
   εὐνῆς ἐπαντείλασαν ὡς τάχος δόμοις
   ὀλολυγμὸν εὐφημοῦντα τῇδε λαμπάδι
   ἐπορθιάζειν, εἴπερ Ἰλίου πόλις
   ἑάλωκεν, ὡς ὁ φρυκτὸς ἀγγέλων πρέπει· (Aeschylus, *Agamemnon* 22–30)

Drill 3: Accentuation 1: The Possibilities of Accent

A. Fill in the blanks.

1. List the three kinds of accents and show how each is written:

_____   _____

_____   _____

_____   _____

2. If an antepenult is accented, the accent must be _____ , and the

ultima must be _____ .

3. A circumflex may/may not (circle one) appear over a short vowel.

4. If a penult is long and is to be accented with a circumflex, the ultima must be long/short (circle one).

5. A grave accent may appear only over the _____ and only

when _____ .

B. Write down from memory the six rules for the possibilities of accent.

1. _____

2. _____

3. _____

4. _____

5. _____

6. _____

C. Applying the rules above, for each word place the correct accent on the indicated syllable.

Example: φρονησις (antepenult)   **φρόνησις**

1. παιδα (penult)   2. θανατος (antepenult)

3. ἐπιστημη (penult)   4. λογους (penult)

5. μητηρ (penult)   6. ἱππον (penult)

7. κατηγορος (antepenult)   8. τειχος (penult)

9. συνουσιᾱ (penult)   10. πρᾱγματα (antepenult)

11. θηριον (penult)   12. πληθος (penult)

D. Applying the rules above, cross out the incorrectly accented word in each pair and state why the accent is not possible.

Example: **ἀνὰγκη, ἀνάγκη** The grave accent appears only over the ultima (rule 1).

1. θεός, θεὸς _____

2. κίνδῡνου, κινδῡ́νου _____

3. οἴκος, οἶκος _____

4. σοφίᾱ, σόφιᾱ _____

5. ἡμε̂ρᾱν, ἡμέρᾱν _____

6. Σῶκρατες, Σώκρατες _____

7. πεῖρα, πείρα _____

8. στρατηγοῦ, στράτηγου _____

9. ἀπόλῡετε, ἀπολῡ́ετε _____

10. πόνους, πὸνους _____

11. χαίρε, χαῖρε _____

12. ἐγέγραφει, ἐγεγράφει _____

E. In the following phrases and sentences, circle the incorrect accents and explain why they are incorrect. Then rewrite the phrase with the correct accents.

1. ἀλλὰ τούς θεούς διὰ τά τούτων αὐτά σημαίνειν ...

_____

_____

2. οὐδὲ τά περί τῆς δίκης ἄρα ἐπύθεσθε ὅν τρόπον ἐγένετο;

_____

_____

3. ἅ μὲν μαθόντας ποιεῖν ἔδοσαν οἱ θεοὶ, μανθάνειν ...

_____

_____

Drill 5: Persistent Accent

A. Write down from memory the six rules for the possibilities of accent.

1. _____

2. _____

3. _____

4. _____

5. _____

6. _____

B. The persistent accent for each of these nouns is given by the first form. Observing the rules for the possibilities of accent, correctly accent the other forms in each series. Assume a pause at the end of each word. Be ready to explain your answers.

1. νόμος	νομοις	νομον	νομου
2. ὄνομα	ὀνοματα	ὀνοματων	ὀνοματος
3. θάλαττα	θαλατταν	θαλαττῃ	θαλατταις
4. τέχνη	τεχνης	τεχνην	τεχνᾱς
5. ῥήτωρ	ῥητορα	ῥητορων	ῥητορ
6. Γαῖα	Γαιᾱς	Γαιαν	Γαιᾳ
7. πρᾶγμα	πρᾱγματι	πρᾱγμασι	πρᾱγματων
8. φιλοσοφίᾱ	φιλοσοφιᾳ	φιλοσοφιᾱν	φιλοσοφιᾱς
9. υἱός	υἱοι	υἱον	υἱους
10. σπονδή	σπονδαι	σπονδᾱς	σπονδην
11. πῆμα	πηματων	πηματα	πημασιν
12. Παλλάς	Παλλαδος	Παλλαδα	Παλλαδι

13. τέκνον	τεκνα	τεκνοις	τεκνου
14. ζεῦγος	ζευγους	ζευγει	ζευγη
15. Ἄτλας	Ἀτλαντος	Ἀτλαντα	Ἀτλαντι
16. ἄγγελος	ἀγγελε	ἀγγελον	ἀγγελῳ
17. βίος	βιοις	βιου	βιον
18. μοῦσα	μουσᾶς	μουσαις	μουσαν
19. δῶρον	δωρα	δωρου	δωροις
20. ἀρετή	ἀρετᾶς	ἀρετην	ἀρεται
21. γένος	γενη	γενους	γενεσιν
22. γεωργός	γεωργοι	γεωργους	γεωργε
23. μοῖρα	μοιρᾶς	μοιραν	μοιρᾳ
24. στάδιον	σταδια	σταδιου	σταδιοις
25. Ἀλέξανδρος	Ἀλεξανδρου	Ἀλεξανδρε	Ἀλεξανδρον
26. οἶνος	οινον	οινων	οινοις
27. χρῆμα	χρηματι	χρηματα	χρηματων
28. Φοῖβος	Φοιβου	Φοιβῳ	Φοιβε
29. πόνος	πονου	πονῳ	πονον
30. Κυθέρεια	Κυθερειᾶς	Κυθερειαν	Κυθερειᾳ

Drill 6: The Greek Noun

Fill in the blanks.

1. The three properties of the Greek noun are _____ , _____ , and

    _____ .

2. Recite from memory the names of the five cases of the Greek noun in order. Then write next to each abbreviation the full name of each case and its basic function(s).

Nom. _____

Gen. _____

Dat. _____

Acc. _____

Voc. _____

3. The idea of means or instrument is expressed in Greek by the _____ case and

    is translated with the English prepositions _____ or _____ . In Greek a preposition would/

    would not (circle one) be used.

4. Greek uses the _____ case to express the subject of a sentence.

5. "From" indicates an idea of _____ and is expressed

    in Greek by the _____ case.

6. In the sentence "The girl will become a woman" the syntax of *woman* would be _____

    _____ .

7. Location in space or time is expressed in Greek by the _____ case.

8. The direct object of a verb appears in Greek in the _____ case.

9. In the sentence "I am going toward the city," the word *city* would be expressed in Greek by the

   _____ case and would/would not (circle one) be preceded by a preposition.

10. In the phrase "the horses of Achilles" the syntax of *of Achilles* in Greek would be _____

    _____.

11. "To" and "for" are English prepositions that would be used to translate a Greek noun in the

    _____ case whose syntax is _____ .

12. The vocative case is used for _____ .

Drill 7–8: The Three Declensions; The First Declension

A. Fill in the blanks.

1. There are _____ families of nouns in Greek, and they are called

   _____ .

2. A full vocabulary entry for a Greek noun contains four elements:

   _____

   _____

   _____

   _____

3. Nouns ending in -ᾱ, -ᾱς or -η, -ης in their vocabulary entries belong to the_____
   declension.

4. When one generates a complete set of forms of a noun, one is said to _____
   that noun.

5. To find the stem of most Greek nouns _____

   _____ .

6. Most nouns of the first declension are _____ in gender. Some are_____ ,

   and there are no _____ nouns in the first declension.

7. The accent on nouns is persistent, but one additional rule of accent for all first-declension nouns is that

   in the genitive plural _____

   _____ .

8. The -αι ending in the nominative/vocative plural of all first-declension nouns counts as _____

for purposes of accent.

9. If a first-declension noun has an acute accent on the ultima in the nominative/vocative singular, the ac-

cent on the ultima in the genitive and dative singular and plural is a _____ .

10. In Attic Greek, long alpha remained in first-declension nouns whose stems end in _____ ,

_____ , and _____ . For all other nouns long alpha changed

to _____ .

B. Recite from memory all the endings singular and plural for long-alpha nouns of the first declension.

C. On a separate sheet decline fully **συμφορά** and **χώρᾱ**. Decline **σοφίᾱ** in the singular only.

D. Recite from memory all the endings singular and plural for eta nouns of the first declension.

E. On a separate sheet decline fully **βουλή** and **γνώμη**. Decline Ἑλένη in the singular only.

F. Write these forms in Greek.

Example: gen. sing. of δίκη   **δίκης**

1. dat. pl. of μάχη _____   2. acc. sing. of εἰρήνη _____

3. voc. sing. of Ἑλένη _____   4. gen. pl. of οἰκίᾱ _____

5. gen. sing. of βουλή _____   6. acc. pl. of γνώμη _____

7. voc. pl. of ψῡχή _____   8. dat. sing. of ἀγορά _____

9. nom. pl. of χώρᾱ _____   10. gen. pl. of δίκη _____

11. acc. sing. of σοφίᾱ _____

12. nom. pl. of γνώμη _____

13. gen. sing. of οἰκίᾱ _____

14. dat. sing. of συμφορά̄ _____

15. acc. pl. of δίκη _____

16. dat. sing. of Ἑλένη _____

17. gen. sing. of εἰρήνη _____

18. nom. pl. of μάχη _____

19. acc. sing. of ἀγορά̄ _____

20. gen. pl. of χώρᾱ _____

G. Identify each form by case, number, and gender; then translate. Give all possibilities.

Example: χώρᾱν   **acc. sing. fem. "country (d.o.)"**

1. βουλῆς _____

2. συμφοραῖς _____

3. εἰρήνη _____

4. ψῡχαί _____

_____

5. οἰκιῶν _____

6. γνώμᾱς _____

7. σοφίᾳ _____

8. Ἑλένη _____

_____

9. χώρᾱς _____

_____

10. ἀγορά̄ν _____

11. ψῡχῇ _____

12. γνῶμαι _____

13. σοφίᾱν _____

14. μαχῶν _____

15. εἰρήνην _____

16. οἰκίᾱς _____

_____

17. χώρᾱ _____

_____

18. Ἑλένης _____

19. ἀγορᾷ _____

20. μάχῃ _____

H. Write in Greek.

1. for a country _____ 2. of souls _____

3. Helen! (d.a.) _____ 4. of peace _____

5. opinion (d.o.) _____ 6. lands (subj.) _____

7. for Helen _____ 8. by misfortune _____

9. of houses _____ 10. peace (subj.) _____

11. by means of justice _____ 12. circumstances (d.o.) _____

13. council (d.o.) _____   14. with wisdom _____

15. of a misfortune _____   16. Helen (d.o.) _____

17. by opinions _____   18. soul (d.o.) _____

19. with peace _____   20. battles (d.o.) _____

I. Give the full vocabulary entry for these nouns.

Example: soul   ψῡχή, ψῡχῆς, ἡ

1. disaster _____

2. peace _____

3. house _____

4. council _____

5. Helen _____

6. wisdom _____

7. marketplace _____

8. opinion _____

9. land _____

10. battle _____

11. justice _____

12. soul _____

Drill 9: The Second Declension

A. Fill in the blanks.

1. Neuter nouns of the second declensions have _____ as the ending in the nominative and accusative singular.

2. The final **-οι** in the nominative/vocative plural of all masculine/feminine second-declension nouns counts as _____ for purposes of accent.

3. The nominative, vocative, and accusative plural ending for neuter second-declension nouns is _____.

4. If a masculine/feminine second-declension noun has an acute accent on the ultima in the nominative singular, the accent on the ultima in the genitive and dative singular and plural is a _____.

5. The vocative singular ending for masculine/feminine second-declension nouns is _____.

B. Recite from memory all the endings, singular and plural, for masculine/feminine nouns of the second declension.

C. On a separate sheet decline fully **πόλεμος, ἑταῖρος**, and **ὁδός**.

D. Recite from memory all the endings, singular and plural, for neuter nouns of the second declension.

E. On a separate sheet decline fully **ἔργον** and **ζῷον**.

F. Write these forms in Greek.

Example: dat. sing. of λόγος   **λόγῳ**

1. gen. pl. of θεός _____

2. acc. sing. of ἑταῖρος _____

3. acc. pl. of ἔργον _____

4. voc. sing. of Πρίαμος _____

5. dat. pl. of ὅπλον _____

6. nom. pl. of νόμος _____

7. dat. sing. of ὁδός _____

8. voc. pl. of τέκνον _____

9. gen. sing. of ζῷον _____

10. dat. pl. of τέκνον _____

11. gen. sing. of νῆσος _____

12. voc. pl. of ἄνθρωπος _____

13. acc. sing. of ὅπλον _____

14. gen. pl. of λόγος _____

15. acc. pl. of νόμος _____

16. gen. sing. of πόλεμος _____

17. dat. sing. of Ἀλέξανδρος _____

18. nom. pl. of ζῷον _____

19. voc. sing. of ἑταῖρος _____

20. dat. pl. of ἔργον _____

G. Identify each form by case, number, and gender; then translate. Give all possibilities.

Example: Πρίαμε   **voc. sing. masc. Priam (d.a.)**

1. πολέμους _____

2. λόγῳ _____

3. ἑταῖροι _____

_____

4. ζῷα _____

_____

_____

5. θεόν _____

6. τέκνων _____

7. ἀνθρώπου _____

8. ὁδοῖς _____

9. Πριάμῳ _____

10. ἔργον _____

_____

_____

11. νόμον _____

12. Ἀλεξάνδρου _____

13. ὅπλοις _____

14. τέκνα _____

_____

_____

15. νῆσον _____

16. ἑταίρου _____

17. πολέμων _____

18. ἄνθρωποι _____

_____

19. Ἀλέξανδρε _____

20. ὁδόν _____

H. Write in Greek.

1. of words _____   2. man (d.a.) _____

3. roads (d.o.) _____   4. by customs _____

5. companions (subj.) _____   6. of a child _____

7. for gods _____   8. of animals _____

9. for Alexander _____   10. with weapons _____

11. Priam (d.a.) _____   12. islands (d.o.) _____

13. war (d.o.) _____   14. by a deed _____

15. of men _____   16. Alexander (d.a.) _____

17. companions (d.o.) _____   18. for Priam _____

19. of wars _____   20. a god (d.o.) _____

I. Give the full vocabulary entry for these nouns.

Example: tool; weapon   **ὅπλον, ὅπλου, τό**

1. god; goddess _____

2. custom, law _____

3. child _____

4. Priam _____

5. war _____

6. deed _____

7. human being _____

8. companion _____

9. animal _____

10. road _____

11. word _____

12. Alexander _____

13. island _____

14. weapon _____

Drill 10: The Article

A. Recite from memory all the forms of the article in Greek.

B. Fill in the blanks.

1. The four forms of the article that have a rough breathing and no accent are _____,

_____, _____, and _____ .

2. A word lacking an accent that is pronounced closely with the word that follows it is called a

_____ .

3. The only form of the article that has a macron is _____ . Its gender, number, and case are

_____, _____, _____ .

4. All the genitive and dative singular and plural forms of the article are accented with a _____ .

5. Whenever a form of the article with an acute accent is followed by another word, the acute accent

_____ .

6. An article always agrees with its noun in _____, _____,

and _____ .

C. On a separate sheet decline fully ἡ ψῡχή, ὁ λόγος, and τὸ ὅπλον. Write the interjection ὦ before vocative forms.

D. Write in front of each of the following nouns all possible forms of the article with accent. Write the interjection ὦ before vocative forms.

Example:_____ σοφίᾱ   **ἡ, ὦ σοφίᾱ**

1. _____ γνώμᾱς   2. _____ συμφορῶν

3. _____ πολέμῳ   4. _____ ἑταῖρε

5. _____ ὅπλα   6. _____ νῆσον

7. _____ χῶραι   8. _____ εἰρήνην

9. _____ βουλῆς   10. _____ λόγοις

11. _____ ζῷον   12. _____ οἰκίᾱς

13. _____ ὁδῷ   14. _____ θεούς

15. _____ ἔργων   16. _____ δίκη

17. _____ Ἑλένη   18. _____ ψῡχαῖς

19. _____ ἄνθρωποι   20. _____ Ἀλεξάνδρου

21. _____ νήσῳ   22. _____ νόμον

Drill 11: Uses of the Article; The Attributive Position

Translate each phrase. Underline any words appearing in the attributive position.

Example: τοὺς <u>ἐν τῇ οἰκίᾳ</u> ἀνθρώπους   **(the) men in the house (d.o.)**

1. αἱ τῶν ἀνθρώπων ψῡχαί _____

2. ἐκ τῆς βουλῆς _____

3. τοῖς τῶν θεῶν τέκνοις _____

4. τὰς συμφορὰς τὰς ἐν τῇ χώρᾳ _____

5. οἱ ἄνθρωποι καὶ οἱ θεοί _____

6. καὶ λόγῳ καὶ ἔργῳ _____

7. τῷ τοῦ Πριάμου ἑταίρῳ _____

8. τὰ ζῷα καὶ τοὺς ἀνθρώπους _____

9. τῇ ὁδῷ τῇ ἐκ τῆς χώρᾱς _____

10. ὦ Ἑλένη _____

11. οἱ ἄνθρωποι οἱ ἐν τῇ βουλῇ _____

12. τὰς τῶν ἀνθρώπων γνώμᾱς τὰς περὶ τῆς ψῡχῆς _____

_____

13. τὰς οἰκίᾱς τὰς τῶν θεῶν _____

14. τῶν ὅπλων τῶν Ἀλεξάνδρου _____

15. καὶ ὁ πόλεμος καὶ ἡ εἰρήνη _____

16. τῇ σοφίᾳ Ἑλένης _____

17. εἰς τὴν μάχην σὺν ὅπλοις _____

18. οἱ τοῦ Ἀλεξάνδρου ἑταῖροι _____

19. σὺν τοῖς θεοῖς _____

20. τὸν ἐν τῇ ἀγορᾷ ἄνθρωπον _____

21. περὶ τῶν λόγων τῆς θεοῦ _____

22. τοῖς ἐν ταῖς νήσοις ἀνθρώποις _____

Exercises, Chapter 1

A. Translate these prepositional phrases.

1. ἐν ἀγορᾷ _____

2. περὶ τὰς τῶν ἀνθρώπων συμφοράς _____

3. εἰς τὴν Πριάμου χώρᾱν _____

4. τὴν βουλὴν περὶ πολέμου καὶ εἰρήνης _____

5. σὺν δίκῃ _____

6. ἐκ τῆς οἰκίᾱς τῆς Ἑλένης _____

7. ἐξ ἀγορᾶς _____

8. εἰς τὴν ὁδὸν ξὺν τοῖς τέκνοις _____

9. τοὺς ἐν ὁδῷ ἑταίρους _____

10. σὺν τῇ θεῷ _____

11. περὶ τῶν νόμων τῆς χώρᾱς _____

12. σὺν θεοῖς _____

13. εἰς μάχην _____

14. περὶ καὶ τῆς εἰρήνης καὶ τοῦ πολέμου _____

15. σὺν ὅπλοις _____

16. αἱ ἐν τῇ χώρᾳ ὁδοί _____

17. ἐξ ἑταίρων _____

18. ξὺν τοῖς τῆς Ἑλένης ἑταίροις _____

19. περὶ τῆς τοῦ Πριάμου γνώμης _____

20. εἰς τὰς νήσους _____

B. Write in Greek.

1. both men and gods (d.o.) _____

2. by the custom of the land _____

3. concerning the justice of the gods _____

4. Priam (d.a.) _____

5. of the misfortunes of Helen _____

6. by the road into the marketplace _____

7. for the companion of the goddess _____

8. the words (d.o.) of Priam _____

9. concerning the wisdom of the god _____

10. out from the marketplace _____

11. the soul (subj.) of the man _____

12. (moving) around the house _____

13. both by words and by weapons _____

14. the children (d.o.) of the gods _____

15. on the islands _____

16. in accordance with justice (justly) _____

17. a companion (d.o.) of the journey _____

18. in the souls of men _____

19. for both Priam and Alexander _____

20. by the wisdom of the goddess _____

21. the misfortunes (d.o.) of battle _____

22. in accordance with the laws (2) _____

_____

23. with a view to justice _____

24. resulting from the deeds of Alexander _____

C. Syntax and Translation

Nominative, Subject	Dative of Reference
Predicate Nominative	Dative of Means
Genitive of Possession	Accusative, Direct Object
Genitive of Separation	Vocative, Direct Address

Choosing from the list above, write the syntax and number above each italicized noun. Note when it requires an article. If the italicized word is a conjunction, label it as such. If a prepositional phrase is italicized, label the preposition and indicate the case and number of the noun that follows. (Remember that not all English prepositional phrases are prepositional phrases in Greek.) Label phrases to be placed in the attributive position. Then write each italicized element in Greek. Consult the vocabulary notes when necessary.

Example:

Syntax:	*Nom., Subj. sing.* *with article*	*Acc., D.O. sing.* *with article*	*prep. + acc. sing.* *with article*	*Gen. of Poss.* *possibly attributive*
Sentence:	*Alexander* sent	*Helen*	*into the house*	*of Priam.*
Translation:	**ὁ Ἀλέξανδρος**	**τὴν Ἑλένην**	**εἰς τὴν τοῦ Πριάμου οἰκίαν.**	

1. Syntax: _____

_____

Sentence:	*Priam* went	*out from the land*	*armed/with arms.*

Translation: _____

2. Syntax: _____

_____

Sentence:	*The men in the marketplace* will cease	*from their deeds.*

Translation: _____

3. Syntax: _____

_____

Sentence: *Justice* is   *the work*   *of the gods.*

Translation: _____

4. Syntax: _____

_____

Sentence: *With words* I persuaded   *Helen*   *and*   *Priam.*

Translation: _____

5. Syntax: _____

_____

Sentence: *Both*   *men*   *and*   *gods,*   *Priam,*   love   *justice.*

Translation: _____

6. Syntax: _____

_____

Sentence: *The child* ran   *into the house.*

Translation: _____

7. Syntax: _____

_____

Sentence: *In the house*   *the children* found   *their companions.*

Translation: _____

8. Syntax: _____

_____

Sentence: *On the road to the marketplace* we saw   *animals*   *and*   *men.*

Translation: _____

9. Syntax: _____

_____

Sentence: When did *the companions*   *of Priam*   cease   *from battle?*

Translation: _____

10. Syntax: _____

_____

Sentence: *Men* make   *both*   *war*   *and*   *peace.*

Translation: _____

11. Syntax: _____

_____

Sentence: *The gods* are honored   *both*   *by the words and by the deeds of men.*

Translation: _____

12. Syntax: _____

_____

Sentence: *Wisdom*   is   *the work*   *of the goddess.*

Translation: _____

13. Syntax: _____

_____

Sentence: *With the aid of the gods*   *men* will make   *peace*   *for their children.*

Translation: _____

14. Syntax: _____

_____

Sentence: *On the island*   *O companion,*   *men* desire   *peace.*

Translation: _____

15. Syntax: _____

_____

Sentence: *For men*   *war* is   *a misfortune.*

Translation: _____

16. Syntax: _____

_____

Sentence: *To (his) children*   *the wisdom*   *of Priam* was great.

Translation: _____

17. Syntax: _____

_____

Sentence: *Helen,* I sacrificed   *animals*   *to both the god and the goddess of war.*

Translation: _____

18. Syntax: _____

_____

Sentence: We heard *the opinion*   *of Priam*   *in the council.*

Translation: _____

19. Syntax: _____

_____

Sentence: *The goddess*   *justly/with justice* punished   *Helen.*

Translation: _____

20. Syntax: _____

_____

Sentence: *Alexander,* will you stand   *in the road*   *armed/with arms?*

Translation: _____

21. Syntax: _____

_____

Sentence: *The men* went   *to the council*   *about the battle on the island.*

Translation: _____

22. Syntax: _____

_____

Sentence: I have written *a speech*   *concerning the souls*   *of men.*

Translation: _____

23. Syntax: _____

_____

Sentence: *Companions,* do   *animals and*   *gods* have   *souls?*

Translation: _____

24. Syntax: _____

_____

Sentence: *The men* will fight   *in battle*   *with weapons.*

Translation: _____

25. Syntax: _____

_____

Sentence: I stopped *the men*   *from war*   *with a speech*   *about peace.*

Translation: _____

26. Syntax: _____

_____

Sentence: *The speeches*   *of the men* were heard   *in the marketplace.*

Translation: _____

27. Syntax: _____

_____

Sentence: *Priam* was seeking   *justice*   *for his child*   *and*   *for Helen.*

Translation: _____

28. Syntax: _____

_____

Sentence: *With the aid of the gods* I shall return   *(out) from the war.*

Translation: _____

29. Syntax: _____

_____

Sentence: *The gods* are often friendly   *to men.*

Translation: _____

30. Syntax: _____

_____

Sentence: *The land* was saved   *by the wisdom*   *of the goddess.*

Translation: _____

31. Syntax: _____

_____

Sentence: *Gods,* do you see   *the misfortunes*   *of men?*

Translation: _____

32. Syntax: _____

_____

Sentence: *Alexander* was   *a companion*   *in war.*

Translation: _____

33. Syntax: _____

_____

Sentence: *Concerning the misfortunes*   *of Helen*   *both gods and men* know.

Translation: _____

34. Syntax: _____

_____

Sentence: *In peace*   *men* make   *speeches*   *concerning war.*

Translation: _____

35. Syntax: _____

_____

Sentence: *O gods,* send   *peace*   *into the souls*   *of men.*

Translation: _____

_____

36. Syntax: _____

_____

Sentence: Are you moved *by the misfortune*   *of Helen,*   *Priam?*

Translation: _____

_____

37. Syntax: _____

_____

Sentence: *The animals, (the ones) for the goddesses,* were driven   *into the road.*

Translation: _____

_____

38. Syntax: _____

_____

Sentence: Do not send *children*   *armed*   *into battle.*

Translation: _____

39. Syntax: _____

_____

Sentence: *Justly* you drove   *Alexander*   *out from the marketplace.*

Translation: _____

40. Syntax: _____

_____

Sentence: *Wars*   *in the lands* are   *misfortunes*   *for men.*

Translation: _____

41. Syntax: _____

_____

Sentence: *The opinions*   *of Helen*   *about the war* are bitter.

Translation: _____

42. Syntax: _____

_____

Sentence: *The souls*   *of men* are dear   *to the gods.*

Translation: _____

43. Syntax: _____

_____

Sentence: *The men* are   *children*   *of a goddess.*

Translation: _____

44. Syntax: _____

_____

Sentence: *The gods* ceased   *from their speeches*   *about men.*

Translation: _____

45. Syntax: _____

_____

Sentence: *For the men on the island*   *peace* is   *the work*   *of the gods.*

Translation: _____

46. Syntax: _____

_____

Sentence: *By the custom of battles*   *Alexander* carries   *the weapons*   *of Priam.*

Translation: _____

Drill 12: Short-Alpha Nouns; First-Declension Masculine Nouns

A. Recite from memory the two sets of endings for short-alpha nouns of the first declension and say when each set is used.

B. On a separate sheet decline fully, both article and noun, ἡ θάλαττα (singular and plural) and ἡ ἀλήθεια (singular only). Write the interjection ὦ before vocative forms.

C. Recite from memory the two sets of endings for masculine first-declension nouns and say when each set is used.

D. On a separate sheet decline fully, both article and noun, ὁ ποιητής (singular and plural), ὁ Γοργίας (singular only), and ὁ Εὐρῑπίδης (singular only). Write the interjection ὦ before vocative forms.

E. Write down from memory the six rules for the possibilities of accent.

1. _____

2. _____

3. _____

4. _____

5. _____

6. _____

F. The persistent accent for each of these nouns is given by the first form. Correctly accent the other forms in each series. Be ready to explain your answers. Assume a pause at the end of each word.

1. Εὐρῑπίδης   Εὐρῑπιδη   Εὐρῑπιδη   Εὐρῑπιδου

2. ἀλήθεια   ἀληθειᾳ   ἀληθειαν   ἀληθειᾱς

3. ποιητής   ποιητα   ποιητην   ποιητου

4. μοῖρα   μοιραν   μοιρᾱς   μοιραι

5. θάλαττα   θαλαττης   θαλαττῃ   θαλατταν

6. νεᾱνίᾱς   νεᾱνιων   νεᾱνιᾳ   νεᾱνιαις

7. Ἀτρείδης   Ἀτρειδην   Ἀτρειδη   Ἀτρειδου

8. δόξα   δοξαι   δοξων   δοξᾱς

9. πολίτης   πολῑτου   πολῑται   πολῑτην

10. Ἅιδης   Ἅιδην   Ἅιδη   Ἅιδου

11. φόβος   φοβου   φοβον   φοβους

12. αἰτίᾱ   αἰτιᾱν   αἰτιων   αἰτιᾱς

13. ἀρχή   ἀρχης   ἀρχαι   ἀρχη

14. Γοργίᾱς   Γοργιᾱ   Γοργιᾱν   Γοργιᾳ

15. δῆμος   δημου   δημον   δημῳ

G. Give the full vocabulary entry for these nouns.

1. young man _____

2. fate _____

3. truth _____ _____

4. citizen _____

5. son of Atreus _____

6. cause _____

7. Euripides _____

8. sea _____

9. opinion _____

10. beginning; rule _____

11. fear _____

12. Hades _____

13. poet _____

14. Gorgias _____

H. Place the correct form of the article or ὦ in front of each noun. Give all possibilities.

1. _____ νεᾱνίαι   2. _____ θαλάττης

3. _____ πολίτης   4. _____ ἀληθείᾳ

5. _____ Εὐρῑπίδην   6. _____ μοῖραν

7. _____ πολίταις   8. _____ ποιητοῦ

9. _____ δοξῶν   10. _____ νεᾱνίᾱς

11. _____ Γοργίᾱ   12. _____ θαλάττᾱς

13. _____ Εὐρῑπίδη   14. _____ φόβον

15. _____ ἀρχῆς   16. _____ δήμου

17. _____ μοίρᾱς   18. _____ αἰτίᾱν

19. _____ πολῖται   20. _____ Ἄιδου

I. Translate each phrase. Then change all singulars to plurals and plurals to singulars.

Example: τὰς τοῦ ποιητοῦ δόξᾱς   **a. the opinions (d.o.) of the poet**
                                  b. τὴν τῶν ποιητῶν δόξαν

1. ἐν τῇ θαλάττῃ   a. _____

                        b. _____

2. τοὺς νεᾱνίᾱς   a. _____

                        b. _____

3. ἡ μοῖρα   a. _____

                        b. _____

4. τοῖς πολίταις   a. _____

                        b. _____

5. ὦ Ἀτρεῖδαι   a. _____

                        b. _____

6. τὴν μοῖραν

a. _____

b. _____

7. εἰς τὰς θαλάττᾱς

a. _____

b. _____

8. τῇ δόξῃ

a. _____

b. _____

9. τῶν πολῑτῶν

a. _____

b. _____

10. περὶ τὴν γνώμην τὴν τοῦ ποιητοῦ

a. _____

b. _____

11. αἱ τῶν νεᾱνιῶν δόξαι

a. _____

b. _____

12. τῶν Ἀτρειδῶν

a. _____

b. _____

13. τὰς τῶν ποιητῶν δόξᾱς

a. _____

b. _____

14. αἱ θάλατται

a. _____

b. _____

J. Write in Greek.

1. both Alexander and Atreides (subj.) _____

2. from the beginning _____

3. concerning the words of Euripides _____

4. the laws (d.o.) of Hades _____

5. of truth _____

6. the glory (d.o.) of Helen _____

7. both Gorgias and Euripides (d.o.) _____

8. for the poet and (his) companions _____

9. into the sea _____

10. the justice (d.o.) of the citizens _____

11. by the wisdom of the poet _____

12. the rule (d.o.) of the land _____

13. a speech (d.o.) of Gorgias _____

14. the souls (subj.) in Hades _____

15. concerning the glory of the goddess _____

16. weapons (d.o.) of the young man _____

17. the truth (d.o.) about the gods _____

18. the fate (subj.) of Priam _____

19. of Hades _____

20. the young man and the poet (d.o.) _____

Drill 13–14: First-Second-Declension Adjectives; Noun-Adjective Agreement

A. On a separate sheet decline fully with the article, singular and plural, **ὁ κακὸς ποιητής**, **ἡ ἄδικος δόξα**, and **τὸ καλὸν ἔργον**. Write the interjection **ὦ** for vocative forms.

B. Supply the correct form of the adjective **ἀγαθός**, **ἀγαθή**, **ἀγαθόν** to modify each noun.

Example: τὴν **ἀγαθὴν** ὁδόν

1. τὰ _____ ἔργα

2. τοῖς _____ ποιηταῖς

3. ὦ _____ ἄνθρωπε

4. τῇ _____ θεῷ

5. τὸ _____ τέκνον

6. τῶν _____ ὅπλων

7. τὰς _____ οἰκίας

8. τοῦ _____ νόμου

9. τὴν _____ δόξαν

10. ὦ _____ πολῖτα

11. τῆς _____ γνώμης

12. ὁ _____ νεᾱνίας

13. τοὺς _____ νεᾱνίᾱς

14. τὴν _____ μοῖραν

C. Supply the correct form of the adjective **ἄδικος, ἄδικον** to modify each noun. Give all possibilities.

1. _____ μοίρᾳ

2. _____ πολίτην

3. _____ νόμους

4. _____ λόγον

5. _____ αἰτίᾱς

6. _____ φίλε

7. _____ γνῶμαι

8. _____ ψῡχῆς

9. _____ πολέμου

10. _____ ἔργον

11. _____ νεᾱνίᾱ

12. _____ φόβοις

13. _____ μάχης

14. _____ ἀρχῇ

D. Translate these phrases.

1. τοὺς λόγους τοὺς ἀθανάτους _____

2. ἐν τῇ καλῇ θαλάττῃ _____

3. Γοργίᾱς μόνος _____

4. τοῖς νεᾱνίαις καὶ τοῖς δικαίοις καὶ τοῖς ἀδίκοις _____

_____

5. ἐς τὴν Λακεδαιμονίᾱν χώρᾱν _____

6. τὴν ἀθάνατον θεόν _____

7. τοὺς ἀνθρώπους τοὺς ταῖς θεοῖς φίλους _____

_____

8. ὦ ἄδικε Εὐρῑπίδη _____

9. περὶ τὰ καλὰ ἔργα τὰ τῶν Ἀτρειδῶν _____

_____

10. λόγῳ μόνῳ _____

11. ἀγαθὸς πολίτης _____

12. δόξαν ἄδικον _____

13. ὦ ἀγαθὲ Γοργίᾱ _____

14. τῆς Λακεδαιμονίᾱς χώρᾱς _____

15. τὴν δεινὴν συμφοράν _____

16. σοφίᾱς μόνης _____

17. ὁ τοῦ Εὐρῑπίδου λόγος _____

18. τῶν φίλων ἑταίρων _____

19. μοῖραν ἐχθράν _____

20. μόναις ταῖς θεοῖς _____

E. Write these phrases in Greek.

1. into the Athenian land _____

2. of the just peace _____

3. by an unjust law _____

4. in the beautiful house _____

5. for the Spartan citizens _____

6. wise Euripides (d.a.) _____

7. with the aid of the good gods _____

8. for Alexander alone _____

9. by an evil fate _____

10. the beautiful sea (d.o.) _____

11. of the friendly gods _____

12. a deathless reputation (subj.) _____

13. a speech (d.o.) both just and beautiful _____

14. a poet (subj.) hostile to Euripides _____

15. fearsome animals (d.o.) _____

16. by peace alone _____

Drill 15: Substantive Use of the Adjective

A. Give the gender, number, and case of these substantives and translate. Give all possibilities.

Example: τοὺς ἀδίκους   **masc. pl. acc., the unjust men**

1. καλά _____

2. αἱ οὐκ ἀγαθαί _____

3. αἱ μὴ ἀγαθαί _____

4. τὸν δίκαιον _____

5. τοῖς καλοῖς _____

6. περὶ τῶν κακῶν _____

7. οἱ Ἀθηναῖοι _____

8. τῇ ἀδίκῳ _____

9. ὁ σοφός _____

10. ὦ κακέ _____

11. τοὺς δικαίους _____

12. τοῖς ἐχθροῖς _____

13. οἱ ἀθάνατοι _____

14. τῆς καλῆς _____

15. ὦ φίλοι _____

16. Λακεδαιμονίων _____

17. τὸν μὴ σοφόν _____

18. τοῦ ἀγαθοῦ _____

19. τὸ ἄδικον _____

20. τὴν Ἀθηναίᾱν _____

21. τὸν φίλον _____

22. τὸ καλόν _____

23. δεινά _____

24. τᾱ̀ς φίλᾱς _____

B. Write these phrases in Greek using *substantives*. Give all possibilities.

1. for the not friendly women _____

2. good things (d.o.) _____

3. of the unjust woman _____

4. not bad men (subj.) _____

5. the terrible thing (subj.) _____

6. wise woman (d.a.) _____

7. not beautiful women (d.o.) _____

8. concerning the just and the unjust thing (2) _____

9. a noble and good man (subj.) _____

10. for an Athenian man _____

11. bad things (subj.) _____

12. for the beautiful woman _____

13. the Spartans (subj.) _____

14. for the Athenians _____

15. an enemy (d.o.) _____

Drill 16–19: Subjective and Objective Genitive; Dative and Accusative of Respect

A. Translate each phrase and give the syntax of the italicized words.

1. περὶ τὸν τῆς *Ἑλένης* φόβον τὸν τοῦ *Ἀλεξάνδρου*

_____

_____

    Ἑλένης _____

    Ἀλεξάνδρου _____

2. τὴν τῶν *κακῶν* αἰτίᾱν

_____

    κακῶν _____

3. πολίτην *λόγῳ* δίκαιον, ἔργῳ ἄδικον

_____

    λόγῳ _____

4. τῷ *λόγους* σοφῷ Εὐρῑπίδῃ

_____

    λόγους _____

5. διὰ τὴν τῶν θεῶν βουλήν

_____

     θεῶν _____

6. πολίτᾱς τὴν ψῡχὴν κακούς

_____

     ψῡχήν _____

7. ἡ τοῦ _Πριάμου_ ἀρχὴ ἡ τῆς χώρᾱς

_____

_____

     Πριάμου _____

     χώρᾱς _____

8. ψῡχὴ τῇ _ἀληθείᾳ_ καλή

_____

     ἀληθείᾳ _____

9. τῷ ποιητῇ τῷ τῶν _λόγων_

_____

     λόγων _____

10. ὁ Πρίαμος ὁ _βουλὴν_ ἀγαθός

_____

     βουλήν _____

11. ἡ αἰτίᾱ τῶν τοῦ Εὐρῑπίδου συμφορῶν

_____

_____

    συμφορῶν _____

12. εἰρήνην οὐ λόγῳ μόνον, ἀλλὰ καὶ ἔργῳ

_____

_____

    ἔργῳ _____

13. οἱ τῶν νόμων ποιηταί

_____

    νόμων _____

14. τῇ τῶν Ἀθηναίων ἀρχῇ τῇ τῆς θαλάσσης

_____

_____

    Ἀθηναίων _____

    θαλάσσης _____

15. περὶ τοῦ ποιητοῦ τοῦ γνώμην ἀδίκου

_____

_____

    γνώμην _____

B. Identify all Subjective and Objective Genitives, Datives and Accusatives of Respect, and Appositives. Then write these phrases in Greek.

1. by the will of the goddess _____

_____

2. a man (subj.) fearsome in battle _____

_____

3. on account of the Spartans' fear of war _____

_____

4. for the Athenians, the makers of the law _____

_____

5. the truly good young men (d.o.) _____

_____

6. concerning the Athenians' fear of the sea _____

_____

7. the gods' rule (subj.) of men _____

_____

8. women (d.o.) wise in respect to beautiful things _____

_____

9. war (d.o.), the cause of misfortunes _____

_____

10. the maker (subj.) of good speeches _____

_____

11. of a friend in word, in fact of an enemy _____

_____

12. in the beginning of the war _____

_____

Drill 20: The Demonstrative Adjective and Pronoun οὗτος, αὕτη, τοῦτο

A. Recite from memory the entire declension of **οὗτος, αὕτη, τοῦτο**.

B. Identify these forms by gender, number, and case. Give all possibilities.

1. τούτους _____

2. τοῦτο _____

3. ταύτης _____

4. τούτῳ _____

5. τοῦτον _____

6. τούτων _____

7. ταύταις _____

8. τούτου _____

9. οὗτος _____

10. ταύτῃ _____

C. Write these forms of **οὗτος, αὕτη, τοῦτο**.

1. fem. sing. gen. _____

2. neut. pl. acc. _____

3. masc. pl. dat. _____

4. neut. sing. nom. _____

5. fem. pl. acc. _____

6. masc. pl. gen. _____

7. fem. pl. nom. _____

8. neut. sing. gen. _____

9. fem. sing. acc. _____

10. masc. sing. dat. _____

D. On a separate sheet decline fully (no vocative) **ὁ ἑταῖρος οὗτος, αὕτη ἡ μοῖρα**, and **τοῦτο τὸ τέκνον**.

E. Provide the correct form of **οὗτος, αὕτη, τοῦτο** to modify each noun and translate each phrase.

	οὗτος, αὕτη, τοῦτο	*Translation*

1. _____ οἱ θεοί _____

2. _____ τῇ γνώμῃ _____

3. _____ τὰ ἀγαθά _____

4. τὸν νόμον _____ _____

5. τῆς χώρᾱς _____ _____

6. Ἀλέξανδρος _____ _____

7. _____ τοὺς λόγους _____

8. _____ τῶν ψῡχῶν _____

9. _____ ἡ ἀρχή _____

10. _____ ταῖς συμφοραῖς _____

11. τοῦ πολέμου _____ _____

12. τῷ πολίτῃ _____ _____

13. _____ τὴν θάλατταν _____

14. Εὐρῑπίδην _____ _____

15. _____ τοῖς νεᾱνίαις _____

16. _____ τὸ ἔργον _____

17. ἡ μάχη _____ _____

οὗτος, αὕτη, τοῦτο		*Translation*
18. τοῦ τέκνου	_____	_____
19. _____	τὰς νήσους	_____
20. Γοργίᾱς	_____	_____

F. Translate these forms of the demonstrative *pronoun.* Give all possibilities.

1. ταῦτα _____

2. τοῦτο _____

3. τούτων _____

4. ταύτῃ _____

5. οὗτοι _____

6. τούτῳ _____

7. τούτους _____

8. τούτου _____

9. ταύταις _____

10. τούτοις _____

G. Translate these phrases.

1. οὗτοι οἱ σοφοί _____

2. τοὺς ἀνθρώπους τούτους _____

3. ἡ τούτου μοῖρα _____

4. μόνος οὗτος _____

5. ταῦτα τὰ ζῷα _____

6. τούτοις τοῖς ὅπλοις _____

7. τούτῳ τῷ ἔργῳ _____

8. ταύτης τῆς μοίρᾱς _____

9. τοῖς φίλοις τούτοις _____

10. τὴν τούτου οἰκίᾱν _____

11. περὶ τοῦτο _____

12. ἐς τοῦτο _____

13. τοῦτον τὸν ποιητήν _____

14. ἐν ταύτῃ τῇ ψῡχῇ _____

15. αὕτη ἡ βουλή _____

16. ἐκ τῆς τούτων χώρᾱς _____

17. εἰς τὸν πόλεμον τοῦτον _____

18. τοῦτο τὸ καλόν _____

19. τῷ ἑταίρῳ τούτῳ _____

20. ταύταις μόναις _____

21. τῶν θεῶν τούτων _____

22. ταῦτα τὰ ἔργα _____

H. Write in Greek.

1. by this deed   _____

2. of these young men   _____

3. this unjust thing (subj.)   _____

4. for these good citizens   _____

5. the misfortune (d.o.) of this woman   _____

6. these things (d.o.)   _____

7. these women (d.o.)   _____

8. the speeches (subj.) of this man   _____

9. of this famous Priam   _____

10. this fear (d.o.)   _____

11. by these opinions   _____

12. of this rule only   _____

13. this thing (subj.)   _____

14. of these things   _____

15. in the house of these women   _____

16. by this word   _____

17. into this war alone   _____

18. the misfortunes (subj.) of these men   _____

19. out of these lands   _____

20. concerning the reputation of this poet   _____

Exercises, Chapter 2

A. Place the correct accents on these phrases and then translate. Assume that the last word in each phrase ends a sentence.

1. εἰς την του Πριαμου μοιραν

_____

_____

2. και των μαχων και των πολεμων

_____

_____

3. περι την ἀρχην του Ἀθηναιων δημου

_____

_____

4. οὐκ ἐν ταις νησοις μονον, ἀλλα και ἐν τη χωρᾳ των Λακεδαιμονιων

_____

_____

5. ἀνθρωπος την ψῡχην ἠ ἀγαθος ἠ κακος

_____

_____

6. περι τᾱς του πολεμου αἰτιᾱς

_____

_____

7. δια την ἀληθειαν και την δικην

_____

_____

8. μονοις τοις πολῑταις ταυτης της χωρᾱς

_____

_____

9. τεκνα καλα και ἑταιρους φιλους

_____

_____

10. ἡ εἰς Ἁιδου ὁδος

_____

_____

B. Syntax and Translation

Nominative, Subject
Predicate Nominative
Genitive of Possession
Genitive of Separation
Subjective Genitive
Objective Genitive
Dative of Reference
Dative of Means
Dative of Respect

Accusative, Direct Object
Accusative of Respect
Vocative, Direct Address
Appositive (give case)

Write in Greek all the italicized words and phrases in these sentences. Then give the syntax of the underlined words.

1. *From the beginning beautiful Helen alone* was *the <u>cause</u> of this <u>war</u>, <u>Alexander</u>.*

_____

_____

cause _____

war _____

Alexander _____

2. *Even for <u>Spartans</u> fear of the <u>sea</u>* is *a <u>bad thing</u>.*

_____

_____

Spartans _____

sea _____

bad thing _____

3. *These <u>young men</u> fearsome in <u>battle</u> are marching through the land toward the sea.*

_____

_____

    young men _____

    battle _____

4. *An evil fate is awaiting the unjust <u>citizen</u>, glory deathless in <u>truth</u> (is awaiting) the just (citizen).*

_____

_____

    citizen _____

    truth _____

5. *To the <u>people</u> of the Athenians, men good in <u>soul</u> are <u>friends.</u>*

_____

_____

    people _____

    soul _____

    friends _____

6. *In this battle both Spartans and Athenians did fearsome <u>deeds</u> with the aid of the good gods.*

_____

_____

    deeds _____

7. *On account of these things alone the <u>sons of Atreus</u> led their noble companions into a just war.*

_____

_____

sons of Atreus _____

8. *On these islands the Athenians are fighting in a <u>truly</u> unjust war.*

_____

_____

truly_____

9. *Not by the <u>wisdom</u> of men but on account of the will of the immortal gods this <u>battle</u> will be stopped.*

_____

_____

wisdom_____

battle _____

10. *Hades justly took this hateful <u>woman</u>, a <u>misfortune</u> for men, away from the Athenian land.*

_____

_____

woman _____

misfortune _____

11. *Gorgias* taught *the <u>young men</u> not with truth but with <u>opinion</u>.*

_____

_____

young men _____

opinion _____

12. *On account of his noble deeds this good citizen* will have *a deathless <u>reputation</u>.*

_____

_____

reputation _____

13. *The law of fate is this: both just and unjust men* go to <u>Hades</u>.

_____

_____

Hades _____

14. We sent *to the island a man just in <u>reputation</u> but in fact unjust and bad.*

_____

_____

reputation _____

15. *Not only wise men but also just citizens* are <u>friends</u> to the <u>gods</u>.

_____

_____

friends _____

gods _____

16. When will *the Athenians* cease *from the <u>rule</u> of the <u>sea</u> not only in <u>word</u> but also in deed?*

_____

_____

rule _____

sea _____

word _____

17. *With good <u>plans</u> and good weapons the Spartans* defeated *the <u>Athenians</u> in this war.*

_____

_____

plans _____

Athenians _____

18. *To these* <u>citizens</u> *good in* <u>judgment</u> *Gorgias is a clever maker of bad* <u>speeches</u>.

_____

_____

citizens _____

judgment _____

speeches _____

19. *To the* <u>son of Atreus</u>, *a wise* <u>human being</u>, *only the will of the immortal ones is the* <u>cause</u> *of his terrible* <u>misfortune</u>.

_____

_____

son of Atreus _____

human being _____

cause _____

misfortune _____

20. *Euripides, either you are a clever* <u>poet</u> *or you write good* <u>speeches</u> *with the aid of the gods.*

_____

_____

poet _____

speeches _____

21. *Both friends and companions of <u>Euripides</u> came into this land.*

_____

_____

    Euripides _____

22. *Not wise men* were praising *the bad <u>opinions</u> of this notorious Gorgias.*

_____

_____

    opinions _____

23. *Truth is a beautiful thing, but this <u>woman's</u> fear of the <u>truth</u> is a <u>bad thing</u>.*

_____

_____

    woman's _____

    truth _____

    bad thing _____

24. *This <u>man</u>, O <u>Gorgias</u>, is not a wise <u>human being</u>, but he alone is a companion to wise men alone.*

_____

_____

    man _____

    Gorgias _____

    human being _____

25. *The wisdom of the* <u>poets</u> *will free* the soul of Helen from <u>fear</u> *of a hateful* <u>fate</u>.

_____

_____

poets _____

fear _____

fate _____

26. *Wise men* are urging *these* <u>citizens</u> *to cease* from fearsome <u>battle</u>.

_____

_____

citizens _____

battle _____

C. Write in Greek all the italicized words in these sentences.

1. *On account of these deeds hateful to gods and men* you are being sent *away from this island.*

_____

_____

2. *A terrible thing* is *fear in the soul of a man.*

_____

_____

3. *These beautiful speeches of Gorgias* hold *either truth or opinion.*

_____

_____

4. *The Athenians' rule of the islands* is *a bad thing for the citizens.*

_____

_____

5. *In the beginning of the war fear* held *the souls of the Spartans, makers of bad laws.*

_____

_____

6. *This hateful and unjust man* wants to take *even the rule away from the people.*

_____

_____

7. *Only these good men* will speak *in the council either about peace or about war.*

_____

_____

8. *Hades* is *a terrible god, companion, but a man noble in soul* does not fear *the Fates.*

_____

_____

9. *A hateful speech* is leading *the people away from the path of truth.*

_____

_____

10. *Not only in word* was *Atreides* revealing *his opinion about Helen, but also in deed.*

_____

_____

11. *The people* suffer *terrible things through wars in this land.*

_____

_____

12. *A wise and clever poet* knows *the causes of these misfortunes.*

_____

_____

13. *Glory in battle* is *the fate of this noble young man, the child of Priam.*

_____

_____

14. *A man bad in soul* desires *not truth but a good reputation, Euripides.*

_____

_____

15. *Not in word but in deed* were *the citizens* seeking *peace on these islands.*

_____

_____

16. *The rule of the gods* is *a fearsome thing for men and animals.*

_____

_____

17. *A not beautiful soul* is *a hateful thing to Hades.*

_____

_____

18. *Alexander alone* refuses to flee *with Helen alone.*

_____

_____

19. *Along with the people of the Athenians the young men* took up *weapons with a view to war.*

_____

_____

20. *Not on account of hateful beliefs but in accordance with the laws the Spartans* are seeking *the beginning of battle.*

_____

_____

21. *Not only friends but also enemies* admired *the truly noble children of Priam.*

_____

_____

Drill 22: Recessive Accent

A. Write down from memory the six rules for the possibilities of accent.

1. _____

2. _____

3. _____

4. _____

5. _____

6. _____

B. The accent on each of these verb forms is *recessive*. Observing the rules for the possibilities of accent, correctly accent each form in each series. Be ready to explain your answers.

1. λεγω	λεγομεν	λελεγμεθα	ἐλελεκτο
2. μελλουσι	ἐμελλετε	μελλω	μελλησω
3. πειθει	πειθετε	ἐπειθον	πειθε
4. παυσον	ἐπαυον	παυε	ἐπαυε
5. ἀρχεις	ἀρχεσθε	ἠρχον	ἠρχε
6. πεμπε	πεμπετε	πεμψει	πεμψομεν
7. ἐθελησει	ἐθελησετε	ἠθελον	ἠθελησεν
8. διδασκομεθα	ἐδιδασκον	διδαχθησεσθε	ἐδιδαξας
9. ἐλεγον	λεγεσθε	ἐλεξατε	λεγετω
10. ἐδιδασκεν	διδαξον	ἐδεδιδαχεσαν	διδασκω

11. μελλομεν   μελλησει   ἐμελλησα   ἐμελλεν

12. ἠθελησας   ἠθελησαμεν   ἠθελεν   ἐθελησω

13. ἠργμεθα   ἠρχθη   ἠρχθε   ἀρχθησεσθε

14. πεισομεν   πειθουσιν   πεισθησομεθα   πειθω

15. ἐπαυομεν   παυσεσθε   παυση   παυσουσιν

16. πεμψεις   πεμπετε   ἐπεμπου   ἐπεμπετο

C. The accent on each of these verb forms is *recessive*. Observing the rules for the possibilities of accent, mark the correct accents for each form in each series. Be ready to explain your answers.

1. ἐλεγετε   λεγετε   λεξουσιν   λεξει

2. ἐπαυετο   ἐπαυσω   ἐπεπαυκετε   ἐπεπαυκειν

3. ἐδιδαχθη   δεδιδαγμεθα   διδαξεις   ἐδιδαξατο

4. ἐπεμποντο   ἐπεμψω   πεμψεσθε   πεμψωμεν

5. μελλησεις   ἐμελλον   μελλετε   ἐμελλησαν

6. ἠθελησα   ἠθεληκατε   ἐθελησομεν   ἐθελομεν

7. ἠρχα   ἀρξει   ἠρχθητε   ἀρχη

8. πεπεικαμεν   πεισον   ἐπεισθη   πεισουσι

9. λεξατω   ἐλεξεν   λεξεις   λελεχθε

10. ἐδεδιδαχειν   διδασκει   διδαξατω   δεδιδαχε

11. θελομεν   ἐθελει   ἠθεληκει   θελω

12. παυσεις   ἐπεπαυκης   ἐπαυθησαν   παυετω

13. ἀρχωμεθα   ἠρχες   ἀρχθησει   ἀρξάτω

14. πεμπη   ἐπεμψατε   πεπομφᾱσιν   ἐπεμπες

15. ἐμελλησας   μελλεις   ἐμελλομεν   μελλησουσι

16. ἐπεπειστο   ἐπεισατο   πεισθησει   ἐπειθου

Drill 23–24: The Finite Greek Verb; The Tenses of the Indicative Mood

A. Fill in the blanks. Do not use abbreviations.

1. The five properties of the finite verb in Greek are: _____

   _____

   _____ .

2. The three voices of the Greek verb are: _____

   _____ .

3. The four moods of the Greek verb are: _____

   _____ .

4. The tense of a Greek verb *always* indicates _____

   and often indicates_____ .

5. The seven tenses of the indicative mood are: _____

   _____

   _____ .

6. A verb that has *simple aspect* represents an action as _____ .

7. A verb that has *progressive aspect* represents an action as _____ .

8. A verb that has *repeated aspect* represents an action as _____ .

9. A verb that has *completed aspect* represents an action as _____ .

10. Primary tenses in Greek are _____ or _____ in time.

11. The four primary tenses are: _____

_____ .

12. Secondary tenses in Greek are _____ in time.

13. The three secondary tenses are: _____

_____ .

B. Give the time and aspect for each tense of the indicative mood. Give all possibilities.

Example: Present: **present time with simple or progressive/repeated aspect**

Imperfect: _____ time with _____ aspect

Future: _____ time with _____ aspect

Aorist: _____ time with _____ aspect

Perfect: _____ time with _____ aspect

Pluperfect: _____ time with _____ aspect

Future Perfect: _____ time with _____ aspect

C. Identify the time and aspect of these English verb phrases. Then name the Greek tense of the indicative that would be used for each.

Example:	*Time*	*Aspect*	*Tense Name*
he brought	**past**	**simple**	**aorist**

	Time	*Aspect*	*Tense Name*
1. you were ruling			
2. they are ruling			
3. he ruled			
4. they have ruled			
5. we had ruled			
6. I shall rule			
7. you are ruling			
8. he will be ruling			
9. we taught (repeatedly)			
10. you taught			
11. I shall have taught			
12. they have taught			
13. she had taught			
14. he was teaching			

	Time	Aspect	Tense Name
15. she will teach	_____	_____	_____
16. I teach	_____	_____	_____
17. she used to teach	_____	_____	_____
18. we are teaching	_____	_____	_____
19. they taught	_____	_____	_____
20. I shall teach (repeatedly)	_____	_____	_____

D. Fill in the blanks.

1. When a verb is in the active voice, the subject _____ the action of the verb.

2. When a verb is in the passive voice, the subject _____ the action of the verb.

E. Identify the voice (active or passive) of each of these English verb phrases.

	Voice		Voice
1. she is seeing	_____	2. they are seen	_____
3. I shall be cooking	_____	4. it was cooked	_____
5. we are going	_____	6. you go	_____
7. he was captured	_____	8. you will be captured	_____
9. it was done	_____	10. she was doing	_____
11. they have pushed	_____	12. you are pushed	_____

F. Identify the voice (active or passive) of these English verb phrases. Then change each phrase from active to passive *or* from passive to active. Keep person, number, and tense (including aspect) the same.

Example:	*Voice*		*Changed Phrase*
she is persuading	**active**		**she is being persuaded**
	Voice		*Changed Phrase*

1. they led

2. they had been led

3. he is being carried

4. we are being seen

5. she teaches

6. she taught

7. he was stopping

8. he will stop

9. we shall say

10. he is carrying

11. you were persuaded

12. you were persuading

13. they are being led

14. they used to lead

15. I was persuading

16. I was persuaded

	Voice	*Changed Phrase*
17. you (pl.) will rule	_____	_____
18. you are ruled	_____	_____
19. they begin	_____	_____
20. they are beginning	_____	_____
21. we used to teach	_____	_____
22. we were taught	_____	_____
23. he will be stopped	_____	_____
24. he will be stopping	_____	_____

Drill 25–26: Principal Parts and Omega Verbs

A. Fill in the blanks. Do not use abbreviations.

1. A vocabulary entry for a verb contains the six _____ and the English meaning(s).

2. Omega verbs are also called _____.

3. The vowel added to certain stems of omega verbs is called a _____

   and is either _____ or _____.

4. A transitive verb is _____

   _____.

5. An intransitive verb is _____

   _____.

B. Give the principal parts of the Greek verbs with these English meanings. Include a blank for any missing principal parts.

1. persuade; *middle,* obey; heed; believe

   _____

   _____

2. be willing, wish

   _____

   _____

3. teach, explain; *middle,* cause to be taught

_____

_____

4. stop (trans.); *middle,* stop (intrans.), cease

_____

_____

5. rule (+ gen.); *middle,* begin (+ gen.)

_____

_____

6. say, speak; tell (of), recount

_____

_____

7. send

_____

_____

8. intend, be about, be likely

_____

_____

C. Fill in the missing principal parts and meanings.

Principal Parts

1	2	3	4	5	6	Meaning
πέμπω						
	μελλήσω					
		ἐδίδαξα				
			πέπεικα			
				λέλεγμαι		
					ἤρχθην	
						be willing, wish
παύω						

Drill 27–35: Present, Imperfect, and Future Active, Middle, and Passive Indicative; Present and Future Active, Middle, and Passive Infinitives of Omega Verbs

A. Study the principal parts of and read carefully the vocabulary notes on the verbs in this chapter. Write a synopsis for each verb in the indicated person and number. Do not include rare forms.

1. ἄρχω, 3rd pl.
2. παύω, 1st sing.
3. πείθω, 2nd pl.
4. λέγω, 3rd sing.
5. ἐθέλω/θέλω, 3rd sing. (active only)
6. πέμπω, 1st pl.
7. διδάσκω, 2nd sing.
8. μέλλω, 1st pl. (active only)

B. Identify each verb form—for finite forms, give person, number, tense, voice, mood; for infinitives give tense and voice. Then translate.

Example: πείθεται (2)

a. **3rd sing. pres. mid. indic.**
b. **he is obeying**
a. **3rd sing. pres. pass. indic.**
b. **he is (being) persuaded**

1. διδάσκει (3)

a. _____

b. _____

a. _____

b. _____

a. _____

b. _____

2. διδάσκῃ (2)   a. _____

                          b. _____

                          a. _____

                          b. _____

3. ἄρξουσι   a. _____

                          b. _____

4. ἄρξει (2)   a. _____

                          b. _____

                          a. _____

                          b. _____

5. λέγετε   a. _____

                          b. _____

6. ἐλέγετε   a. _____

                          b. _____

7. πεμφθήσομαι   a. _____

                          b. _____

8. πέμπειν   a. _____

                          b. _____

9. ἔπαυε   a. _____

                          b. _____

10. παύσεται

a. _____

b. _____

11. μελλήσετε

a. _____

b. _____

12. ἔμελλον (2)

a. _____

b. _____

a. _____

b. _____

13. ἐθέλειν

a. _____

b. _____

14. ἤθελεν

a. _____

b. _____

15. ἐθελήσειν

a. _____

b. _____

16. ἤρχοντο (2)

a. _____

b. _____

a. _____

b. _____

17. ἄρχονται (2)   a. _____

                              b. _____

                              a. _____

                              b. _____

18. ἀρχθήσονται   a. _____

                              b. _____

19. πείθομεν   a. _____

                              b. _____

20. πείθεσθαι (2)   a. _____

                              b. _____

                              a. _____

                              b. _____

21. πεισόμεθα   a. _____

                              b. _____

22. ἐδιδάσκου (2)   a. _____

                              b. _____

                              a. _____

                              b. _____

23. διδάσκεται (2)   a. _____

                            b. _____

                            a. _____

                            b. _____

24. διδαχθήσει   a. _____

                            b. _____

25. πεμπόμεθα   a. _____

                            b. _____

26. ἐπέμποντο   a. _____

                            b. _____

26. πέμψεις   a. _____

                            b. _____

27. λέγειν   a. _____

                            b. _____

28. ἔλεγες   a. _____

                            b. _____

29. λεχθήσεται   a. _____

                            b. _____

30. ἔπαυον (2)   a. _____

                        b. _____

                        a. _____

                        b. _____

31. ἐπαύου (2)   a. _____

                        b. _____

                        a. _____

                        b. _____

32. παύσεσθαι   a. _____

                        b. _____

33. ἄρχει (3)   a. _____

                        b. _____

                        a. _____

                        b. _____

                        a. _____

                        b. _____

34. ἀρξόμεθα   a. _____

                        b. _____

35. ἦρχεν   a. _____

                        b. _____

36. θέλεις

a. _____

b. _____

36. ἐθελήσεις

a. _____

b. _____

37. ἐθέλουσι

a. _____

b. _____

38. ἐπείθετο (2)

a. _____

b. _____

a. _____

b. _____

39. πείθομαι (2)

a. _____

b. _____

a. _____

b. _____

40. πεισθήσομαι

a. _____

b. _____

C. Identify the tense and voice of each verb phrase and then write it in Greek. Give all possibilities. Include movable nus in parentheses.

Example:	*Tense and Voice*	*Greek Verb*
you used to send	**imperfect active**	ἔπεμπες

	Tense and Voice	*Greek Verb*

1. I was obeying _____ _____

2. they are persuading _____ _____

3. we say _____ _____

4. to be saying _____ _____

5. he will say _____ _____

6. you (pl.) were beginning _____ _____

7. we used to rule _____ _____

8. to be ruled (repeatedly) _____ _____

9. they will begin _____ _____

10. she will be sent _____ _____

11. to be sent (repeatedly) _____ _____

12. to be going to send (once) _____ _____

13. I am being stopped _____ _____

14. you are stopping (intrans.) _____ _____

15. they were stopping (trans.) _____ _____

16. we were wishing _____ _____

	Tense and Voice	*Greek Verb*
17. you will wish		
18. he wishes		
19. they were being taught		
20. I shall teach		
21. you are causing to be taught		
22. he is trying to persuade		
23. we were intending		
24. to be likely (repeatedly)		
25. I am stopping (trans.)		
26. it will be stopped		
27. you used to be stopped		
28. you (pl.) are being ruled		
29. you will be ruled		
30. you are persuading		
31. you will be persuaded		
32. to obey (repeatedly)		
33. they say		
34. to be said (repeatedly)		

Tense and Voice	*Greek Verb*

35. to be going to be said _____ _____

36. I was being taught _____ _____

37. she used to teach _____ _____

38. you used to wish _____ _____

39. to wish (repeatedly) _____ _____

40. I was trying to stop (trans.) _____ _____

41. it used to be said _____ _____

42. they will begin _____ _____

D. Write these forms in Greek. Include movable nus in parentheses.

Example: 2nd pl. pres. act. indic. of ἐθέλω (2)   **ἐθέλετε, θέλετε**

1. 1st pl. imperf. act. indic. of πέμπω _____

2. 3rd pl. pres. mid. indic. of ἄρχω _____

3. fut. act. infin. of μέλλω _____

4. 1st sing. fut. act. indic. of ἐθέλω _____

5. pres. pass. infin. of διδάσκω _____

6. 2nd sing. imperf. pass. indic. of πείθω _____

7. 3rd sing. pres. act. indic. of λέγω _____

8. pres. act. infin. of παύω _____

9. 2nd pl. fut. pass. indic. of παύω _____

10. 1st pl. fut. act. indic. of μέλλω _____

11. 1st pl. pres. act. indic. of ἐθέλω (2) _____

12. 1st sing. imperf. pass. indic. of διδάσκω _____

13. 2nd sing. pres. act. indic. of μέλλω _____

14. 3rd pl. fut. pass. indic. of πείθω _____

15. pres. mid. infin. of ἄρχω _____

16. 2nd pl. pres. mid. indic. of παύω _____

17. 3rd pl. imperf. pass. indic. of πέμπω _____

18. pres. act. infin. of λέγω _____

19. 1st sing. imperf. act. indic. of ἐθέλω _____

20. 2nd sing. imperf. pass. indic. of διδάσκω _____

21. 3rd sing. pres. mid. indic. of πείθω _____

22. 3rd pl. imperf. act. indic. of ἄρχω _____

23. 1st pl. pres. pass. indic. of λέγω _____

24. 1st sing. imperf. mid. indic. of παύω _____

25. fut. pass. infin. of διδάσκω _____

26. 2nd pl. fut. act. indic. of πείθω _____

27. 2nd sing. pres. pass. indic. of πέμπω (2) _____

28. 3rd sing. imperf. act. indic. of ἐθέλω _____

29. 2nd sing. fut. mid. indic. of ἄρχω (2) _____

30. pres. pass. infin. of πέμπω _____

E. Change these *active* forms to the *passive*. Keep person, number, tense, and mood the same, changing *voice only.*

Example: *Active* *Passive*

  ἄρχω **ἄρχομαι**

Active	*Passive*	*Active*	*Passive*
1. παύει _____		2. διδάξετε _____	
3. πέμπομεν _____		4. ἔλεγε _____	
5. ἄρχετε _____		6. ἔπειθες _____	
7. διδάσκουσιν _____		8. πέμψω _____	
9. παύω _____		10. ἤρχομεν _____	
11. ἄρξειν _____		12. λέξει _____	
13. ἐπέμπετε _____		14. ἔπειθον (2) _____	
		_____	
15. διδάσκει _____		16. ἄρξεις (2) _____	
		_____	

Active	Passive	Active	Passive

17. λέγουσιν _____   18. πείθομεν _____

19. ἔπαυον (2) _____   20. πείσουσι _____

_____

21. ἄρχεις (2) _____   22. πέμπω _____

_____

23. διδάσκειν _____   24. ἐδιδάσκετε _____

25. ἄρξετε _____   26. λέγει _____

27. ἦρχε _____   28. ἔπειθες _____

29. πέμψομεν _____   30. λέξειν _____

F. Translate these *middle voice* verb forms.

1. παύῃ _____

2. πείθεσθαι _____

3. παύσεσθε _____

4. ἤρχετο _____

5. διδασκόμεθα _____

6. πείθομαι _____

7. ἄρξει _____

8. παύεσθε _____

9. παύεσθαι _____

10. ἠρχόμην _____

11. πείσεται _____

12. ἐδιδάσκου _____

13. ἐπαυόμην _____

14. ἄρχει _____

15. διδάσκονται _____

16. ἀρξόμεθα _____

17. ἐπείθετο _____

18. ἤρχοντο _____

19. διδάσκεσθαι _____

20. παύεται _____

21. πείθεσθε _____

22. διδάξεσθε _____

G. Place correct accents on these verb forms.

1. λεγομεν

2. παυθησονται

3. ἠρχε

4. πειθεσθαι

5. μελλησει

6. ἐπεμπετο

7. παυουσιν

8. διδασκειν

9. ἠθελεν

10. πεμπονται

11. πεισθησεται

12. ἐμελλεν

13. λεγεις

14. παυσεται

15. ἀρχειν

16. ἐδιδασκοντο

17. λεξειν

18. θελει

19. ἐπειθου

20. μελλει

21. ἐπαυομην

22. ἐλεγον

23. ἀρξεσθαι

24. παυω

25. ἠρχες

26. διδασκεσθαι

27. ἐπαυου

28. ἐθελουσι

29. πειθει

30. λεξομεν

Drill 36–38: Short Sentences and Syntax

Object Infinitive
Genitive of Personal Agent
Dative of Indirect Object

Translate these short sentences with some regard for good English usage, and from the list above give the syntax of the italicized words.

Example: ὅπλα μόνοις τοῖς *Λακεδαιμονίοις* πέμπομεν.
> **We are sending weapons to the Spartans alone.**
> **Λακεδαιμονίοις: Dative of Indirect Object**

1. οἱ Λακεδαιμόνιοι ὑπὸ τῶν *Ἀθηναίων* *ἄρχεσθαι* οὐκ ἐθέλουσιν.

_____

_____

Ἀθηναίων _____

ἄρχεσθαι _____

2. τοῦτο *Ἑλένῃ* πρὸς τοῦ *Πριάμου* σὺν δίκῃ ἐλέγετο.

_____

_____

Ἑλένῃ _____

Πριάμου _____

115

3. ὁ φίλος ὁ ἀγαθὸς τοῦτον τὸν νεᾱνίᾱν πείθει τὴν ἀλήθειαν ἐξ ἀρχῆς λέγειν.

_____

_____

λέγειν _____

4. λόγος καλὸς ἐν τῇ ἀγορᾷ ὑπὸ τοῦ *Γοργίου* λεχθήσεται.

_____

_____

Γοργίου _____

5. ταῦτα τὰ τέκνα διδάξομεν τοῖς νόμοις *πείθεσθαι.*

_____

_____

πείθεσθαι _____

6. ταύτᾱς τὰς συμφορὰς μόνοις τοῖς *ἀνθρώποις* τοῖς ἐν τῇ νήσῳ ἡ ἀθάνατος θεὸς ἔπεμπεν.

_____

_____

ἀνθρώποις _____

7. πειθόμεθα πολέμου ἄρχεσθαι.

_____

_____

    ἄρχεσθαι _____

8. μόνος μόνοις τοῖς *νεᾱνίαις* τὰ ἐν πολέμῳ ἔργα ἔλεγον.

_____

_____

    νεᾱνίαις _____

9. ζῷον καλὸν ὑπὸ Ἀλεξάνδρου πέμπεται ἐς ἀγορᾱν.

_____

_____

    Ἀλεξάνδρου _____

10. τούτῳ τῷ ἀγαθῷ μόνῳ σοφίᾱν πέμψει ἡ θεὸς ἡ δεινή.

_____

_____

    ἀγαθῷ _____

Exercises, Chapter 3

A. Place the correct accents on these phrases and sentences and then translate. Assume that the last word in each phrase ends a sentence.

1. τα κοινα του δημου και της βουλης

_____

_____

2. τοις μεν ξενοις, τοις δε φιλοις

_____

_____

3. οἱ μαχην δεινοι ἀνθρωποι

_____

_____

4. και Γαια και Οὐρανος, δεινοι θεοι

_____

_____

5. ὑπο του δημου των Ἀθηναιων

_____

_____

6. ἐς την των ξενων γαιαν

_____

_____

7. ἐν τη γη ταυτη ἠ πολεμος ἠ εἰρηνη

_____

_____

8. συμφορᾱν τῳ φιλῳ δεινην

_____

_____

9. ἀρα ἐθελεις περι το κοινον εὐ λεγειν των πολῑτων;

_____

_____

10. αἰσχρα και δεινα, ὠ γη και θεοι, Γοργιᾱς οὑτος ἐλεγε τῳ Εὐρῑπιδη.

_____

_____

B. Translate these sentences.

1. οἱ θεοὶ τοὺς ἀνθρώπους πολέμου παύουσιν.

_____

_____

2. οἱ ἄνθρωποι, ὦ ξένε, πρὸς τῶν θεῶν πολέμου παύονται.

_____

_____

3. σὺν θεοῖς, ὦ ξένοι, οἱ ἄνθρωποι πολέμου παυθήσονται.

_____

_____

4. πότε, ὦ πολῖται, τοῖς ἀδίκοις πείθεσθαι οὐκ ἐθελήσετε;

_____

_____

6. πότε τὰς τοῦ πολέμου αἰτίᾱς οὗτοι λέξουσιν ἐν τῇ βουλῇ;

_____

_____

7. πολλάκις ἔλεγον οἱ Ἀθηναῖοι καὶ περὶ τῆς ἀρχῆς τοῦ δήμου καὶ περὶ τοῦ κοινοῦ ἀγαθοῦ.

_____

_____

8. οὐκ, ὦ ξένε, διὰ τὴν τῶν θεῶν βουλὴν ἀλλὰ πρὸς τῶν ἀνθρώπων νῦν ὁ πόλεμος παύεται.

_____

_____

9. καὶ τοῖς συμμάχοις καὶ τοῖς φίλοις οἱ Ἀθηναῖοι ὅπλα ἔπεμπον. καὶ γὰρ οἱ Λακεδαιμόνιοι πολέμου ἤρχοντο.

_____

_____

10. οἱ μὲν κακοὶ πολέμου ἄρχεσθαι ἤθελον, οἱ δὲ ἀγαθοὶ περὶ τῆς εἰρήνης ἔλεγον.

_____

_____

11. ὁ Γοργίᾱς ἐθέλει οὐ μόνον ἄρχειν ταύτης τῆς χώρᾱς, ἀλλὰ καὶ τοὺς πολίτᾱς διδάσκειν μὴ τοῖς νόμοις πείθεσθαι. διὰ δὲ ταῦτα μέλλω λόγου τοῦτον παύσειν.

_____

_____

_____

_____

12. τοῖς μὲν κακοῖς κακὰ πέμπουσιν πολλάκις οἱ θεοί, τοῖς δὲ ἀγαθοῖς ἀγαθά. ἢ πῶς ταῦτα λέγεις, ὦ Γοργίᾱ;

_____

_____

_____

13. πρὸς θεῶν μόνῳ τούτῳ τῷ αἰσχρῷ νεᾱνίᾳ λόγον οὐ λέξω. οὐ γὰρ ἐθέλει διδάσκεσθαι.

_____

_____

14. Α. τὴν τῶν ποιητῶν σοφίᾱν τὴν περὶ τὴν ψῡχὴν σὺν θεοῖς διδάσκω.
    Β. ἀλλὰ ὁ Ἅιδης τῶν ψῡχῶν ἄρχει. ταύτην λέγεις τὴν σοφίᾱν;

_____

_____

_____

_____

15. οἱ σύμμαχοι πολέμου ἄρξεσθαι ἐν ταῖς νήσοις μέλλουσιν. ἐθέλω οὐκ ἐν τῇ βουλῇ μόνον λέγειν τὴν περὶ τούτων γνώμην, ἀλλὰ καὶ ἐν τῷ Ἀθηναίων δήμῳ.

_____

_____

_____

_____

16. ὁ πολίτης ὁ τῇ ἀληθείᾳ ἀγαθὸς καὶ ἄρχειν καὶ ἄρχεσθαι ἐθέλει. τοῦτο μόνον λέγειν ἤθελον.

_____

_____

17. πότε, ὦ ξένε, λόγον τέκνοις περὶ τῶν ἐν Ἅιδου ψῡχῶν λέγειν ἐθελήσεις;

_____

_____

18. ὁ Πρίαμος ἐθέλει Ἑλένην πέμπειν ἀπὸ τῆς χώρᾱς ταύτης, ἀλλὰ τῷ τούτου λόγῳ ὁ Ἀλέξανδρος πείθεσθαι οὐκ ἐθελήσει. διὰ δὲ τὴν αἰτίᾱν ταύτην οὐχ αὕτη πεμφθήσεται.

_____

_____

_____

19. παύεται ξὺν ἀληθείᾳ ὁ πόλεμος ὁ ἄδικος. ἀλλὰ γάρ, ὦ πολῖται, οἱ νεᾱνίαι τῶν πολέμου ἔργων οὐ παύσονται τῶν κακῶν.

_____

_____

_____

_____

20. Α. ταύτης τῆς νήσου οἱ σύμμαχοι εὖ ἦρχον σὺν τῷ δήμῳ Ἀθηναίων.
    Β. καὶ πῶς, ὦ πολῖτα, τῆς γῆς ἦρχον οἱ μὴ ἀγαθοί;

_____

_____

_____

_____

21. οἱ νεᾱνίαι πέμπεσθαι σὺν ὅπλοις εἰς πόλεμον οὐκ ἤθελον. πρὸς δὲ τούτοις μόνοι λόγους καλοὺς περὶ τῶν εἰρήνης ἀγαθῶν τοῖς ἐν ἀγορᾷ πολίταις μόνοις ἔλεγον. νῦν δέ, ὦ φίλοι, λόγου παύομαι.

_____

_____

_____

_____

22. πολλάκις γῇ καὶ οὐρανῷ Ἑλένη αὕτη Ἀλεξάνδρου μόνη τὰ αἰσχρὰ ἔργα ἔλεγεν, τὰς αἰτίᾱς τῶν συμφορῶν.

_____

_____

23. τῆς μὲν γῆς οἱ ἄνθρωποι ἄρχουσι, τοῦ δὲ οὐρανοῦ οἱ θεοί. καὶ ἄνθρωποι τῆς θαλάσσης καὶ θεοὶ ἄρχειν ἐθέλουσιν. πῶς γὰρ ταῦτα σὺν δίκῃ οὐ λέγω;

---

24. περὶ τῶν κακῶν λόγων τοῦ Εὐρῑπίδου λέγειν ἠρχόμην ἀλλὰ παύομαι. νῦν γὰρ ὁ ποιητὴς εὖ λέγει.

---

25. σὺν δίκῃ τοῦ πολέμου ἤρχεσθε, ὦ σύμμαχοι, ἀλλὰ σὺν ὅπλοις τοῦτον παύσομεν.

---

26. Α. ὁ δίκαιος διὰ σοφίᾱν δίκαια μέλλει ἐν τῇ βουλῇ λέξειν.
    Β. πῶς γὰρ οὔ; καὶ ὁ ψῡχὴν ἄδικος ἄδικα.

---

27. "Διὰ φόβον τοῖς Ἀτρείδου τούτου λόγοις πειθόμεθα, ἀλλὰ πειθόμεθα." ταῦτα ἔλεγον οἱ τούτου ἑταῖροι.

_____

_____

_____ .

28. καὶ λόγῳ καὶ ἔργῳ ὑπὸ τούτου τοῦ πολίτου τὴν γνώμην περὶ τοῦ δικαίου τὰ τέκνα ἐδιδάσκετο.

_____

_____

29. αὗται μόναι ἐκ τῆς γῆς σὺν τοῖς τέκνοις πέμπεσθαι μέλλουσιν. κακὰ γὰρ πολλάκις ἔλεγον περὶ τῶν Ἀτρειδῶν.

_____

_____

_____

30. ἀδίκους μὲν λόγους ἐλέγετε, ὦ ἑταῖροι, τὴν δὲ ἀλήθειαν οὔ. διὰ τοῦτο ἐκ ταύτης τῆς χώρᾱς νῦν πέμπεσθε.

_____

_____

_____

31. διὰ μάχᾱς δεινὰς πεμφθήσονται τῷ Ἅιδῃ, τῷ ὑπὸ γῆς θεῷ, καὶ οἱ καλοὶ καὶ οἱ μὴ καλοί. πότε παυθήσεται ὁ πόλεμος οὗτος;

_____

_____

_____

32. ἆρα ὑπὸ Εὐρῑπίδου τούτου, ὦ φίλε ἑταῖρε, περὶ τοῦ καλοῦ ἐδιδάσκου καὶ τοῦ αἰσχροῦ;

_____

_____

33. ἦρχον μὲν ζῴων καὶ ἡ Γαῖα καὶ ὁ Οὐρανός. νῦν δὲ οὗτοι πρὸς τῶν ἀγαθῶν θεῶν σὺν δίκῃ ἄρχονται.

_____

_____

34. διὰ τοὺς τοῦ ποιητοῦ λόγους πόνου ἐπαυόμεθα. μόνος γὰρ ἔλεγε καλὰ καὶ ἀγαθά.

_____

_____

35. ἢ λόγοις πείσομεν ἢ ὅπλοις τοὺς τοῖς Ἀθηναίοις ἐχθροὺς μὴ μάχης ἐν ταύτῃ ἄρχεσθαι τῇ νήσῳ.

_____

_____

36. Α. ἦρχον μὲν οἱ Ἀθηναῖοι τῆς θαλάσσης, νῦν δὲ παύονται πρὸς τῶν Λακεδαιμονίων.
    Β. ταῦτα, ὦ πολῖται, τοῖς συμμάχοις οὐ πείθομαι.

_____

_____

_____

37. τῆς ψῡχῆς καὶ τούτου τοῦ ἀνθρώπου, ποιητοῦ λόγων καλῶν, οἱ ἐν Ἅιδου νόμοι ἄρχουσιν.

_____

_____

38. ὁ τῇ ἀληθείᾳ σοφὸς πολλάκις τοῖς Ἀθηναίοις λέγει μὴ πολέμου ἀδίκου ἄρχεσθαι, ἀλλὰ οὐ τούτῳ
    πείθονται.

——

——

——

39. ἐν ἀρχῇ μὲν ἠρχόμην τῷ τῶν ἀθανάτων φόβῳ, νῦν δὲ τούτου τοῦ δεινοῦ φόβου παύομαι.

——

——

40. ἐν τῇ γῇ τῇ τῶν Ἀθηναίων πολέμου οἱ Λακεδαιμόνιοι ἤρχοντο. οὗτοι γὰρ ἄρξειν ἔμελλον τῶν νήσων.

——

——

41. τούτους καλὰ σὺν πόνῳ Εὐρῑπίδης ὁ ποιητὴς καὶ δεινὰ διδάσκει.

——

——

42. διὰ κακὴν μοῖραν σὺν φίλῳ τέκνῳ ἐκ τῆς χώρᾱς πεμφθήσει ταύτης εἰς τὴν γῆν τὴν τῶν ἐχθρῶν.

——

——

43. μόνῳ τῷ Πριάμῳ ἡ Ἑλένη μόνη περὶ τῶν συμφορῶν λέγει. τῇ γὰρ ἀληθείᾳ ἐθέλει ἀπὸ τῆς γῆς
    πέμπεσθαι.

——

——

44. ἡ ἀθάνατος θεὸς τοῖς ἀνθρώποις λέγει μὴ ὑπὸ φόβου ἄρχεσθαι, ἀλλὰ οἱ ἄνθρωποι τὸν πόλεμον ἔργον λέγουσι κακὸν τῆς θεοῦ.

45. περὶ μὲν εἰρήνης οἱ Λακεδαιμόνιοι ἔλεγον, τοῦ δὲ πολέμου ἤρχοντο.

46. πῶς Γαῖα καὶ Οὐρανὸς ἐπαύοντο τῆς ἀρχῆς πρὸς τῶν δικαίων θεῶν;

47. οὐ λόγοις ἀλλὰ ἔργοις τοῖς καλοῖς ἐπείθοντο οἱ πολῖται ἄρχεσθαι.

48. πότε καὶ πῶς ταύτᾱς καὶ τοὺς τούτων ἑταίρους ἐδίδασκες, ὦ Εὐρῑπίδη, τὴν τῶν ποιητῶν σοφίᾱν;

49. οὗτοι οἱ ξένοι, σύμμαχοι ταύτης τῆς χώρᾱς, λόγῳ πείθουσι δικαίῳ καὶ κοινῷ τὸν δῆμον μὴ πολέμου πρὸς τοὺς Λακεδαιμονίους ἄρχεσθαι.

50. πολλάκις λόγους πρὸς τοὺς θεοὺς ὁ Γοργίας λέγει. διὰ δὲ τοῦτο ἐκ τῆς γῆς οὗτος ὁ κοινὸς ἐχθρὸς πεμφθήσεται ὑπὸ τῶν πολῑτῶν.

51. τοῖς τῶν Ἀθηναίων νόμοις πειθόμεθα. διὰ δὲ τοῦτο καὶ οἱ σύμμαχοι πείσονται.

52. τὴν γνώμην τὴν περὶ τῆς τῶν θεῶν δίκης τοῖς ἐν οἰκίᾳ φίλοις ἔλεγον.

53. τὰ ἔργα τοῦ Ἀτρείδου τὰ οὐ καλὰ τοὺς νεᾱνίᾱς πείθει αἰσχρὰ λέγειν περὶ τῆς τούτου δόξης.

54. οἱ Ἀτρεῖδαι ἐν ἀγορᾷ ἔλεγον καὶ διὰ τῶν λόγων τὰ δεινὰ τοῦ πολέμου ἐδιδάσκοντο οἱ νεᾱνίαι.

55. καὶ τοὺς φίλους καὶ τοὺς ξένους πείθειν ἐθέλομεν περὶ τῆς εἰρήνης.

56. οὗτος ὁ πολίτης ὁ αἰσχρὸς καὶ ἄδικος τοὺς ἐν ἀγορᾷ ἀνθρώπους ἐδίδασκεν. νῦν δὲ ἐκ τῆς γῆς πέμπεται· τοῖς γὰρ νεᾱνίαις ἔλεγε μὴ τοῖς νόμοις πείθεσθαι τοῖς κοινοῖς καὶ τῶν Ἀθηναίων καὶ τῶν συμμάχων.

_____

_____

_____

_____

57. ἀπὸ μὲν τῶν θεῶν ἄρχονται αἱ Ἑλένης συμφοραί, ἐκ δὲ τῆς Ἑλένης ἄρχεται ὁ πόλεμος.

_____

_____

58. πῶς, ὦ δῆμε, τοῖς τούτων λόγοις πείθεσθαι ἐθέλεις τῶν ἀδίκων;

_____

_____

59. τοὺς νεᾱνίᾱς μόνος διδάσκομαι περὶ τὸν κοινὸν ἐχθρὸν τῶν δικαίων καὶ τῶν ἀγαθῶν.

_____

_____

60. ἆρα τὸν Εὐρῑπίδην φίλον λέγεις, ὦ ἑταῖρε; τοῦτον γὰρ ἐχθρὸν λέγω.

_____

_____

61. τὰς γνώμᾱς περὶ πολέμου καὶ εἰρήνης οἱ σύμμαχοι ἔλεγον. οὗτος δὲ ὁ πολίτης ὁ ταῦτα σοφὸς τὸν δῆμον ἔπειθε μὴ τοῖς Λακεδαιμονίοις ὅπλα πέμπειν.

_____

_____

_____

62. πόλεμος περὶ τὴν τῆς θαλάσσης ἀρχὴν τὴν κοινὴν ὑπὸ τῶν Ἀθηναίων παύεται. ἆρα οὐ λέγω τὴν ἀλήθειαν;

_____

_____

_____

C. Write these sentences in Greek.

1. We are refusing to obey Gorgias, the maker of unjust speeches. For this man often speaks not well in the presence of the people.

_____

_____

_____

2. How was the evil goddess alone persuading the men to begin this battle? She was sending evil opinions into their souls.

_____

_____

_____

3. The gods not only send the terrible toil of war to men, stranger, but they also teach these men about peace.

_____

_____

_____

4. I shall cause my children to be taught the truth not only about the rule of heaven but also about the gods under the earth. And in addition to these things they will be taught the deeds of the gods.

_____

_____

_____

5. The just gods many times send opinions not unjust into the souls of men. Or how do you say this thing, companion?

_____

_____

_____

6. Are you beginning the toils of war, young men, or are you ceasing from these noble deeds? For often the hostile gods do not intend to stop the misfortunes of men.

_____

_____

_____

7. These wise women are recounting the misfortunes of Helen and Alexander to their dear children alone.

_____

_____

_____

8. When shall we be sent on the sea to the land of the truly noble and good Athenians?

_____

_____

9. On account of the Athenians' rule of the sea both the Spartans and the allies were likely to begin a war.

_____

_____

_____

10. Were the children being taught well about the just and unjust things of war by the stranger from the Spartan land?

_____

_____

_____

11. How will the wise man persuade the young man to obey unjust laws? For he is not willing (to obey these laws).

_____

_____

_____

12. A man not truly good will speak beautiful speeches among the people, but when will he stop the young men from their wicked and unjust deeds?

_____

_____

_____

13. A. Were you telling your children not to be ruled by fear of war?
    B. Indeed how not?

_____

_____

_____

14. Aren't citizens good in judgment willing both to rule and to be ruled?

_____

_____

15. We were trying to persuade the strangers to speak publicly about the distress of the citizens on the islands.

_____

_____

_____

Drill 40: Contracted Verbs 1: -έω

A. Study the principal parts of and read carefully the vocabulary notes on the epsilon-contracted verbs in this chapter. Then write these verb phrases in Greek twice, first in the *uncontracted* form, then in the *contracted* Attic form. Accent both forms correctly.

Example: *Uncontracted Form*   *Contracted Form*
we are making war   **πολεμέομεν**   **πολεμοῦμεν**

	Uncontracted Form	*Contracted Form*

1. we were loving _____ _____

2. I was being loved _____ _____

3. to be loving _____ _____

4. to be being loved _____ _____

5. they are loving _____ _____

6. you are doing wrong _____ _____

7. I am being wronged _____ _____

8. you (pl.) were doing wrong _____ _____

9. he was being wronged _____ _____

10. to be wronged (repeatedly) _____ _____

11. they used to make war _____ _____

12. we are being treated as enemies _____ _____

13. to make war (repeatedly) _____ _____

	Uncontracted Form	*Contracted Form*

14. you (pl.) make war _____ _____

15. he was making war _____ _____

16. she is making (2) _____ _____

_____ _____

17. it is being made _____ _____

18. to be making (2) _____ _____

_____ _____

19. you were considering _____ _____

20. I was doing (2) _____ _____

_____ _____

B. Write a synopsis for each verb in the indicated person and number. Do not include rare forms.

1. φιλέω, 3rd sing.   2. ἀδικέω, 2nd pl. (no middle)
3. ποιέω, 1st sing.   4. πολεμέω, 3rd pl. (no middle)

C. Supply the resulting contraction for each.

ε + ε _____   ε + ο _____

ε + ω _____   ε + ει _____

ε + η _____   ε + ου _____

D. Translate these forms, giving all possibilities. Both regular omega verbs and epsilon-contracted verbs are included.

1. λέγεται _____

2. φιλεῖται _____

3. πολεμήσειν _____

4. μελλήσει _____

5. ἦρχε _____

6. ἠδίκει _____

7. ἀδικήσει _____

8. ἐθέλετε _____

9. πολεμεῖτε _____

10. πείθω _____

11. ποιῶ _____

12. ἀδικεῖσθαι _____

13. παύεσθαι (2) _____

14. ἐφιλούμεθα _____

15. ἐδιδασκόμεθα (2) _____

16. πέμπειν _____

17. ποιεῖν _____

18. ἔλεγεν _____

19. ἐπολέμει _____

20. ἔμελλον (2) _____

21. ἐφιλούμην _____

22. ἐπαυόμην (2) _____

23. ἠδικοῦ _____

24. ἐδιδάσκου (2) _____

25. ποιήσονται _____

26. ποιοῦνται (2) _____

Drill 41: Contracted Verbs 2: -άω

A. Study the principal parts of and read carefully the vocabulary notes on the alpha-contracted verbs in this chapter. Then write these verb phrases in Greek twice, first in the *uncontracted* form, then in the *contracted* Attic form. Accent both forms correctly.

	Uncontracted Form	*Contracted Form*
Example:		
they were winning	ἐνίκαον	ἐνίκων

	Uncontracted Form	*Contracted Form*
1. she is being honored	_____	_____
2. to honor (repeatedly)	_____	_____
3. you are honored	_____	_____
4. he was deeming worthy	_____	_____
5. we were being honored	_____	_____
6. to be (being) conquered	_____	_____
7. they are being conquered	_____	_____
8. he was winning	_____	_____
9. you (pl.) are winning	_____	_____
10. you were conquering	_____	_____
11. to be ending	_____	_____
12. he is dying	_____	_____
13. I was finishing	_____	_____

	Uncontracted Form	*Contracted Form*

14. they are ending _____ _____

15. we were accomplishing _____ _____

16. I was being conquered _____ _____

17. we are being honored _____ _____

18. you (pl.) were dying _____ _____

19. I was conquering _____ _____

20. they honor _____ _____

B. Write a synopsis for each verb in the indicated person and number. Do not include rare forms.

1. νῑκάω 3rd sing.   2. τελευτάω, 2nd pl. (no middle)
3. τῑμάω, 1st sing.   4. τῑμάω, 3rd pl.

C. Supply the resulting contraction for each.

α + ω _____   α + ο _____

α + ου _____   α + ε _____

α + ει _____   α + η _____

D. Translate these forms, giving all possibilities. Regular omega verbs and contracted verbs are included.

1. ἐτίμᾱ _____

2. ἤθελεν _____

3. ποιεῖ (3) _____

4. πείθει (3) _____

_____

5. ἀρξόμεθα _____

6. ἀδικηθησόμεθα _____

7. τελευτᾶν _____

8. ἀδικεῖν _____

9. ἄρχεται (2) _____

10. νῑκᾶται _____

11. ἐπέμπομεν _____

12. ἐτῑμῶμεν _____

13. παύεσθαι (2) _____

14. ποιεῖσθαι (2) _____

15. νῑκήσετε _____

16. ἐνῑκᾶσθε _____

17. ἐνίκᾱ _____

18. ἔλεγε _____

19. ἐτελεύτων (2) _____

20. ἐπαύου (2) _____

21. ἐτῑμῶ (2) _____

22. νῑκᾷ (2) _____

23. τῑμᾶσθαι (2) _____

24. ἐνίκων (2) _____

25. μέλλεις _____

26. τῑμήσεις _____

27. ἐφίλει _____

28. πολεμοῦσιν _____

29. ἐνίκω _____

30. τῑμᾶν _____

Drill 42: Contracted Verbs 3: -όω; New Verbs

A. Study the principal parts of and read carefully the vocabulary notes on the omicron-contracted verbs in this chapter. Then write these verb phrases in Greek twice, first in the *uncontracted* form, then in the *contracted* Attic form. Accent both forms correctly.

Example: *Uncontracted Form*   *Contracted Form*
he is making clear   **δηλόει**   **δηλοῖ**

                        Uncontracted Form   *Contracted Form*

1. they were making clear _____   _____

2. to be showing _____   _____

3. I was making clear _____   _____

4. you are making clear_____   _____

5. you were showing_____   _____

6. we were thinking worthy_____   _____

7. you (pl.) are being thought worthy _____   _____

8. I was expecting _____   _____

9. to be thinking (it) right _____   _____

10. she was being thought worthy _____   _____

11. they are making clear _____   _____

12. you (pl.) were showing_____   _____

13. I am making clear _____   _____

	Uncontracted Form	*Contracted Form*
14. she is making clear	_____	_____
15. he was showing	_____	_____
16. to be thought worthy (repeatedly)	_____	_____
17. I am being thought worthy	_____	_____
18. you are being thought worthy	_____	_____
19. it is being thought worthy	_____	_____
20. we require	_____	_____

B. Write a synopsis for each verb in the indicated person and number. Do not include rare forms.

1. δηλόω, 3rd sing.   2. ἀξιόω, 1st pl.
3. δηλόω, 3rd pl.   4. ἀξιόω, 2nd sing.

C. Supply the resulting contraction for each.

ο + ε _____   ο + ο _____

ο + ω _____   ο + ει _____

ο + η _____   ο + ου _____

D. Translate these forms, giving all possibilities. Regular omega verbs and contracted verbs are included.

1. ποιηθήσονται _____

2. ἔμελλεν _____

3. δηλοῖ _____

4. ἀξιοῦν _____

5. ἠξίουν (2) _____

6. πείθεσθε (2) _____

7. ἀδικεῖς _____

8. δηλοῖς _____

9. ἠξιοῦτε _____

10. ἀξιώσετε _____

11. φιληθήσεσθαι _____

12. ἐδήλου _____

13. δηλοῦν _____

14. πέμψομεν _____

15. τελευτῶσιν _____

16. ἐφίλουν (2) _____

17. μελλήσετε _____

18. ἀξιούμεθα _____

19. παυόμεθα (2) _____

20. ποιεῖσθαι (2) _____

21. ποιήσεσθαι _____

22. ἀρχθήσει _____

23. πολεμεῖς _____

24. ἐδηλοῦμεν _____

25. ἐπείθου (2) _____

26. ἀξιοῖ (2) _____

E. Translate these short sentences containing contracted verbs.

1. τοῦτο δηλώσω τοῖς νεᾱνίαις.

_____

_____

2. τοῖς Λακεδαιμονίοις ἐπολεμοῦμεν.

_____

_____

3. ἆρα ἠδικοῦ ὑπὸ τῶν ξένων;

_____

_____

4. εὖ τελευτήσει ἡ μάχη. τὴν μάχην εὖ τελευτήσει.

_____

_____

5. ὁ αἰσχρὸς ἄνθρωπος ταύτην ἀδικεῖ.

_____

_____

6. τὴν τούτου τοῦ πολέμου αἰτίᾱν ἐδήλουν.

_____

_____

7. τοὺς πόνους τῶν πολῑτῶν ἐθέλομεν τελευτᾶν.

_____

_____

8. σὺν θεοῖς ὅπλα ἀγαθὰ ποιῶ.

_____

_____

9. ἆρα φιλεῖσθαι οἱ θεοὶ θέλουσι πρὸς τῶν ἀνθρώπων;

_____

_____

10. ὁ ποιητὴς καλοῖς τῑμᾷ λόγοις τούτους τοὺς πολίτᾱς.

_____

_____

11. τοῦτο μόνον δηλοῦν μέλλω· αἰσχρὰ ποιεῖτε, ὦ κακοί.

_____

_____

12. οἱ Ἀθηναῖοι νῑκηθήσονται ἐν τούτῳ τῷ πολέμῳ.

_____

_____

F. Study the principal parts of and read the vocabulary notes on all the verbs in this chapter. Then give the principal parts of these verbs.

1. conquer _____

_____

2. love _____

_____

3. make clear _____

_____

4. end, finish _____

_____

5. do wrong _____

_____

6. think worthy _____

_____

7. make war (upon) _____

_____

8. honor _____

_____

9. make, do _____

_____

10. have, hold _____

_____

G. Write a synopsis for ἔχω in each indicated person and number.

1. ἔχω, 3rd sing.   2. ἔχω, 1st pl.

Drill 43: The Demonstrative Adjective and Pronoun ὅδε, ἥδε, τόδε

A. Recite from memory the entire declension of **ὅδε, ἥδε, τόδε**.

B. Identify these forms by gender, number, and case. Give all possibilities.

1. τῇδε _____

2. τόνδε _____

3. τοῖσδε _____

4. τάδε _____

5. ὅδε _____

6. τόδε _____

7. τοῦδε _____

8. αἵδε _____

9. τῆσδε _____

10. τῶνδε _____

C. Write these forms of **ὅδε, ἥδε, τόδε**.

1. masc. sing. dat. _____ 2. neut. pl. acc. _____

3. fem. pl. gen. _____ 4. neut. sing. nom. _____

5. masc. pl. acc. _____ 6. fem. sing. acc. _____

7. masc. pl. nom. _____   8. neut. pl. dat. _____

9. fem. pl. acc. _____   10. masc. sing. gen. _____

D. On a separate sheet decline fully (no vocative) **ὅδε ὁ ποιητής**, **ἥδε ἡ δόξα**, and **τὸ ἔργον τόδε**.

E. Provide the correct form of **ὅδε**, **ἥδε**, **τόδε** to modify these nouns and translate each phrase.

ὅδε, ἥδε, τόδε		*Translation*
1. _____	τοὺς θεούς	_____
2. _____	τῆς θαλάσσης	_____
3. _____	τὰ αἰσχρά	_____
4. τῇ αἰτίᾳ _____		_____
5. τοῦ λόγου _____		_____
6. τὸ τέκνον _____		_____
7 _____	τὰς ὁδούς	_____
8. _____	τὸν ἑταῖρον	_____
9. _____	τῷ νεανίᾳ	_____
10. _____	οἱ φόβοι	_____
11. τῶν φίλων _____		_____
12. τῇ μοίρᾳ _____		_____
13. _____	τὸ ὅπλον	_____
14. _____	τὸν ξένον	_____

ὅδε, ἥδε, τόδε		Translation

15. _____ τοῖς πολίταις   _____

16. _____ τοὺς δικαίους   _____

17. ἡ Ἑλένη _____   _____

18. τοῦ συμμάχου _____   _____

19. _____ τὴν δόξαν   _____

20 τὰ κακὰ _____   _____

F. Translate these forms of the demonstrative pronoun. Give all possibilities.

1. αἵδε _____

2. τόδε _____

3. τῶνδε _____

4. τῆσδε _____

5. τούσδε _____

6. τοῖσδε _____

7. οἵδε _____

8. τάδε _____

9. τοῦδε _____

10. ταῖσδε _____

G. Translate these phrases.

1. τοῖσδε τοῖς ἀνθρώποις _____

2. περὶ τῶνδε _____

3. ἥδε ἡ θεός _____

4. τὰς τοῦδε γνώμᾱς _____

5. τῷδε τῷ πόνῳ _____

6. ἀπὸ τῆς οἰκίᾱς τῆσδε _____

7. διὰ τάδε _____

8. τόδε τὸ ἀγαθόν _____

9. ἐν τῇδε τῇ γῇ _____

10. ὑπὸ τῶν συμμάχων τῶνδε _____

11. οἱ τῆσδε φίλοι _____

12. οὐχ ὅδε ἀλλὰ ἥδε _____

13. τάδε τὰ καλά _____

14. τῇ ἀληθείᾳ τῇδε _____

15. περὶ τῆς τοῦδε ψῡχῆς _____

16. πρὸς τούσδε μόνους _____

17. τάσδε τὰς συμφορᾱς _____

18. ἐν τῇ τῶνδε χώρᾳ _____

19. τήνδε τὴν σοφίᾱν _____

20. εἰς τὸν πόλεμον τόνδε _____

H. Write these phrases in Greek using forms of **ὅδε, ἥδε, τόδε**.

1. through this land _____

2. the opinion (subj.) of this man _____

3. these things (d.o.) _____

4. (out) from this sky _____

5. by this plan _____

6. these laws (subj.) _____

7. this cause (d.o.) _____

8. for these allies _____

9. concerning this thing _____

10. the children (d.o.) of this woman _____

11. by these companions _____

12. either for this man or for this woman _____

_____

13. with the aid of this goddess _____

14. by this peace _____

15. not only these women (d.o.) but also these men (d.o.) _____

_____

16. the weapons (d.o.) of these young men _____

17. this animal (subj.) _____

18. on account of these causes _____

19. this good citizen (subj.) _____

20. on this island _____

Drill 44: The Demonstrative Adjective and Pronoun
ἐκεῖνος, ἐκείνη, ἐκεῖνο

A. Recite from memory the entire declension of ἐκεῖνος, ἐκείνη, ἐκεῖνο.

B. Identify these forms by gender, number, and case. Give all possibilities.

1. ἐκείνην _____

2. ἐκεῖνοι _____

3. ἐκείνοις _____

4. ἐκείνῃ _____

5. ἐκεῖνο _____

6. ἐκείνων _____

7. ἐκεῖνα _____

8. ἐκεῖνον _____

9. ἐκείνᾱς _____

10. ἐκείνους _____

C. Write these forms of ἐκεῖνος, ἐκείνη, ἐκεῖνο.

1. fem. pl. nom. _____   2. neut. sing. acc. _____

3. masc. sing. dat. _____   4. neut sing. nom. _____

5. fem. sing. gen. _____   6. masc. pl. nom. _____

7. fem. pl. dat. _____   8. neut. pl. nom. _____

9. masc. sing. acc. _____   10. neut. pl. gen. _____

D. On a separate sheet decline fully (no vocative) **ἐκεῖνος ὁ φίλος, ἡ αἰτίᾱ ἐκείνη**, and **ἐκεῖνο τὸ ζῷον**.

E. Provide the correct form of **ἐκεῖνος, ἐκείνη, ἐκεῖνο** to modify these nouns and then translate each phrase.

	ἐκεῖνος, ἐκείνη, ἐκεῖνο	*Translation*
1.	_____ τὴν θεόν	_____
2.	_____ τῶν πολῑτῶν	_____
3.	_____ τῷ φόβῳ	_____
4. τὰ ἔργα	_____	_____
5. τὸν νεᾱνίᾱν	_____	_____
6. ταῖς γνώμαις	_____	_____
7.	_____ τὸ κακόν	_____
8.	_____ τοῦ ξένου	_____
9.	_____ τὰς νήσους	_____
10. οἱ λόγοι	_____	_____
11. τῇ ἀγαθῇ	_____	_____
12.	_____ τῷ ὅπλῳ	_____
13.	_____ ἡ ὁδός	_____
14. Γοργίᾱν	_____	_____

ἐκεῖνος, ἐκείνη, ἐκεῖνο	*Translation*
15. τοὺς ἑταίρους _____	_____
16. _____ τῶν καλῶν	_____
17. _____ τοὺς πόνους	_____
18. _____ ἡ γῆ	_____
19. τὸ τέκνον _____	_____
20. τοῖς νόμοις _____	_____

F. Translate these forms of the demonstrative pronoun. Give all possibilities.

1. ἐκεῖνον _____

2. ἐκεῖναι _____

3. ἐκείνου _____

4. ἐκείνους _____

5. ἐκείνη _____

6. ἐκεῖνο _____

7. ἐκεῖνα _____

8. ἐκείναις _____

9. ἐκείνᾱς _____

10. ἐκείνῳ _____

G. Translate these phrases.

1. ὑπὸ τοῖς σοφοῖς ἐκείνοις _____

2. ἐκεῖναι αἱ συμφοραί _____

3. ἐν ἐκείνῃ τῇ χώρᾳ _____

4. εἰς ἐκεῖνα _____

5. τοὺς συμμάχους ἐκείνους _____

6. περὶ ἐκείνων _____

7. οὐχ ὅδε ἀλλὰ ἐκεῖνος _____

8. ἀπὸ τῆς οἰκίας ἐκείνης _____

9. εἰς ἐκεῖνον τὸν πόλεμον _____

10. ἐκείνῳ τῷ πόνῳ μόνῳ _____

11. τοῖς πολίταις ἐκείνοις _____

12. πρὸς ἐκείνους τοὺς ἀνθρώπους _____

13. οὐ μόνον ἐκεῖνοι ἀλλὰ καὶ ἐκεῖναι _____

14. ὑπὸ τῆς θεοῦ ἐκείνης _____

15. ἐκείνῳ τῷ ἔργῳ _____

16. περὶ τῶν αἰσχρῶν ἐκείνων _____

H. Write these phrases in Greek using forms of **ἐκεῖνος, ἐκείνη, ἐκεῖνο**.

1. out from that land _____

2. for those allies on that island _____

3. resulting from that thing alone _____

4. the opinions (subj.) of those men _____

5. that guest (d.o.) _____

6. through those lands _____

7. in the beginning of that war _____

8. of those unjust speeches _____

9. on that road _____

10. by those poets _____

11. that child (subj.) _____

12. of those young men _____

13. concerning that advice _____

14. that justice (d.o.) of the gods _____

15. in that house _____

16. in reply to those men _____

17. that good thing (d.o.) _____

18. those beautiful gods (subj.) _____

Drill 45: Comparison of **οὗτος**, **ὅδε**, and **ἐκεῖνος**

Translate these sentences containing forms of **οὗτος**, **ὅδε**, and **ἐκεῖνος**.

1. ἀδίκου πολέμου οἱ Ἀθηναῖοι ἄρχονται. ταῦτα ὑπὸ τῶν Λακεδαιμονίων λέγεται.

_____

_____

2. σὺν τοῖς θεοῖς ἐκείνων τῶν νήσων ἄρξομεν, ἀλλὰ τῶνδε οὔ.

_____

_____

3. οὐκ ἐπείθοντο τοῖς ἐκείνων λόγοις οὗτοι οἱ ἀγαθοὶ πολῖται.

_____

_____

4. ὁ ἐν τῇδε τῇ γῇ πόλεμος νῦν παύεται· τοῦτο, ὦ σύμμαχοι, λέγετε;

_____

_____

5. οἱ μὲν νεᾱνίαι διδάσκεσθαι ἐθέλουσιν, οἱ δὲ τούτων ἑταῖροι οὔ. καὶ τούτους καὶ ἐκείνους ὁ Γοργίᾱς
   διδάσκειν ἐθέλει.

_____

_____

6. Εὐρῑπίδης ἐκεῖνος ἔλεγε τάδε· Τοῖς πολίταις λέγω μὴ τῷ κακῷ λόγῳ τῷ τοῦ Γοργίου πείθεσθαι.

_____

_____

7. μόναι αἱ καλαὶ γνῶμαι ἄρχουσι τῆσδε τῆς ψῡχῆς.

_____

_____

8. τόδε τῷ φίλῳ πέμπω, ἀλλὰ ἐκεῖνο πέμπειν μέλλεις.

_____

_____

9. ταῦτα τὰ τέκνα περὶ τῶν νόμων εὖ διδαχθήσεται.

_____

_____

10. οἱ σύμμαχοι περὶ τῆς εἰρήνης καὶ τοῦ πολέμου λέγουσιν. τούτου μὲν παύεσθαι ἐθέλουσιν, ἐκείνης δὲ ἄρχεσθαι.

_____

_____

Drill 46: The Irregular Adjectives μέγας, μεγάλη, μέγα and πολύς, πολλή, πολύ

A. On a separate sheet decline fully these phrases. Write the interjection ὦ before vocative forms.

1. ὁ μέγας θεός
2. ἡ μεγάλη οἰκίᾱ
3. πολλὰ ὅπλα (pl. only)
4. πολὺς πόνος
5. μέγας σύμμαχος
6. τὸ μέγα ἔργον

B. Supply the correct form of the adjective μέγας, μεγάλη, μέγα to modify each noun.

1. _____ θάλασσαν   2. _____ λόγοι

3. _____ ζῷα   4. _____ αἰτίαις

5. _____ ἄνθρωπον   6. _____ ἔργων

7. _____ δόξῃ   8. _____ οὐρανός

9. _____ ζῷον   10. _____ νῆσος

11. _____ φόβῳ   12. _____ ὅπλον

13. _____ σύμμαχε   14. _____ θεοῖς (2)

_____

15. _____ ποιητῶν   16. _____ ἔργου

C. Supply the correct form of the adjective **πολύς**, **πολλή**, **πολύ** to modify each noun.

1. _____ οὐρανόν

2. _____ ὅπλων

3. _____ λόγος

4. _____ ψῡχᾱ́ς

5. _____ θεῶν

6. _____ ἔργον

7. _____ συμμάχοις

8. _____ χώρᾱς (2)

   _____

9. _____ πόνον

10. _____ νεᾱνίαι

11. _____ ζῷα

12. _____ θεοί (2)

    _____

13. _____ ποιητᾱ́ς

14. _____ ξένοις

15. _____ αἰτιῶν

16. _____ ἔργα

D. Translate these phrases.

1. ὦ μεγάλε Πρίαμε _____

2. πολλῶν λόγων _____

3. περὶ τῆς μεγάλης θαλάσσης _____

4. πολλοῖς σὺν ὅπλοις _____

5. μεγάλα καὶ πολλά _____

6. πολλοὶ καὶ ὅπλα πολλά _____

7. ἐν νήσοις μεγάλαις _____

8. τὸ πολὺ ἔργον _____

9. μέγα ἔργον _____

10. πολὺν φόβον _____

11. οἱ πολλοί _____

12. ἐκ πολλῶν αἰτιῶν _____

13. δόξαν μεγάλην _____

14. πολλὰ καὶ δεινά _____

15. σοφίᾱν οὐ πολλὴν _____

16. πολλοῖς τέκνοις _____

17. μέγα καὶ καλόν _____

18. μέγαν πόλεμον _____

Drill 47–50: Partitive Genitive; Genitive of Value; Substantive Use of the Article; Adverbs

Underline and identify all substantives, Partitive Genitives, Genitives of Value, and adverbs in these sentences. Then translate.

1. τὸ τέκνον ὁ μὲν διδάσκει, ὁ δὲ διδάσκεται.

_____

_____

_____

2. ἥδε ἡ γῆ ὑπὸ τῶν τῆς νήσου καλῶς ἄρχεται.

_____

_____

_____

3. περὶ τῶν νῦν λέξω καὶ τοὺς ἀγαθοὺς τῶν νεāνιῶν πείσω.

_____

_____

_____

4. πολλοῦ δὴ τοὺς Γοργίου λόγους ἐποιούμην.

_____

_____

_____

5. τῶν πολῑτῶν μόνους τούτους τῑμώμεθα ἀρχῆς.

_____

_____

_____

6. ὁ τῶν Ἀθηναίων δῆμος δικαίως ἦρχεν τῶν ἐκείνης τῆς χώρᾱς.

_____

_____

_____

7. ὁ σοφὸς τῷ δήμῳ λέγειν μέλλει τὰ ἐν τῇ βουλῇ.

_____

_____

_____

8. ὁ δῆμος τοῦτον τὸν πολίτην διὰ τὰ καλὰ ἔργα τῑμᾶται δόξης καλῆς.

_____

_____

_____

9. οὕτω τῶν ἑταίρων τοὺς μὲν ὁ Γοργίᾱς ἔπειθεν, τοὺς δὲ οὔ.

_____

_____

_____

10. τὰ τοῦ πολέμου ὑπὸ τούτου τοῦ ποιητοῦ ἐδιδασκόμεθα.

_____

_____

_____

11. ἆρα οὐ περὶ πολλοῦ εἰρήνην ὁ Πριάμου ποιήσεται;

_____

_____

_____

12. τοῦτο, ὦ φίλε, σὺν τῷ δικαίῳ λέγεις.

_____

_____

_____

13. τῶν πολῑτῶν οἱ περὶ Εὐρῑπίδην ὑπὸ τούτων διδάσκεσθαι οὐκ ἐθέλουσιν.

_____

_____

_____

14. τούτῳ μόνῳ τῶν Ἀθηναίων πείσεται ὁ δῆμος.

_____

_____

_____

15. τοῖς Ἀθηναίων νόμοις αἱ ἀπὸ τῶν νήσων οὐκ ἐπείθοντο.

_____

_____

_____

16. ὧδε ἔπειθον τὸν δῆμον· εὖ γὰρ καὶ καλῶς ἔλεγον.

_____

_____

_____

17. τῶν φίλων τοὺς μὲν εἰς ἀγορὰν πέμψομεν, τοὺς δὲ εἰς οἰκίᾱν.

_____

_____

_____

18. οἱ Λακεδαιμόνιοι οὐκ ἐτῑμῶντο τῆς τῶν νήσων ἀρχῆς τοὺς Ἀθηναίους.

_____

_____

_____

Drill 51: Elision and Crasis

A. Rewrite these phrases and sentences *without* elision or crasis. *Do not translate.*

Example: ταῦθ' ὁ Πρίαμος   **ταῦτα ὁ Πρίαμος**

1. τἄδικα _____

2. ἀπ' ἀρχῆς _____

3. τἀν τῇ γῇ _____

4. χαὖται _____

5. κοὐ _____

6. ὠγαθέ _____

7. ἀλλ' οὐ _____

8. κἀς ὁδόν _____

9. ὁ δ' ἦρχεν. _____

10. τοῦθ' οἱ ἑταῖροι ἔλεγον. _____

B. Rewrite these phrases and sentences using *elision. Do not translate.*

1. οἱ δὲ ἐν ἀγορᾷ _____

2. ὑπὸ ἀνθρώπων _____

3. ἀπὸ οὐρανοῦ _____

4. ὑπὸ Ἑλένης _____

5. κακὰ ἐν πολέμῳ _____

6. ἐπέμπεσθε ἐκ τῆς γῆς. _____

7. πῶς τοῦτο ἔλεγεν; _____

8. πότε, ὦ Εὐρῑπίδη, τοῦτο ἔλεγες; _____

C. Rewrite these phrases using *crasis*.

1. ὁ ἄνθρωπος _____

2. καὶ ἡ τύχη _____

3. τὸ ἔργον _____

4. καὶ οὗτος _____

5. τὸ ἀγαθόν _____

6. τῷ ἀνθρώπῳ _____

7. τὰ ἀπὸ τῆς εἰρήνης ἀγαθά _____

8. καὶ ὁ θεός _____

9. ὦ ἄνθρωποι _____

10. καὶ ἐκείνων _____

11. καὶ ἐκ κακῶν _____

12. τὸ ἐν οἰκίᾳ τέκνον _____

Exercises, Chapter 4

A. Place the correct accents on these phrases and sentences and then translate. Assume that the last word in each phrase ends a sentence.

1. ὁ ἐπι τους πολεμιους των Ἀθηναιων λογος

_____

_____

2. νῑκαν και νῑκασθαι

_____

3. μετα του ταυτης υἱου και των τουτου ἑταιρων

_____

_____

4. τα ὑπο γης

_____

5. ἀφ' Ἑρμου ἀρχεσθαι και τελευταν

_____

6. πως, ὠγαθε, ἐχεις;

_____

7. πολλακις ὑπ᾽ ἐχθρου ἠδικου.

_____

8. δεινα ποιειν, ὦ πολῖται, ἀξιουτε;

_____

9. ὀλιγοι προς πολλους ἐπολεμουν.

_____

10. ἐτελευτᾱ ἡ μαχη.

_____

B. Translate these sentences.

1. κακὸν ἐκείνᾱς ποιεῖτ᾽, ὦ πονηροί.

_____

_____

2. τοῦ δικαίου μόνος εἰχόμην.

_____

_____

3. πῶς δὴ τοῦτο ἔχει; οὕτως.

_____

_____

4. φίλους κακῶς ἀδικεῖν οὐκ ἠξίουν.

_____

_____

5. κακοὺς καλῶς ποιεῖν οὐκ ἔχω.

_____

6. οἱ νέοι ἀδικεῖν φιλοῦσιν. τοῦτο γὰρ δηλώσω.

_____

_____

7. ἆρ' ἐτελεύτᾱ ὑφ' ἑταίρων;

_____

8. πότε τόδε τὸ ἔργον οὐκ ὀλίγον, ὠγαθέ, ποιήσειν μέλλεις;

_____

_____

9. τοῦ δήμου οἱ μὲν εὖ λέγουσιν, οἱ δὲ κακῶς.

_____

_____

10. πολλάκις καὶ ἐν ταῖς ὁδοῖς, ὦ Ἑρμῆ, τῑμᾷ.

_____

_____

11. μετὰ πολλῆς ἔλεγες, ὦ φίλ᾽ ἑταῖρε, ἀληθείας.

_____

_____

12. τὸν ταύτης υἱὸν μετὰ ταύτην φιλῶ.

_____

_____

13. θέλω τοῖς φίλοις μόνοις τούτους τελευτᾶν τοὺς πόνους.

_____

_____

14. τῶνδε τῶν συμμάχων οἱ μὲν ἐκείνην τὴν μάχην ἐνίκων, οἱ δ᾽ ἐνῑκῶνθ᾽ ὑπὸ τῶν πολεμίων. τούτους δὲ τῑμᾶσθαι οὐκ ἀξιοῦμεν.

_____

_____

_____

15. τὸ τῆς τύχης αἰτίᾱν ἔχει πολλὴν τῶν βίου συμφορῶν, ὁ δὲ ποιητὴς ἔχει τοῦτο τοῖς πολίταις δηλοῦν.

_____

_____

_____

16. περὶ τούτων λέγειν τῶν αἰσχρῶν δι᾽ αἰτίᾱς πολλὰς οὐκ ἤθελον, νῦν δὲ ἀρχὴν λόγου ποιοῦμαι.

_____

_____

17. μέγας καὶ δεινός, ὦ γῆ καὶ θεοί, ἔχει τὸν δῆμον φόβος τῶν νῦν ἐν τῇδε τῇ χώρᾳ κακῶν.

_____

_____

18. αἰτίᾱν ἔχεις, ὦ πονηρέ, τῆσδε τῆς συμφορᾶς. ἐκ δὲ τούτου πέμπῃ ἀπὸ τῆς γῆς.

_____

_____

_____

19. πολλάκις δὴ ὅδε ὁ πολίτης ὁ τὴν περὶ πολέμου σοφίᾱν δεινὸς λόγους ἐν τῇ βουλῇ ἐποιεῖτο.

_____

_____

20. εἰρήνην δὴ πρὸς τοὺς πολεμίους οἱ Ἀθηναῖοι ποιεῖσθαι ἠξίουν. οἱ δὲ πολεμεῖν ἐπαύοντο.

_____

_____

21. πολεμίους οἱ Ἀθηναῖοι τοὺς Λακεδαιμονίους σὺν δίκῃ ἔλεγον. ἐκεῖνοι γὰρ ὑπὸ τούτων μόνων ἐπολεμοῦντο.

_____

_____

_____

22. τοῖς μὲν νόμοις τῶν Ἀθηναίων, ὦ νέοι, εὖ ἐπείθεσθε καὶ δικαίως τοὺς θεοὺς ἐτῑμᾶτε—τῶν γὰρ φίλων ἐνῑκᾶσθε λόγοις—τὰ δὲ δὴ μετὰ ταῦτα ποιεῖτε οὐ καλῶς.

_____

_____

_____

23. ὑπὸ χαλεπῆς τύχης καὶ τῶν ἐχθρῶν θεῶν οἵδε οἱ βροτοὶ οἱ μάχην ἀγαθοὶ ἐνῑκῶντο.

_____

_____

24. οὐ μόνον οὐκ ἐποίει κακὰ καὶ αἰσχρὰ ἐκεῖνος ὁ καλὸς κἀγαθὸς ἄνθρωπος, ἀλλ᾽ ἔπαυε δὴ τούτων πολλοὺς τῶν ἑταίρων ταῖς ἀρεταῖς οὐκ ὀλίγαις. μετὰ δὲ ταῦτα ἐτῑμᾶτο.

_____

_____

_____

25. πόλλ᾽ οὐκ τῆς νήσου ξένος τὸν νέον διδάσκειν ἔχει. ὁ δὲ διὰ τὴν αἰτίᾱν ταύτην ἑταῖρον ποιεῖσθαι τοῦτον ἐθελήσει.

_____

_____

_____

26. λέγεται τάδε τὰ νέα περὶ Λακεδαιμονίων καὶ Ἀθηναίων· οὗτοι μὲν γὰρ τὰ χαλεπά διδάσκειν τὰ πολέμου
ἤθελον καὶ τἀγαθὰ εἰρήνης, ἐκεῖνοι δὲ, πολλοὶ καὶ πονηροί, λόγους περὶ νίκης αἰσχρῶς ἐποιοῦντο.

_____

_____

_____

27. ἐπὶ τὰς τοῦ δήμου γνώμᾱς ὀλίγοι τῶν ξένων λέγειν ἐθέλουσιν, ἀλλ᾽ ὅδε τὴν γνώμην δηλοῖ.

_____

_____

28. μετὰ τὴν νίκην τοὺς φίλους τοὺς ὑπὸ γαίᾱς τῑμᾶν ἀξιώσουσιν οἱ καλοὶ κἀγαθοί.

_____

_____

29. ὁ σοφὸς καὶ ψῡχὴν ἀγαθὸς νῦν ὑπ᾽ ἐχθρῶν τελευτᾷ τὸν βίον. ὀλίγου γὰρ οὗτοι τὴν τούτου μεγάλην
ἐποιοῦντο ἀρετὴν καὶ τὰς σοφὰς γνώμᾱς.

_____

_____

_____

30. τὸν υἱὸν ὁ σοφὸς ἐδίδασκε μὴ μεθ᾽ ὅπλων ἀλλὰ διὰ λόγων δεινῶν πολεμεῖν πρὸς τοὺς πολεμίους. ὁ δὲ
σὺν δίκῃ ἐπείθετο.

_____

_____

_____

31. οἱ μὲν μὴ σοφοὶ ἄρχειν ἐθέλουσιν, οἱ δὲ δὴ καλοὶ κἀγαθοὶ τῶν πολλῶν νῦν ἄρχουσιν. σοφὰς γὰρ γνώμας ἔχουσιν.

_____

_____

_____

32. τὸν μὲν μέγαν οὐρανὸν οἱ ἀθάνατοι ἔχουσιν, τὴν δὲ γῆν τήνδε οἱ ἄνθρωποι μετὰ τῶν ζῴων. ταῦθ᾽ οὕτως ἔχει.

_____

_____

_____

33. τοὺς μὲν Ἀθηναίους οἱ πολλοὶ ἐν αἰτίᾳ ἐκείνου τοῦ πολέμου εἶχον, τοὺς δὲ Λακεδαιμονίους μόνους μετὰ δίκης ἐτίμων.

_____

_____

_____

34. τοῖς νεανίαις λέγεις, ὦ πολῖτα, μὴ τῷ νόμῳ τῷδε πείθεσθαι. οὕτως ἄδικον καὶ αἰσχρὸν ποιεῖς, θεοῖς ἐχθρέ.

_____

_____

_____

35. οἵδε οὐ διὰ τύχην ἀλλὰ ἀρετῇ καὶ πόνῳ καλῶς μάχην νῑκῶσιν. καὶ γὰρ νῦν ἔχει μέγας φόβος τοὺς
πολεμίους.

_____

_____

_____

36. διὰ τὰ κάκ᾽ ἔργα καὶ δεινὰ ἐπέμπετο ἐκ τῆς χώρᾱς ὁ Γοργίᾱς. μετὰ δὲ τοῦτον καὶ ὁ Εὐρῑπίδης. τούτους
νῦν ἐχθροὺς οἱ πολῖται λέγουσιν.

_____

_____

_____

37. διὰ τὴν τῶν Λακεδαιμονίων νίκην οἱ σύμμαχοι δικαίως ἐτῑμῶντο ὑπὸ τοῦ Ἀθηναίων δήμου.

_____

_____

_____

38. μεγάλη δὴ ἀρετῇ αὕτη τοὺς ἀνθρώπους οὐ διδάσκει μόνον, ἀλλὰ καὶ οὕτω τοὺς πολίτᾱς εὖ ποιεῖ. ἐκ
δὲ τούτων τῑμηθήσεται.

_____

_____

_____

39. οὐ τοὺς λόγους ἀλλὰ τὸν βίον ἐκείνου τοῦ ποιητοῦ μεγάλως τῑμήσομεν. κακὰ μὲν γὰρ λέγει, καλὰ δὲ
ποιεῖ.

_____

_____

_____

40. πολλοὺς δὴ δι' ὀλίγους ἀξιοῖ ὁ πολέμου θεὸς ὁ χαλεπὸς ἐς Ἅιδου πέμπεσθαι. ἆρ' οὐχ ὧδ' ἔχει;

_____

_____

_____

41. ὀλίγοις δὴ ἀνθρώπων οἱ μεγάλοι θεοὶ τύχην ἀγαθὴν πέμπουσιν. καὶ γὰρ ὀλίγους φιλοῦσιν.

_____

_____

42. οὐξ ἀρχῆς φίλος μὲν, ἐχθρὸς δὲ νῦν, τοῦτον αἰσχρῶς ἀδικεῖ. ὁ δὲ κακῶς ἔχει.

_____

_____

_____

43. ὅδε ὁ ἀγαθὸς πολίτης φόβον οὐκ εἶχε θανάτου, ἀνθρώπων τύχης κοινῆς. καὶ γὰρ τοῦ βίου νίκην ἐτῑμᾶτο τὴν ἐν ἐκείνῃ τῇ μάχῃ.

_____

_____

_____

44. καὶ πῶς, ὦ Γοργίᾱ, τούτους εὖ μὲν ποιεῖς, κακῶς δὲ λέγεις;

_____

_____

45. τοὺς υἱοὺς ἐφίλει ὁ Πρίαμος, ἀλλ’ ἐς μάχην τούτους πολλάκις ἔπεμπεν.

_____

_____

46. τοὺς μὲν φίλους αὕτη πολλοῦ ποιεῖται, τοὺς δ’ ἐχθροὺς οὔ. οὗτως εὖ ἔχει ὁ βίος.

_____

_____

47. καὶ οἱ κακοὶ πεισθήσεσθαι μέλλουσι μὴ τοὺς συμμάχους ἀδικεῖν ἀλλὰ τὴν ἀρετὴν φιλεῖν. τούτοις γὰρ
    δηλοῦμεν τὰ ἔργα τοῦ βίου τοῦ καλοῦ.

_____

_____

_____

48. Α. ἆρ’ οὐκ ἄρχει ἐν ταῖς ψῡχαῖς τῶν μὲν τὸ ἀγαθόν, τῶν δὲ τὸ κακόν;
    Β. οὕτω γὰρ ἔχει.

_____

_____

_____

49. χαλεπὰ λέγει ἡ Ἑλένη μόνη τῷ καλῷ Πριάμου υἱῷ μόνῳ. ὁ δ’ οὐ μέλλει πολεμεῖν.

_____

_____

50. πῶς ὁ Πρίαμος τῷ νέῳ υἱῷ ἐδήλου τὸ δίκαιον καὶ τὸ μὴ δίκαιον;

_____

_____

51. Α. τοῖς νεᾱνίαις λέγω μὴ ἀδικεῖν, ἀλλ᾽ οὐ πείθονται.
    Β. οὐ γὰρ ἔχουσιν ἄρχεσθαι οἱ νεᾱνίαι.

_____

_____

_____

52. καλῶς ποιεῖ ἡ δικαίᾱ Τύχη· ὁ μὲν γὰρ πονηρὸς κακῶς τελευτᾷ, ὁ δ᾽ ἀγαθὸς εὖ.

_____

_____

53. οἱ βροτοὶ περὶ τοῦ δικαίου καὶ ἀδίκου τοὺς θανάτους καὶ τὰς μάχᾱς ποιοῦσιν. καὶ γὰρ τὴν δόξαν νῑκᾶν ἢ νῑκᾶσθαι ἐθέλουσιν.

_____

_____

_____

54. λόγῳ μὲν οἱ Λακεδαιμόνιοι πρὸς τῶν Ἀθηναίων ἐπολεμοῦντο, ἔργῳ δ᾽ ἐκεῖνοι ἀπ᾽ ἀρχῆς ἐπολέμουν.

_____

_____

55. οἱ τῶν νήσων ὑπὸ πολέμου καὶ συμφορῶν κακῶν κακῶς ἔχουσιν. καὶ δὴ κακῶς, ὦ Ἀθηναῖοι, πολλοὶ
   τελευτῶσιν. πότε παύσονται οἱ τούτων πόνοι;

_____

_____

_____

_____

56. πῶς οὗτος ὁ λόγος, ὦ δῆμε, τελευτήσει; ἆρ᾽ οἱ πολλοὶ πείθονται δικαίως μὴ τοὺς κακοὺς τῖμᾶν ἀλλὰ
   τούτους πέμπειν ἐκ τῆσδε τῆς γῆς;

_____

_____

_____

_____

_____

57. ὅδε ὁ τῇ ἀληθείᾳ δίκαιος τῶν νόμων ἔχεται τῶν ἀνθρώποις καὶ θεοῖς κοινῶν κοὐκ ἐθέλει ἀδικεῖν. διὰ δὲ
   ταῦτα οὗτος μόνος ὑπὸ τοῦ δήμου τῖμᾶται.

_____

_____

_____

58. τοῖς πολεμίοις πολεμεῖν σὺν ὅπλοις ἐθέλω, ἀλλ᾽, ὦ μεγάλαι Μοῖραι, φόβον θανάτου ἔχω οὐκ ὀλίγον.

_____

_____

59. τελευτᾶν, ὠγαθοί, ἐθέλω καὶ ἄρχεσθαι ἀπὸ τῆσδε τῆς γνώμης· αἱ βίου συμφοραὶ πολλάκις τοῖς βροτοῖς τὴν ἀρετῆς ὁδὸν δηλοῦσιν.

_____

_____

_____

60. ταῦτα ποιεῖτ᾽ ἐπ᾽ αἰσχραῖς αἰτίαις, καὶ ἀδικεῖτε δὴ τοὺς υἱοὺς τοὺς Ἀθηναίων. ἐπὶ δὲ τούτοις νῦν πολλοὶ ἐν μάχῃ τελευτῶσιν.

_____

_____

_____

61. μεγάλην μὲν χώραν καὶ καλὴν εἴχομεν, εἰς ὀλίγην δὲ πεμπόμεθα οὐ δικαίως νῆσον.

_____

_____

C. Write these sentences in Greek.

1. I was trying to persuade that young man not to end his life, but he was refusing to be taught by good opinion and judgment.

_____

_____

2. The great battle on the sea begins well for the Athenians, but it will end badly. When, O earth and gods, will this terrible war be stopped?

_____

_____

_____

3. Helen along with Alexander has the responsibility for the great misfortune of this war. This thing is this way.

_____

_____

4. A. The people do not think it right to make war in a friendly land. For they are refusing to do wrong to the allies.
   B. Indeed they are doing this thing justly and nobly.

_____

_____

_____

5. Many good citizens were ending life in that fearsome battle. Thus is the fate of death for mortals.

_____

_____

6. How is it, O earth and gods, that many allies are willing to make war upon the Spartans, but the people of the Athenians are not? When will you be able, citizens, to make clear the cause of this shameful circumstance?

_____

_____

_____

_____

7. With harsh speeches we were explaining well the great toil of that fearsome battle on the sea. In this way we were trying to persuade the noble and good ones of the citizens to refuse to make war.

_____

_____

_____

_____

8. Some of the Athenians are accustomed to do(ing) wrong, others to obey(ing) the laws. The majority indeed think it right to be taught concerning the noble thing and the shameful thing. How, O Gorgias, will you accomplish this thing?

_____

_____

_____

_____

9. Euripides, clever, of course, in respect to speeches, teaches the majority in the following way: he speaks beautifully about the laws of this land and the works of virtue.

_____

_____

_____

10. I am intending to stop this shameful speech about the Athenians and their allies; for the latter certainly are dying nobly at the hands of hostile foreigners, but the former are unjustly being honored both in the council and among the people.

_____

_____

_____

_____

11. Many men were thinking it right to make war in the land of the foreigners (along) with the sons of Atreus, and indeed many men are ending life (along) with a noble reputation.

_____

_____

_____

_____

12. On account of her responsibility for that war, beautiful Helen was wishing either to be sent to the land of the Lacedaemonians or to die shamefully in this land.

_____

_____

_____

_____

Drill 52: Noun Morphology: Third Declension, Consonant Stems 1

A. Recite from memory the set of endings for third-declension masculine/feminine nouns.

B. On a separate sheet decline fully **ἡ ἀγαθὴ ἐλπίς, οὗτος ὁ Ἕλλην** (no vocative), and **ὁ καλὸς Ἕκτωρ** (singular only). Write the interjection **ὦ** before vocative forms.

C. Recite from memory the set of endings for third-declension neuter nouns.

D. On a separate sheet decline fully **αἰσχρὸν χρῆμα** and **τὸ μέγα δῶμα** (no vocative). Write the interjection **ὦ** before vocative forms.

E. Give the full vocabulary entry for these nouns.

1. desire _____

2. body _____

3. commander _____

4. heart; mind _____

5. public speaker _____

6. Hector _____

7. child; slave _____

8. expectation _____

9. grace, favor _____

10. Zeus _____

11. divinity; spirit _____

12. house _____

13. Greek _____

14. thing _____

F. Write these forms in Greek.

1. acc. sing. of ἐλπίς _____   2. nom. pl. of Ἕλλην _____

3. voc. sing. of Ζεύς _____   4. dat. pl. of παῖς _____

5. gen. sing. of ἄρχων _____   6. voc. pl. of δαίμων _____

7. gen. pl. of χρῆμα _____   8. dat. sing. of φρήν _____

9. nom. pl. of δῶμα _____   10. gen. pl. of παῖς _____

11. voc. sing. of ῥήτωρ _____   12. acc. pl. of χάρις _____

13. gen. sing. of ἔρως _____   14. voc. pl. of ἄρχων _____

15. dat. pl. of σῶμα _____   16. acc. sing. of χάρις _____

17. gen. sing. of Ζεύς _____   18. dat. pl. of δαίμων _____

19. acc. pl. of χρῆμα _____   20. dat. pl. of ἄρχων _____

21. voc. sing. of παῖς _____   22. acc. sing. of ἔρως _____

G. Supply the correct form of the article or ὦ and the correct form of the adjective **καλός, καλή, καλόν** for each noun. Give all possibilities.

1. _____ δαίμονες

2. _____ σώματα

3. _____ φρενός

4. _____ παῖδας

5. _____ ἐλπίδων

6. _____ χάριτι

7. _____ χρήμασι

8. _____ ἐρώτων

9. _____ δῶμα

10. _____ Ἕκτορα

H. Supply the correct form of the article or ὦ and the correct form of the adjective **ἄδικος, ἄδικον** for each noun. Give all possibilities.

1. _____ ἄρχον

2. _____ ῥήτορος

3. _____ δαίμοσι

4. _____ φρήν

5. _____ ἔρωτα

6. _____ Ἕλληνες

7. _____ παισίν

8. _____ χάριν

9. _____ δαῖμον

10. _____ ἄρχοντες

I. Translate these phrases.

1. τοῖς ἄρχουσι τῶν Ἀθηναίων _____

2. διὰ τὸν τῆς σοφίᾱς ἔρωτα _____

3. τὴν καλὴν χάριν _____

4. ὑπὸ τοῦ ῥήτορος τοῦ ἀγαθοῦ _____

5. ὦ Ζεῦ καὶ δαίμονες _____

6. Ἕκτορα, τὸν Πριάμου _____

7. τῷ σώματι τῷ καλῷ _____

8. περὶ τὰ τῶν Ἑλλήνων χρήματα _____

9. τὴν Διὸς φρένα _____

10. καὶ τῷ Πριάμῳ καὶ τῷ Ἕκτορι _____

11. δώματα καλά _____

12. τοῖς Ἕλλησι μόνοις _____

J. Write these phrases in Greek.

1. in the mind of Zeus _____

2. the body (d.o.) of the child (m.) _____

3. O noble Hector _____

4. for the good ruler _____

5. with the aid of a just divinity (m.) _____

6. on account of the hopes of the Spartans _____

7. the Graces (subj.) _____

8. by (the agency of) Zeus (2) _____

_____

9. the rulers (d.o.) of the Athenians _____

10. of this unjust public speaker _____

11. Helen's love (d.o.) of her country _____

12. with the money of the Greeks _____

Drill 53: The Relative Pronoun and Relative Clauses

A. Recite from memory the forms of the relative pronoun in Greek.

B. Identify these forms by gender, number, and case. Give all possibilities.

1. ἅς _____

2. οἵ _____

3. ἦ _____

4. οὖ _____

5. αἷς _____

6. ᾧ _____

7. ὅς _____

8. ἅ _____

9. ἦς _____

10. αἵ _____

11. ὅ _____

12. ἥ _____

13. οἷς _____

14. ἥν _____

15. ὧν _____

16. ὅν _____

C. In these sentences, underline the relative clause once and the relative pronoun twice. Then explain the gender, number, and case of the relative pronoun. Finally, translate the sentence.

Example: τῇ θεῷ πειθόμεθα <u>ἀφ' ῆς τὰ ἀγαθὰ τοῖς ἀνθρώποις ἄρχεται</u>.

      ῆς = **fem. sing. to agree with antecedent (θεῷ)**

        = **gen., object of preposition ἀφ'**

      We obey the goddess from whom good things for men begin.

1. οἱ νεᾱνίαι πεμφθήσονται εἰς τὴν γῆν ἣ ὑπὸ τῶν σοφῶν ἄρχεται.

_____

_____

_____

_____

2. καὶ ὑπὸ τοῦ δήμου ἐφιλεῖτο ὁ πολίτης οὗ τῇ γνώμῃ οἱ ξένοι ἐπείθοντο.

_____

_____

_____

_____

3. τὸ τέκνον ταύτην τὴν σοφίαν διδάσκω ᾗ καὶ ἐν ἀγορᾷ εὖ λέξει καὶ ἐν τῇ βουλῇ.

_____

_____

_____

_____

_____

4. ἆρα πείθει, ὦ φίλε, τοῖς νόμοις οἷς πείθομαι;

_____

_____

_____

_____

5. τοὺς νεανίας οὓς οὐκ ἐδίδασκον οἱ ποιηταὶ διδάσκειν ἐθέλω.

_____

_____

_____

_____

6. τῷ λόγῳ ὃν ἔλεγεν ὁ Πρίαμος ἐπείθετο ὁ Ἀλέξανδρος.

_____

_____

_____

_____

7. ταῦτα τὰ ζῷα ἃ εἰς ἀγορὰν πέμπειν ἔμελλες τοῖς ἑταίροις ἐπέμπετο.

_____

_____

_____

_____

8. τοῦ πόνου οὗ ἄρχῃ, ὦ Ἑλένη, νῦν παυόμεθα.

_____

_____

_____

_____

9. αὗται αἱ δόξαι αἳ πρὸς τοῦ Εὐρῑπίδου ἐλέγοντο τοὺς πολίτᾱς οὐκ ἔπειθον.

_____

_____

_____

_____

10. αἱ ψῡχαὶ ὧν ὁ Ἅιδης ἄρχει παύεσθαι τῶν πόνων ἐθέλουσιν.

_____

_____

_____

_____

D. Translate these sentences. Identify the relative pronouns with *generic* antecedents. Identify instances of *attraction.*

1. ὧν ἔχομαι εἰς ἀρετήν, ἆρα ταῦτ' ἔχεις, ὦ παῖ;

_____

_____

_____

2. πρὸς τοὺς φίλους ἐθέλω νῦν ὀλίγα λέγειν τούτων ὧν ἐν τῇ βουλῇ λέξω.

_____

_____

_____

3. πολλοὺς δὴ κακῶς ἐδίδασκεν ὅδε ὁ ποιητής. πρὸς ὃν ἔλεγον ταῦτα, τοῦτον τῑμᾷς;

_____

_____

_____

4. οὐ τῑμῶ ἐν τῇδε τῇ χώρᾳ πολλούς, ὦ πολῖται, καλῶν κἀγαθῶν ἀνθρώπων υἱούς, οἳ νῦν κακῶς τὸν δῆμον ποιοῦσιν.

_____

_____

_____

5. οἵδε οἱ ξένοι ὑπ᾽ ἐκείνων τῶν Ἀθηναίων πολλὰ καὶ καλὰ διδαχθήσονται· ἐξ ὧν μεγάλην σχήσουσιν ἀρετήν, δι᾽ ἣν πρὸς τῶν πολῑτῶν τῑμηθήσονται.

_____

_____

_____

6. πότ', ὦ Ἀθηναῖοι, ἀξιώσετε τὴν γνώμην λέγειν περὶ τῶν συμμάχων ὧνπερ ἐπέμπομεν εἰς μάχην;

_____

_____

_____

7. ἃ λέγεις περὶ τῆς ψῡχῆς, ὦ ποιητά, ταῦτα δὴ πολλοῦ τῑμῶμαι.

_____

_____

_____

8. ὧν ἦρχον οἱ Λακεδαιμόνιοι, τούτους ἠδίκουν οἱ Ἀθηναῖοι.

_____

_____

_____

9. ἃ φιλεῖς φιλῶ καὶ δὴ ἃ μὴ φιλεῖς οὐ φιλῶ.

_____

_____

10. τῶν πολῑτῶν οἵδε οἱ σοφοὶ ταύτην μὲν τὴν ἀρετὴν ἥνπερ ἔχουσι πέμπειν εἰς τὰς τῶν πολεμίων ψῡχὰς ἐθέλουσιν.

_____

_____

_____

11. ταύτᾱς τὰς δόξᾱς ἃς περὶ τῶν Λακεδαιμονίων ἔχω τοὺς νεᾱνίᾱς διδάξω τοὺς ἐν τῇδε τῇ χώρᾳ.

_____

_____

_____

12. ταῦθ' ἃ ποιεῖς, ὦγαθέ, τὴν τῆς ψῡχῆς ἀρετὴν δηλοῖ.

_____

_____

E. Write in Greek these sentences containing relative clauses.

1. Those Athenians by whom noble deeds are being done will be honored by the citizens.

_____

_____

2. We shall have our sons taught the art of words by Gorgias, on account of whose wisdom they will wish to do good.

_____

_____

3. The men who do wrong to their children, these ones will end life badly.

_____

_____

4. The things that mortals love many of the gods do not love.

_____

_____

5. That man has noble virtue, which even his enemies deem worthy of much.

_____

_____

6. We were about to be persuaded by those things that Gorgias was saying, but we were indeed clinging to the things that the wise ones of the citizens were making clear.

_____

_____

_____

7. In accordance with the laws that in this country we were always heeding, the citizens now are ruling.

_____

_____

8. I shall make clear the things about which I have come.

_____

_____

Drill 54: Enclitics

A. Fill in the blanks.

1. *No change* of accent occurs when the word preceding an enclitic (one or two syllables) is accented with

   an _____ or a _____ on the ultima.

2. When an enclitic (one or two syllables) directly follows a proclitic, _____

   _____ .

3. When a monosyllabic enclitic follows a word with an acute accent on the penult, a change of accent does/

   does not occur. (Circle one.)

4. When a disyllabic enclitic follows a word with an acute accent on the penult, the enclitic _____

   _____ .

5. When a word with an acute accent on the antepenult is followed by an enclitic (one or two syllables),

   the word _____ .

6. An additional accent (acute) is added to the ultima of a word followed by an enclitic (one or two

   syllables) when the word has a _____ accent on the penult.

7. When an enclitic (one or two syllables) is directly followed by another enclitic, _____

   _____ .

B. The following phrases and sentences contain enclitic words. Place correct accents on each phrase or sentence. Assume that the last word in each phrase ends a sentence. Do *not* translate.

1. οὐ παυει ποτε.

2. νομοι γε

3. οὐ παυεται ποτε.

4. οἱ γε νομοι

5. οὐ ποτε

6. ἀλλα γε

7. οὐ ποιει ποτε.

8. της γε χωρᾱς

9. ἀγαθοι και πολλοι γε

10. αἱ γε τοι καλαι

11. οὐκ ἠρχε ποτε.

12. ψῡχη τοι

13. οὐ ποτ᾽ ἠρχεν.

14. ἀνθρωποι γε

15. τουτο δε τοι

16. οὐ γαρ πονου ποτε παυεται.

17. δια γε τον τουτου λογον

18. το γαρ τοι ἐργον

19. οὐ ποιειται ποτε.

20. ἀνθρωπος γε τοι

21. την γε ψῡχην ποτε

22. ἡ γε τοι ψῡχη

23. ὡδε πως

24. και πως πειθομεθα γε.

25. οὐκ ἐπεμπομεν ποτε

26. χωρᾱ γε

27. εἰς τουτον ποτε τον λογον

28. αἱ γ᾽ ἀρεται

29. τουτων ποτε ἠρχον.

30. ἀγαθον τοι

31. και οὐ λεγει ποτε

32. ταις γ᾽ ἀρεταις τοι

33. ἐλεγε πως

34. νησους γε

35. λεγειν ποτε

36. νησοι γε

C. After reading carefully the vocabulary note on **τε**, accent correctly and translate these sentences.

1. ἐν γῃ τε και θαλαττῃ παυεται ὁ πολεμος.

_____

_____

2. περι πολεμου εἰρηνης τ᾽ ἐλεγον.

_____

_____

3. τους τε πολῑτᾱς και τους ξενους Γοργιᾱς ἐδιδασκεν.

_____

_____

4. ἀρχει τε ἀρχεται τε ὁ ἀγαθος πολῑτης.

_____

_____

5. φιλους συμμαχους τε πεισειν ἐμελλομεν.

_____

_____

6. οἱ τε σοφοι και οἱ μη σοφοι εὐ λεγουσιν.

_____

_____

7. καλον τε αἰσχρον τε λεγεις.

_____

_____

8. διδάσκειν τε καὶ διδάσκεσθαι ἤθελον.

_____

_____

D. Write each sentence in Greek in four *different* correct ways using the conjunction τε.

1. She is saying these things to gods and men.

_____

_____

_____

_____

2. War will be stopped by Spartans and Athenians.

_____

_____

_____

_____

Drill 55: The Verb εἰμί; Partial Deponents; New Verbs

A. Study the principal parts of and read carefully the vocabulary note on εἰμί. Write a synopsis for εἰμί in each indicated person and number.

1. εἰμί, 2nd sing.

2. εἰμί, 3rd pl.

B. Write these phrases in Greek.

1. to be _____

2. we were _____

3. he will be _____

4. you (pl.) are _____

5. there is _____

6. I am _____

7. you used to be _____

8. you will be (2) _____

_____

9. they are _____

10. she was _____

11. I shall be _____

12. you (pl.) used to be _____

C. Translate these forms.

1. ἐσμέν _____

2. ἔσεσθαι _____

3. ἦσαν _____

4. ἐστί _____

5. ἔσται _____

6. ἦν (2) _____

7. ἔσονται _____

8. εἶ _____

9. ἦ _____

10. εἰσίν _____

11. ἔσομαι _____

12. εἰμί _____

D. Study the principal parts of and read carefully the vocabulary notes on **ἀκούω** and **μανθάνω**. Write a synopsis for each verb in the indicated person and number.

    1. ἀκούω, 1st pl.   2. μανθάνω, 3rd pl.   3. εἰμί, 3rd sing.

E. Translate these forms. Give all possibilities.

1. ἀκούσεσθε _____

2. ἀκούετε _____

3. μανθάνειν _____

4. μαθήσονται _____

5. ἔστι _____

6. ἔσται _____

7. ἤκουον (2) _____

8. ἀκούσει _____

9. ἦσαν _____

10. εἶναι _____

11. ἔσει _____

12. εἶ _____

13. μαθήσῃ _____

14. μανθάνει _____

15. ἀκούουσι _____

16. ἀκούσῃ _____

17. ἐσόμεθα _____

18. ἐστέ _____

19. ἐμάνθανεν _____

20. μαθήσεται _____

F. Write these phrases in Greek.

1. you will be (2) _____

2. we were learning _____

3. they will hear _____

4. they will learn _____

5. you (pl.) will be heard _____

6. to be about to be _____

7. you are being heard (2) _____

8. I shall be _____

9. she is learning _____

10. I am _____

11. he is spoken of _____

12. to be about to hear _____

13. to be _____

14. you (pl.) are _____

15. we shall hear _____

16. he will learn _____

17. to be heard _____

18. she will be _____

19. to be learning _____

20. to be about to learn _____

21. it will be heard _____

22. we are called _____

G. Study the principal parts of and read carefully the vocabulary notes on **ἄγω**, **δεῖ**, and **ἥκω**. Write a synopsis for each verb in the indicated person and number.

1. δεῖ, 3rd sing.   2. ἥκω, 3rd pl.   3. ἄγω, 2nd sing.

H. Give the principal parts of these verbs.

1. listen (to), hear (of) _____

_____

2. learn _____

_____

3. be; exist _____

_____

4. have come, be present _____

_____

5. lead, bring _____

_____

6. it is necessary _____

_____

Drill 56–58: Short Sentences and Syntax

Nominative, Subject
Predicate Nominative
Nominative, Predicate Adjective
Subject Accusative
Subject Infinitive

A. Translate these short sentences, and from the list above give the syntax of the italicized word(s). Identify nominal sentences.

1. ἦσθα μὲν *αἰσχρός*, νῦν δὲ καλὸς εἶ, ὦ φίλε, κἀγαθός.

_____

_____

    αἰσχρός_____

2. οὐ δεῖ *νεᾱνίᾱν* ταῦτα τὰ αἰσχρὰ *ποιεῖν*.

_____

_____

    νεᾱνίᾱν_____

    ποιεῖν_____

3. ἆρ᾽ ἔστιν ἐν τῇ ψῡχῇ ἡ *ἀρετή*;

_____

_____

    ἀρετή_____

4. καλὴ ἡ τῆς ἀληθείᾱς ὁδός, ὦ παῖ.

_____

_____

      καλή_____

5. ἆρ' ἔστιν ὑπὸ φίλων φίλους ἀδικεῖσθαι;

_____

_____

      φίλους _____

      ἀδικεῖσθαι _____

6. δίκαιοί ἐστε ἄνθρωποι, ἀλλὰ δίκαια οὐ ποιεῖτε.

_____

_____

      ἄνθρωποι _____

7. ἀγαθὸν καὶ καλὸν ἦν τοὺς υἱοὺς τῷ Πριάμῳ πείθεσθαι.

_____

_____

      υἱούς _____

8. καλὸν τοὺς ψῡχὴν ἀγαθοὺς τῑμᾶσθαι.

_____

_____

      τῑμᾶσθαι _____

9. δεῖ, ὦ σύμμαχοι, τήνδε τὴν μάχην τελευτᾶν.

_____

_____

   τελευτᾶν _____

10. πολλὰ διδάσκῃ, ὦ τέκνον. νέος γὰρ εἶ.

_____

_____

   νέος _____

11. τὰς τῶν σοφῶν γνώμᾱς ἦν νῑκᾶν.

_____

_____

   γνώμᾱς _____

12. καλόν ἐστι τόδε τὸ ἔργον.

_____

_____

   καλόν _____

13. δεινόν γε τοῖς πολεμίοις πολεμεῖν.

_____

_____

   πολεμεῖν _____

14. ἦμεν ὀλίγοι ἀλλὰ νὴ Δία μεγάλοι.

_____

_____

ὀλίγοι _____

15. ἔδει τοὺς ξένους ἀπὸ τῆς γῆς πέμπεσθαι.

_____

_____

πέμπεσθαι _____

16. χαλεπὸν ἔσται ἐς κοινὸν λέγειν.

_____

_____

χαλεπόν _____

B. Write these sentences in Greek. (If a form of the verb "to be" is in parentheses, treat the sentence as a _nominal sentence._)

1. Often we were in the marketplace. For it was possible to speak to many men.

_____

_____

_____

2. You are not in a friendly land, Athenians.

_____

_____

3. It is necessary for just men to be at war with unjust men.

_____

_____

4. The men on the islands were allies to the Spartans.

_____

_____

5. We are doing great things, but we are not gods.

_____

_____

6. The reputation of good men (is) immortal.

_____

_____

7. I am a poet, and I am making beautiful things.

_____

_____

8. The son of a god was in this land at some time.

_____

_____

9. There are among the Spartans many ways of war.

_____

_____

10. To obey the laws (is) just and good.

_____

_____

11. That man must not prevail in his opinion.

_____

_____

12. When will it be possible to conquer in battle?

_____

_____

13. War (is) always a misfortune for mortals.

_____

_____

Exercises, Chapter 5

A. Place the correct accents on these sentences and then translate.

1. Γαια τουδ' ἐχει το θνητον σωμα, ἀλλ' Ἀιδης την ψῡχην την ἀθανατον.

2. ἀρ' εἰ ὡδε βαρβαρος, ὡ ξενε, φρενα; οὐ γαρ ἐθελεις τοις της γης τησδε νομοις πειθεσθαι.

3. ῥᾳδιον τοι ἐστιν, ὡ παι, περι των φιλων πολλα τε και δικαια δηλουν.

4. αὑτη ἠν ἐτῑμωμεν μονην των ἀλλων καλᾱς τοι εἰχε φρενας και καλως ἠκουεν.

5. χαλεπον ὁ βιος, ἀλλ᾽ οὐ δια τουθ᾽ ὁ Ἑκτωρ τελευταν ἐθελει. ἀει πως τουτῳ εἰσι πολλοι πονοι.

_____

_____

_____

6. αἰτιᾱ πολλων γ᾽ ἀνθρωποις ὁ φοβος κακων.

_____

_____

7. χαλεπος των θνητων ὁ βιος και χαλεποι της ἀναγκης οἱ νομοι, οἷς δει πειθεσθαι και τους θεους.

_____

_____

_____

8. πολῖται Ἀθηναιοι οὐποτ᾽ ἐσονται οἱδε οἱ ξενοι. και οἱ τουτων θεοι εἰσι βαρβαροι.

_____

_____

_____

9. ἐξ ἐκεινων των ξενων μελλετ᾽, ὦ βουλη, την γ᾽ ἀληθειαν ἀκουσεσθαι.

_____

_____

10. ὅ γε λόγος τὴν τοῦδε τοῦ ποιητοῦ δηλοῖ πως ἀρετήν.

_____

_____

11. ἆρ᾽ ἠξίους ποτὲ τοὺς ἀδίκους τὴν τῶν θεῶν χάριν ἔχειν;

_____

_____

12. Α. οὐ μὰ Δι᾽ εὖ ἔχει τὰς φρένας ὁ Εὐρῑπίδης.
    Β. κακῶς λέγεις, ὦ ξένε, κοὐκ ἐκ τῆς ἀληθείᾱς.

_____

_____

_____

B. Translate these sentences.

1. περὶ τῶν κοινῶν γνώμᾱς ἄλλοι ἄλλᾱς ἔλεγον.

_____

_____

2. οὐ φιλεῖ τοι ἡ νέου φρὴν ἐκ συμφορῶν μανθάνειν.

_____

_____

3. ξένοις φίλος ἐστὶν ὅδε ὁ ψῡχὴν ἀγαθός.

_____

_____

4. δεῖ δὴ τὰ τῆς χώρᾱς ταύτης καλῶς ἔχειν.

_____

_____

5. τοὺς ποιητὰς Ἔρως διδάσκει καὶ μετὰ τῶν νέων ἀεί ἐστιν.

_____

_____

6. ἧκον σὺν τοῖς τέκνοις εἰς τὴν γῆν ἐκείνην. νέου γὰρ ἔδει βίου.

_____

_____

7. πολλὰ χρήματ' ἔχεις, ἀλλ' οὐ μὰ τὸν Δία κατὰ τὸ δίκαιον. οὔποτ' ἀδικήσω χρημάτων χάριν.

_____

_____

8. θνητὸν μὲν ζῷόν εἰμι, ἀθάνατος δὲ ἡ ψῡχὴ ἣ τοῦδε τοῦ σώματος ἄρχει τοῦ θνητοῦ.

_____

_____

9. Ἕλληνες ἀεὶ παῖδές ἐστε. νέοι γάρ ἐστε τὰς ψῡχάς. ἆρα τούτοις δὴ πείθεσθε οἷς λέγω; παρά γε τοῖς
   βαρβάροις κακῶς ἀκούετε.

_____

_____

_____

10. Α. εὖ ἔχει, ὦ νεᾱνίᾱ, παρὰ τῶν σοφῶν μανθάνειν τὴν σοφίᾱν. ἆρ' οὔ;
    Β. νὴ τοὺς θεοὺς εὖ γε λέγεις καὶ σοφοῦ γ' ἐστι ἐθέλειν τοὺς νεᾱνίᾱς διδάσκειν.

_____

_____

_____

11. Α. πολλὰ δεήσει χρήματα παρὰ τῶν ἐν ταῖς νήσοις συμμάχων πέμπεσθαι.
    Β. ὅπλων γὰρ δεῖ νὴ Δία εἰς πόλεμον.

_____

_____

_____

12. τῶν διδασκάλων οἵ γ' ἀγαθοὶ ὑπὸ τῶν μαθητῶν ὧν εὖ διδάσκουσι τῑμηθήσονται, οἱ δ' ἄλλοι οὔ.

_____

_____

_____

13. ἄλλος μὲν ὁ τῶν φίλων ἔρως, ἄλλος δὲ ὁ τοῦ δικαίου τε καὶ καλοῦ.

_____

_____

14. κοινὸς τοῖς τε κακοῖς ὁ θάνατος καὶ τοῖς ἀγαθοῖς, ἀλλ' ἀθάνατος ἡ τῶν ἀγαθῶν δόξα.

_____

_____

_____

15. Α. ἔρως τε θνητοὺς ἔχει βίου καὶ θανάτου φόβος.
     Β. ἀλλὰ παρὰ τοῦτον ὃν ἐλέγομεν ὁ θάνατος ἥκει οὐ κατὰ μοῖραν.

_____

_____

_____

_____

16. τῆς ἀφ' ὁδοῦ τῆσδ' ἥξομεν πολλῷ σὺν φόβῳ—Ἕλληνες γάρ ἐσμεν—ἐς τὴν τῶν βαρβάρων γαῖαν.
     πολλὴ ἀνάγκη ἔσται τοῖς τούτων νόμοις πείθεσθαι.

_____

_____

_____

17. οὐ μὰ τὸν Δί᾽ ὀλίγος πόνος ὅδε· διδάσκειν μαθητὰς τοὺς νέους τὸν τῆς ἀρετῆς ἔρωτα.

---

18. πολλάκις ἠδίκουν τὰς παῖδας καὶ δὴ ἐπὶ ταύτῃ μόνῃ νὴ τοὺς θεοὺς τῇ αἰτίᾳ τελευτᾶν ἔμελλον.

---

19. τὸ τῆς τύχης αἰεὶ μετ᾽ Ἀθηναίων ἔσται καὶ ἡ τούτων δόξα ἔσται ἐς αἰεί. ἃ γὰρ ποιοῦσιν Ἀθηναῖοι εὖ
τελευτᾷ.

---

20. μέγας τε θεὸς καὶ δεινός ἐστιν ὁ Ἔρως καὶ ἐν ἀνθρώποις καὶ ἐν θεοῖς. οὐκ ἔστι μὴ τούτῳ τῷ δαίμονι
πείθεσθαι.

---

21. πολὺς φρένας τοῦτον ἔχει φόβος. πέμπεται γὰρ ξὺν ὅπλοις ἐς μάχην. δι᾽ ὃ ἢ καὶ ἄλλως πως τελευτήσει.
οὕτω γὰρ ἔχει ἡ τούτου μοῖρα.

---

22. τοὺς Ἀθηναίους πολέμου παύεσθαι μόνοι τῶν συμμάχων ῥᾳδίως πείσομεν. καὶ δὴ καὶ νῦν ἔσται ἥ γε εἰρήνη.

_____

_____

_____

23. ἃ οἱ πολλοὶ λέγουσιν, τούτοις πολλάκις οὐ πείθομαι. χρῆμα οὐκ ἀγαθόν ἡ τοῦ δήμου ἀρχή, ἀλλ᾽ ἐκ φρενὸς τὸν δῆμον τῶν Ἀθηναίων φιλῶ.

_____

_____

_____

_____

24. καλὸς ἄνθρωπος ἦσθα κἀγαθός. εὖ γὰρ νὴ τὰς Χάριτας ἦγες σὺν δαίμοσι τὸν βίον. πῶς νῦν γ᾽ ἐχθρὸς εἶ τοῖς τε θεοῖς καὶ τοῖς θνητοῖς;

_____

_____

_____

25. Α. μήποτ᾽ ἐθέλειν παρὰ τῶν μαθητῶν μανθάνειν οὐκ ἔστι διδασκάλου σοφοῦ.
    Β. οὐ μὰ τὸν Δία, ὦ ξένε.

_____

_____

_____

26. Α. ἆρ’ οὐ τὸ δίκαιον τόδε, τοὺς μὲν φίλους εὖ ποιεῖν, τοὺς δ’ ἐχθροὺς κακῶς;
    Β. οὐ κατὰ τὴν γνώμην τήν γε τῶν σοφῶν οἳ ἄλλως περὶ τοῦ δικαίου λέγουσιν.

_____

_____

_____

_____

27. οὐ δεῖ τοὺς πολεμίους ταύτην τὴν μάχην νῑκᾶν. Ζεῦ ἄλλοι τε θεοί, τάδ’ ἀκούετε;

_____

_____

28. δεινά τοι τὰ τῆς θαλάττης καί πως μέγας ἐν τοῖς πολλοῖς ἐστι ὁ ἐκείνης φόβος.

_____

_____

29. τὴν μὲν μάχην οἱ βάρβαροι παύουσιν, τὸν δὲ πόλεμον παύειν οὐκ ἐθέλουσιν οἱ Ἀθηναῖοι.

_____

_____

30. ἐπὶ τοῖς δεινοῖς ἔργοις κἀδίκοις ἀχθήσει, ὦ πονηρέ, εἰς δίκην. μετὰ δὲ τοῦτο ὑπὸ τῶν πολλῶν ὧν ἠδίκεις κακῶς ἀκούσει.

_____

_____

_____

31. τῶν μὲν ἀνθρώπων σὺν ἀνάγκῃ ἀδικεῖν, τῶν δὲ δαιμόνων τούτους ἄγειν ἐς τὸ δίκαιον.

_____

_____

32. Α. φίλοι τε καὶ σύμμαχοι ἦμεν ἐκ παίδων, νῦν δ᾽ ἐχθροί ἐσμεν.
    Β. πῶς οὕτως ἔχει;

_____

_____

_____

33. παρὰ δόξαν ὁ Γοργίᾱς τοὺς υἱοὺς τῶν Ἀθηναίων καλούς τε κἀγαθοὺς ἐποίει τήν γε ἀρετήν. ἐκείνην γὰρ εἶχε τὴν τέχνην.

_____

_____

_____

34. πονηρῶν γ᾽ ἔργων νὴ Δία διδάσκαλος ἦσθ᾽, ὦ ξένε, καὶ αἰτίᾱ τοῖς νεᾱνίαις κακῶν, οὓς χρημάτων γε χάριν καὶ ἀδικεῖν ἐδίδασκες.

_____

_____

_____

_____

35. ἐν ἀνάγκαις, ὦ ἄρχοντες, τὸν δῆμον μετὰ γνώμης ἤγετε. ἐκ δὲ τούτου μεγάλην σχήσετε δόξαν ἐπὶ σοφίᾳ.

_____

_____

36. παρὰ τὴν τῶν ἀρχόντων δόξαν κατὰ γῆν τε καὶ κατὰ θάλασσαν ἐνῑκῶντο οἱ Ἀθηναῖοι. τὰ δὲ μετὰ ταῦτα λόγον νῦν ποιοῦμαι.

———

———

———

37. μαθητὴς εἶναι ἐκείνου τοῦ ῥήτορος θέλω τοῦ τῇ ἀληθείᾳ σοφοῦ. οὐ γὰρ ἔχω τὴν λόγων τέχνην.

———

———

———

38. μόνοι τῶν Ἑλλήνων τὸν πόλεμον φιλοῦσιν οἱ Λακεδαιμόνιοι. χαλεπόν τοι ἔργον τοὺς Λακεδαιμονίους πείθειν εἰρήνην ἄγειν, ἀλλ᾽ εὖ τόδε σὺν δαίμοσι τελευτήσεις.

———

———

———

———

39. καλὸς εἶ σῶμά τε ψῡχήν τε. διὰ δὲ τοῦτο πολλά τ᾽ ἀγαθὰ ῥᾳδίως σχήσεις καὶ πολλὴν βίου χάριν.

———

———

———

40. Α. ἢ πολεμεῖν ἢ ἄγειν δεῖ εἰρήνην. ἢ πῶς λέγεις;
    Β. κακὸν τὸ χρῆμα, ἀλλ᾽ οὕτως ἔχει.
    Α. λόγῳ μὲν οἱ βάρβαροι εἰρήνην πολλοῦ ποιήσονται, ἔργῳ δ᾽ οὔ.
    Β. καὶ δεινοί γ᾽ ἔσονται μάχην.

_____

_____

_____

_____

_____

41. τὴν κατ᾽ ἄνθρωπον σοφίᾱν σοφός ἐστιν οὗτος μόνος. πολλὰ γὰρ ἐμάνθανε παρά τε τῶν ἄλλων ποιητῶν
    καὶ τοῦ Εὐρῑπίδου. καὶ νῦν δὴ καλῶς ἀκούει καὶ μέλλει τοὺς Ἀθηναίους μεγάλων διὰ πόνων ἄγειν ἐπ᾽
    ἀρετήν.

_____

_____

_____

_____

42. τὸν παῖδα ἦγον ἐπὶ τὰ Εὐρῑπίδου δώματα. παρὰ γὰρ τούτῳ ἔμελλε τὴν τῶν ποιητῶν σοφίᾱν τε καὶ τὴν
    τούτων τέχνην μαθήσεσθαι.

_____

_____

_____

43. ἀγαθοὶ δή εἰσιν οἱ ἀρετῆς διδάσκαλοι, ἀλλ' ἀπὸ τούτου τοῦ ῥήτορος οἱ παῖδες μανθάνουσι τὰ κακὰ
    τάδε· ξένους τε κακῶς ποιεῖν καὶ πόλεμον φιλεῖν. κακὸν δὴ διδάσκειν ἅπερ οὗτος διδάσκει.

_____

_____

_____

_____

_____

44. δεῖ δὴ τοὺς λόγους ἐκείνου μὴ ἀκούειν τοῦ αἰσχροῦ ῥήτορος· κακὰ γὰρ ποιεῖν τοὺς παῖδας διδάσκει.

_____

_____

45. ἀγαθόν ἐστι μάχης τοὺς Λακεδαιμονίους, ὧν φρένας φόβος ἔχει αἰσχρός, παύεσθαι, ἀλλ' οὔποτ', ὦ
    μεγάλε Ζεῦ, πολεμεῖν παυσόμεθα. τῶν γὰρ τέκνων χάριν πολεμοῦμεν κοὐκ ἀδίκως.

_____

_____

_____

_____

46. οἱ μὲν Ἀθηναῖοι ἐλπίδ᾽ ἀεὶ ἔχειν μεγάλην φιλοῦσι τῆς νίκης ἐπὶ τοὺς πολεμίους, ἀλλ᾽ εὖ πολεμοῦσιν οἱ βάρβαροι καὶ μέλλουσι δὴ νῑκᾶν ποτε.

_____

_____

_____

47. Α. πολέμου δεῖ ἄρχεσθαι, ὦ ἄρχον, καὶ τοὺς νέους πέμπειν εἰς μάχην.
    Β. ἀλλ᾽ οὐκ ὀλίγον ἔργον ἐστὶ ταῦτα τὸν δῆμον πείθειν.
    Α. καλῶν δὴ δεήσει λόγων. τὴν γὰρ εἰρήνην φιλεῖ ὁ δῆμος.

_____

_____

_____

_____

48. ἐκεῖνος ὁ ἄρχων τοὺς ἄλλους πολίτᾱς καὶ τούσδε τοὺς ἀγαθοὺς εἰς νίκην ἄξει καὶ σὺν θεοῖς δὴ τὸν πόλεμον τελευτήσει· τὰς μὲν ἐλπίδας εἶχον ταύτᾱς, νῦν δὲ πολὺν ἀκούω πόνον τὸν τῶν ἐν μάχῃ.

_____

_____

_____

_____

49. καὶ πῶς, ὦ Εὐρῑπίδη, τούτους γε τοὺς ξένους λέγεις ποιητὰς σοφούς; ἆρ' ἔχουσί τε τὴν λόγων τέχνην καὶ διδάσκουσιν; δεινοὶ μὲν ἀκούουσιν, μέλλεις δὲ πολλὰ παρὰ τούτων μαθήσεσθαι;

_____

_____

_____

_____

_____

50. οὐ πολλοὶ μὲν ἄνθρωποι ἐθέλουσι διδάσκεσθαι (οὐ γὰρ ἔρωτ' ἔχουσι τέχνης)· ἐν δὲ τοῖσδε μόνοις τοῖς νεᾱνίαις εἰσὶν ἐλπίδες· νέοι γάρ. τοὺς δὲ λόγους ἀκούσονται τοὺς τῶν ποιητῶν καὶ τὸν ἔρωτα δὴ τοῦ καλοῦ μαθήσονται.

_____

_____

_____

_____

_____

51. οὔ τοι καλοὺς μέλλω ποιεῖσθαι λόγους πρὸς τούς τε πολίτᾱς καὶ τοὺς ξένους περὶ τούτων τῶν αἰσχρῶν χρημάτων. δεινὸς γὰρ ἦν ὁ τοῦδε λόγος.

_____

_____

_____

_____

52. θνητοὶ μέν εἰσιν οἱ ποιηταί, καλοὺς δὲ κἀθανάτους σὺν δαίμοσι ποιοῦσι λόγους.

_____

_____

53. πρὸς τὸν δῆμον λέξω, ὦ Ἀθηναῖοι, περὶ τούτου τοῦ δικαίου πολέμου. μετὰ δὲ ταῦτα πεμφθήσεται παρὰ
τῶν συμμάχων ὅπλα τε καὶ χρήματα. ῥᾳδίως δὲ τοὺς ἄλλους νīκήσομεν Ἕλληνας.

_____

_____

_____

_____

54. οὔ ποτε μὰ τὸν Δία καὶ τοὺς ἄλλους θεοὺς πεισόμεθα τοῖς τε δεινοῖς κἀδίκοις νόμοις τῶν
Λακεδαιμονίων, ὑφ᾽ ὧν νῦν γ᾽ ἀρχόμεθα.

_____

_____

_____

55. πολλά τοι τελευτᾶν οὐχ ἕξεις, ἀλλ᾽ ἐκεῖνό γε ῥᾳδίως ποιήσεις· τὸν παῖδα διδάξεις τὸ ἀγαθὸν φιλεῖν.

_____

_____

56. δεινὸν ἦν κατά γε τὴν γνώμην τὴν τούτου τοῦ ῥήτορος τοὺς πολλοὺς ὑπὸ τοῖς ὀλίγοις εἶναι. καὶ νῦν αὕτη ἡ γνώμη νῑκᾷ. διὰ δὲ τὴν αἰτίᾱν ταύτην ἕξεται ὁ τῶν Ἀθηναίων δῆμος τῆς ἀρχῆς ἐς ἀεί.

_____

_____

_____

_____

_____

57. παρά γε τῶν Λακεδαιμονίων πολεμεῖν ἐμανθάνομεν. ταύτην γὰρ εἶχον τὴν τέχνην καὶ ἄλλους διδάσκειν ἤθελον.

_____

_____

_____

58. Α. καὶ οἱ ἄνθρωποι εὖ τὰ σώματα ἔχουσιν ἐκ πολλῶν πόνων;

　　Β. πῶς γὰρ οὔ;

　　Α. καὶ τὸ τοῦ πόνου ἔργον γε τόδ' ἐστίν· καλοὺς ποιεῖν τοὺς ἀνθρώπους τὰ σώματα κοὐκ αἰσχρούς.

　　Β. νὴ Δί' εὖ λέγεις.

　　Α. ἆρ', ὦ παῖ, ἐν τοῖς θεοῖς εἰσιν οἱ πόνοι;

　　Β. οὔ ποτε μὰ τοὺς θεούς.

　　Α. διὰ δὲ ταύτην τὴν αἰτίαν αἰσχροὶ οἱ θεοὶ τὰ σώματα;

　　Β. ἀνάγκη νὴ τὸν Ἑρμῆν, ἀλλ' οὐ τὰς φρένας.

　　Α. καὶ ὁ Ζεὺς κατά γε τοῦτον τὸν λόγον αἰσχρὸς μὲν τὸ σῶμα, καλὸς δὲ τὴν φρένα. τοῦτο οὐχ οὕτω πως λέγεις;

_____

_____

_____

_____

_____

_____

_____

_____

_____

59. Α. ἆρα δεῖ ποτ' ἀδικεῖν;

    Β. οὔποτε μὰ τὸν Δία, κατά γε τοὺς σοφούς.

    Α. καὶ ἀδικεῖσθαί γε;

    Β. πολλάκις ὑπ' ἐχθρῶν ἀδικοῦμαί γε.

    Α. ἆρ' ὑπ' ἀνάγκης ποιοῦσιν ἄδικον ἢ ἐς χάριν;

    Β. οὐ δὴ ἐς χάριν.

    Α. ἀνάγκη ἐκ τούτων τοὺς ἐχθροὺς ἀδικεῖν.

    Β. πῶς δή; ἃ γὰρ λέγεις οὐ μανθάνω.

_____

_____

_____

_____

_____

_____

_____

_____

_____

C. Write these sentences in Greek.

1. I shall send my child to Gorgias; for from that rhetor alone he will learn to speak well, and with this marvelous art he will persuade many men in the council.

_____

_____

_____

_____

2. Necessity is a harsh thing, you know, for Hector and for the rest of mortal men. Even the Fates must obey this fearsome goddess.

_____

_____

_____

_____

3. You will hear words not with a view to delight, citizens, but I shall speak from the heart; for I am trying to persuade the people of the Athenians to keep the peace in this land.

_____

_____

_____

_____

4. Zeus great in mind and the rest of the gods used to bring harsh justice down from heaven to wicked mortals. These things were this way.

_____

_____

_____

_____

5. Alexander, at the hands of great passion and harsh necessity, will somehow lead Helen out from the land of the Greeks, and, by Zeus, this woman, whom Eros rules, will be willing to be led. And after these things, the sons of Atreus will make war on the non-Greeks.

_____

_____

_____

_____

_____

_____

6. Are you intending, beloved companion, to learn the art of war from those fearsome foreigners who are always accustomed to making (to make) war? To do this thing will be difficult, you know.

_____

_____

_____

_____

7. Never, by Hermes, will that wicked public speaker, whom the citizens refuse to heed, send this truly good man from the land. With the aid of the divinities he will be stopped somehow from this shameful deed.

_____

_____

_____

_____

8. It is, of course, necessary for a good friend, at least, to lead his companions through much suffering by the path of truth and justice.

_____

_____

_____

9. These students have come to the agora, and by Gorgias they are being taught virtue. On account of this thing they will think it right to honor their teacher with fine speeches *and* with much money.

_____

_____

_____

10. The things that a young man hears, those things he always believes. Easily indeed are the souls of children persuaded by clever teachers. Because of this it is a necessity for teachers always to tell the truth to their students.

_____

_____

_____

_____

11. Some gods are persuaded by the words of some mortals, others (are persuaded) by the words of others. O Zeus, will you ever hear these citizens and will you send favor?

_____

_____

_____

12. From childhood I was trying to learn to make beautiful speeches; for I was wishing to be a good public speaker. But now, contrary to expectation, I love not beautiful speeches but truth, and I do not wish to say the very things that Gorgias says.

_____

_____

_____

_____

Drill 60: First Aorist Active and Middle Indicative and Infinitives

A. Translate these forms.

1. ἦρξεν _____

2. ἄρξει (2) _____

3. ἤρξατο _____

4. ἄρξεται _____

5. ἠθέλησας _____

6. ἐθελῆσαι _____

7. ἠθέλησαν _____

8. ἐθελήσουσι _____

9. ἐποιήσασθε _____

10. ποιήσεσθε _____

11. ἐποιήσω _____

12. ποιήσω _____

13. ἐπείσαμεν _____

14. πείσομεν _____

15. ἐπείθοντο (2) _____

16. πείσονται _____

17. μελλῆσαι _____

18. μελλήσει _____

19. ἔπεμψα _____

20. πέμψω _____

21. ἐτῑμήσατε _____

22. τῑμήσετε _____

23. ἐτῑμησάμεθα _____

24. τῑμησόμεθα _____

25. παύσασθαι _____

26. παύσεσθαι _____

27. ἐπαυσάμην _____

28. ἐπαυόμην (2) _____

29. ἠξίωσας _____

30. ἀξιῶσαι _____

B. Write these verb phrases in Greek.

1. to teach (once) _____

2. to be about to teach _____

3. to cause to be taught (once) _____

4. I accomplished _____

5. they accomplished _____

6. they were accomplishing _____

7. you (pl.) made war _____

8. you (pl.) were making war _____

9. we were conquering _____

10. we conquered _____

11. to conquer (once) _____

12. you will injure _____

13. you injured _____

14. it was necessary _____

15. to be necessary (repeatedly) _____

16. it is necessary _____

17. you ceased _____

18. you (pl.) ceased _____

19. to cease (once) _____

20. she began _____

21. she will begin _____

22. to begin (once) _____

23. I valued _____

24. we valued _____

25. to persuade (once) _____

26. to obey (repeatedly) _____

27. to obey (once) _____

28. he was showing _____

29. he showed _____

30. he shows _____

Drill 61: Second Aorist Active and Middle Indicative and Infinitives

A. Translate these forms.

1. εἶπον (2) _____

2. ἔλεγον (2) _____

3. ἠγάγου _____

4. ἤγου (2) _____

5. ἐμάθετε _____

6. ἐμανθάνετε _____

7. ἐσχόμεθα _____

8. εἰχόμεθα (2) _____

9. ἔλεξας _____

10. εἶπας _____

11. εἶπες _____

12. ἐσχόμην _____

13. ἕξομαι _____

14. σχέσθαι _____

15. ἔχεσθαι (2) _____

16. σχήσεσθαι _____

17. ἠγάγοντο _____

18. ἤγοντο (2) _____

19. μαθεῖν _____

20. μανθάνειν _____

21. μαθήσεσθαι _____

22. εἶπεν _____

23. ἔπαυεν _____

24. ἠγαγόμην _____

25. ἀγαγεῖν _____

26. εἴπομεν _____

27. εἴχομεν _____

28. ἠγάγετε _____

29. ἀγαγέσθαι _____

30. σχεῖν _____

B. Write these verb phrases in Greek.

1. you (pl.) learned _____

2. you said (3) _____

_____

3. we held on to _____

4. we were holding on to _____

5. to lead (repeatedly) _____

6. to lead (once) _____

7. to say (once) (2) _____

8. he married _____

9. she began _____

10. I said (2) _____

11. they learned _____

12. they were learning _____

13. I learned _____

14. you carried away with yourself _____

15. I clung to _____

16. I was being held _____

17. we said (2) _____

18. we were saying _____

19. he learned _____

20. he was learning _____

21. they carried away with themselves _____

22. you (pl.) held on to _____

23. to marry (once) _____

24. to be marrying _____

25. to occupy (once) _____

26. to be occupying _____

Drill 62–63: Aorist Active, Middle, and Passive Indicative and Infinitives

A. Write a synopsis for each of the following verbs in the indicated person and number.

1. πείθω, 2nd sing.
2. δηλόω, 3rd sing.
3. μανθάνω, 1st pl.
4. ἔχω, 2nd pl.
5. ἄρχω, 3rd pl.
6. λέγω, 3rd sing.
7. φιλέω, 1st pl.
8. ἄγω, 1st sing.

B. Translate these forms.

1. ἠκούσθη _____

2. ἠκούεσθε _____

3. ἐπαύθην _____

4. ἔπαυον (2) _____

5. παυθήσομαι _____

6. ἤρχθητε _____

7. ἤρχετε _____

8. ἀρχθῆναι _____

9. ἀρχθήσονται _____

10. δηλῶσαι _____

11. δηλοῦν _____

12. ἐδιδάχθημεν _____

13. ἐδιδαξάμεθα _____

14. ἐδιδάξαμεν _____

15. ἀδικῆσαι _____

16. ἀδικηθῆναι _____

17. ἠδικήθης _____

18. ἠδικοῦ _____

19. ἐπέμφθησαν _____

20. ἔπεμψαν _____

21. ἠξίουν (2) _____

22. ἠξίωσαν _____

23. ἐνῑκήθη _____

24. ἐνίκᾱ _____

C. Write these verb phrases in Greek.

1. we were treated as an enemy _____

2. we made war upon _____

3. they were ruled _____

4. they began _____

5. I was led _____

6. I led _____

7. it was stopped _____

8. it was being stopped _____

9. you (pl.) were loved _____

10. you (pl.) will be loved _____

11. you (pl.) loved _____

12. to be sent (once) _____

13. to be about to be sent _____

14. to send (repeatedly) _____

15. it was said _____

16. to be said (once) _____

17. they said (2) _____

18. you were defeated _____

19. you (pl.) were defeating _____

20. you defeated _____

D. Write these forms in Greek.

1. 3rd pl. aor. act. indic. of πέμπω _____

2. 2nd sing. imperf. mid. indic. of πείθω _____

3. 1st pl. aor. pass. indic. of παύω _____

4. aor. mid. infin. of ἄγω _____

5. 3rd pl. aor. pass. indic. of ἀξιόω _____

6. 3rd pl. aor. act. indic. of μανθάνω _____

7. pres. act. infin. of τῑμάω _____

8. 3rd sing. imperf. pass. indic. of λέγω _____

9. 2nd pl. pres. mid. indic. of διδάσκω _____

10. 1st sing. imperf. mid. indic. of ἄρχω _____

11. 2nd sing. aor. mid. indic. of ἄρχω _____

12. 1st pl. pres. pass. indic. of ἀδικέω _____

13. fut. act. infin. of πολεμέω _____

14. 3rd sing. imperf. act. indic. of εἰμί _____

15. 2nd pl. fut. act. indic. of ἐθέλω _____

16. aor. pass. infin. of νῑκάω _____

17. 2nd pl. fut. pass. indic. of ποιέω _____

18. 2nd sing. imperf. act. indic. of δηλόω _____

19. 1st sing. fut. mid. indic. of ἀκούω _____

20. 3rd pl. aor. act. indic. of διδάσκω _____

21. aor. mid. infin. of παύω _____

22. 2nd sing. imperf. act. indic. of μέλλω _____

23. 3rd sing. aor. act. indic. of ἔχω _____

24. pres. act. infin. of εἰμί _____

25. 1st pl. fut. mid. indic. of μανθάνω _____

26. 3rd pl. aor. pass. indic. of πείθω _____

Drill 60–64: The Aorist Indicative and Infinitives

A. Translate these sentences.

1. τοῖς ἀνθρώποις τούτοις οὐκ ἐθέλομεν πολεμῆσαί ποτε.

_____

_____

2. ὑπὸ τῶνδε τῶν ποιητῶν ἐδιδάχθη καὶ πολλὰ ἔμαθε δίκαια.

_____

_____

3. ἄλλα τε πολλὰ καὶ δὴ τὴν Ἑλένην ἐκ τῆς Λακεδαιμονίᾱς γῆς ἠγάγετο ὁ Ἀλέξανδρος πρὸς τὴν Πριάμου γαῖαν.

_____

_____

_____

4. σοφοὶ τὰ μὲν τῆς ἀρετῆς ἔμαθον, τοὺς δὲ ἀγαθοὺς οὐκ ἠδίκησάν ποτε.

_____

_____

5. ταῦτα μὲν τὰ καλὰ καὶ ἄλλα πόλλ᾽ ἐδίδαξε ὁ ποιητὴς τοὺς παῖδας τοὺς τοῦ ἄρχοντος, ἀλλ᾽ οὐκ ἀγαθοὺς ἐποίησε τούτους.

_____

_____

_____

6. πολλοὺς νὴ τὸν Δία τῶν πολῑτῶν ἠδικήσατε καὶ νῦν δὴ ἐκ ταύτης τῆς γῆς πεμφθήσεσθε.

_____

_____

7. ἐνίκων οἱ πολέμιοι, ἀλλὰ μάχης ἐπαύσαντο. τὴν τούτου αἰτίᾱν δηλώσειν μέλλω.

_____

_____

8. ἐκεῖνος ὁ ῥήτωρ ὁ αἰσχρὸς τὸν Εὐρῑπίδην οὐκ ἠξίωσε περὶ πολλοῦ ποιεῖσθαι.

_____

_____

9. τόνδε νῦν τῑμῶμεν· τῇ γὰρ τούτου ἀρετῇ ἐνῑκήσαμεν οὐ μόνον ταύτην τὴν μάχην, ἀλλὰ καὶ τὸν ἄλλον πόλεμον. μεγάλην δὲ δόξαν διὰ τοῦτον αὕτη ἡ γαῖα ἔσχεν.

_____

_____

_____

10. πότε τοῖς τῶν σοφῶν λόγοις ὁ δῆμος πεισθῆναι ἐθελήσει;

_____

_____

B. Write these sentences in Greek.

1. The commander led these men with arms against the foreigners who had come into the land.

_____

_____

2. On account of this thing, Athenians, that wicked orator was never honored by the Spartans and will not be honored.

_____

_____

3. After the war, that noble and good man became ruler with the aid of the gods.

_____

_____

4. I was loving my sons, but they were sent somehow out from the land.

_____

_____

5. Divinities make great hopes and fears in the minds of mortals.

_____

_____

6. Did you think your son worthy to be ruling this land?

_____

_____

7. It was necessary to learn (once) these things, but these students refused to listen (repeatedly) to the words of the teacher.

_____

_____

8. The Spartan spoke well, and somehow he persuaded the Athenians to keep (repeatedly) the peace.

_____

_____

Drill 65: Deponents; New Verbs

A. Study the principal parts of and read carefully the vocabulary notes on the new verbs in this chapter. Write a synopsis for each of the following verbs in the indicated person and number.

1. βούλομαι, 2nd sing.

2. γίγνομαι, 3rd sing.

3. ἔρχομαι, 2nd pl.

4. ὁράω, 1st sing.

5. δέχομαι, 3rd pl.

B. Translate these forms.

1. βούλει _____

2. ἐβουλήθη _____

3. ἐγίγνετο _____

4. ἐγένου _____

5. μαθήσεσθε _____

6. μανθάνει _____

7. εἶ _____

8. ἔσει _____

9. ἐδέξω _____

10. δέξασθαι _____

11. ἤλθετε _____

12. ἔρχῃ _____

13. ὀφθῆναι _____

14. ὄψει _____

15. ἦν (2) _____

16. ἔσται _____

17. ἰδεῖν _____

18. εἴδομεν _____

19. ἐβούλου _____

20. βουληθῆναι _____

C. Write these verb phrases in Greek.

1. to be seeing _____

2. to see (once) _____

3. they are going _____

4. he will go _____

5. you were welcoming _____

6. we shall welcome _____

7. to be (repeatedly) _____

8. I used to be (2) _____

9. she learned _____

10. she will learn _____

11. you (pl.) will become _____

12. to become (once) _____

13. they were wanting _____

14. to want (once) _____

15. they became _____

16. to be going to be _____

17. I saw _____

18. they were seen _____

Drill 66: The Intensive Adjective αὐτός, αὐτή, αὐτό

A. Translate these phrases and sentences.

1. εἰς τὰς αὐτὰς συμφοράς _____

2. εἰς αὐτὰς τὰς συμφοράς _____

3. τῷ λόγῳ αὐτῷ _____

4. τῷ αὐτῷ λόγῳ _____

5. αὐτὰ τὰ ἔργα _____

6. τὰ ἔργα τὰ αὐτά _____

7. αὐτὸ τοῦτο _____

8. ταὐτὰ ταῦτα _____

9. ταὐτὸν ἐκείνοις ἐποιοῦμεν. _____

10. αὐτοὶ ὑπὸ τοῦ δήμου τῑμηθήσεσθε. _____

_____

11. αὕτη τὴν αὐτὴν ἔχει γνώμην τοῖς πολλοῖς. _____

_____

12. αὐτοὺς τοὺς νέους οὔποτ᾽ ἀδικήσω. _____

_____

13. ἆρ᾽ ἐκεῖνα τὰ πονηρὰ αὐτὸς ἐποίεις; _____

_____

14. τοῖς αὐτοῖς Πριάμῳ ὅπλοις πολεμοῦμεν. _____

_____

15. ταὐτὰ ἔλεγεν ὁ Γοργίᾱς καὶ ἐν ἀγορᾷ καὶ ἐν δώματι φίλων. _____

_____

16. ἆρ᾽ ἦν τὸν μαθητὴν αὐτὸν σοφίᾱν μαθεῖν; _____

_____

17. αὐτὸς τὸ αὐτὸ τὸν υἱὸν διδάσκειν ἐθέλω. _____

_____

18. εἰς τὴν αὐτὴν γαῖαν πρὸς τοῦ αὐτοῦ πέμπονται. _____

_____

19. οὐκ ἄλλο λέγω, αὐτὰ δὲ τάδε. _____

_____

20. τὸ ἔργον αὐτὸ τὴν τούτου ἀρετὴν ἐδήλου. _____

_____

B. Write these phrases and sentences in Greek.

1. for the same divinities _____

2. Zeus himself (d.o.) _____

3. in the same war _____

4. these same things (subj.) _____

5. justice itself (d.o.) _____

6. for the sake of truth itself _____

7. The very archons were wronging the people of the Athenians. _____

_____

8. Hector himself is the hope of the non-Greeks. _____

_____

9. Both Helen and Alexander are ruled by the same passion. _____

_____

10. I shall tell these misfortunes to the very gods in the sky. _____

_____

11. You yourselves, children, are dear to this woman. _____

_____

12. He will say the same things to Priam himself. _____

_____

13. I am the same, but you have another mind. _____

_____

14. It is necessary for the foreigners to obey (repeatedly) the same laws as the citizens.

_____

_____

Drill 67: Personal Pronouns and Possessive Adjectives

A. Write these pronouns in Greek using *non*-enclitic forms.

1. of us _____

2. her (d.o.) _____

3. for me_____

4. you (subj.) _____

5. for him _____

6. we _____

7. of me _____

8. for you_____

9. you (pl.) (d.o.) _____

10. them (d.o.) (f.) _____

11. it (d.o.) _____

12. of you (pl.) _____

13. us (d.o.) _____

14. of you _____

15. me (d.o.) _____

16. you (pl.) (subj.) _____

17. for them (m.) _____

18. I _____

19. you (d.o.) _____

20. for us _____

B. Write these phrases in Greek. Express possession in *one* possible correct way, but *do not use the article to express possession.*

1. for me and for my companions _____

2. by his favor _____

3. in your body _____

4. her (d.o.) and her child (d.o.) _____

5. on account of their (m.) words _____

6. with him in his house _____

7. our teacher (subj.) _____

8. my great hope (d.o.) _____

9. by her skills _____

10. into your (pl.) land _____

11. you alone (f. subj.) _____

12. concerning your excellence _____

13. both you and me (d.o.) _____

14. of those men and of their allies _____

15. his fate (subj.) _____

16. either for us or for them (f.) _____

17. in addition to our fear _____

18. to me, at least _____

19. my money (d.o.) _____

20. according to your wisdom _____

21. her enemies (subj.) _____

22. to me alone (m.) _____

C. Translate these sentences containing personal pronouns and possessive adjectives.

1. οἱ ἄρχοντες ἡμᾶς εἰς μάχην πέμπουσιν, ἀλλ᾽ ἔγωγ᾽ οὐκ ἐθελήσω ὑπ᾽ αὐτῶν ἄγεσθαί ποτε.

_____

_____

2. σύ γ᾽ ἐμὲ οὔποτ᾽, ὦ ἑταῖρε, ταῦτα πείσεις.

_____

_____

3. τῶν δαιμόνων οἱ μὲν ὑμῶν, ὦ παῖδες, ἀκούειν φιλοῦσιν, οἱ δ᾽ οὔ.

_____

_____

4. οὗτος τὰ ὑμέτερα ἔχει χρήματα· ὑμεῖς γε τὰ αὐτοῦ;

_____

_____

5. οὐκ ἀγαθόν ἐστι κατά γ᾽ ἐμὴν δόξαν αὐτοὺς ἄρχειν τῆσδε τῆς γῆς.

_____

_____

6. πρὸς ὑμᾶς, ὦ βουλή, πολλὰ δηλοῦν ἐθέλω.

_____

_____

7. ἆρ' ἐπὶ τούτῳ αὐτὴν μόνῳ δεῖ ἐμὲ τῑμᾶν;

_____

_____

8. ἔμοιγε ἔργον οὐ ῥᾴδιόν ἐστι τοὺς σοὺς παῖδας τὴν σοφίᾱν μου διδάσκειν.

_____

_____

9. ἐκείνη ἡμῖν ἔλεγεν ἀεὶ τὰς θεοὺς φιλεῖν.

_____

_____

10. ὑφ' ὑμῖν οὐκ ἔσονται οἱ πολῖται, ὦ ῥήτορες. μέλλω γὰρ ἔγωγ' ἄρξειν αὐτῶν.

_____

_____

11. ἐγὼ μὲν πόνου παύομαι. σὺ δ', ὦ τέκνον, παύσεσθαι μέλλεις;

_____

_____

12. μεγάλη νὴ Δία ἥκει ἐπ' αὐτοὺς συμφορά.

_____

_____

13. ὑμεῖς, ὦ Ἀθηναῖοι, αὐτῶν ἄρχετε ἢ ὑμῶν ἄρχουσιν αὐτοί;

_____

_____

14. σοῦ γε ἠκούομεν ἀλλ᾽ οὐκ αὐτοῦ.

_____

_____

15. οὐκ ἔστι τοῖς ἡμετέροις φίλοις ἡμᾶς ἀδικεῖν.

_____

_____

16. ὁ ἔρως οὐχ ὁ πόλεμός με νῑκήσει.

_____

_____

17. νῦν ἐκεῖνος μὲν ὑμᾶς διδάσκει, ὑμεῖς δ᾽ αὐτοὺς διδάξετε.

_____

_____

18. τὰ τούτου τέκνα ἀξιῶ ἐξ οἰκίᾱς πέμπεσθαι.

_____

_____

19. τῷ σῷ ἑταίρῳ ἔλεγον φόβου παύεσθαι.

_____

_____

20. τῷ ὑμετέρῳ λόγῳ δεῖ ἡμῖν πείθεσθαι.

_____

_____

Drill 68: The Adjectives πᾶς, πᾶσα, πᾶν and ἅπᾱς, ἅπᾱσα, ἅπαν

A. Supply the correct form of **πᾶς, πᾶσα, πᾶν** for each phrase and then translate.

πᾶς, πᾶσα, πᾶν	Translation

1. _____ τὴν ἀλήθειαν   _____

2. _____ τοὺς βαρβάρους   _____

3. _____ τὰ ἔργα   _____

4. ὁ _____ ἄνθρωπος   _____

5. ἐν _____ μάχῃ   _____

6. _____ τοῖς ξένοις   _____

7. _____ τῶν νήσων   _____

8. κατὰ _____ τὰς χώρᾱς   _____

9. _____ οἱ ἐμοὶ πόνοι   _____

10. τῇ _____ φρενί   _____

B. Supply the correct form of **ἅπᾱς, ἅπᾱσα, ἅπαν** for each phrase and then translate.

ἅπᾱς, ἅπᾱσα, ἅπαν	Translation

1. _____ τὰ ἀγαθά   _____

2. διὰ _____ τῆς γῆς   _____

3. _____ τὸν λόγον   _____

ἅπᾶς, ἅπᾶσα, ἅπαν   *Translation*

4. τὸ _____ δῶμα   _____

5. περὶ _____ τῶν θεῶν   _____

6. _____ ἡ βουλή   _____

7. τῷ _____ βίῳ   _____

8. _____ οἱ βροτοί   _____

9. _____ τῇ γνώμῃ   _____

10. παρὰ _____ τοῖς Ἕλλησιν   _____

C. Write these phrases in Greek.

1. all things (d.o.) concerning the divinities _____

2. through the whole sky _____

3. for quite all the people _____

4. in respect to all things _____

5. all the citizens (subj.) _____

6. in every misfortune _____

7. quite all the money (d.o.) _____

8. by all weapons _____

9. every fear (d.o.) _____

10. quite all the children (subj.) _____

D. After studying the vocabulary in Chapter 6, on a separate sheet decline fully these phrases.

1. ὁ ἡμέτερος δεσπότης
2. ὁ μέγας ἀγών
3. τὸ πᾶν ἔργον
4. ὅδε ὁ ἀνήρ
5. ἡ ὀρθὴ ὁδός
6. αὐτὸ τὸ χρῆμα
7. τὸ θνητὸν σῶμα
8. ὁ ἐμὸς μαθητής
9. ἡ ὀλίγη ἐλπίς
10. ἅπᾱσα ἡ συμφορά

Drill 69: Indirect Statement 1

A. Translate these sentences containing indirect statements.

1. λέγω ὡς οὗτος ὁ πολίτης ἀδικεῖ.

_____

_____

λέγω ὡς οὗτος ὁ πολίτης ἠδίκησεν.

_____

_____

λέγω ὡς οὗτος ὁ πολίτης οὐκ ἀδικήσει.

_____

_____

2. εἶπον ὅτι ὑπ᾽ ἐκείνου πείθομαι.

_____

_____

εἶπον ὅτι ὑπ᾽ ἐκείνου ἐπείσθην.

_____

_____

εἶπον ὅτι ὑπ' ἐκείνου πεισθήσομαι.

_____

_____

3. δεῖ τοῖς νέοις δηλῶσαι ὅτι ἀθάνατός ἐστιν ἡ ψῦχή.

_____

_____

4. ἆρ' ἔλεγες ὡς ὁ πόλεμος ἐν ταῖς νήσοις ἤρξατο;

_____

_____

5. δῆλον ὅτι οὐκ εὖ τὸ σῶμα ἔχεις.

_____

_____

6. ἤκουσα, ὦ φίλοι, ὡς τοῦτο ἐποιήσατε.

_____

_____

7. οὔποτ' ἐπείσθην ὅτι οἱ Λακεδαιμόνιοι πολεμεῖν ἐθέλουσιν.

_____

_____

8. δῆλόν ἐστιν ὅτι τὸ δίκαιον ποιήσετε.

_____

9. οὐκ ἔχω εἰπεῖν ὡς ταῦτα μανθάνω.

_____

_____

10. εἶπεν ὅτι τοῖς ἀδίκοις νόμοις οὐ πείσεται.

_____

_____

11. δηλοῖ δὴ ὁ ποιητὴς ὅτι οὐκ ἀεὶ οἱ θεοὶ τοὺς ἀνθρώπους φιλοῦσιν.

_____

_____

12. ὅδε ὁ σοφὸς λέγει ὡς πολλοὶ δι᾽ ἔρωτα ἀδικεῖν ἤθελον.

_____

_____

13. μετά γε τὴν μάχην δῆλον ἔσται ὅτι περὶ τούτων τὴν ἀλήθειαν εἶπον.

_____

_____

14. διδάξω δὴ τοὺς μαθητὰς ὡς ἡ σοφίᾱ ἀγαθόν ἐστιν.

_____

_____

15. παρ᾽ ἄλλων ἐμάθομεν ὅτι οἱ φίλοι χρήματα πέμπουσιν.

_____

_____

16. λέγειν φιλοῦμεν ὅτι Ἀνάγκη τῶν ἄλλων ἄρχει δαιμόνων.

_____

_____

17. ἆρ' οὐ μανθάνεις, ὦ παῖ, ὡς Ἑρμῆς τὰς τέχνᾱς τοὺς θνητοὺς ἐδίδαξεν;

_____

_____

18. πῶς οἱ νεᾱνίαι πεισθήσονται ὅτι οὐ δεινά ἐστι ταῦτα;

_____

_____

19. ὁ Γοργίᾱς λέξει ὡς τοὺς πολίτᾱς τὴν ἀρετὴν διδάσκει.

_____

_____

20. ἐκ παίδων ἔμαθον ὡς δεῖ τοὺς θεοὺς τῑμᾶσθαι.

_____

_____

21. δεῖ τοὺς συμμάχους πείθειν εἰρήνην ἄγειν. δῆλον ὅτι οὕτως ἔχει.

_____

_____

22. τοῖς γ’ ἑταίροις ἐδήλου λόγῳ ὡς οὐ ῥᾴδιον ἔσται πολεμεῖν.

_____

_____

B. Write these sentences in Greek.

1. These students will easily learn that the body is ruled by the soul.

_____

_____

2. It was clear to the Greeks that Alexander had wished to marry Helen.

_____

_____

3. With the aid of the gods you will understand that good men, at least, have a great love of virtue.

_____

_____

4. Priam was revealing to Hector that the Greeks had many weapons.

_____

_____

5. Are you saying, companion, that it is not possible for men to be just?

_____

_____

6. That the sufferings of mortals will never end is clear from these things.

_____

_____

7. From the strangers we learned that the sons of the Athenians had been sent into battle.

_____

_____

8. I heard that the citizens would at some time honor both Zeus and Hermes.

_____

_____

9. The child said that he was not willing to learn the art of war.

_____

_____

10. It is clear that those non-Greeks will somehow end life at the hands of the Greeks.

_____

_____

Exercises, Chapter 6

A. Place the correct accents on these sentences and then translate.

1. διδασκαλος παντων ἀνθρωπων ὁ λογος· πολλα γαρ δια τουτου μονου ἐμαθομεν τε και μαθησομεθα.

_____

_____

_____

2. προς ὑμᾱς, ὠ Λακεδαιμονιοι, ἐπολεμησαν αὐτοι οἱ Ἀθηναιοι ὑπερ της των συμμαχων ἐλευθεριᾱς.

_____

_____

_____

3. των πολῑτων οἱ μεν ἐλεγον ὡς συμφορᾱ οὐκ ὀλιγη ὁδε ἐσται ὁ πολεμος, οἱ δε πολεμειν ἐβουλοντο.

_____

_____

_____

4. οὐκ ὀρθῶς ἐκεινοι εἶπον, ὑμεις δε μου ἀκουσεσθε, ὦ ἀνδρες Ἀθηναιοι, πᾶσαν την
ἀληθειαν. ποθεν ποτ' ἀρξομαι λεγειν;

_____

_____

_____

5. οἵδε οἱ ἀνδρες τους αὐτους αἰει περι των αὐτων λογους λεγουσιν.

_____

_____

6. κακως δη εἰχον νη Δι' οἱ δουλοι ὑπο τῳ χαλεπῳ δεσποτῃ.

_____

_____

7. ὁ αὐτος εἰμι τῃ γε γνωμῃ ταυτῃ· ἀει γαρ ἐπεισθην ὁτι φιλον πᾶσιν ἐστι το καλον.
τουτο μονον ἐμαθον.

_____

_____

_____

8. εἰρηνη προς θεων γενησεται και οἱ ἡμετεροι ἀνδρες πονων παυσονται. ἐλευθεραι δη
φοβου και αὐται ἐσομεθα.

_____

_____

_____

9. συ γε λεγεις ὡς εἰρηνην δει ἀγειν· ἀναγκη οὐν και ἡμῖν ταὐτον ποιειν.

_____

_____

10. ἀρ' ἀνηρ καλος κἀγαθος βουλει γενεσθαι; χαλεπα τοι τα της ἀρετης.

_____

_____

B. Translate these sentences.

1. ἐμοί ἐστιν ὅπλα καλά, ἃ σοὶ δηλῶ. ἆρ' αὐτὰ ὁρᾷς;

_____

_____

2. μεγάλαι μοι ἐλπίδες ἦσαν ὡς οἱ δίκαιοι ἄρξουσι τῆς γῆς τῆσδε, ἧς ἦρχον οἱ κακοὶ κἄδικοι.

_____

_____

3. πόθεν ἐκεῖνοι ἥκουσιν οἱ ξένοι; οὐκ ἐν ταῖς ὁδοῖς μόνον ἀλλὰ καὶ ἐν ἀγορᾷ αὐτοὺς εἴδομεν.

_____

_____

4. πάντα τοι δεινοί εἰσιν οἱ τούτου τοῦ ῥήτορος λόγοι, ὡς ἀκούετε, ἀλλ' ἐξ ἐμοῦ γε μόνου τὴν ἀλήθειαν μαθήσεσθε περὶ ὧν λέγει αὐτός.

_____

_____

_____

5. ποῦ γῆς εἰμι; ποῖ μετὰ τῶν τέκνων ἥκω; μέλλεις ταῦτά μοι δηλώσειν, ὦ δέσποτα;

_____

_____

6. ὁ ἀνὴρ ὁ ἀγαθὸς λέγει ὅτι οὔ ποτε τοὺς φίλους ἀδικήσει.

_____

_____

οἱ ἀγαθοὶ ἄνδρες ἔλεγον ὅτι τοὺς φίλους οὔποτ' ἀδικήσουσιν.

_____

_____

7. δῆλόν ἐστιν ὅτι οἱ πολῖται ἡμῶν τοὺς ἀγῶνας ἐνίκησάν τε καὶ τῑμᾶσθαι ἠξιώθησαν.

_____

_____

πᾶσι δῆλον ἐγένετο ὅτι οἱ ἡμέτεροι πολῖται τοὺς ἐν Ἀθήναις ἀγῶνας ἐνίκησαν. νῦν γε τῑμᾶσθαι
ἀξιοῦνται.

_____

_____

_____

8. ἐχθρὸς μέν ἐστιν ὁ ξένος οὗτος, ἀλλὰ καὶ αὐτὸν ἄνευ φόβου δέξομαι εἰς τὴν οἰκίᾱν ὅτι πᾶσίν εἰμι φίλος.

_____

_____

_____

9. μέλλομεν μετὰ τήνδε τὴν μάχην ὄψεσθαι πολλὰ κατὰ γῆν ἀνδρῶν ἀγαθῶν σώματα.

_____

_____

10. δῆλον ὅτι ἡ ἀνδρὸς θνητοῦ ψῡχὴ οὐ δέχεται θάνατον, ὡς σὺ πολλάκις λέγεις.

_____

_____

11. πολλαὶ καὶ καλαὶ τοῖσδε ἐλπίδες τοῖς δούλοις εἰσὶν ἐλευθερίᾱς, ἥνπερ βούλονται πάντες οἱ ἄνθρωποι.

_____

_____

12. φίλος εἶ ἐμοί· ταὐτὰ οὖν ἐμοὶ βούλει.

_____

_____

13. ἤδε ἡ τύχη πόθεν ἧκεν; αὐτὸς γὰρ αὐτὸν τὸν θεὸν ἐν ἀγορᾷ εἶδον μετὰ τῶν ἄλλων δαιμόνων. ὦ Ἑρμῆ, ποῦ νῦν εἶ; ποῖ ποτ᾽ ἦλθες; ὑμεῖς δὲ, ὦ τέκνα, πείθεσθ᾽ οἷς λέγω;

_____

_____

_____

_____

14. εἰς τὴν βουλὴν ἦλθον καὶ ἠρξάμην ὧδέ πως· Οὐχ ὁρᾶτ᾽, ὦ πολῖται, τόνδε τὸν ἄνδρα ὅτι ἄνευ γνώμης πάντων ἄρχειν βούλεται;

_____

_____

_____

15. ἔστι τοῖς τ᾽ ἀνθρώποις καὶ τοῖς θεοῖς καὶ τοῖς ζῴοις ὁ κοινὸς νόμος ὅδε· τέκνα φιλεῖν. ὑπὲρ ὧν πολλοὶ ἡμῶν καὶ τελευτᾶν θέλουσιν τὸν βίον.

_____

_____

_____

16. Α. παρὰ τοῦδε τοῦ ἀνδρὸς τὴν λόγων τέχνην μαθήσει.
    Β. ποῦ δὲ καλοὶ κἀγαθοὶ γίγνονται ἄνθρωποι;

_____

_____

_____

17. τοῖσδε τοῖς ἀνδράσιν εἶπον μήτε πολέμου ἄρξασθαι μήτε σὺν ὅπλοις εἰς τὴν τῶν πολεμίων γῆν ἐλθεῖν
ὅτι ἠξίουν τὴν εἰρήνην ἄγειν.

---

18. λέγεις ὅτι ὁ ἐμὸς ἀνὴρ ἐκ τῆσδε τῆς γῆς ἐπέμφθη. ποῖ οὖν ἦλθεν; ποῦ γῆς ἐστιν;

---

19. ἐκεῖνος ὁ ἀνὴρ εἰς μάχην ἡμᾶς ἤγαγεν· νῦν δὲ ἀκούομεν ὅτι αὐτός τ' ἐτελεύτησε καὶ ἄλλοι πολλοὶ τῶν
σὺν αὐτῷ. ἆρ' ἄλλως πως ταῦτα λέγεις;

---

20. τόδ' ἐξ ἀρχῆς εἶπον, ὅτι ἐλπὶς ἡμῖν οὐκ ἔστιν οὔτε νίκης οὔτε τύχης οὔτε βίου. ποῖ οὖν ἐλθεῖν μέλλομεν;

---

21. λέξω, ἄνδρες Ἀθηναῖοι, ἐν τῇ βουλῇ ὅτι τὸν πρὸς τοὺς βαρβάρους πόλεμον ῥᾳδίως τελευτήσομεν, ἀλλ' οὔ μοι πείσεσθε. ὃ γὰρ παρὰ δόξαν γίγνεται, χαλεπῶς τούτῳ ὁ δῆμος πείθεται.

_____

_____

_____

_____

22. τῆς γνώμης ἀεὶ τῆς αὐτῆς εἰχόμην· οὐκ ἔστι φίλους γενέσθαι τούς τε θεοὺς καὶ τοὺς βροτοὺς ὅτι βίον οὗτοι μὲν πολλοῦ ποιοῦνται, ἐκεῖνοι δ' οὔ. πῶς δὴ δῆλον ὑμῖν πᾶσι ποιῆσαι τοῦτο ἔξω;

_____

_____

_____

_____

23. οὔθ' ὅπλα, ὦ Ἀθηναῖοι, οὔτε σύμμαχοι ὑμῖν εἰσιν. δεῖ οὖν ὑμᾶς εἰρήνην τ' ἄγειν καὶ τὸν πόλεμον δὴ λέγειν μεγάλην συμφοράν. τοῦτο γὰρ ταὐτόν ἐστιν ἐκείνῳ.

_____

_____

_____

_____

24. Α. πολλὰ μὲν παρὰ Γοργίου ἔμαθον, μαθήσει δὲ παρ' ἐμοῦ τὴν ὁδὸν τῆς ἐμῆς γνώμης· οὐ δὴ θεὸς ἀλλὰ
    θνητός ἐστιν ὁ Ἔρως. τήν γ' αὐτὴν ἔχεις σὺ γνώμην;
    Β. ἀλλ' ἔμοιγε δῆλόν ἐστιν ὅτι δεινὸς δαίμων ὁ Ἔρως. καὶ δὴ καὶ μέγας μοί ἐστιν αὐτοῦ φόβος. ταύτην
    τὴν γνώμην ἔχω ἔγωγε.

25. ἡ αὐτὴ ὑμῖν δόξα ἐστὶ καὶ ἡμῖν. διὰ δὲ τοῦτο, ὦ σύμμαχοι, πολεμεῖν δεήσει τοῖς Ἀθηναίοις, τοῖς νῦν
    ὑμετέροις δεσπόταις.

26. ἐγὼ ὑμᾶς, ὦ ἄνδρες Ἀθηναῖοι, τιμῶ μὲν καὶ φιλῶ, πείσομαι δὲ δὴ ταῦτα τῷ θεῷ. πῶς οὖν τὸ δίκαιον οὐ
    ποιήσω; δηλοῖ γὰρ ὁ θεὸς ὃ δεῖ θνητοὺς ποιῆσαι.

27. Α. ἔρχεται ὁ θάνατος ἐπὶ τὸν ἄνθρωπον· τὸ μὲν θνητὸν σῶμα αὐτοῦ τελευτᾷ, ἡ ψῡχὴ δ' οὔ.

B. οὐχ ὁ πᾶς οὖν ἄνθρωπος κατά γε τὸν σὸν λόγον βροτός, ἀλλὰ τὸ σῶμα μόνον.

Α. ὀρθῶς λέγεις, ὦ παῖ.

B. ἔμοιγε φόβος οὐκ ἔσται θανάτου· ἀθάνατος γὰρ ἡ ψῡχή μου.

_____

_____

_____

_____

_____

_____

28. πολλοί τοι αὐτῶν τῶν νεᾱνιῶν οἳ τὸν σὸν λόγον ἤκουσαν, ὦ Γοργίᾱ, βούλονται μαθηταί σου γενέσθαι. ἆρα σὺ διδάσκαλος γενήσει πως τούτων;

_____

_____

_____

29. τοῖς τέκνοις εἶπον μήτε δοῦλον μήτε ἐλεύθερον εἰς δῶμα δέξασθαι. πότε τόνδε ἐδέξαντο τὸν ξένον;

_____

_____

_____

30. πάντα τοι τὰ τῆς ἀρετῆς ἔργα δέχεται ἡ ψῡχή. ἢ πῶς τοῦτο λέγεις, ὦ Γοργίᾱ;

_____

_____

31. μέλλετε πρὸς τῶν θεῶν, ὦ ἄνδρες, εἰς τὸν ἀγῶνα πέμπεσθαι τὸν ψῡχῆς πέρι. ὑμῖν οὖν δεήσει φρενῶν τε
    καὶ ὅπλων ἀγαθῶν.

_____

_____

_____

32. χρήμασιν οὐκ ἐμὲ πείσεις, ὤνθρωπε, δέξασθαι εἰς δῶμα τούσδε τοὺς ξένους. βάρβαροι γάρ εἰσιν κοὐκ
    αὐτοῖς λέγειν ἔχω.

_____

_____

_____

33. μετὰ τὴν μάχην εἶδον αὐτὸν τὸν Ἀλέξανδρον, πρὸς ὃν ἦν ἡμῖν πᾶς ὑπὲρ τῆς Ἑλένης ἀγών.

_____

_____

34. Α. περὶ πολλοῦ ἐποιοῦντο οἱ Ἕλληνες τὴν ἐλευθερίᾱν. διὰ δὲ τοῦτο νῑκηθῆναι ὑπὸ τῶν βαρβάρων οὐκ
       ἠθέλησαν.
    Β. δῆλα δὴ καὶ ταῦτα.

_____

_____

_____

35. δεῖ δὴ ὑμᾶς, ὦ ἄνδρες Ἀθηναῖοι, πᾶσαν ἀκοῦσαι περὶ τούτων τὴν ἀλήθειαν, ὡς ὁ νόμος λέγει. καὶ νῦν ἐγὼ κατὰ τοῦτον τὸν νόμον ἥκω πρὸς ὑμᾶς. ἆρα τούς τ᾽ ἐμοὺς δέξεσθε λόγους κἀμοὶ πείσεσθε;

_____

_____

_____

_____

36. ἄδηλά τοι τὰ τοῦ πολέμου· νῑκῶσί ποτε οἱ πολέμιοι, νῑκῶνταί ποτε. ἡμῖν μὲν οὖν καὶ τοῖς Λακεδαιμονίοις νίκης ἡ αὐτὴ ἐλπίς ἐστιν, οὐ δὲ δὴ ἄνευ πόνου ἐν τῇδε πολεμήσομεν τῇ μάχῃ, ἧς αὐτοί, ὦ ἄνδρες, ἀρχόμεθα.

_____

_____

_____

_____

37. σύ γε λέγεις ὅτι οὗτος μόνος ὑπὲρ πάντων εὖ ἐποιήσατο τῶν πολῑτῶν. κἀγὼ αὐτὸς οὐκ ἄνευ δίκης τὰ καλοῦ κἀγαθοῦ ἀνδρὸς ἔργα τῑμῶ.

_____

_____

_____

38. Α. πόθεν ἦλθες εἰς Ἀθήνᾱς;

    Β. ἐκ τῆς γῆς τῶν βαρβάρων.

    Α. δοῦλός ποτ' ἦσθα;

    Β. ἦν γάρ.

    Α. πῶς οὖν ἐγένου ἀνὴρ ἐλεύθερος;

    Β. χρήματα δέχεσθαί πως παρ' ἐμοῦ ὁ δεσπότης ἠθέλησεν.

_____

_____

_____

_____

_____

_____

39. μέλλομεν, ὦ ἄνδρες σύμμαχοι, τοῖς βαρβάροις πολεμήσειν. μεγάλην δ' ἔχομεν ἐλπίδα ὡς τὸ τῆς τύχης ἔσται μεθ' ἡμῶν. ὃ οὖν αὐτοὶ βουλόμεθα, ἆρα τοῦτο καὶ ὑμεῖς;

_____

_____

_____

40. Α. ὦ δέσποτα, ἐγὼ δὴ ταῦτα τοῦτον ἐποίησα σὺν δίκῃ.

    Β. οὐ μὰ τοὺς θεοὺς οὔτε πείσομαι σοῖς, ὦ πονηρέ, λόγοις οὔτ' ἔργοις.

_____

_____

_____

41. ἆρ' ἀπὸ τῆς ψῡχῆς οὕτω με φιλεῖς ὡς ἐγὼ σέ; ἔρωτα γὰρ δεῖ ἡμῖν εἶναι τὸν αὐτόν.

_____

_____

42. πῶς δή, ὦ ἑταῖρε, κακὸς ἐγένου ἐξ ἀγαθοῦ; νῦν γὰρ ἐμὲ αἰσχρῶς ἀδικεῖς.

_____

_____

43. οἵδε οἱ ῥήτορες οἱ δεινοὶ εἰς Ἀθήνᾱς ἦλθον ἐπὶ τόδε· τούς γε νέους διδάσκειν ἐβούλοντο ὡς ἀγαθόν ἐστι τοὺς πολίτᾱς πεῖσαι πολλὰ ποιῆσαι παρὰ τὸν νόμον. αὐτοὺς οὖν δεῖ παῦσαι.

_____

_____

_____

_____

44. οὗτοι σὺν ὅπλοις ἤλθομεν, ὦ Ἀθηναῖοι, ἐς τὴν ὑμετέρᾶν γαῖαν. πῶς δὴ οὖν αὐτοὶ ἡμῖν ὧδε πολεμεῖτε;
    ἡμεῖς γ᾽ εἰρήνην ἀξιοῦμεν ἄγειν καὶ βουλόμεθα.

_____

_____

_____

_____

45. οἱ μὲν ἠδίκησαν, οἱ δ᾽ ἠδικήθησαν, ἀλλ᾽ ἄδηλοι ἦσαν οἱ ψῡχὴν ἀγαθοί· πολλοὶ γάρ τοι λόγῳ μὲν εὖ
    ἔχουσιν, ἔργῳ δ᾽ οὔ. ἃ δὴ λέγουσιν, ταῦτ᾽ οὐ ποιοῦσιν.

_____

_____

_____

_____

46. μετὰ τὴν τῶν Ἑλλήνων νίκην δοῦλοι οἱ ξένοι ἐγένοντο πάντες ἐν τῇδε τῇ γῇ. οὗτος γὰρ ὁ νόμος ὁ
    αὐτὸς καὶ τοῖς Ἕλλησιν ἦν καὶ τοῖς βαρβάροις.

_____

_____

_____

_____

47. πολλάκις οἱ μὲν πολλοὶ λέγουσιν ὅτι θνητοῖς φίλοι οἱ θεοὶ οὔποτε γενήσονται, ἀλλὰ Ζεὺς καὶ οἱ ἄλλοι θεοὶ ἀεὶ ὑπὲρ ἐμοῦ τελευτῶσιν ἀγαθά. ὡς γὰρ πρὸς φίλους, οὕτως αὐτοὺς πρὸς τοὺς θεοὺς ἔχω.

_____

_____

_____

_____

48. οἱ ἐμοὶ υἱοὶ ὑπ' ἄλλων διδαχθήσονται ἀλλ' οὐχ ὑπ' ἐμοῦ. οὐ γὰρ ῥᾴδιον ἔσται αὐτοὺς πεῖσαι ὅτι καὶ τοὺς ἐχθροὺς δεῖ δικαίως ποιεῖν.

_____

_____

_____

_____

49. παρ' ὑμῶν ἀκούομεν ὡς ὅπλα τ' ἐστὶ καὶ σύμμαχοι ἐπὶ πόλεμον. ἀλλὰ γάρ, ὦ ἄνδρες, πάντα ταῦτα τἀγαθὰ καὶ τῶν πολεμίων ἐστίν. νῦν γὰρ αὐτοὺς ὁρᾶτε, ὅτι οὐκ ἄνευ γνώμης πρὸς ἡμᾶς πολεμῆσαι ἤρξαντο.

_____

_____

_____

_____

50. τοῦτο πᾶσι δῆλον ἐγένετο, ὅτι ὁ ἡμέτερος διδάσκαλος, ἀνὴρ καλὸς κἀγαθός, τὸν βίον τελευτᾷ. ὃς ἡμῖν χαλεπῶς εἶπεν· Οὐκ, ὦ ἑταῖροι, τὴν ἐμὴν ψῡχὴν ὁρᾶτε, ὅτι ἔστιν, ἀλλὰ ἔργοις πείθεσθε τοῖς ἐμοῖς ὡς ἐν τῷδε τῷ θνητῷ σώματι τῇ ἀληθείᾳ αὕτη ἐστίν. ὑμῖν δ᾽ ἐκ φρενὸς λέγω ὅτι ἀθάνατός γε ἥδε ἡ ψῡχή. τοῦτ᾽ εἶπεν καὶ ἐτελεύτησεν.

_____

_____

_____

_____

_____

_____

51. ἐν Ἀθήναις τοὺς λόγους ἐκείνων ἤκουον τῶν ῥητόρων. ἔλεγον μὲν ὡς εὖ περὶ ἁπάντων λέγειν ἐστὶν ἡ ἀρετὴ αὐτῶν, χαλεπὸν δὲ ἦν τὴν ἀλήθειαν παρ᾽ αὐτῶν μαθεῖν.

_____

_____

_____

_____

52. οὔτ᾽ ἔστι τὰ τῶν θεῶν μανθάνειν τῇ ἡμετέρᾳ σοφίᾳ οὔτ᾽ αὐτοὶ οἱ θεοὶ κατὰ τὸν σὸν λόγον δεσπόται ἡμῶν εἰσιν. ἆρ᾽ οὐκ ἐχθρὸς ἔσει διὰ τὴν γνώμην ταύτην τοῖς τε θνητοῖς καὶ θεοῖς;

_____

_____

_____

_____

53. ἐκείνων τῶν δούλων χαλεπῶς ἤρχομεν. οἱ δ᾽ ἐγένοντο ἐλεύθεροι καὶ νῦν ἄλλων πολλῶν εἰσιν δεσπόται χαλεποί.

_____

_____

_____

54. οὗτος ὁ ἀνὴρ πολλοὺς τῶν ὑμετέρων πολῑτῶν ἐς ἐλευθερίᾱν ἤγαγέν τε καὶ δόξαν ἐκ τούτου ἔσχ᾽ ἐν Ἀθήναις ἀθάνατον. οὗ τὴν ἀρετὴν παντὶ δεῖ τῷ δήμῳ δηλοῦν.

_____

_____

_____

55. ἆρ᾽ ἀγαθὸν ἔσται ὁ θάνατος; ἄδηλον γὰρ τοῦτο παντὶ θνητῷ, ἀλλ᾽ οὐ τῷ θεῷ.

_____

_____

56. δεινὸν ἔμοιγε ἡ δίκη, ὦ τέκνον, ἥ γε τῶν δαιμόνων. λέγω ὅτι ἅπαντας τοῖς νόμοις δεῖ πείθεσθαι τοῖς ὑμετέροις, ὦ Ζεῦ καὶ ἄλλοι θεοί.

_____

_____

_____

57. A. σὺ δ’, ὦ θεοῖς ἐχθρέ, ποῖ;
    B. εἰς Ἀθήνας ἐλθεῖν βούλομαι ἔγωγε.

_____

_____

_____

58. εὖ γ’ ἐπολέμουν οἱ ἡμέτεροι ἄνδρες, ἀλλ’ οἱ βάρβαροι ἐνίκησαν. πολλοὶ μὲν νῦν τῶν ἐλευθέρων ἐκ τῆς χώρας ἔρχονται, ἡμεῖς δὲ δοῦλοι ἐσόμεθα τῶν βαρβάρων. ποῖ δὴ ἡμᾶς ἄξουσιν;

_____

_____

_____

_____

59. Α. τῷ γε δικαίῳ παρὰ τῶν θεῶν πολλὰ γίγνεται ἀγαθά.

    Β. καὶ τῷ ἀδίκῳ δὲ κακά.

    Α. ἀλλ' ἔγωγε νῦν κακῶς ἀδικοῦμαι.

    Β. ταῦτ' οὖν ὁ θεός, ὦ φίλ' ἄνερ, οὐκ ὀρθῶς ποιεῖ.

_____

_____

_____

_____

_____

60. Α. ποῦ ὁ σὸς φίλος;

    Β. νῦν μὲν γὰρ οὐκ ἔχω εἰπεῖν· δῆλον δὲ ὅτι ἦν παρ' ἐμοί.

    Α. ποῖ ποτ' ἦλθεν;

    Β. ἀπὸ ταυτῆς δή, ὦ ξένε, τῆς χώρᾱς μετὰ σῶν συμμάχων.

_____

_____

_____

_____

61. A. σὺ δ’ ἦσθα ποῦ ποτε;
    B. ἐν ταῖς γ’ Ἀθήναις· ἐβουλόμην γὰρ αὐτὸς τὰ μεγάλα ἰδεῖν τῶν ἐλευθέρων ἀνδρῶν ἔργα.

62. A. τὸ φίλον σῶμα ποῦ παιδός μου;
    B. ἆρ’ αὔτ’ οὐκ εἶδες μετὰ τὴν μάχην;
    A. οὐκ εἶδον. ποῦ γῆς ἐστι τέκνον ἐμόν; ὦ Ζεῦ, ποῖ ποτ’ ἤγαγές με;

63. A. ἅπαντα νῦν σοφὸς εἶ. πάντα γὰρ παρ’ ἐμοῦ ἔμαθες.
    B. ἀλλ’ ὡς ἄδικοί εἰσιν οἱ ἀγαθοί, ποῦ δὴ ἐγὼ τοῦτο ἔμαθον;
    A. τοῦτό γε οὐ μὰ Δί’ οὐκ ἐμοῦ πάρα.
    B. ποῖ δὴ τελευτᾷ νῦν ἡμῖν οὗτος ὁ λόγος;

C. Write these sentences in Greek.

1. I myself caused my son to be taught the art of war by a Spartan man because I wanted him to become (once) a man without the fear of death. Will you, poet, do the same thing that I did?

_____

_____

_____

2. How and from where will you learn, child, that the soul of a just man is not ever ruled by unjust opinions? Don't you want to be taught (repeatedly) by that good teacher? For you will not see another man so wise.

_____

_____

_____

3. It is clear that for men to become (once) truly wise is a difficult thing. This thing, at least, I learned from boyhood; for I had fortune as a teacher.

_____

_____

_____

4. Not easy is it, as you yourselves see, to persuade (once) the people that Gorgias does not speak the truth. For he always makes beautiful and clever speeches.

_____

_____

_____

5. I married beautiful Helen, but she herself went from my house to a foreign land with another man. And now on account of her shameful love you (pl.) with the sons of the Greeks must make war on the non-Greeks.

_____

_____

_____

_____

6. On account of his excellence Hector was spoken of well and was honored by many men. He had, of course, a noble soul. (Write the second sentence twice, once with ἔχω and once with the Dative of the Possessor.)

_____

_____

_____

_____

7. In the country of the non-Greeks you will have many enemies and few friends, but in Athens you will see that the majority (of men) are just and good. (Write the first clause twice, once with ἔχω and once with the Dative of the Possessor.)

_____

_____

_____

_____

8. To where shall we ourselves be led after the war that is ending now? For the non-Greeks are likely to become (once) masters of all. *My* mind is ruled by fear.

_____

_____

_____

_____

9. As the soul has one virtue, so the body has another. It is clear to me, at least, that justice itself is the virtue of the soul.

_____

_____

_____

10. After the war against the non-Greeks, the Athenians got the rule of many of the islands, but it became clear to the Spartans that it would be necessary to make war upon (once) them.

_____

_____

_____

11. I, at least, often used to see (repeatedly) your noble son in the agora, but his companions say that he went away from Athens on account of a misfortune about love. Did I hear the truth from them?

_____

_____

_____

12. Priam along with his sons wanted to cease (once) from battle, but neither did he send another man to the sons of Atreus nor did he go himself.

_____

_____

_____

Drill 72: Quantitative Meter and Scansion

A. Fill in the blanks.

1. Write out from memory the scheme of the iambic trimeter. Mark metron divisions.

_____

2. Write out from memory the scheme of the dactylic hexameter. Mark foot divisions.

_____

3. Write out from memory the scheme of the elegiac couplet. Mark foot divisions.

_____

_____

4. Resolution is _____

_____ .

5. A caesura occurs when _____

_____ .

6. A principal or main caesura occurs when _____

_____ .

7. In a line of iambic trimeter, the principal caesura occurs most often _____

_____ .

Somewhat less common is a principal caesura after _____

_____ .

8. In a dactylic hexameter line, each dactyl may be replaced by a _____ .

A dactyl is *rarely* replaced by a spondee in the _____ foot.

9. Synizesis is _____

_____ .

10. Epic correction is _____

_____ .

B. Scan the following lines, marking long (‾) and short (˘) syllables, foot or metron divisions (|), and each principal caesura (‖) or diaeresis (⫴).[1]

Iambic Trimeter

1. ἀεί ποθ᾽ ἥδε γαῖα τοῖς ἀμηχάνοις

   cὺν τῷ δικαίῳ βούλεται προcωφελεῖν.

   τοιγὰρ πόνουc δὴ μῡρίουc ὑπὲρ φίλων

   ἤνεγκε, καὶ νῦν τόνδ᾽ ἀγῶν᾽ ὁρῶ πέλαc.

2. τὰ μὲν διδακτὰ μανθάνω, τὰ δ᾽ εὑρετὰ

   ζητῶ, τὰ δ᾽ εὐκτὰ παρὰ θεῶν ἠτηcάμην.

3. Ἥλιε, cε γὰρ δεῖ προcκυνεῖν πρῶτον θεῶν,

   δι᾽ ὃν θεωρεῖν ἔcτι τοὺc ἄλλουc θεούc.

1. The lines for scansion practice have been taken from the readings in Chapter 6.

4. πενίᾱν φέρειν οὐ παντός, ἀλλ' ἀνδρὸς σοφοῦ.

Elegiac Couplet

5. οὔποθ' ὕδωρ καὶ πῦρ συμμείξεται· οὐδέ ποθ' ἡμεῖς

   πιστοὶ ἐπ' ἀλλήλοις καὶ φίλοι ἐσσόμεθα.

6. Καρτερὸς ἐν πολέμοις Τῑμόκριτος, οὗ τόδε σᾶμα·

   Ἄρης² δ' οὐκ ἀγαθῶν φείδεται, ἀλλὰ κακῶν.

7. Δοῦλος Ἐπίκτητος γενόμην, καὶ σῶμ' ἀνάπηρος,

   καὶ πενίην Ἶρος, καὶ φίλος ἀθανάτοις.³

8. τῆς ἀρετῆς τὸν πλοῦτον, ἐπεὶ τὸ μὲν ἔμπεδον αἰεί,

   χρήματα δ' ἀνθρώπων ἄλλοτε ἄλλος ἔχει.

Dactylic Hexameter

9. Κλειώ τ' Εὐτέρπη τε Θάλειά τε Μελπομένη τε

   Τερψιχόρη τ' Ἐρατώ τε Πολύμνιά τ' Οὐρανίη τε

   Καλλιόπη θ'. ἡ δὲ προφερεστάτη ἐστὶν ἁπᾱσέων.

10. νῦν μὲν γὰρ Μενέλᾱος ἐνίκησεν σὺν Ἀθήνῃ,

    κεῖνον δ' αὖτις ἐγώ· παρὰ γὰρ θεοί εἰσι καὶ ἡμῖν.

2. The alpha of Ἄρης here scans long.
3. The first alpha of ἀθανάτοις here scans long.

Drill 73: Present and Aorist Participles

A. Write in Greek these *present* participle forms.

Example: act. neut. sing. nom. of εἰμί   **ὄν**

1. act. masc. pl. gen. of πέμπω _____

2. pass. neut. pl. nom. of ποιέω _____

3. mid. fem. sing. dat. of βούλομαι _____

4. act. fem. pl. gen. of τῑμάω _____

5. mid. masc. sing. gen. of διδάσκω _____

6. pass. fem. pl. acc. of ὁράω _____

7. act. neut. sing. acc. of δηλόω _____

8. act. masc. pl. dat. of μανθάνω _____

9. mid. neut. pl. nom. of γίγνομαι _____

10. act. fem. pl. voc. of ἄγω_____

11. mid. masc. sing. nom. of δέχομαι _____

12. pass. neut. pl. nom. of λέγω _____

13. act. masc. sing. acc. of ἐθέλω (2) _____

14. act. fem. sing. acc. of ἀδικέω _____

15. mid. masc. pl. gen. of ἄρχω _____

16. pass. fem. sing. nom. of ἀκούω _____

17. act. neut. pl. dat. of πείθω _____

18. mid. fem. pl. nom. of ἔχω _____

19. act. masc. sing. dat. of ἥκω _____

20. pass. neut. sing. nom. of φιλέω _____

21. act. masc. sing. acc. of εἰμί _____

22. act. masc. pl. dat. of ἔχω _____

23. pass. neut. pl. acc. of πέμπω _____

24. act. fem. pl. gen. of εἰμί_____

B. Write in Greek these *aorist* participle forms.

1. act. masc. sing. acc. of ἔρχομαι _____

2. pass. masc. pl. nom. of βούλομαι _____

3. act. neut. sing. dat. of πείθω _____

4. mid. fem. pl. dat. of ποιέω _____

5. pass. masc. sing. dat. of πέμπω _____

6. act. masc. pl. gen. of ἔχω _____

7. mid. fem. sing. acc. of δέχομαι _____

8. act. fem. sing. nom. of ὁράω _____

9. pass. neut. pl. acc. of ἄγω _____

10. mid. masc. pl. dat. of παύω _____

11. act. fem. sing. gen. of ἀκούω _____

12. pass. masc. pl. acc. of ἀδικέω _____

13. mid. neut. pl. nom. of γίγνομαι _____

14. act. masc. sing. gen. of πολεμέω _____

15. pass. fem. pl. acc. of ἄρχω _____

16. act. masc. sing. nom. of μανθάνω _____

17. mid. fem. pl. nom. of διδάσκω _____

18. pass. neut. sing. acc. of φιλέω _____

19. act. fem. sing. dat. of ἐθέλω _____

20. pass. masc. pl. gen. of νῑκάω _____

21. mid. fem. sing. acc. of πείθω _____

22. pass. neut. sing. nom. of λέγω _____

23. pass. masc. pl. dat. of δηλόω _____

24. pass. masc. pl. acc. of ὁράω _____

Drill 73–74: Present and Aorist Participles; New Verbs

A. Write a synopsis for each of the following verbs in the indicated person and number. Give the participles in the indicated gender, number, and case.

1. ἄγω, 3rd sing.; masc. sing. acc.
2. ἀκούω, 3rd pl.; masc. pl. dat.
3. πείθω, 1st sing.; fem. sing. dat.
4. δέχομαι, 2nd sing.; masc. sing. voc.
5. ἀδικέω, 2nd pl.; masc. pl. acc.
6. τῑμάω, 1st pl.; fem. pl. nom.
7. ἀξιόω, 1st pl.; fem. pl. nom.
8. ὁράω, 3rd sing.; neut. sing. nom.

B. Write these participle forms in Greek.

Example: pres. act. masc. sing. acc. of ἥκω   **ἥκοντα**

1. aor. mid. fem. sing. nom. of διδάσκω _____

2. aor. pass. masc. pl. acc. of πέμπω _____

3. pres. pass. neut. sing. acc. of ποιέω _____

4. pres. act. masc. pl. dat. of ἀκούω _____

5. aor. act. masc. pl. nom. of νῑκάω _____

6. aor. mid. fem. pl. acc. of ἄρχω _____

7. pres. mid. neut. pl. gen. of γίγνομαι _____

8. pres. act. masc. sing. acc. of εἰμί _____

9. aor. pass. neut. pl. nom. of λέγω _____

10. aor. act. fem. sing. nom. of ἔρχομαι _____

11. pres. pass. masc. sing. dat. of φιλέω _____

12. pres. mid. masc. sing. gen. of ἔχω _____

13. aor. act. masc. sing. nom. of μανθάνω _____

14. aor. pass. fem. pl. dat. of ἀδικέω _____

15. pres. act. neut. pl. nom. of μέλλω _____

16. pres. act. fem. pl. gen. of ἄγω _____

17. aor. mid. masc. pl. acc. of δέχομαι _____

18. aor. act. masc. sing. nom. of ὁράω _____

19. pres. pass. neut. pl. acc. of δηλόω _____

20. pres. mid. fem. pl. nom. of βούλομαι _____

21. aor. pass. masc. sing. nom. of ἄρχω _____

22. pres. pass. neut. pl. gen. of διδάσκω _____

23. pres. mid. fem. gen. pl. of δέχομαι _____

24. aor. pass. neut. sing. acc. of φιλέω _____

C. Identify these participle forms by giving tense, voice, gender, number, and case.

1. ὄντας _____

2. οὖσιν (2) _____

3. ὁρώμενα (3) _____

_____

4. ἰδόντα (4) _____

_____

5. πεισθεῖσαν _____

6. πείθοντας _____

7. διδασκομέναις (2) _____

8. διδαξάμενοι (2) _____

9. δηλοῦντι (2) _____

10. δηλώσαντι (2) _____

11. γενομένης _____

12. γιγνομένῃ _____

13. ἐλθόντι (2) _____

14. ἐθέλοντι (2) _____

15. δεχομένους _____

16. δεξαμένᾱς _____

17. ἔχουσι (2) _____

18. σχόντι (2) _____

19. εἰπόντων (2) _____

20. λεχθέντων (2) _____

21. ποιήσᾱς (2) _____

22. ποιησάσᾱς _____

23. μανθάνων (2) _____

24. μαθών (2) _____

25. βουληθεῖσαι (2) _____

26. βουλόμεναι (2) _____

27. ἀξιωθεισῶν _____

28. ἀξιώσᾱσιν (2) _____

29. νῑκῶντας _____

30. νῑκήσαντας _____

D. Study the principal parts of and read the vocabulary notes on the new verbs in this chapter. Write a synopsis for each of the following verbs in the indicated person and number. Give the participles in the indicated gender, number, and case.

1. ἀποπέμπω, 3rd pl.; fem. pl. acc.   2. διαλέγομαι, 1st sing.; masc. sing. nom.
3. ζηλόω, 2nd pl.; fem. pl. gen.   4. πάρειμι, 3rd sing.; neut. sing. acc.
5. πάσχω, 2nd sing.; masc. sing. dat.   6. πρᾱ́ττω, 1st pl.; fem. pl. nom.
7. προσέχω, 3rd pl.; masc. pl. acc.   8. χαίρω, 2nd sing.; fem. sing. gen.

E. Translate these forms and phrases.

1. ἐχάρη _____

2. προσεῖχες _____

3. πάσχομεν _____

4. τὰ πρᾱχθέντα _____

5. ζηλοῦσθαι _____

6. ἀποπέμψαι _____

7. διαλέγει _____

8. τὸ παρόν _____

9. ἐχαίρετε _____

10. πρᾶξαι _____

11. προσέξουσι _____

12. ἐζήλωσας _____

13. τοῖς παθοῦσι _____

14. ἀποπεμφθήσεσθαι _____

15. τοῖς διαλεγομένοις _____

16. πάρεισιν _____

17. τοὺς πράττοντας _____

18. παθεῖν _____

19. χαιρήσεις _____

20. παρῆσθα _____

F. Write these verb phrases in Greek.

1. it was practiced (once) _____

2. to be deemed fortunate (repeatedly) _____

3. she sent away _____

4. they will envy _____

5. men who enjoyed (subj.) _____

6. I used to hold to _____

7. for the women being present _____

8. the man suffering (d.o.) _____

9. to be going to bring about _____

10. we shall discuss _____

11. they were rejoicing _____

12. the men who sent away (d.o) _____

13. he used to envy _____

14. to converse (once) _____

15. we were present _____

16. we enjoy _____

17. they were faring _____

18. you applied _____

19. you (pl.) were envying _____

20. to be sent away (once) _____

Drill 75: Attributive and Substantive Participles

A. Translate these phrases containing attributive and substantive participles.

Example: τὸν ὑπὸ τοῦ δήμου τῑμώμενον ἄνδρα
the man being honored by the people (d.o.)

1. τοῖς μαθηταῖς τοῖς παρὰ τοῦ διδασκάλου πολλὰ μανθάνουσιν _____

_____

2. τὰ μέλλοντα _____

3. τῇ Ἀθήνᾱς εὖ φιλούσῃ θεῷ _____

4. οἱ τῶν πολῑτῶν ἄρχοντες ἄνδρες _____

_____

5. τῷ ὄντι _____

6. τοὺς νῑκηθέντας μάχῃ _____

7. τοῦ ῥήτορος τοῦ εἰς τὴν ἡμετέρᾱν γῆν ἐλθόντος _____

_____

8. τὰ αὐτοὺς πείθοντα _____

9. τοῖς ἀκούουσιν _____

10. τῶν Λακεδαιμονίων τῶν τοῖς Ἀθηναίοις πολεμησάντων _____

11. οἱ μὴ ἔχοντες χρήματα _____

12. ἄνδρες εἰς μάχην πεμφθέντες _____

13. ἐν τῇ χώρᾳ τῇ ὑπ' Ἀθηναίων ἀρχομένῃ _____

_____

14. τὰ γενόμενα _____

15. ἐμοὶ τοὺς δούλους δέχεσθαι ἐθέλοντι _____

_____

16. τῶν Ἀθηναίων οἱ εὖ εἰπόντες _____

17. τὸ φιλούμενον _____

18. τὴν κακῶς ποιουμένην παῖδα _____

19. τοῖς τὴν χάριν τῶν δαιμόνων ἔχουσιν _____

_____

20. τοὺς ὑφ' ὑμῶν διδαχθέντας νεανίας_____

B. Translate these sentences containing attributive and substantive participles.

1. τῷ βουλομένῳ ἔστι τὴν λόγων τέχνην μαθεῖν.

_____

_____

2. πολλὰ τῶν νῦν λεγομένων ἐστὶν ἃ παρ' αὐτῶν ἤκουσας.

_____

_____

3. τοῖς τὰς νήσους ἔχουσιν οὐκ ἦσαν δοῦλοι.

_____

_____

4. οἱ ὑπ᾽ ἐκείνων τῶν πολῑτῶν αἰσχρῶς ἀδικηθέντες ἀπ᾽ Ἀθηνῶν ἔρχονται.

_____

_____

5. καλὴ δὴ ἡ δόξα τῶν τούς τε θεοὺς καὶ τοὺς τῶν θεῶν παῖδας τῑμώντων.

_____

_____

6. τὰ μέλλοντα ἔσεσθαι οὐκ ἔστι εἰπεῖν, τὰ δὲ γενόμενα λέξω.

_____

_____

7. πολλὰς συμφορὰς καὶ δεινὰς ὁ θεὸς ἔπεμψε τοῖς ἀδικοῦσι βροτοῖς.

_____

_____

8. πολεμήσουσιν οἱ Ἕλληνες τῷ Ἀλεξάνδρῳ τῷ τὴν Ἑλένην ἀγαγομένῳ εἰς τὴν τῶν βαρβάρων γῆν.

_____

_____

9. οὗτος ἦν ὁ ἀδικήσᾱς, ὦ βουλή, καὶ ὑμεῖς ἦτε οἱ ἀδικηθέντες.

_____

_____

10. ἠθέλομεν τῶν λέγειν ἀξιωθέντων ἀνδρῶν ἀκοῦσαι.

_____

_____

11. δεήσει δὴ δικαίως τῆς νῑκηθείσης χώρᾱς ἄρχειν.

_____

_____

12. τοῖς ὑπὲρ ὑμῶν ἐν τῇ μάχῃ τελευτήσᾱσιν, ὦ πολῖται, ἀθάνατος ἔσται ἡ δόξα.

_____

_____

13. δεινόν ἐστι τὸ ὑπὸ τοῦ δήμου ὁρώμενόν τε καὶ ἀκουόμενον.

_____

_____

14. ἔγωγε οὐ πείθομαι τῷ ποιητῇ τῷ περὶ τῶν ἐν Ἅιδου λέγοντι.

_____

_____

15. τελευτήσουσί ποθ' οἱ ἄρχοντες ὑπὸ τῶν ἄλλως πως βουλομένων ἄρχεσθαι.

_____

_____

Drill 76: Supplementary Participles

Translate these sentences containing supplementary participles.

1. καλῶς ἐποίησεν ἐκεῖνος τελευτήσᾱς τὸν βίον. ἐπολέμει γὰρ ὑπὲρ τῶν παίδων.

_____

_____

2. πῶς μόνοι, ὦ ἄνδρες σύμμαχοι, ὑμεῖς παύσετε τοὺς πολεμίους εἰς τὴν ἡμετέρᾱν χώρᾱν ἐλθόντας;

_____

_____

3. τὸ σὸν τέκνον οὐκ ἠδίκησεν τούς γε ξένους δεξάμενον εἰς οἰκίᾱν.

_____

_____

4. τοὺς ἄλλους ἐνίκησας περὶ τῶν ἑταίρων εὖ λέγων.

_____

_____

5. κακῶς ἐποίουν οἱ πολλοὶ ὑπ' ἐκείνων τῶν ῥητόρων πειθόμενοί τε καὶ ἀγόμενοι.

_____

_____

6. ἠρξάμην τόνδε τὸν ἄνδρα τῑμῶν ἐξ ἔργων αὐτοῦ· νῦν δὲ περὶ τῆς ψῡχῆς λέγειν βούλομαι.

_____

_____

_____

7. ἀδικεῖτε πολέμου ἀρχόμενοι, ὦ Ἀθηναῖοι, ἀλλ᾽ οὔποτε παυσόμεθα σύμμαχοι ὄντες ὑμέτεροι.

_____

_____

8. τούτους τοὺς ξένους οὐκ ἦν παῦσαι γενομένους τοῖς νῑκήσᾱσι δούλους.

_____

_____

9. τοὺς νεᾱνίᾱς ἄρξομαι διδάσκων φιλεῖν τε τοὺς δαίμονας καὶ τῑμᾶν.

_____

_____

10. οὐκ ἐμὲ νῑκήσουσιν τὴν τῶν Ἀθηναίων νίκην τῑμῶντες.

_____

_____

Drill 77–78: Third Declension, σ-Stems and ι-Stems

A. Recite from memory the set of endings for third-declension σ-stem nouns of the **Σωκράτης** type. Recite from memory the set of endings for third-declension σ-stem nouns of the **γένος** type.

B. On a separate sheet decline fully **ὁ Δημοσθένης** (singular only) and **τοῦτο τὸ ἔπος** (no vocative). Write the interjection **ὦ** before vocative forms.

C. Recite from memory the set of endings for third-declension ι-stem nouns.

D. On a separate sheet decline fully **πᾶσα ἡ δύναμις** and **ἡ πονηρὰ φύσις**.

E. Give the full vocabulary entry for these nouns.

1. insolence _____

2. word _____

3. power _____

4. race, descent _____

5. Socrates _____

6. city _____

7. nature _____

8. experience _____

9. Demosthenes _____

F. Write these forms in Greek.

1. gen. pl. of δύναμις _____

2. dat. sing. of ὕβρις _____

3. nom. pl. of πάθος _____

4. gen. pl. of γένος _____

5. voc. pl. of πόλις _____

6. acc. pl. of φύσις _____

7. gen. sing. of Δημοσθένης _____

8. voc. sing. of Σωκράτης _____

9. dat. pl. of γένος _____

10. acc. sing. of ἔπος _____

11. nom. pl. of ὕβρις _____

12. voc. sing. of φύσις _____

13. dat. pl. of δύναμις _____

14. gen. sing. of ἔπος _____

15. acc. pl. of πάθος _____

16. acc. sing. of πόλις _____

17. nom. pl. of ἔπος _____

18. gen. sing. of δύναμις _____

G. In front of each noun place the correct form of the article or ὦ and the correct form of the adjective **καλός, καλή, καλόν**. Give all possibilities.

1. _____ φύσει

2. _____ γένος

3. _____ ὕβριν

4. _____ Δημόσθενες

5. _____ Σώκρατη

6. _____ δυνάμεις

7. _____ πόλεων

8. _____ ἔπη

9. _____ πάθεσιν

10. _____ γένει

Drill 79: Third-Declension Adjectives 1: -ης, -ες

A. Recite from memory the set of endings for third-declension **-ης, -ες** adjectives.

B. On a separate sheet decline fully **ἡ ἀληθὴς δόξα** and **αὐτὸ τὸ ἀληθές**.

C. Write these phrases in Greek.

1. by true judgments _____

2. a false speech (d.o.) _____

3. a sure friend (subj.) _____

4. of false opinions _____

5. of real excellence _____

6. the real causes (subj.) _____

7. by a clear law _____

8. clear speeches (d.o.) _____

9. true nature (d.o.) _____

10. real expectations (subj.) _____

D. Translate these sentences.

1. μόνοι οἱ τἀληθῆ λέγοντες τοὺς πολλοὺς ῥᾳδίως πείσουσιν.

_____

_____

2. αὕτη σοι λέγειν οὐκ ἔχει σαφεῖς λόγους.

_____

_____

3. δεῖ τἀληθὲς λέγειν.

_____

_____

4. ἐμοὶ ἦν φίλος σαφὴς καὶ ἀγαθός.

_____

_____

5. οἱ ἔχοντές τ' ἀληθεῖς δόξᾱς καὶ λόγους οὐ ψευδεῖς λέγοντες τὸν δῆμον ἔπειθον.

_____

_____

6. παρὰ τούτου τοῦ ἀνδρὸς ψευδεῖς ἀκούσεσθε λόγους.

_____

_____

Drill 80–82: Short Sentences and Syntax

Genitive of Cause
Dative of Cause
Dative with a Compound Verb

After studying the new vocabulary of this chapter, translate these short sentences, and from the list above give the syntax of the italicized words.

1. Εὐρῑπίδην ζηλοῦσιν οἱ ἄλλοι ποιηταὶ τῆς *τέχνης*.

_____

_____

    τέχνης _____

2. ἀγαθά *σοι* πάντα παρέσται ἐν τῇδε τῇ γῇ.

_____

_____

    σοι _____

3. τοῖς βαρβάροις ἐπολεμοῦμεν *ἀνάγκῃ* ἀλλ᾽ ἄνευ δίκης.

_____

_____

    ἀνάγκῃ _____

4. ἆρ᾽ ἐθέλεις προσέχειν τοῖς *ῥήτορσι* τούτοις τὴν γνώμην;

_____

_____

   ῥήτορσι _____

5. οἱ ἐλεύθεροι χάριν οὐκ ἔχουσι τῆς *ἐλευθερίας* τοῖς δεσπόταις.

_____

_____

   ἐλευθερίας _____

6. ἆρ᾽ ἔστι *φόβῳ* τελευτῆσαι;

_____

_____

   φόβῳ _____

7. οἱ Λακεδαιμόνιοι τῇ *νίκῃ* ἔχαιρον τῇ τῶν Ἀθηναίων.

_____

_____

   νίκῃ _____

8. παρῆν τῷ *δώματι* τοῦ Εὐρῑπίδου μετὰ τῶν ἑταίρων.

_____

_____

   δώματι _____

Exercises, Chapter 7

A. Place the correct accents on these sentences and then translate.

1. οἱ πολλα και δεινα παθοντες γνωμην οὐκ ἀγαθην ἐσχον περι ἡμᾶς.

_____

_____

2. ὀλιγοι τοι οἱ την ἐν τῃ ψῡχῃ ἀρετην ὁρωντες, ἀλλ' ἐγω σοι δηλωσω αὐτο τουτο.

_____

_____

3. σαφως ὁρᾱται ὁ φυσει την δικην τῑμων ἐν τουτοις των ἀνθρωπων ἐν οἱς ῥᾳδιον ἀδικειν.

_____

_____

_____

4. καλως ἐποιησεν ἡ μητηρ μου εἰς τᾱς Ἀθηνᾱς ἐλθουσα συν παισιν. ὀντως γαρ ἀγαθον ἐν τῃ πολει βιον ἠγομεν.

_____

_____

_____

5. που ποτ᾽ εἰ, Ζευ πατερ; τουτ᾽ ἀκουεις το ἐπος; τηνδε ὁρᾳς την ὑβριν;

_____

_____

6. οὐ μονον ἀληθη τα ἐπη ἐκεινου του ποιητου ἀλλα και ὡς ἐπος εἰπειν ἀθανατα ἐστιν.

_____

_____

7. ἐκειν᾽ οὐχ ὁρᾱτ᾽, ὠ βουλη, ὡς οὑτος οὐ προσεχει ὑμῑν τον νουν οὐδε τοις της πολεως νομοις;

_____

_____

_____

8. ἡδε ἐστιν ἡ γυνη μονη ἡ σοι παντ᾽, ὠ δεσποτα, λεξει σαφως.

_____

_____

9. δικαιον που παντα των τεκνων χαριν πρᾱττειν τον γε πατερα.

_____

_____

10. οὐδεποτε τοι φιλον Ἑλλησι το βαρβαρον γενησεται γενος.

_____

_____

B. Translate these sentences.

1. ἀνὴρ ἀγαθός, ὦ Δημόσθενες, ἀληθῆ λέγειν καὶ ποιεῖν φιλεῖ καὶ πάντα κατὰ φύσιν ὁρᾶν.

_____

_____

2. πότ' ἐγένετο ἡ τῶν Ἀθηναίων πόλις; τοῦτό ποθεν ἔχεις μαθεῖν;

_____

_____

3. εὖ καὶ καλῶς λέγειν μανθάνειν θέλω. οὐ γάρ που ἥδε ἐστὶν ἡ λόγων δύναμις, ὦ Γοργία, σοὶ μόνῳ.

_____

_____

4. λέξεις που ὡς Δημοσθένει πολλάκις μόνος μόνῳ διελεγόμην, ἀλλὰ τοὺς ἡμετέρους λόγους ἤκουσάς ποτε; ἆρα μεθ' ἡμῶν παρῆσθα;

_____

_____

5. προσέχουσιν αἱ μητέρες τοῖς παισίν· τοῦτο γὰρ τὸ τῶν γυναικῶν ἔργον.

_____

_____

6. οἱ νέοι μετὰ τὸν τοῦ Γοργίου λόγον ἐν νῷ εἶχον τῷ Σωκράτει διαλέγεσθαι περὶ τῆς ἀρετῆς φύσεως.

_____

_____

7. πρὸς τὰ ἐκείνου ἔπη τὸν νοῦν λέγω σοι, ὦ παῖ, προσέχειν. δεῖ γὰρ δή που τῷ πατρὶ πείθεσθαι.

_____

_____

8. τοῖς νεᾱνίαις τοῖς περὶ τῆς ψῡχῆς διαλεγομένοις ὁ Σωκράτης εἶπεν ὧδέ πως· ἡ θνητὴ φύσις κατὰ τὴν δύναμιν βούλεται αἰεί τε εἶναι καὶ ἀθάνατος.

_____

_____

_____

9. ἆρ' οὐχ ὑμεῖς, ὦ πολῖται, τὰ δέοντα ποιεῖν βούλεσθε; οὐκ ἀποπέμψετέ ποι τήνδε τὴν γυναῖκα, κοινὴν ὡς ἔπος εἰπεῖν πάσης τῆς Ἑλλάδος συμφοράν;

_____

_____

_____

10. πῶς σύ, ὦ πονηρέ, ἐχθρὸς ἐγένου τοῖς τε θεοῖς κἀμοὶ καὶ παντὶ ἀνθρώπων γένει; οὐ γὰρ δή που ταύτην ἀεὶ τὴν μοῖραν εἶχες.

_____

_____

_____

11. ὁ εἰς τὴν πόλιν ἐλθὼν ξένος ἡμῖν ἔλεξε χώρᾱν καὶ γένος καὶ συμφοράς, ὥσπερ αὐτὸς ἤκουσας, ἀλλὰ ψευδῆ εἶπε καὶ οὐ τὰ ὄντα.

_____

_____

_____

12. ὃς δι᾽ ἀρετὴν καλῶς ἐν Ἀθήναις τε καὶ καθ᾽ Ἑλλάδα ἤκουεν, οὗτος παρὰ δόξαν πολέμιος τοῦ δήμου τοῦ Ἀθηναίων αὐτὸς καὶ γένος πᾶν ἐγένετο.

_____

_____

_____

13. εἶπας ὡς βάρβαρος ἄνθρωπος εἰς πόλιν ἦλθέ ποθεν. πονηροί τοι καἰσχροὶ οἱ ψευδῆ λέγοντες.

_____

_____

_____

14. ἀνὴρ καλὸς κἀγαθὸς ὃς ἐπὶ τοῖς ἀγαθοῖς τῶν φίλων ὡς ἀληθῶς χαίρει οὐδέποτ᾽ αὐτοὺς πλούτου ζηλοῖ.

_____

_____

_____

15. δεινὰ ἦν τὰ ἔργα ἐν τῇ μάχῃ ἐκείνῃ, τὰ μὲν δι᾽ ἀνάγκης γιγνόμενα, τὰ δὲ διὰ νοῦ πρᾱττόμενα.

_____

_____

_____

16. δῆλον ὅτι οἱ ἐχθροί σου ἀποπέμψαι ποι σὲ βούλονται σὺν τῇ γυναικὶ ἐκ τῆς πόλεως. ζηλοῦσίν σε δή που ἐπὶ πλούτῳ καὶ γένει καὶ δόξῃ.

_____

_____

_____

17. δεῖ ἐν μεγάλῃ πόλει καὶ ἀρχὴν ἐχούσῃ ἄνδρας ἐλευθέρους τὰ πράγματα πράττειν τὰ τῶν πολῑτῶν.

---

18. ὄντως ἐστὶν ἀληθὲς τὸ ὑπὸ τοῦ ποιητοῦ λεχθέν· πόλις ἄνδρα διδάσκει.

---

19. τοῖς Λακεδαιμονίοις, οἳ τότε καὶ δόξαν καὶ δύναμιν μεγάλην εἶχον, τῶν Ἀθηναίων ὀλίγοι μὲν πολεμεῖν ἤθελον, πᾶσι δ᾽ ὡς ἔπος εἰπεῖν ἐν τῇ πόλει κοινὴ ἦν ἡ γνώμη ἥδε· ἔδει τῆς τῶν νήσων ἀρχῆς ἔχεσθαί πως.

---

20. οὐ μὰ Δία χαιρήσεις ἀκούουσ᾽, ὦ γύναι, ὡς ὁ φίλος Σωκράτης ὑπ᾽ ἐχθρῶν ἐτελεύτησε τὸν βίον.

---

21. ὅδε ὁ μαθητὴς τῇ τῶν ποιητῶν σοφίᾳ οὐδέποτε προσέχει τὸν νοῦν οὐδ' οἷς λέγει ὁ διδάσκαλος. πῶς οὖν ἀγαθὸς εἶναι ψῡχὴν διδαχθήσεταί ποτε;

22. πῶς οὐκ ἀδικεῖς καὶ δεινὰ ποιεῖς ὁ νῦν πολεμῶν τούτοις ὧν παρὰ τὴν δόξαν τότ' οὐκ εἶχες λέγειν;

23. οὐκ ἔμοιγε σαφής ἐστιν ἡ αἰτίᾱ δι' ἣν ταῦτα ὡς ἀληθῶς ἐγένετο, καὶ οὐ φρένα πείθομαι ὑπὸ τούτου τοῦ ἀνδρός, ὃς ὀλίγα μὲν τῷ ὄντι ἀληθῆ, πολλὰ δὲ ψευδῆ λέγει.

24. ἀληθῶς δή που ἀδικεῖτ', ὦ παῖδες, οὐ μόνον ψευδῆ λέγοντες ἀλλὰ καὶ πράττοντες αἰσχρά.

25. δύναμίς τοι τῆς ψῡχῆς ἐστιν ἡ δίκη. διὰ δὲ ταύτην τὴν αἰτίᾱν ἀνδρὶ δικαίῳ ἐστὶν ἡ δικαίᾱ ψῡχή. ἢ οὔ;

26. χαίρουσιν οἱ ἐχθροί σου ὁρῶντές σε, ὅτι κακὰ πάσχεις. ζηλοῦσι γάρ που τῆς τύχης.

_____

_____

27. τότε μὲν οἱ ἡμέτεροι πατέρες ὑπὲρ ἁπάσης τῆς Ἑλλάδος πρὸς τήν τε τῶν βαρβάρων δύναμιν καὶ τὸν πλοῦτον ἐπολέμησαν· νῦν δ' ἡμεῖς οἱ πόλεμον παύσαντες τὴν εἰρήνην παρὰ τὴν ἐκείνων γνώμην ἄγομεν.

_____

_____

_____

_____

28. πολλάκις τοι ὁ Σωκράτης, ὃς γένος Ἀθηναῖος ἦν, ἔχαιρεν ἄλλοις πολίταις τε καὶ ξένοις διαλεγόμενος καὶ ἐν ταῖς ὁδοῖς καὶ ἐν ἀγορᾷ. καὶ γὰρ ὀλίγοι τῶν ἑταίρων αὐτὸν παῦσαί ποτε λέγοντα εἶχον.

_____

_____

_____

_____

29. πολλάκις πολλοὶ τῶν Ἀθηναίων τὸν Σωκράτη εἰς δώματά ποθεν ἐδέχοντο. διαλέγεσθαι γὰρ αὐτῷ
    ἕκαστος τὴν τῶν ὄντων φύσιν ἐβούλετο καί πως ἀνὴρ καλὸς κἀγαθὸς γενέσθαι.

    _____

    _____

    _____

    _____

30. ἆρ' οὐ τῑμήσετε, ὦ πολῖται, τούσδε τοὺς ἄνδρας τοὺς πάντα ὑμῖν κατὰ γνώμην πρᾱ́ξαντας καὶ
    νῑκήσαντας τοὺς πολεμίους καὶ ὑπὲρ ὑμῶν τελευτήσαντας καὶ οὐδέποτ' ὑμεῖς εἰρήνην ποιήσεσθε;

    _____

    _____

    _____

    _____

31. ῥᾴδιον μὲν ἦν καὶ τοῖς μὴ χρήματα ἔχουσιν Σωκράτει διαλέγεσθαι καὶ παρ' αὐτοῦ πολλὰ ἀκούειν·
    χαλεπὸν δέ που τὴν σοφίᾱν αὐτοῦ μαθεῖν.

    _____

    _____

    _____

    _____

32. τότε μὲν κακὰ ἐπάσχομεν αὐτοὶ ὑπὸ τῶν παρὰ νόμους ἀρχόντων, νῦν δ᾽ εὖ πράττουσιν ἅπαντες ἐν πόλει ὅτι οἱ ἄρχοντες οὕτω τοῦ δήμου ἄρχουσιν ὥσπερ οἱ πατέρες τῶν υἱῶν.

_____

_____

_____

_____

33. ὁ εἰς Ἀθήνας ὑπὸ τῶν Λακεδαιμονίων πεμφθεὶς πρὸς τὸν δῆμον λόγον περὶ τῆς εἰρήνης ἐποιήσατο. οἱ δ᾽ Ἀθηναῖοι ἐδέξαντό τε τοὺς λόγους αὐτοῦ καὶ προσεῖχον τὴν γνώμην. ἐκ δὲ τούτων δῆλον ἦν ὅτι οἱ Λακεδαιμόνιοι ἀληθῶς ἐβούλοντο πολεμοῦντες παύσασθαι.

_____

_____

_____

_____

34. Α. εἶπεν ὁ Σωκράτης ὅτι θνητὸν δεῖ θνητὰ πράττειν τε καὶ πάσχειν.
    Β. ἀλλὰ φύσει ἀνὴρ ἕκαστος πράττει ἃ πράττειν φιλεῖ;
    Α. κατά γε τὴν ἐμὴν δόξαν νόμος τῶν ἔργων ἄρχει ἅπαντος ὡς ἔπος εἰπεῖν ἀνθρώπου.

_____

_____

_____

_____

35. οἱ Ἀθηναῖοι οἵ γε νοῦν καὶ φρένας ἔχοντες λέγουσιν ὡς ἐκεῖνοι οἱ ἄρχοντες, ὅ τε τελευτήσᾱς καὶ ὁ νῦν ὤν, ὑπὲρ ταύτης τῆς πόλεως πάντ᾽ ἀγάθ᾽ ἔπρᾱττον. οὗ χάριν αὐτοὺς δεήσει ὑπὸ τῶν τῑμηθῆναι πολῑτῶν.

---

36. αἰεὶ καὶ παρὰ θεοῖς καὶ παρ᾽ ἀνθρώποις πρᾱ́ξομεν κατὰ νοῦν, ὡς ἐστὶν ὁ τῶν γε σοφῶν λεγόμενος λόγος.

---

37. κακὸν μὲν ταῖς ἄλλων χαίρειν συμφοραῖς, ἀγαθὸς δὲ δὴ ὃς μὴ αὐτὸ τοῦτο πράττει.

---

38. τοῖς νέοις, ὦ Σώκρατες, διαλέγῃ, ὅπερ πράττοντες οἵ τε ἄλλοι χαίρουσι ῥήτορες καὶ ὁ Γοργίᾱς.

---

39. πάρεστιν ἀνὴρ τῷ ὄντι χρηστός, ὦ αἰσχροὶ πολῖται, ὃς ὑμᾶς παύσει ὕβριν τῆσδε τῆς γυναικὸς ποιοῦντας.

_____

_____

_____

40. τὰ τότε λεγόμενα σαφῶς ἤκουσα, ταῦτα δὲ τὰ ἔπη τοῦ ποιητοῦ οὔτ᾽ ὀρθῶς οὔτε καλῶς εἶπες. οὐ μὰ τὸν Δία τῷ σῷ λόγῳ οὐκ ἐχάρην τῷ ψευδεῖ.

_____

_____

_____

41. τὰ μὲν κακὰ λεγόμενα ἀγαθὰ τοῖς ἀδίκοις ἐστίν, τοῖς δὲ δικαίοις κακά. τὰ δ᾽ ἀγαθὰ τοῖς μὲν ἀγαθοῖς ὄντως ἀγαθά, τοῖς δὲ κακοῖς κακά. ἢ πῶς ταῦτα λέγεις, ὦ φίλ᾽ ἑταῖρε;

_____

_____

_____

42. αὐτὸς τοῦ θεοῦ ἤκουσα τοῦ λέγοντός πως τὸ μέλλον, ὅτι δεσπόται ἁπάσης Ἑλλάδος ἔσονται οἱ Ἀθηναῖοι. τὸ δὲ ἔπος τοῦτο βούλεται λέγειν ὡς τοῦτον τὸν μέγαν νῑκηθήσονται πόλεμον οἱ βάρβαροι ὑπὸ τῶν Ἀθηναίων. ἀληθῆ ἔλεγεν ὁ δαίμων;

---

43. παρὰ μὲν ἀρετήν, κατὰ δὲ τὸ δέον ἐκεῖνα ἔπρᾱξα, ἃ ἀκούοντες, ὦ πολῖται, οὐ χαίρετε. ἐμὲ γὰρ ἦγε δαίμων ποθέν.

---

44. νὴ τὸν Ἑρμῆν, ὦ φίλε Σώκρατες—δεῖ γὰρ πρός σε τἀληθῆ λέγειν—μέγας τοῦ θανάτου μ᾽ ἔχει φόβος, ὑφ᾽ οὗ πολλάκις δεινὰ καὶ πολλὰ ἔπαθον. δῆλον παντὶ ὅτι δύναμις ὑπὲρ ἄνθρωπον ὁ Ἅιδης.

---

45. ἀληθῆ ἦν τὰ ὑπὸ σοῦ λεχθέντα περὶ τούτων ὧν τὰς δόξᾱς ζηλοῖς. πολλὰ δ' ἔχω εἰπεῖν, ἀλλὰ διὰ τὴν τοῦ πρᾱγματος φύσιν παύσομαι λέγων.

_____

_____

_____

_____

46. πολλὰ ἐλέγετο περὶ τῆς παρούσης δόξης καὶ ἐν τῇ βουλῇ καὶ κατὰ τὴν πόλιν. τοῖς γὰρ γένος οὖσι πολίταις πολὺς ἦν φόβος τῶν ξένων τῶν ἐκ τῆς ἄλλης Ἑλλάδος ἐλθόντων.

_____

_____

_____

_____

47. Α. ἆρ' αὐτὸς παρῆσθα, ὦ φίλε, τῷ Σωκράτους θανάτῳ;
   Β. καὶ πολλά γε αὐτῷ διελεγόμεθα, ἐγώ τε καὶ ἄλλοι οἱ αὐτὸν ἀληθῶς φιλοῦντες. ἀλλὰ τὸν θάνατον αὐτὸν οὐκ εἶδον· οὐδέποτε γὰρ ἐβουλήθην τὸ ἐκείνου πάθος ἰδεῖν οὐδὲ ἄλλοι πολλοί.

_____

_____

_____

_____

_____

48. ἄλλα μὲν κακὰ γίγνεται ἢ τῇ τύχῃ ἢ τῇ θνητῇ φύσει τῇ τῶν ἀνθρώπων, ἄλλα δ' ἡμεῖς αὐτοὶ ποιοῦμεν. οὔποθ' ἡμεῖς, οἱ παθόντες καὶ ποιήσαντες, παυόμεθα αἰσχρῶς ἀδικούμενοί τε καὶ ἀδικοῦντες.

_____

_____

_____

_____

_____

49. τάσδε τὰς γυναῖκας τὰς χρηστὰς δέξεσθαί τε μέλλομεν καὶ καλῶς ποιήσειν· εὖ μὲν γὰρ ἀκούουσιν ὑφ' ἁπάντων, ἀγαθοὶ δὲ τῷ ὄντι εἰσὶν οἱ ἄνδρες αὐτῶν.

_____

_____

_____

50. Α. ἆρα πείθῃ ὡς τὸν νοῦν τοῖς ξένοις τοῖς κακῶς πάσχουσιν οἱ ἡμέτεροι ἄρχοντες προσεῖχον;
    Β. οὐκ ἔγωγε, μὰ τὸν Δία, οὐδὲ νῦν δίκαια πράττουσιν, κατά γ' ἐμὴν δόξαν.

_____

_____

_____

51. Α. λέγει που ὁ ποιητὴς ὅτι οἱ πρὸς Δίκης γε κακὰ πάσχοντες μαθήσονται ἕκαστος. πάθει γὰρ σοφοὶ γενήσονται.

    Β. δικαίως μὲν οὗτοι πάσχουσιν, ἀλλ᾽ οὐκ ἀεὶ κατὰ δίκην εἰσὶν αἱ θνητῶν τύχαι.

_____

_____

_____

_____

52. οὗτοι κατὰ γένος ἀλλὰ δι᾽ ἀρετὴν μόνην ὁ δῆμος τῶν Ἀθηναίων ἄνδρας τ᾽ ἐτίμησε καὶ γυναῖκας.

_____

_____

_____

53. ὅτι πάντες τῶν ἐπῶν ποιηταὶ οἱ χρηστοὶ οὐκ ἐκ τέχνης ἀλλὰ σὺν τοῖς δαίμοσι ταῦτα τὰ καλὰ ποιοῦσιν δῆλόν ἐστιν.

_____

_____

_____

54. Α. οὗτοι οἱ δεινοὶ πολέμιοι ἔχειν οὐ μόνον τὴν κατὰ γῆν ἀρχὴν βούλονται ἀλλὰ καὶ τὴν κατὰ θάλατταν.
    Β. νῦν δὴ σύ σαφῶς πρὸς θεῶν λέγεις ἃ οἱ ἄλλοι ἐν νῷ ἔχουσιν μέν, λέγειν δὲ οὐκ ἐθέλουσιν.

_____

_____

_____

_____

_____

55. οὔτε τῆς δυνάμεως τοῦτον ζηλῶ οὔτε τοῦ πλούτου. ταῦτ᾽ ἔχει οὗτός γε, κἀγὼ οὐκ ἔχω, ἀλλὰ κοινὸς δή
    ἐστιν οὐρανὸς πᾶσιν βροτοῖς καὶ γαῖα, ἐν ᾗ δώματ᾽ ἔχομεν.

_____

_____

_____

_____

56. τόδε γε σαφές, ὅτι παρὰ τὴν θάλατταν ἐκείνη ἡ μάχη ἐγένετο. νῦν δὲ δι᾽ ἁπάσης ὡς ἔπος εἰπεῖν τῆς
    χώρᾱς πολεμοῦμεν.

_____

_____

_____

57. ποῖ ποθ᾽ ἡ τῆς πόλεως ἦλθεν δύναμις καὶ ποῦ, ὦ ἄνδρες, ὀφθήσεται; ἀεί πως ἄδηλα τὰ μέλλοντα ἅπασιν ἀνθρώποις, ἀλλὰ μέγας ἔσται καὶ χαλεπὸς ὁ ἀγὼν πρὸς τὸν βάρβαρον, καὶ πολέμου ἄρξασθαι διὰ τὰς νῦν τῶν ξυμμάχων ὕβρεις ἀξιοῦμεν.

_____

_____

_____

_____

_____

58. ἐκ παίδων ἀεὶ μαθεῖν τάς τε αἰτίας ἑκάστου τοῦ πράγματος ἐβουλόμην καὶ τὰ περὶ τὸν οὐρανόν τε καὶ τὴν γῆν πάθη, ἀλλ᾽ ἐμοὶ τούτων τότ᾽ οὐκ ἦν διδάσκαλος νοῦν ἔχων.

_____

_____

_____

_____

59. βούλομαι ὀλίγα ὑμῖν, ὦ ἄνδρες Ἀθηναῖοι, εἰπεῖν περὶ τῶν κοινῶν. παρῆτε γὰρ ἐν τῇ βουλῇ, ἐν ᾗ περὶ τῆς εἰρήνης διελέχθην, ἀεὶ δ᾽ ἐμάθετέ με, ὅτι εἰς τὸ τῆς πόλεως κοινὸν ἀγαθὸν ἔλεγον· καὶ τότε καὶ νῦν ὑμᾶς παύσασθαι δεῖ πολεμῶντας τούτοις τοῖς ξένοις τοῖς φίλοις οὖσιν.

_____

_____

_____

_____

_____

60. Α. τὸ ἔχον ἀρχήν, ἆρα δεῖ καὶ τελευτῆσαι;

    Β. ἀλλ' ἄρχεταί τε ὁ βίος ἀνθρώπου καὶ κατ' ἀνάγκην τελευτᾷ. ἢ οὔ;

    Α. ἀληθῆ λέγεις.

    Β. ἀρχὴν δὲ ὁ βίος ἔχει δαίμονος, ἀλλ' οὐ τελευτᾷ ποτε. Ζεύς τοι ἐγένετο, ἀλλὰ τὸν θάνατον οὐ πείσεται.

    Α. καὶ ταῦτ' ἀληθῆ λέγεις.

    Β. λέγομεν οὖν ὅτι οἱ ἀεὶ ὄντες θεοὶ ἤρξαντο μέν, τελευτῶσιν δ' οὔ.

    Α. καὶ τοῦτό γε λέγω, ὅτι παντὸς ἀνθρώπου ἀθάνατον ἡ ψυχὴ καὶ ἔσονται ἡμῶν αἱ ψυχαὶ ὄντως ἐν Ἅιδου.

_____

_____

_____

_____

_____

_____

_____

_____

_____

C. Write these sentences in Greek.

1. You are saying, I suppose, that you do all things because of chance and not because of judgment, but you do not see the soul, that it is really ruling the body itself.

_____

_____

_____

2. From the things that he said to the men being present Hector revealed his true opinion about you, Alexander, and he never stopped saying terrible things. And resulting from this (thing) you now have a bad reputation.

_____

_____

_____

_____

3. You say true things, Socrates. Now this thing alone I wish to learn (once): is it possible for the just man to do wrong (once), and are the deeds of the unjust man ever just?

_____

_____

_____

_____

4. I tell you, child, that your father will end life at the hands of a fearsome mortal woman. For I, your dear mother, will somehow do this great thing.

_____

_____

_____

5. From boyhood I used to enjoy hearing the epic poems of the good poets. Even now those men who nobly made war against the non-Greeks are present, so to speak, to the ones listening.

6. I did not experience the same thing as the strangers who had come from somewhere and were then occupying Athens; for I was not in Athens but in another city.

7. You do wrong, young man, (in) not believing the things that you hear from your wise mother. This woman, you know, understands the nature of reality and many other things.

8. Many, I suppose, are the acts of violence, Demosthenes, that the citizens in conquered cities experience at some time at the hands of the ones who conquered.

9. Did you hear the speech of Socrates? Not without justice, you know, he was saying that it was necessary for commanders to pay (repeatedly) attention to some opinions, to others (it was) not.

_____

_____

_____

_____

10. From where, therefore, did this terrible deed arise? It is clear that you did violence against your wife at the hands of a wicked nature and not through reason and judgment.

_____

_____

_____

_____

11. It is not possible to believe (repeatedly) those worthless rhetors to whom many of the young (men) pay attention; for the man wanting to persuade (repeatedly) others considers reputation and not true judgment of much value.

_____

_____

_____

_____

12. It is clear that the companions of Socrates were not envying him because of his wealth—for he did not have (wealth)—but because of the excellence of his soul.

_____

_____

_____

Drill 83: Perfect and Pluperfect Active Indicative of Omega Verbs; Perfect Active Infinitive of Omega Verbs

A. Name the tense of these verbs and then translate.

1. πεποίηκας _____

2. ἐπεποιήκης _____

3. ἔμαθον (2) _____

4. ἐμεμαθήκη _____

5. πεπράχαμεν _____

6. πεπράγαμεν _____

7. ἤρχειν _____

8. ἦρχεν (2) _____

9. ἑορᾱκέναι _____

10. ἑωράκᾱσι _____

11. ἐπεπόνθετε _____

12. ἐπάθετε _____

13. ἀπεπεπόμφεσαν _____

14. ἀπέπεμπον (2) _____

15. ἐδίδασκες _____

16. ἐδεδιδάχης _____

17. πεπεικέναι _____

18. πεπείκᾱσιν _____

19. ἔσχηκε _____

20. ἔσχε _____

21. ἠκηκόειν _____

22. ἀκήκοεν _____

23. ἠδικηκέναι _____

24. ἠδικήκει _____

25. ἐτελεύτησας _____

26. τετελεύτηκας _____

27. νενῑκήκατε _____

28. ἐνῑκᾶτε _____

29. γεγονέναι _____

30. ἐγεγόνει _____

31. ἐζήλωκα _____

32. ἐζήλωσα _____

B. Write these verb phrases in Greek.

1. we have envied _____

2. to have envied _____

3. she had honored _____

4. she will honor _____

5. we had led _____

6. we were leading _____

7. I was willing _____

8. I have been willing _____

9. to have made war _____

10. they have made war _____

11. you have heard _____

12. to have heard _____

13. they were stopping (trans.) _____

14. they had stopped (trans.) _____

15. she has fared _____

16. to have fared _____

17. I have seen (2) _____

18. I had seen (2) _____

19. we have learned _____

20. we learned _____

Drill 84–85: Perfect and Pluperfect Active and Middle/Passive Indicative and Perfect Active and Middle/Passive Infinitives; New Verbs

A. Write a synopsis for each of the following verbs in the indicated person and number. Give the participles in the indicated gender, number, and case.

1. ἄγω, 3rd sing.; masc. sing. nom.
2. πείθω, 2nd pl.; fem. pl. gen.
3. ὁράω, 3rd pl.; masc. pl. dat.
4. πράττω, 1st sing.; masc. sing. dat.
5. ἄρχω, 2nd sing.; fem. sing. gen.
6. νῑκάω, 3rd pl.; masc. pl. acc.
7. ποιέω, 1st pl.; fem. pl. acc.
8. δηλόω, 3rd sing.; neut. sing. nom.

B. Name the tense and voice of these verbs and then translate. Give all possibilities.

1. πεφιλῆσθαι _____

2. πεφιληκέναι _____

3. πέπαυνται _____

4. ἐπέπαυντο _____

5. κεχάρηκας _____

6. ἐχάρης _____

7. ἐπεπείσμην _____

8. πέπεισαι _____

9. τετίμηται _____

10. τετῑμηκέναι _____

11. ἑώρᾱται _____

12. ἑωρᾶτο _____

13. ἐπεπράγεσαν _____

14. πέπρᾱκται _____

15. ἠθέληκα _____

16. ἠθελήκη _____

17. διειλέγμεθα _____

18. διελέχθημεν _____

19. δεδίδαχθε _____

20. ἐδεδίδαχθε _____

21. ἠξίωτο _____

22. ἠξίωται _____

23. ὤφθη _____

24. ὦπται _____

25. γεγένησθε _____

26. γεγενῆσθαι _____

27. ἐπεπέμμην _____

28. πέπεμψαι _____

C. Write these verb phrases in Greek.

1. we have been seen (2) _____

2. we were seen _____

3. to have sent _____

4. to have been sent _____

5. she had persuaded _____

6. she had been persuaded _____

7. they will hear _____

8. they have heard _____

9. you have done _____

10. you have fared _____

11. to be led (once) _____

12. to have been led _____

13. I have accomplished _____

14. I had accomplished _____

15. you (pl.) have begun _____

16. you (pl.) had begun _____

17. to have become (2) _____

18. they have become (2) _____

19. he learned _____

20. he had learned _____

21. we have thought worthy _____

22. we have been thought worthy _____

23. they have come (2) _____

24. they had come (2) _____

25. you were conversing _____

26. you have conversed _____

D. Study the principal parts of and read the vocabulary notes on the new verbs in this chapter other than **φάσκω** and **φημί**. Write a synopsis for each of the following verbs in the indicated person and number. Give the participles in the indicated gender, number, and case.

1. ἀποθνῄσκω, 3rd pl.; neut. pl. gen.   2. ζάω, 3rd sing.; masc. sing. nom.
3. μάχομαι, 2nd sing.; masc. sing. voc.   4. οἴομαι/οἶμαι, 2nd pl.; fem. pl. dat.
5. ——, ἐρῶ, 1st pl.; masc. pl. acc.   6. κτείνω, 1st sing.; fem. sing. acc.

E. Translate these forms and phrases.

1. ἐχρῆν _____

2. κτενεῖ _____

3. ᾤμην _____

4. οἱ ζῶντες _____

5. ἐροῦσι _____

6. τεθνᾶσιν _____

7. ἀποκτεῖναι _____

8. εἰρήκαμεν _____

9. ἐμεμάχηντο _____

10. εἴρηντο _____

11. ἀπέκτονε _____

12. χρῆσται _____

13. μαχεῖσθαι _____

14. ζῆν _____

15. ᾠήθητε _____

16. τὰ ῥηθέντα _____

17. κτείνειν _____

18. ἐρεῖ _____

19. οἰήσει _____

20. ἀποθανεῖ _____

F. Write these verb phrases in Greek.

1. they were living _____

2. we shall fight (2) _____

3. she died (2) _____

4. he was supposing _____

5. we shall say (2) _____

6. you have killed _____

7. to be necessary (repeatedly) (2) _____

8. it has been said (2) _____

9. you suppose (2) _____

10. to fight (once) (2) _____

11. we shall live _____

12. he is dead _____

13. the women living (d.o.) _____

14. I suppose (2) _____

15. you (pl.) had killed _____

16. to have fought (2) _____

17. the men who fought (subj.) (2) _____

18. I used to live _____

19. by the thing said (once) (2) _____

20. to have died _____

Drill 83–86: Perfect and Pluperfect Indicative
and Perfect Infinitives; Dative of Agent

A. Translate these sentences and underline each Dative of Agent.

1. ἄδικα ἐπεπόνθεσαν οἱ Ἀθηναῖοι ὑπὸ τῶν Λακεδαιμονίων, ἀλλὰ πολέμου οὐκ ἤρχοντο.

_____

_____

2. πῶς τὸν νοῦν τῷ τοῖς θεοῖς ἐχθρῷ ποιητῇ προσεῖχες ᾧ ἐπεποίητο τάδε τὰ ἔπη τὰ καλά;

_____

_____

3. περὶ τούτων ἡμεῖς μὲν τοῦ Σωκράτους ἀκούειν πεφιλήκαμεν, σὺ δέ που Γοργίου ἀκήκοας.

_____

_____

4. τῶν ἐν πόλει γυναικῶν αἱ μὲν ἡμῖν τετίμηνται, τὰς δὲ μετὰ τὸν πόλεμον τῖμήσομεν.

_____

_____

5. ἡ μάχη ἐπέπαυτο, ἀλλ' ἐπολέμουν οἱ βάρβαροι.

_____

_____

6. τὰ τοῦ ποιητοῦ ἔπη μεμάθηκα τὰ περὶ τὰ καλῶν κἀγαθῶν ἀνδρῶν ἔργα.

_____

_____

7. διδασκάλοις πονηροῖς δεδίδαχθε, ὦ παῖδες.

_____

_____

8. ἆρ᾽ ἀγαθὸν τοὺς ξένους δεδέχθαι εἰς τὴν χώρᾱν;

_____

_____

9. δεινὸν γεγένηται τόδε· τὸν Σωκράτην θανάτου οἱ Ἀθηναῖοι ἠξιώκᾱσιν.

_____

_____

10. ἄνευ ὅπλων εἰς τὴν ὑμετέρᾱν γῆν, ὦ Ἀθηναῖοι, πεπέμμεθα τοῖς ἄρχουσι τῶν Λακεδαιμονίων.

_____

_____

_____

B. Write these sentences in Greek.

1. This rhetor has made a fine speech, which many of the citizens have heard.

_____

_____

2. Our father was not present in the city; for he had been sent away by the archons.

_____

_____

3. All Hellas has paid attention to these disgraceful acts of violence that have been done by you, Euripides.

_____

_____

4. Your slave has been seen by many men somewhere in the land of the Spartans. For he wants to become free.

_____

_____

5. Alexander had carried off Helen for himself, and this deed alone had become the cause of a great war.

_____

_____

6. Gorgias had been stopped from his speech by the companions of Socrates.

_____

_____

7. Those good young men had been honored by the people for skill and wisdom.

_____

_____

8. From the strangers we have learned that war has begun on the islands.

_____

_____

Drill 87: The Verbs φημί and φάσκω

A. Study the principal parts of and read the vocabulary notes on **φημί** and **φάσκω**. Write a synopsis for **φημί/φάσκω** in each indicated person and number. Give the participles in the indicated gender, number, and case.

1. φημί/φάσκω, 2nd sing.; masc. sing. acc.

2. φημί/φάσκω, 3rd pl.; fem. pl. dat.

B. Translate these forms and phrases.

1. φησί _____

2. φᾱσί _____

3. φῆσαι _____

4. ἔφαμεν _____

5. φατέ _____

6. φήσει _____

7. ἔφην _____

8. ἔφασαν _____

9. ἔφατε _____

10. φαμέν _____

11. ἔφησεν _____

12. ἔφασκεν _____

13. φάσκειν _____

14. φήσουσιν _____

15. τὸν φάσκοντα _____

16. αἱ φάσκουσαι _____

17. ὁ φήσᾱς _____

18. ταῖς φησάσαις _____

19. ἔφασκον (2) _____

20. ἔφη _____

C. Write these forms of **φημί** or **φάσκω**.

1. to assert (repeatedly) (2) _____

2. you are asserting _____

3. I said _____

4. he was saying (2) _____

5. you will assert _____

6. you (pl.) will assert _____

7. you were asserting (3) _____

8. we shall say _____

9. we said _____

10. we used to say (2) _____

11. I am asserting _____

12. to be about to assert _____

13. the men asserting (d.o.) _____

14. of the women who asserted _____

15. they asserted _____

16. they were asserting (2) _____

17. of the man saying _____

18. the woman asserting (subj.) _____

19. to say (once) _____

20. I was saying (2) _____

Drill 88: Indirect Statement 2

Translate the these sentences containing indirect statements. Underline each Subject Accusative and infinitive.

1. οἰόμεθα αὐτοὺς κακῶς πράττειν/πρᾶξαι/πράξειν.

_____

_____

_____

2. οἰόμεθα κακῶς πράττειν/πρᾶξαι/πράξειν.

_____

_____

_____

3. ᾠήθημεν αὐτὴν εὖ πράττειν/πρᾶξαι/πράξειν.

_____

_____

_____

4. οἰήσεσθε αὐτὴν εὖ πράττειν/πρᾶξαι/πράξειν.

_____

_____

_____

5. οἱ ποιηταὶ λέγουσί που μητέρα ἀνθρώπων καὶ ζῴων εἶναι Γαῖαν.

_____

_____

6. οἱ ποιηταὶ ἔλεγόν που μητέρα ἀνθρώπων καὶ ζῴων εἶναι Γαῖαν.

_____

_____

7. ἐρεῖν μέλλω τοῦτον τὸν πόλεμον συμφορὰν εἶναι δεινήν.

_____

_____

8. πολλάκις εἴρηκα τοῦτον τὸν πόλεμον συμφορὰν ἔσεσθαι δεινήν.

_____

_____

9. Σωκράτης φησὶ τὸ ἀγαθὸν φιλεῖν δεῖν.

_____

_____

10. ἔφη Σωκράτης τοῦ θνητοῦ σώματος ἄρχειν τὴν ψῡχήν.

_____

_____

11. ἆρ᾽ οἴει αὐτὸν κακὸν εἶναι ψῡχήν;

_____

_____

12. ἆρ’ οἴεται κακὸς εἶναι ψῡχήν;

_____

_____

13. φᾱσὶ Σωκράτη ἄλλους νῑκῆσαι τοὺς νεᾱνίᾱς διδάσκοντα τὴν περὶ ἄνθρωπον σοφίᾱν.

_____

_____

14. ἐλπίδα οὐκ ὀλίγην ἔχω τὸν ἀγῶνα νῑκήσειν.

_____

_____

15. ἐλπίς ἐστί μοι ἡμετέρους τὸν ἀγῶνα νῑκῆσαι.

_____

_____

16. εἰς τὴν Ἑλλάδα αὐτὴν ᾠόμην τοὺς βαρβάρους ἥκειν.

_____

_____

17. οὐκ ἔγωγε αὐτοὺς οὐδέποτε πείσειν οἴομαι.

_____

_____

18. ἆρ’ ᾤου ἐκ τῆς πόλεώς ποι ἐμὲ ἀποπεμφθῆναι;

_____

_____

19. τὸν Δία ἄρχειν τῶν ἄλλων δαιμόνων οἱ πολλοὶ λέγουσιν.

_____

_____

20. οὗτοι οὐκ ᾤοντο δεῖν ἐν τοῖς λόγοις τῑμᾶσθαι, ἀλλ᾽ ἐν ταῖς φρεσὶ τῶν εὖ παθόντων.

_____

_____

_____

21. φήμ᾽ ἡμᾶς ἔσεσθαι συμμάχους τῶν ἐν ταῖς νήσοις.

_____

_____

22. ἀεὶ ἄδικα τὰ τῶν ἀδίκων ἔργα εἶναί φησιν.

_____

_____

23. ἆρ᾽ αὐτὸς εἶ ὅν φησιν οὗτος ἢ ἄλλος ἀνήρ;

_____

_____

24. πόθεν οἴει ἕξειν χρήματα; ἀλλ᾽ οὐ γάρ που παρ᾽ ἐμοῦ.

_____

_____

Drill 89: Indirect Statement 3

Translate these sentences containing indirect statements. Underline each Subject Accusative and supplementary participle.

1. τούς γε παῖδας ἀκούομεν τὸν πατέρα αἰσχρῶς ἀδικοῦντας/ἀδικήσαντας.

_____

_____

2. ἑώρων οὐ νῑκῶντες/οὐ νῑκήσαντες.

_____

_____

3. οὐχ ὁρᾶν ἔχεις ἐκεῖνον τὸν νεᾱνίᾱν μαθητὴν ὄντα τοῦ Γοργίου;

_____

_____

4. τοὺς βαρβάρους οὗτος ἔμαθεν ἐς τὴν τῶν Ἑλλήνων χώρᾱν ἐλθόντας ποθέν.

_____

_____

5. ἀκούσεσθε, ὦ ἄνδρες, ψευδῆ ἐμὲ ἐν τῇ βουλῇ εἰπόντα, ἀλλ' οὐ μὰ Δία τοῦτ' ἔπρᾱξα.

_____

_____

6. πῶς ἔσται σαφῶς δηλοῦν καλὴν οὖσαν τὴν τοῦ καλοῦ ψῡχὴν ἀνθρώπου;

_____

_____

7. εἴδομεν ἅπαντες ἡμεῖς οὐ πειθόμενον τὸν ἑταῖρον τοῖς Σωκράτους λόγοις.

_____

_____

8. τῆς μητρὸς ἤκουσα τὸν πατέρα πρὸς πάντων καὶ ἀνδρῶν καὶ γυναικῶν καὶ ξένων καὶ πολῑτῶν μεγάλως τῑμώμενον.

_____

_____

_____

9. οὔτ᾽ ἀκούσει οὔτ᾽ ὄψει τούτους τούς γ᾽ ἐλευθέρους δούλους γενομένους τῶν βαρβάρων.

_____

_____

10. τῶν νῦν ἀρχόντων ὁρῶμεν πάντα τὰ ἔργα ὄντα περὶ τὸ κοινόν.

_____

_____

Drill 90: Personal Constructions

Translate these sentences.

1. λέγεται ὁ ἄρχων τῶν πολεμίων τελευτήσειν.

_____

_____

2. λέγεται τὸν ἄρχοντα τῶν πολεμίων τελευτήσειν.

_____

_____

3. δίκαιόν ἐστι τὴν αἰτίᾱν τοῦτον ἔχειν.

_____

_____

4. τὴν αἰτίᾱν οὗτός ἐστι δίκαιος ἔχειν.

_____

_____

5. λέγεται αὕτη ἡ γυνὴ τοὺς Ἕλληνας πεῖσαι τοῦ πολέμου τοῦ πρὸς τοὺς βαρβάρους ἄρξασθαι.

_____

_____

6. ἆρ᾽ οὐ δῆλος εἶ ταῦτα εἰπὼν ψευδῆ;

_____

_____

7. πῶς οὖν δέχεσθαι τὸν πλοῦτον αὐτοῦ τοῦ πατρὸς δίκαιος εἶ, ὦ ἄνερ;

_____

_____

8. δῆλός ἐστιν ὅτι τήνδε τὴν γυναῖκα βούλεται ἀγαγέσθαι.

_____

_____

9. καὶ ἐν τῷ παρόντι δίκαιός εἰμι πράττειν ἃ πράττειν οἱ πατέρες ἠξίουν.

_____

_____

10. ἆρ᾽ οὐκ ἐγὼ ἦν δικαίᾱ ἐπὶ ταῖς τῶν ἐχθρῶν συμφοραῖς χαίρουσα;

_____

_____

Drill 91: Articular Infinitive

A. Translate these phrases containing articular infinitives.

1. τῷ τοῦ δήμου δικαίως ἄρχειν

_____

2. τὸ τὸν Σωκράτη θανάτου ἀξιοῦσθαι

_____

3. διὰ τὸ πολλὰς πεπονθέναι συμφοράς

_____

4. φόβος τοῦ τὸν βίον τελευτῆσαι

_____

5. μετὰ τὸ τὰς γυναῖκας ἀποπεμφθῆναι εἰς τὴν νῆσον

_____

6. τῷ μὴ αἰσχρὰ πράττειν

_____

7. τὸ τοὺς Ἀθηναίους νῑκᾶσθαι

_____

8. πρὸς τῷ τὰ χρήματα δέξασθαι

_____

9. τῷ τοῖς ἄρχουσι πείθεσθαι

_____

10. τὸ μὴ βούλεσθαι τὰ δέοντα ποιεῖν

_____

B. Write in Greek these phrases containing articular infinitives.

1. a speech (subj.) about wronging (repeatedly) and being wronged (repeatedly)

_____

_____

2. for the sake of conversing (repeatedly) with Socrates

_____

3. by being present in the city

_____

4. after learning (once) the truth about Demosthenes

_____

5. the slaves' being willing (repeatedly) (subj.) to pay attention (repeatedly) to the words of the master

_____

_____

6. a great hope (subj.) of being honored (once) by the citizens

_____

_____

7. on account of its being necessary (repeatedly) to make war (once)

_____

8. in respect to speaking (once) cleverly

_____

9. envying (subj.) (repeatedly) that man for his wealth

_____

10. because of Alexander's having married Helen

_____

C. Translate these sentences containing articular infinitives.

1. ὑπὲρ τοῦ μὴ ὑπ' ἐχθρῶν ὁρᾶσθαι ἐκ τῆς πόλεώς ποι ἦλθον.

_____

_____

2. καλὸν τὸ τοὺς πολίτᾱς τούτους εἶναι ἐλευθέρους.

_____

_____

3. ἆρ' οὐκ ἐχάρης ἐπὶ τῷ τὸν ἀγῶνα νῑκῆσαι;

_____

_____

4. τῷ εἰς Ἀθήνας ἥκειν, ὦ ξένοι, ἐδηλώσατε ὅτι τὴν ἐλευθερίᾱν φιλεῖτε.

_____

_____

5. ἔχουσί που καὶ οἱ ἄνδρες καὶ αἱ γυναῖκες τὴν αὐτὴν ἐλπίδα τοῦ βίου εὖ ἄγειν.

_____

_____

6. εἰρήνην ἦγον οὐ διὰ τὸ ὑπὸ φόβου ἄρχεσθαι ἀλλ' ὅτι ὅπλ' αὐτοῖς οὐκ ἦν.

_____

_____

7. χρηστὸν τὸ δικαίους εἶναι νόμους εἰς τὸ τὴν πόλιν εὖ πράττειν.

_____

_____

8. διὰ τὸ πολέμιος δήμῳ γενέσθαι ὁ ἄρχων κακῶς ἀκούει.

_____

_____

9. ἀγαθὸν τὸ υἱὸν τὰ τοῦ πατρὸς ἔπη ἀκοῦσαι.

_____

_____

10. αἰσχρὸν τὸ τῇ τῶν πολεμίων νίκῃ χαίρειν.

_____

_____

Exercises, Chapter 8

A. Place the correct accents on these sentences and then translate.

1. φαμεν που ὀλιγην το πληθος ἐχειν σοφιᾱν περι γε την της πολεως ἀρχην.

_____

_____

_____

2. οὐχ ὑπερ των ἰσων ὑμῖν και τοις ἀλλοις ἐσθ᾽ ὁ κινδῡνος, ὠ ἀνδρες στρατιωται.

_____

_____

_____

3. βουλει, ὠ στρατιωτα, κακως ζην ἠ καλως ἀποθανειν; ἠ γαρ τουτο ἠ ἐκεινο πρᾱξαι δεησει.

_____

_____

_____

4. ὕβρεις οἵδε μόνοι τῶν Ἀθηναίων πεπρᾶχᾶσι πλούτου χάριν. ὡς ἠδίκησαν σαφές ἐστιν
   πᾶσιν ἐν τῷ πλήθει.

   _____

   _____

   _____

   _____

5. ἦλθεν εἰς τὴν πόλιν ὁ στρατηγὸς καὶ λέγων ἤρξατο ὧδε πως· Τῶν στρατιωτῶν οἱ μὲν
   τεθνᾶσιν, οἱ δ' ἔτι μάχονται. μεγάλη ἐν αὐτοῖς ἡ νίκης ἐστὶν ἐλπίς.

   _____

   _____

   _____

   _____

6. ὁ υἱὸς ὁ μετὰ τὸ τὸν πατέρα θανεῖν τὴν ἀρχὴν δεξάμενος εἶχε μὲν πολλά, ἔπρᾶττε δ'
   ὀλίγα.

   _____

   _____

   _____

7. τῶν ὑπὸ σοῦ λεχθέντων τὰ μὲν ὄντως, ὦ Σώκρατες, μανθάνω· τὰ δὲ πως οὐ πάνυ ἐστὶ
σαφῆ.

---

8. λεγεται που ἴση τὴν δύναμιν εἶναι αὕτη ἡ νῆσος τῇ τῶν Ἀθηναίων πόλει.

---

9. ὁ Ἀλέξανδρος ἔφασκεν Διὸς υἱὸς εἶναι· ὅπερ ψευδὲς ὂν ἑώρων οἱ τούτου στρατιῶται.

---

10. ᾤμην τῶν ἡμετέρων στρατιωτῶν τὸ πλῆθος ἀποθανεῖσθαι ὑπὸ τῶν πολεμίων, ἀλλ᾽
ἐγένετο τοὐναντίον.

B. Translate these sentences.

1. ὁρῶμεν πάντα ἀληθῆ ὄντα ἃ εἴπετε.

_____

_____

ὁρῶμεν ὅτι πάντα ἀληθῆ ἐστιν ἃ εἴπετε.

_____

_____

2. δῆλον ὅτι αὐτὸς τὸν ἄρχοντα ἀπέκτεινεν.

_____

_____

δηλώσω αὐτὸν ἀποκτεῖναι τὸν ἄρχοντα.

_____

_____

δῆλός ἐστι τὸν ἄρχοντα ἀποκτείνᾱς.

_____

_____

3. φαμὲν τὰς γνώμᾱς αὐτῶν ἐναντίᾱς εἶναι τῶν ὑμετέρων.

_____

_____

ἔφαμεν πάντα ἐναντίοι αὐτοῖς εἶναι.

_____

_____

4. οὐκέτ᾽ ἦν ἴση ἡ ἐν πόλει ἀρχή· οὗτος γὰρ ὁ ἀνὴρ τῶν ἄλλων μόνος ἦρχεν καὶ οὐ κατὰ δίκην.

_____

_____

5. πρὸς τὴν βουλὴν ἐρῶ ὅτι ὁ τῶν Ἀθηναίων στρατὸς οὐκέτι ὑπὸ τῶν βαρβάρων νῑκᾶται.

_____

_____

6. χαίρεις πως τῷ αἰεὶ παρεῖναι τοῖς κινδύνοις τῶν φίλων, οὓς εἰς σωτηρίᾱν ἄγειν ἔχεις.

_____

_____

7. πολλοὶ μὲν ἐν τῷ πλήθει οἴονται ἀγαθὸν εἶναι τὸ τὸν πάντα βίον ἐν ἡδοναῖς ἄγειν. ἐγὼ δέ φημι χρῆναι λύπᾱς παθεῖν πρὸς ταῖς ἡδοναῖς.

_____

_____

_____

8. οἵδε οἱ οὐκέτι ζῶντες ἴσην μοῖραν ἔπαθον· πάντας γὰρ ἐν μάχῃ ἐκτείναμεν, ἀλλ' οὐ δή που ἴσως τῑμηθήσονται πάντες.

_____

_____

_____

9. οὐ πολὺ εἴρηκας περὶ τῆς μάχης. ζῇ ἔτι ἡ ψῡχὴ αὐτοῦ ἢ τέθνηκεν ὁ φίλος μου;

_____

_____

10. πρὸ τοῦ ἄρχων γεγονέναι ὁ ἐμὸς πατὴρ τὴν τοῦ δήμου χάριν ἔσχεν. νῦν δὲ στρατηγὸς εἶναί φησι βούλεσθαι.

_____

_____

_____

11. ἐν ἐκείνῃ τῇ μάχῃ τὸ πλῆθος τῶν στρατιωτῶν τῶν συμμάχων οἱ πολέμιοι ἀπέκτειναν. καὶ δὴ πάνυ ὀλίγοι ἔτ' ἔζων Ἀθηναῖοι καὶ οὗτοι δεινῶς ἔπασχον.

_____

_____

_____

12. τὸ ζῆν φημι κοινὸν εἶναι τοῖς τε ἀνθρώποις καὶ τοῖς θεοῖς καὶ τοῖς ζῴοις. τοῦ δὲ ἀποθνήσκειν πέρι (οὐ γὰρ ἀποθνήσκουσιν οἱ δαίμονες) οὔ φημι ταὐτόν.

_____

_____

_____

13. καλὸν τὸ νῑκᾶν, ἀλλ’ οὐ χρὴ τοὺς νῑκήσαντας πάνυ κακῶς ποιεῖν τοὺς νῑκηθέντας. παλαιός ἐσθ’ ὁ νόμος
οὗτος καὶ καλῶς ἔχων.

_____

_____

_____

_____

14. Α. φήσεις ἴσως δίκαιον εἶναι τὸ πάντας ἔχειν ἴσον ἀλλήλοις.
    Β. οὕτω γ’ ἔφασκον οἱ παλαιοί.

_____

_____

_____

15. εἰς δῶμα ἧκον κοὐκ ἐχάρην ἀκούσᾱς τὸν ἐμὸν ἑταῖρον ταὐτὸν ἄλλοις πολίταις παθόντα· ἀπεπέμπετο
γὰρ ἄνευ τε πλούτου καὶ φίλων ἐκ τῆς πόλεως.

_____

_____

_____

16. ἡ συμφορὰ ἡ ἐν τῇ θαλάσσῃ γενομένη οὐχ ἡμῖν μόνον ἀλλὰ καὶ τοῖς ἄλλοις Ἕλλησιν ἐδήλωσεν ὅτι ἡ
τῆς πόλεως τῆσδε δύναμις ὡς ἔπος εἰπεῖν ἁπάσης τῆς Ἑλλάδος ἦν σωτηρίᾱ.

_____

_____

_____

17. ἐχθρὸς εἶ τοῖς τε θεοῖς καὶ ἐμοὶ καὶ δὴ πρὸ μοίρᾱς ἀποθανεῖ, ὦ πάτερ. αὐτὸς γὰρ τήνδ᾽ ἀπέκτονας ἧς τέκνον εἰμί.

_____

_____

_____

18. ἴσαι πως ἦσαν αἱ δόξαι τῶν στρατηγῶν τούτων, ἀλλ᾽ ὁ μὲν πολλοὺς ἔκτεινε πολεμίους, ὁ δ᾽ οὐ πάνυ ἔκτεινε ἀλλ᾽ εἰρήνην πρὸς πολεμίους ἐποιήσατο.

_____

_____

_____

19. περὶ ἀρετῆς μακροὺς λόγους εἴρηκα καὶ πρὸς πολλούς, καὶ πάνυ εὖ, ὡς ἐγῷμαι. πότε ἀκούσει, ὦ ἑταῖρε, τοὺς ἐμοὺς λόγους;

_____

_____

_____

20. τὴν τῶν βαρβάρων νίκην τετελευτήκαμεν. καὶ δὴ πέπρᾱκται τὸ ἔργον πόνῳ οὐ μακρῷ. διὰ γὰρ πολλῶν κινδύνων, ὥσπερ καὶ πρὸ τοῦ, δαίμονός που χάρις ἡμᾶς ἐς σωτηρίᾱν ἦχεν.

_____

_____

_____

21. μετὰ τὸν πόλεμον οὐκ ἴσην μοῖραν ἐπεπόνθεσαν οἱ νῑκήσαντες καὶ οἱ νῑκηθέντες.

_____

_____

22. Α. τῷ καὶ σμῑκρὸν νοῦν ἔχοντι ἀεὶ ἄδικόν ἐστι τὸ ἐναντίως τοῖς νόμοις πράττειν.
    Β. ἴσως.
    Α. οὐκ ἴσως δή, ὦ φίλ' ἑταῖρε, ἀλλ' ἀνάγκη ἐκ τῶν ὑφ' ἡμῶν πρὸ τοῦ λεχθέντων.

_____

_____

_____

_____

23. πάνυ δικαίᾱ, ὡς ἐγῷμαι, ἦν ἡ τοῦ Σωκράτους ψῡχή· οὗτος γὰρ μόνος τῶν Ἀθηναίων πάντα ἤθελεν πάσχειν πρὸ τοῦ ἀδικεῖν.

_____

_____

_____

24. ὑμῖν εἶπον, ὦ ἄνδρες στρατιῶται, μηκέτι τοῖς ἐν τῷ τείχει μάχεσθαι πολεμίοις, ἀλλ' ὁρῶ ὑμᾶς ἔτι καὶ νῦν πολεμοῦντας. αἰσχρὸν δὴ τὸ τῷ στρατηγῷ μὴ πείθεσθαι.

_____

_____

_____

25. περὶ τοῦ ζῷα πάντα θνητὰ τήν τε ἡδονὴν πάσχειν καὶ τὴν λύπην πάνυ εὖ εἴρηκας, ὦ Δημόσθενες, καὶ δὴ καὶ τὸ πλῆθός γε πέπεικας τῶν ἀκουόντων, ἀλλ᾽ ἔγωγε ἐν νῷ ἔχω ἄλλως πως λέγειν περὶ τούτων καὶ σοῦ ἐναντίως.

_____

_____

_____

_____

_____

26. εὖ γέ που πράττετε, ὦ στρατιῶται, ἐν τῇ παρούσῃ σωτηρίᾳ, ἀλλὰ πῶς ποθ᾽ ἕξουσιν ἐν κινδύνοις δεινοῖς αἱ φρένες ὑμῶν;

_____

_____

_____

_____

27. καλὸν φὴς πρᾶγμα εἶναι τὸν πόλεμον. ἴσως δὲ ταῦτα μὲν ὀρθῶς οἴονται οἱ πολλοὶ λέγεσθαι, ἀλλὰ τὸ ἐναντίον ἐρῶ ἀληθές. ἑώρακα γὰρ αὐτὸς τὰ μὴ καλὰ πάθη τὰ τῶν στρατιωτῶν.

_____

_____

_____

_____

_____

28. A. πρὸ τῆς νίκης καὶ οἱ βάρβαροι εὖ ἐμαχέσαντο καὶ οἱ Ἀθηναῖοι, ἴσοι πρὸς ἴσους.

B. ἀλλὰ περὶ τῆς μεγάλης ἡμῖν ἀκήκοα νίκης.

A. σὺ δ᾽ ἴσως ᾤου με ἐρεῖν ὡς τοῦ στρατοῦ τὸ πλῆθος οὐκέτι ζῇ.

B. ἀλλ᾽ οὐ πάνυ οὕτως ᾤμην.

_____

_____

_____

_____

_____

_____

29. ἐκεῖνος ὁ στρατιώτης ὃς ἐν τῷ πλήθει τῶν πολεμίων ἐμεμάχητο, πρὸ τοῦ πάνυ καλῶς θανεῖν ἔφησε Δία εἶναι τὸν πατέρα, ἀλλ᾽ ἐκ θνητῆς γυναικὸς γενέσθαι.

_____

_____

_____

_____

30. τὰ ὑπὸ τῶν πολλῶν λεγόμεν᾽ ἀγαθὰ οὐκ ὀρθῶς εἴρηται. ταῦτα γὰρ ἀγαθὰ μόνοις τοῖς στρατηγοῖς ἐστιν οὐδὲ τοῖς στρατιώταις.

_____

_____

_____

31. πολλὰ δή, ὦ ἄνδρες Ἀθηναῖοι, καὶ περὶ ὧν τὸν στρατὸν ἠδίκηκεν ἐκεῖνος ὁ στρατηγὸς ἔχω λέγειν, ὥσπερ εἶπον ἐν ἀρχῇ τοῦ λόγου.

_____

_____

_____

_____

32. τὸν νοῦν αἰεί πως πλούτῳ προσέχεις καὶ κατὰ τοῦτο οἴει μακρὸν εἶναι αὐτόν, ἀλλὰ δεῖ, ὦ φίλε Δημόσθενες, τῆς ἀρετῆς, ὡς ἐγῷμαι, τοῦ τὴν ψῡχὴν ἀληθῶς εὖ πράττειν χάριν.

_____

_____

_____

_____

33. διὰ τὸ μήτε πόνων ἐν μάχῃ πεπαῦσθαι μήθ’ ὑπὸ φόβου ἦρχθαι δέξεται οὗτος ὁ στρατηγὸς πλοῦτόν τ’ οὐ σμῑκρὸν καὶ μεγάλην παρὰ τοῦ δήμου χάριν.

_____

_____

_____

_____

34. ἐν εἰρήνῃ μὲν πάνυ πολλὰ χρήματα εἰς τὴν πόλιν ἐπέπεμπτο τοῖς συμμάχοις ἡμῶν, ἐν πολέμῳ δὲ πάντα ταῦτα οἱ στρατηγοὶ ἐδέχοντο ὑπὲρ τοῦ πολεμεῖν.

_____

_____

_____

_____

35. ὦ φίλε Γοργίᾱ, ποῖ δὴ καὶ πόθεν; ὄντως παρὰ σοῦ οἱ νεᾱνίαι περὶ τοῦ δικαίου μεμαθήκᾱσιν ἢ ἄλλην αὐτοὺς σοφίᾱν δεδίδαχας ἄνευ νοῦ καὶ δίκης;

_____

_____

_____

36. μετὰ πολλὰς μάχᾱς καὶ δεινὰς οἵ τε Λακεδαιμόνιοι καὶ οἱ Ἀθηναῖοι εἰρήνην πρὸς ἀλλήλους ἐποιήσαντο καὶ ἦγον, ἀλλ' ἔτ' ἐμάχοντο οἱ ἐν ταῖς νήσοις.

_____

_____

_____

37. δῆλον ὅτι, ὥς φησιν ἐκεῖνος ὁ σοφός, ἅπαντα τὰ τῶν θνητῶν πάθη ἢ λῦπαί ἐστιν ἢ ἡδοναὶ ἢ οὐκ ἄνευ λύπης ἢ ἡδονῆς.

_____

_____

_____

38. πρὸ τῶν μακρῶν τειχῶν ἦσαν πολέμιοι σὺν ὅπλοις, ἀλλ' αὐτοὺς οἱ ἡμέτεροι στρατιῶται οὐκ ἑοράκεσαν. διὰ δὲ τὴν αἰτίᾱν τήνδε πάνυ ῥᾳδίως ἐνῑκήθησαν.

_____

_____

_____

39. τοὺς ἄνδρας οἳ ὑπὲρ τῆς ὑμετέρας σωτηρίας ἐν τῇ μάχῃ τεθνᾶσι τīμήσετε; ἕκαστος γὰρ αὐτῶν ἔρωτι τῆς γῆς ταύτης θάνατον πεπόνθᾱσιν.

_____

_____

_____

40. περί γε τῆς τῶν πολῑτῶν σωτηρίᾱς, ὦ ἄνδρες, ἐμὲ ἔδει λόγους εἰπεῖν ἐναντίους ταῖς ὑμετέραις γνώμαις. νῦν δὲ κοινὸς καὶ ὑμῖν ὁ νοῦς καὶ ἐμοί.

_____

_____

_____

41. οἱ ἄλλοι θεοὶ καὶ ὁ Ζεὺς τοῖς τοῦ πολέμου ἔργοις χαίρουσι, καὶ πράττοντες καὶ ὁρῶντες. τοῦτ᾽ εἰρήκᾱσιν ὡς ἀληθῶς οἱ παλαιοὶ τῶν ποιητῶν.

_____

_____

_____

42. οἱ Ἀθηναῖοι τοῖς ἄλλοις Ἕλλησιν ἐδεδηλώκεσαν ὅτι κατὰ γῆν ἔστι τοὺς πολεμίους νῑκηθῆναι ὑπ᾽ ὀλίγων πολλούς, κατὰ δὲ θάλασσαν ἔτι ἦν ἄδηλον. δόξαν γὰρ εἶχον οἱ βάρβαροι δεινοὶ εἶναι καὶ πλήθει καὶ πλούτῳ καὶ τέχνῃ.

_____

_____

_____

_____

43. ὡς ὑμεῖς, ὦ ἄνδρες φίλοι, ἐν τῷ παρόντι χαίρετέ μου ἀκούοντες, οὕτως ἐγὼ χαίρω λέγων. μετὰ δὲ ταῦτα ὑμεῖς γ᾽ ἐρεῖτε κἀγὼ ἀκούσομαι. τῷ γὰρ πρὸς ἀλλήλους πολλὰ φάσκειν τὴν ἀλήθειαν ἔσται μαθεῖν.

_____

_____

_____

_____

44. τῶν ἡμετέρων στρατιωτῶν οἱ μὲν ὑπὸ τῶν Λακεδαιμονίων ἔπασχόν τε κακῶς καὶ ἀπέθνησκον, οἱ δὲ πρὸς τῷ μεγάλῳ τείχει ἐμάχοντο καὶ εἰς σωτηρίᾱν ἄγεσθαι σὺν τοῖς συμμάχοις οὐκ ἤθελον οὐδὲ πολέμου ἐπαύοντο. ᾤοντο γὰρ τοὺς πολεμίους οὐκέτι ἔχειν τὴν πόλιν.

_____

_____

_____

_____

45. φησὶ ὁ Δημοσθένης οὐ πάνυ ἠδικηκέναι, ἀλλ᾽ ἐδήλωσα σαφῶς τοῖς ἐν ἀγορᾷ ἀκούουσιν, ὥσπερ ὑμῖν δηλώσω, ὦ ἄνδρες Ἀθηναῖοι, ἅπαντα τὰ ὑπὸ τοῦδε κακῶς κἀδίκως πρᾱχθέντα.

_____

_____

_____

46. ἅπᾶσι τοῖς ἐν τῇ πόλει παροῦσι σαφῶς ἐρεῖν μέλλω τὰς αἰτίᾱς τοῦ τοῦτον ἀδικεῖν. πολλοὶ δὴ θνητῶν τοῦτο πεπόνθᾱσι τὸ αὐτὸ κακόν· πλοῦτον γὰρ ἔχειν ἐβουλήθησαν ἀλλ᾽ αὐτὸν ἔσχον οὔποτε.

_____

_____

_____

_____

_____

47. πάντα μέν φημι ἐν νῷ ἔχειν τοὺς θεούς, τά τε λεγόμενα καὶ πρᾱττόμενα ὑπ᾽ ἀνθρώπων, ἐν ἁπάσαις δὲ ταῖς πόλεσιν παρεῖναι καὶ τοὺς ἀνθρώπους περὶ τῶν γενομένων καὶ γιγνομένων διδάσκειν. ταῦτά γε μανθάνω.

_____

_____

_____

_____

_____

48. οὐ δή που χαίρει ὁ ἀγαθὸς πολίτης τἀναντία πράττων τῷ τε νόμῳ καὶ τοῖς τὸν νόμον ποιησαμένοις.

_____

_____

_____

49. ἔπαυσας, ὦ στρατιῶτα, τὸν δεινὸν πολέμιον ἀποκτείνοντα τὸν στρατηγὸν ἡμῶν. διὰ δὲ τοῦτο τὸ ἔργον οὐ σμῑκρὸν ἔσται θνητοῖς ἐς ἀεὶ λόγος μέγας τῆς σῆς ἀρετῆς.

_____

_____

_____

_____

50. ἔτι παῖδα μῑκρὸν ἐμὲ περὶ τὰ πάνυ παλαιὰ ὁ πατὴρ ἐδιδάξατο. ᾤετο γάρ που πολίτην καλὸν κἀγαθὸν οὕτω πως γενήσεσθαι τὸν υἱόν.

_____

_____

_____

C. Write these sentences in Greek.

1. You have suffered many and terrible pains, soldiers, on behalf of our beloved city and the long walls. You ought, therefore, to be honored (repeatedly) not only with just words but also with wealth not small.

_____

_____

_____

2. I deny that Alexander has come out from the house of (his) father; for he is paying attention to the words of Helen not without pleasure.

_____

_____

_____

3. Death in battle is the fate of each soldier, but dying on behalf of the freedom and safety of the country is a noble thing. And these things have been said before this by the greater part of men.

_____

_____

_____

_____

4. In front of the walls the generals were discussing with one another the (being) present dangers for the army and other things.

_____

_____

_____

5. It is a terrible thing, you know, for a general not to lead (repeatedly) an army into dangers because of fear, but to live (repeatedly) shamefully without accomplishing a noble victory. For we assert that in this way he will not be thought worthy of great glory.

_____

_____

_____

_____

6. Do you suppose, sons of Atreus, that it is necessary for all the soldiers whom you are leading to be present (repeatedly) beside the sea? A few of them, at least, must fight near the walls.

_____

_____

_____

_____

7. Were you denying that men at that time had fought against one another? Perhaps you believe that we shall not think those men who fought worthy of rule. *I do not have the same opinion.*

---

8. Both the Greeks and the foreigners understand that the struggle now arising against one another will be the cause of many evils for us all. Is it possible to discuss (repeatedly) these things publicly?

---

9. Who will enjoy hearing that fearsome enemies killed the good commander, who had been spoken of exceedingly well before the victory over the enemies? From where have you learned these things, companion?

---

10. The small sons had seen that their dear father was no longer living. They learned from a slave in the house that this man had died at the hands of a foreign woman.

_____

_____

_____

_____

11. The students asserting that both the body and the soul of a mortal (man) experience equal pleasures have said things not at all correct and not true. For the pleasures of the body are somehow small and worthless; contrary to which, the (ones) of the soul are deathless.

_____

_____

_____

_____

12. You have heard from somewhere that the army that fought against the enemies upon the wall and in front of the wall fared badly because of its being small, but you ought to pay (repeatedly) attention to the things being said by each of the still living soldiers.

_____

_____

_____

_____

Drill 92: The Verb οἶδα; New Verbs

A. Write a synopsis of **οἶδα** in each indicated person and number.

1. οἶδα, 2nd sing.

2. οἶδα, 3rd pl.

B. Write these verb phrases in Greek using **οἶδα**.

1. we know _____

2. I knew _____

3. you (pl.) knew _____

4. they will know _____

5. she knows _____

6. you knew _____

7. to know _____

8. you will know _____

9. they know _____

10. they knew _____

11. he will know _____

12. you know _____

13. he knew _____

14. you (pl.) know _____

15. you (pl.) will know _____

16. I shall know _____

17. we knew _____

18. we shall know _____

19. to be about to know _____

20. I know _____

C. Read carefully the vocabulary note on **οἶδα** and then translate these sentences.

1. οἶδα τοῦτον τὸν παῖδα οὐκέτι ὄντ᾽ ἀγαθόν καὶ δὴ καὶ πολλὰ κακὰ πράττοντα.

_____

_____

2. οἶσθ' ὅτι ἀγαθὸς πολλὰ ἔσται οὗτος ὁ παῖς.

_____

_____

3. οὐκέτι ἔχων ἐλθεῖν εἰς τὴν ἡμετέραν χώραν εὖ ᾔδει.

_____

_____

4. τὸν ἄρχοντα ἴσμεν εἰς πόλιν ἐλθόντα. ἆρ' οἶδεν εὖ ἄρχειν;

_____

_____

5. ἴσμεν ὅτι ταῦθ' ὑμεῖς ἐποιεῖτε, τὸν δὲ Δημοσθένη οὐκ οἰόμεθα.

_____

_____

6. ὅτι μαχοῦνται ὑπὲρ ταύτης τῆς πόλεως σαφῶς οἶδ' ἐγώ.

_____

_____

7. ταῦτα ἐπράξαμεν ὑπὲρ ὑμῶν καὶ ταύτης τῆς γῆς. ᾖσμεν γὰρ ὑμᾶς ὑπ' ἐκείνου τοῦ πονηροῦ δεινῶς πάσχοντας.

_____

_____

8. οὗτος πᾶν τὸ αἰσχρὸν πράττειν ἐθέλει ὁ φάσκων οὐκ εἰδέναι τοὺς ἡμετέρους ἀποθανόντας ἐν μάχῃ.

_____

_____

9. τὴν αὐτὴν ἐβουλόμην δύναμιν ἥνπερ ᾔδειν τὴν βουλὴν ἔχουσαν.

_____

_____

10. οἶσθά που ὅτι οἱ Λακεδαιμόνιοι τῇδε τῇ νίκῃ ἔχαιρον.

_____

_____

D. Write these sentences in Greek.

1. We know clearly that those men died well. (Express the indirect statement in two ways.)

_____

_____

_____

2. Did you know that few men were able to hold (repeatedly) power but many were desiring (it)? (Express the indirect statement in two ways.)

_____

_____

_____

3. We knew this thing, that neither our general nor the soldiers would cease from the battle.

_____

_____

4. That our men will prevail I know well.

_____

5. There were many things about the soul that Socrates both knew and was practicing.

_____

_____

6. You know that we are suffering many terrible things at the hands of this shameful rhetor, whom you believe you will be able to send away (once) from this land.

_____

_____

_____

7. A stranger has come to our city. Perhaps he will know the things that ought to be done (repeatedly) concerning this terrible misfortune.

_____

_____

_____

8. Do you believe that you know how to rule (repeatedly) according to the law?

_____

_____

9. He knew that he was doing the opposite things to the ones that it was necessary (to do).

_____

_____

_____

10. You all know power, that it is a difficult thing for mortals.

_____

_____

E. Study the principal parts of and read the vocabulary notes on the new verbs in this chapter. Write a synopsis for each of the following verbs in the indicated person and number. Give the participles in the indicated gender, number, and case.

1. λαμβάνω, 1st sing.; masc. sing. acc.   2. φεύγω, 2nd sing.; masc. sing. dat.
3. ὑπολαμβάνω, 2nd pl.; fem. pl. nom.   4. φέρω, 3rd pl.; neut. pl. gen.
5. μένω, 3rd sing.; neut. sing. acc.   6. διαφθείρω, 1st pl.; fem. pl. acc.
7. ἕπομαι, 1st sing.; masc. sing. dat.

F. Translate these forms and phrases.

1. ὑπολαβεῖν _____

2. ὑπειλήφειν _____

3. ὑπολήψει _____

4. ἔμεινας _____

5. ἐμεμενήκης _____

6. μενεῖς _____

7. ἐνεγκεῖν _____

8. ἐνήνεκται (2) _____

9. οἴσονται _____

10. εἴληφα _____

11. ἐλήφθη _____

12. λαβέσθαι _____

13. διέφθειρεν (2) _____

14. διεφθάρμεθα (2) _____

15. διαφθαρῆναι _____

16. τοὺς ἑπομένους _____

17. εἵποντο _____

18. ἕσπου _____

19. ἐφέρομεν _____

20. τοῖς φέρουσιν (2) _____

21. οἴσεις _____

22. φυγεῖν _____

23. φεύξεται _____

24. πέφευγε _____

G. Write these verb phrases in Greek.

1. they were remaining _____

2. they will remain _____

3. the thing remaining (subj.) _____

4. we were seized _____

5. we have been seized _____

6. we shall seize _____

7. you (pl.) fled _____

8. you (pl.) flee _____

9. the men who fled (d.o.) _____

10. the men exacting punishment (subj.) _____

11. she endured _____

12. she will win _____

13. I supposed _____

14. I had supposed _____

15. I was supposing _____

16. you are carrying _____

17. you will carry _____

18. they endured (2) _____

19. to follow (repeatedly) _____

20. to follow (once) _____

21. we shall follow _____

22. he has ruined (2) _____

23. the men who destroyed (once) (subj.) _____

24. to corrupt (once) _____

Drill 93: The Interrogative Pronoun and Adjective τίς, τί

A. Write these forms of the interrogative pronoun in Greek.

1. for whom (2) _____

_____

2. who (pl.) (subj.) _____

_____

3. what (d.o.) _____

4. whose (pl.) _____

5. whom (d.o.) _____

6. what (subj.) _____

7. of whom (2) _____

_____

8. who (subj.) _____

_____

9. for whom (pl.) _____

10. with what (Dat. of Means) _____

B. Translate these forms of the interrogative pronoun. Give all possibilities.

1. τίνι _____

2. τίνος _____

3. τίνες _____

4. τίσιν _____

5. τῷ _____

6. τίνα _____

7. τί _____

8. τίς _____

9. τίνων _____

10. τοῦ _____

C. Translate these interrogative sentences. Identify each interrogative pronoun and adjective.

1. τίς ταῦτ᾽ εἶπεν;

_____

_____

   τίς ἀνὴρ τοῦτ᾽ εἶπεν;

_____

_____

2. τίνας τῶν πολῑτῶν ἀποπέμψεις;

_____

_____

   τίνας πολῑτᾱς ἀπέπεμψας;

_____

_____

3. τί οὖν τοῦτ᾽ ἔστιν; δῆλον ὅτι κακόν.

_____

_____

4. διὰ τίν᾽ αἰτίᾱν τούτῳ νῦν ἐστὶ τῷ δούλῳ μέγας πλοῦτος;

_____

_____

5. ἐν τῇ γ᾽ ἡμετέρᾳ πόλει τίνας τίνων ἄρχειν δεῖ;

_____

_____

6. τίσι ποτ᾽ ἔπεσιν τοὺς Ἀθηναίους ἔπεισαν οἱ Σωκράτους ἐχθροὶ θανάτου τοῦτον ἀξιῶσαι;

_____

_____

7. τίνας τούσδ᾽ ἐν δώματι ὁρῶ ξένους;

_____

_____

8. τῷ ὑμῶν οὐ φίλος ἦν ὁ Ἀλέξανδρος;

_____

_____

9. τί ἐν νῷ ἔχεις, ὦνερ; τί χρῆμα; ποῦ ποτ᾽ εἶ φρενῶν;

_____

_____

10. τί μοι ἄλλο ἀγαθὸν τελευτήσουσιν οὗτοι οἱ ξένοι;

_____

_____

11. τίνας ἐν ἀρχῇ πολέμου συμμάχους εἶχεν ἡ πόλις καὶ τίνας δυνάμεις;

_____

_____

12. τίνι δίκῃ, ὦ δέσποτα, ἐπὶ θάνατον οἴδ' ἄγουσί σε;

_____

_____

13. πῶς, ὦ Γοργίᾱ, αὐτοὺς πείσεις καὶ τίνι λόγῳ;

_____

_____

14. περὶ τίνος ἐστὶν αὐτῷ ὁ φόβος;

_____

_____

15. πρὸς τοῦ ἐπείσθης; τίνος δὴ λόγοις;

_____

_____

16. ὑπὲρ τίνων ἐπολεμήσατε; διὰ τί εἰρήνην ἐποιήσασθε;

_____

_____

17. ἐκ τίνος τοῦτ᾽ ἤκουσας τὸ ἔπος;

_____

_____

18. παρὰ τοῦ τὴν σοφίᾱν ἐμάνθανες ταύτην;

_____

_____

19. εἰς τί ἔργον ἥκουσι ἢ τίνος γνώμης χάριν;

_____

_____

20. διὰ τί ἀπ᾽ Ἀθηνῶν ἤλθετε;

_____

_____

D. Write these sentences in Greek.

1. Whom (pl.) in the world is it necessary to believe (repeatedly) and whom (pl.) not?

_____

2. By what man was this woman loved?

_____

3. What do you want? Who has what you want?

_____

4. Whose son was Alexander?

_____

5. Whose wife was Helen?

_____

6. Is it the work of Demosthenes or whose is this (work)?

_____

7. Of the things that Gorgias says, about which do you understand well?

_____

8. Of what father are you? Of what mother?

_____

9. From whom (pl.) do children learn virtue?

_____

10. What weapons are yours?

_____

11. Whom did you welcome into the city?

_____

12. With whom (pl.) were you conversing? What things were said?

_____

13. On account of what experience did you become wise?

_____

14. The Spartans ruled whom (pl.) after the peace?

_____

15. Who (pl.) will be thought worthy of rule?

_____

16. Who (are you) and from where are you present in our city?

_____

Drill 93–94: The Interrogative Pronoun and Adjective τίς, τί and the Enclitic Indefinite Pronoun and Adjective τις, τι

A. Place the correct accents on these phrases containing forms of the enclitic indefinite adjective and then translate. Assume that they are the last words in a sentence.

1. ἀνθρωπος τις _____

2. ἀνθρωποις τισιν _____

3. κακον τι _____

4. κακα τινα _____

5. κακον τινα _____

6. γυναικων τινων _____

7. γυναικος τινος _____

8. δαιμονι τινι _____

9. δαιμονες τινες _____

10. ἀγων τις _____

11. ἀγωνα τινα _____

12. ὑβρεως τινος _____

13. ὑβριν τινα _____

14. χρήματα τινα _____

15. χρῆμά τι _____

16. αἰτίᾳ τινι _____

17. αἰτίᾱ τις _____

18. αἰτίᾱς τινας _____

19. ἀνδράσι τισιν _____

20. ἀνδρός τινος _____

B. Translate these sentences containing interrogative and indefinite pronouns and adjectives. Identify each such word.

1. τίνες τότε τοῦ δήμου ἦρχον;

_____

_____

2. ἆρ' ἤκουσας νέον τι παρ' αὐτῶν; ἐγὼ γὰρ πόλλ' ἄττα καὶ δεινά.

_____

_____

3. οἵ τι ἔχοντες εὖ ἔπρᾱξαν, κακῶς οἱ μή.

_____

_____

4. πέμπειν τινὰ δεῖ τῶν πολῑτῶν εἰς τὴν γῆν τῶν βαρβάρων. τίς οὖν πεμφθήσεται;

_____

_____

5. τέχνην τίνα ποτ᾽ ἔχεις ἧς χάριν τῑμᾷ;

_____

_____

6. ἆρα τότε διελέγετό τινι ὁ Σωκράτης; τίνι διελέγετο;

_____

_____

7. ἢ τισι λόγοις πεῖσαι ἢ χρήμασι τοὺς συμμάχους ἕξομεν.

_____

_____

8. ὦ Ζεῦ, τί ποτε βούλει ποιεῖν; τίνα πείσομαι;

_____

_____

9. ταῦτ᾽ ἐτελευτήσαμεν σύν τινι δὴ θεῶν.

_____

_____

10. ἀρετῆς τινος πᾶς ἀνὴρ ζηλοῦται.

_____

_____

11. παρῆν ἡμῖν σοφός τις, ἀλλὰ ξένος.

_____

_____

12. τίς οὖν ἦν ὁ μετὰ τοῦτον λόγος;

_____

_____

13. ἀκοῦσαι οὐκ ἐθέλετε, ὦ Ἀθηναῖοι, ἀλλ᾽ ἄττα λέγω ἃ δεῖ ἀκοῦσαι.

_____

_____

14. ὑπ᾽ αἰσχροῦ τινος καὶ πονηροῦ μεγάλην ἔπαθον ὕβριν.

_____

_____

15. τίνων ῥητόρων ἀκούων χαίρεις; δεινοί τινες νῦν λέγουσιν.

_____

_____

16. συμφορᾷ τίνι δεινῶς πάσχεις;

_____

_____

17. ἆρα ταῦτ᾽ εἶπεν ἢ ἄλλ᾽ ἄττα; τίν᾽ ἔπη ἔλεξεν;

_____

_____

18. τίσιν ὁ Σωκράτης διελέχθη περὶ τῆς φύσεως τῆς ψῡχῆς;

_____

_____

19. τί πρᾱττουσα, ὦ γύναι, ἔχαιρες; τίν᾽ ἔπρᾱττες;

_____

_____

20. δαίμονές τινες θνητοὺς οὐ φιλοῦσιν.

_____

_____

C. Write these sentences in Greek.

1. Were those weapons made with any skill?

_____

2. Some students are conversing with Socrates.

_____

3. Has anyone come from any of the islands?

_____

4. Your slaves, Demosthenes, have some hope of freedom.

_____

5. We shall send someone of the men to the council.

_____

6. With a view to the contest there will be need for you of both some wits and some fortune.

_____

_____

7. Were any things said about the insolence of the archons?

_____

8. The people are willing to obey (repeatedly) the word of anyone of the ones speaking well.

_____

_____

9. I wish to say (once) something. Will anyone listen?

_____

10. For some reason (cause) I do not like him.

_____

Drill 95: The Adjectives εἷς, μία, ἕν and
οὐδείς, οὐδεμία, οὐδέν/μηδείς, μηδεμία, μηδέν

Translate these sentences.

1. οὐκ οὐδενὶ πέπεισμαι τῶν ἐν τῇ βουλῇ λεγόντων.

_____

_____

2. οὔτ᾽ ἄνδρα οὐδένα πλούτου ζηλῶ οὔτε οὐδεμίαν γυναῖκα.

_____

_____

3. τοῖς τέκνοις εἶπον μὴ μηδένα ἀνθρώπων μήποτε ἀδικεῖν.

_____

_____

4. οὐδεὶς τῶν ὑπὲρ τῆς χώρᾱς πολεμησάντων οὐκ ἐβούλετο τῑμηθῆναι.

_____

_____

5. οὐδὲν ἀγαθὸν παρὰ τῶν ἐχόντων οὔποτ᾽ ἐδεξάμην.

_____

_____

6. πολλὰ μὲν ἀκήκοα ἐγὼ περὶ τῶν τότε γενομένων, ἓν δὲ μαθεῖν βούλομαι παρ' αὐτοῦ τοῦ θεοῦ.

_____

_____

_____

7. τούτους τοὺς ξένους μία τύχη ἔχει οὓς πάντας δεήσει ἐκ τῆς πόλεως πέμπεσθαι.

_____

_____

8. ἄδηλα ἔσται ταῦτα τοῖς μὴ θέλουσι μηδὲν ὁρᾶν μηδ' ἀκούειν.

_____

_____

9. οὐδεμία εἰς οὐδὲν οὐδενὸς γυναικῶν οὔποτε ἀξιωθήσεται.

_____

_____

10. οὐδεὶς ἐν ἀγορᾷ τὸν Γοργίαν οὐκ εἶδεν.

_____

_____

11. ὁ λόγος ἑνὸς ἀνδρὸς τὸν πάντα δῆμον ἔπεισεν.

_____

_____

12. ἕν γε δῆλόν ἐστιν· οὐχ αἵδε οὐδὲν κακὸν ἔπρᾶξαν.

_____

_____

Drill 96: Conditional Sentences 1

A. Identify each type of conditional sentence and then translate.

1. εἰ οἱ σοφοὶ τὴν δύναμιν ἔχουσι τὴν ἐν τῇ πόλει, πάντα ἐς τὸ ἀγαθὸν πράττεται.

_____

_____

_____

εἰ οἱ σοφοὶ τὴν δύναμιν εἶχον τὴν ἐν τῇ πόλει, πάντα ἐς τὸ ἀγαθὸν ἐπράττετο.

_____

_____

εἰ οἱ σοφοὶ τὴν δύναμιν εἶχον τὴν ἐν τῇ πόλει, πάντ᾽ ἂν ἐς τὸ ἀγαθὸν ἐπράττετο.

_____

_____

2. τὰ τῆς πόλεως κατὰ δίκην ἂν ἐποίουν οἱ σοφοὶ εἴπερ τὴν δύναμιν εἶχον, ὡς ἐγῷμαι. νῦν δὲ ἄδικα πάσχομεν.

_____

_____

_____

3. ἐκεῖνος ὁ νεανίᾱς, εἰ ἐν πολέμῳ μὴ ἀπέθανεν, νῦν ἂν Σωκράτει παρῆν καὶ πολλὰ διελέγετο.

_____

_____

_____

4. οὐκ ἂν ποτε ἐκεῖνον τὸν δεσπότην εὖ ἐδεξάμεθα εἰ αὐτὸν ἠκούσαμεν οὕτω κακὸν ὄντα.

_____

_____

_____

5. πολλὰ ἔστι παρὰ τῶν ποιητῶν μανθάνειν εἰ διδάσκεσθαί πως ἐθέλεις τοῖς ἔπεσιν αὐτῶν.

_____

_____

_____

6. εἰ ἡ ἐκ τῆς νήσου ἤκουσα τὴν ἀλήθειαν εἶπε περὶ τὴν ὑπὸ τοῦ ἀνδρὸς πρᾱχθεῖσαν ὕβριν, οὐκ ἂν δεινὰ ἔπαθεν ὑφ᾽ ἡμῶν.

_____

_____

_____

7. ἔγωγ᾽, εἰ εἶπον ἃ σύ, ὦνερ, περὶ τοῦ ἡμετέρου ἄρχοντος, πολλὰ ἂν ἔπασχον καὶ δικαίως.

_____

_____

_____

8. ἆρ' ὑπὲρ τῆς πόλεως σωτηρίας μαχεῖσθ', ὦ στρατιῶται, εἰ εἰς μεγάλους ἀχθήσεσθε κινδύνους ὑπὸ τούτου τοῦ στρατηγοῦ τοῦ δεινοῦ;

_____

_____

_____

_____

9. τοῖς γε ἄρχουσι τὸν νοῦν προσείχομεν ἂν εἰ αὐτοὺς ᾠόμεθα τὰ τῆς πόλεως μανθάνειν.

_____

_____

_____

B. Identify each type of conditional sentence and then write it in Greek.

1. If you had paid attention to those having much money, you would now be rejoicing in (because of) great wealth.

_____

_____

2. If we thought that Socrates was going to be speaking, we always went to the agora with his companions.

_____

_____

3. If you were really wanting to learn my opinion about these things, Gorgias, you would be listening to my words.

_____

_____

4. Would I envy Socrates for (because of) his wisdom if I were not wishing to become wise myself?

_____

_____

5. If we desire to learn about the soul, we discuss it and many other things with Socrates. For he is a marvelous teacher.

_____

_____

_____

Drill 97: Third-Declension Adjectives 2: **-ων, -ον**

A. On a separate sheet decline fully **ἡ εὐδαίμων γυνή**, **τὸ εὔδαιμον γένος**, and **ὁ σώφρων ἀνήρ**.

B. Supply the correct form of the article or **ὦ** and the adjective **εὐδαίμων, εὔδαιμον** to agree with each noun. Give all possibilities.

1. _____ πόλιν   2. _____ ποιητά

3. _____ στρατηγούς   4. _____ Ἀθῆναι

5. _____ υἱῷ   6. _____ μητέρων

7. _____ πολίταις   8. _____ βίου

C. Supply the correct form of the article or **ὦ** and the adjective **σώφρων, σῶφρον** to agree with each noun. Give all possibilities.

1. _____ Σώκρατες   2. _____ γνώμη

3. _____ τέκνον   4. _____ γυναιξίν

5. _____ δεσπότα   6. _____ διδασκάλου

7. _____ ἑταίρων   8. _____ μαθητά

Drill 98–99: Short Sentences and Syntax

Dative of Manner
Adverbial Accusative

After studying the new vocabulary of this chapter, translate these short sentences, and from the list above give the syntax of the italicized words.

1. *οὐδέν* σε φιλῶ. *τί* οὖν ἐμὲ φιλεῖς;

_____

_____

   οὐδέν _____

   τί _____

2. παρὰ Σωκράτους σοφίᾱν μαθήσεσθαι μέλλω. *τούτῳ τῷ τρόπῳ* διδάσκαλος τῶν νεᾱνιῶν γενήσομαί ποτε.

_____

_____

   τρόπῳ _____

3. *μέγα* σοι ἠδίκημαι, ὦ ἑταῖρε. ἔπη γὰρ ψευδῆ εἶπες περὶ τῶν ἔργων μου.

_____

_____

   μέγα _____

4. σὺ γέ τι μανθάνεις τοῦτον τὸν λόγον;

_____

_____

    τι _____

5. ταύτῃ τὸν ἄρχοντα τοῦ δήμου δεῖ ἄρχειν ἢ τὸν πατέρα τῶν τέκνων.

_____

_____

    ταύτῃ _____

    ἢ _____

6. οὐδὲ σμῑκρὸν ἐχάρην ἐπὶ ταύτῃ τῇ συμφορᾷ οὕτω δεινῇ.

_____

_____

    σμῑκρόν _____

7. τίνα τρόπον ὑπὸ τῶν παίδων ταῦτα τὰ κακὰ ἐτελευτήθη; αὐτὰ ἐτελεύτησαν τρόπον τινά.

_____

_____

    τρόπον _____

8. τί γέγονεν, ὦ μαθηταί; τί νῦν ἐναντίον λέγετε τῶν σοφῶν διδασκάλων;

_____

_____

τί _____

ἐναντίον _____

9. ὑπὸ τοῦ στρατηγοῦ διὰ πολλῶν κινδύνων ἠγόμεθα, τέλος δ᾽ εἰς σωτηρίᾱν ἤλθομεν.

_____

_____

τέλος _____

10. σέ γε πολὺ ζηλῶ τῆς σῆς τέχνης τοῦ λέγειν.

_____

_____

πολύ _____

Exercises, Chapter 9

A. Place the correct accents on these sentences and then translate.

1. τις οὐκ ἀν χαλεπως ἠνεγκεν εἰ ὁ στρατηγος τοις στρατιωταις εἰπεν συν ὁπλοις μενειν, ἀλλ᾽ ἐκ μαχης ἐφυγεν αὐτος;

_____

_____

_____

2. εἰ τις τον ἀρχοντα ἀποκτενει, δικην ὁ δημος ληψεται πως.

_____

_____

3. προς τινας χρη εἰρηνην ποιεισθαι και τισιν πολεμειν και τινα τροπον;

_____

_____

_____

4. τινος δη χαριν ταυτα σοι εἰρηται, ὦ Σωκρατες; οὐ γαρ δη που ἡμᾶς πεισεις τῳ ἀμαθει ἑπεσθαι διδασκαλῳ ἐκεινῳ.

_____

_____

_____

5. τις γη; τι ποτε γενος; τινας ὁρω ἐχοντας τηνδε την χωρᾶν;

_____

_____

6. φημι οὐδεν κακον θνητοις εἶναι ἀνθρωποις τον θανατον.

_____

_____

7. ἰσως οὐκ οἰσθ' ὁτι οὑτοι ὑπ' ἀμαθιᾶς οὐ σοι ἑψεσθαι μελλουσιν εἰς την των πολεμιων νησον.

_____

_____

_____

8. τινι τροπῳ οἱ νεοι διαφθειρονται και τινες οἱ διαφθειροντες; ἐγωγε λεγω ὁτι οἰδε ἰσᾱσιν ἀλλ' οὐ φᾱσιν εἰδεναι.

_____

_____

_____

9. ἀθλιως ἀν ἐπρᾱττον ἐγω εἰ τους ἐχθρους ἠδη ἐν τῃ πολει μενοντας. νυν δε πεφευγᾱσιν ἁπαντες.

_____

_____

_____

10. οἱ στρατιῶται οἱ τοῦ βασιλέως τοὺς μὲν διέφθειραν τῶν Ἀθηναίων, τοὺς δε οἱ ἔφευγον ἔλαβον.

_____

_____

_____

B. Translate these sentences.

1. εἴ τις νέον τινὰ ἐν τῇ πόλει διέφθειρεν, ἔλαβον ἄν που δίκην οἱ πολῖται.

_____

_____

εἴ τις νέον τινὰ ἐν τῇ πόλει διαφθερεῖ, λήψονταί που δίκην οἱ πολῖται.

_____

_____

εἴ τις νέον τινὰ ἐν τῇ πόλει διέφθειρεν, ἐλάμβανον ἄν που δίκην οἱ πολῖται.

_____

_____

2. ποῦ φὴς ξένους πολλούς τινας ἐν τῇ πόλει ζῆν; ἆρ᾽ ἐκεῖ μένειν ἐν νῷ ἔχουσιν;

_____

_____

3. τῷ φάσκοντι ἃ οὐ χρὴ οὐδένα φάναι, τί ἄρ᾽ ἐρεῖς; τί ἔσται τὸ τέλος τούτων ἡμῖν;

_____

_____

4. τί ποτ', αἰσχρέ, ἐφίλεις τὸν μὲν ἄνδρα τοῦτον, ὃν δὲ χρῆν φιλεῖν ἀποκτεῖναι ἐβούλου;

_____

_____

5. τὰ τοῦ δήμου χρήματ' εἰληφέναι φησὶν ἐμὲ ὁ αὐτὸς ὃς αἰσχρῶς ἔλαβεν. ἀπὸ τῶν ἔργων καὶ τοὺς τρόπους αὐτοῦ οἶμαι δήλους ἔσεσθαι.

_____

_____

_____

6. λέγεται μία εἶναι ἐν τῇ ψῡχῇ ἡ δικαιοσύνη, ἣν ἔχει καὶ ὁ ἀδικῶν, ὥσπερ πολλάκις ὁ Σωκράτης εἴρηκεν.

_____

_____

_____

7. οὐδεὶς πώποτ' ἄλλος ἀνθρώπων οὕτως ὥσπερ σὺ οὔτ' ἐν Ἕλλησιν οὔτ' ἐν βαρβάροις τὸν ὑπὲρ τῆς νίκης ἤνεγκε πόνον. καλῶς μὲν γὰρ ἐμαχέσω, τέλος δ' ἐνίκησας.

_____

_____

_____

8. πῶς σὺ οὐκ εὖ ἐποίησας ἀμαθίᾱς παύσᾱς τὴν ἐμὴν ψῡχήν; μόνος γὰρ μ' ἐδίδαξας τῶν ὄντων τήν τε ἀλήθειαν καὶ τὴν φύσιν.

_____

_____

9. ἄνδρα οὐκ εἶδον πω, μὰ Δία, ὃς δόξαν μὲν ἀνδρείᾱς τε καὶ φρονήσεως ἔλαβεν, τέλος δ' οὐκ ἠθέλησε πρὸ τοῦ τείχους μάχεσθαι.

_____

_____

_____

10. Α. πολλοὶ ἡμῖν λέγουσιν ὡς ὁ σὸς πατὴρ ἐν χώρᾳ τῇ βαρβάρῳ ἔζη κἀκεῖ ἀθλίως ἀπέθανεν.
    Β. οὐκ ἀληθῆ ἀκήκοας, ἀλλ' ἐν Ἀθήναις πρὸ τῆς μοίρᾱς. δεήσει δὲ τὴν ἀλήθειαν εἰδέναι πάντας.
    Α. τίνα οὖν τρόπον τοῦτο τελευτήσεις;
    Β. τρόπον τινὰ τοῦτο τελευτήσω.

_____

_____

_____

_____

_____

11. χρήματα πάνυ πολλὰ νῦν παρ' ἡμῶν δέδεξαι καὶ ἃ ἔφης ποιήσειν ἡμῖν ἀγαθά, τούτων οὐδὲν οὐ τετελεύτηκας. τοῖς γε σώφροσι δῆλόν ἐστιν ὅτι χρηστὸς εἶ πολίτης.

_____

_____

_____

12. τὸ θνητὸν σῶμα τοῦ υἱοῦ τοῦ ὑπὸ κακῆς τύχης ἀποθανόντος τῷ ἀθλίῳ ἐνήνεκτο πατρὶ ἐς δῶμα. περὶ τὰ μετὰ ταῦτα ἐκεῖ γενόμενα ἄλλος ἄλλο εἶπεν. τί τῶν λεχθέντων οἴει ἀληθὲς εἶναι; ἢ ὑπολαμβάνεις πάντα εἰρῆσθαι ψευδῆ;

_____

_____

_____

_____

_____

13. φῂς καὶ δούλους ἀθλίους ἔχειν περὶ τὰ τῆς φρονήσεως καὶ σωφροσύνης καὶ δικαιοσύνης ἔργα μανθάνειν. τίς ἄρα αὐτοὺς διδάξει; οὐ γὰρ πάνυ ὁ δεσπότης.

_____

_____

_____

_____

14. οὐδεμίαν πω τῶν βαρβάρων εἰλήφεμεν πόλιν καὶ δεινῶς ἔτ' ἐπολεμοῦμεν. τέλος δ' ἠκούσαμεν πολλάς τινας μετ' ἀνδρείᾱς οὐ σμῑκρᾶς ὑπὸ τοῦ στρατοῦ τῶν Ἀθηναίων διαφθαρείσᾱς.

_____

_____

_____

_____

15. ὁ τῶν πολεμίων στρατηγὸς εἶδε σὺν μὲν τῷ ἡμετέρῳ ἄρχοντι πολλούς τε καὶ καλοὺς καὶ ἀγαθοὺς ἑπομένους, σὺν αὐτῷ δὲ ὀλίγους τε καὶ ὀλίγου τῑμωμένους, ἃ χαλεπῶς ἔφερεν.

_____

_____

_____

_____

_____

16. εἰσί τινες οἳ ὑπειλήφᾱσιν ὡς ἀνδρείᾱ καὶ σοφίᾱ καὶ δικαιοσύνη ταὐτόν ἐστι καὶ φύσει οὐδὲν αὐτῶν ἔχομεν. οἱ αὐτοὶ λέγουσι φρόνησιν εἶναι τὴν ἀρετήν, ἥπερ οὐ πάνυ ἔχει διδάσκεσθαι ἀλλ' ἐν ψῡχαῖς γίγνεται.

_____

_____

_____

_____

17. εἴ ποτέ τις ἐρεῖ ὡς χρὴ πρὸς Λακεδαιμονίους εἰρήνην ποιήσασθαι, ληψόμεθά τ' αὐτὸν καὶ ἐκ τῆς πόλεως ἀποπέμψομεν.

_____

_____

_____

18. περὶ τούτων ὁρῶ ὑμᾶς ἔγωγ', ὦ βουλή, τὴν αὐτὴν τῷ πλήθει ἔχοντας γνώμην. πολλοὶ μὲν γὰρ ἐροῦσι δίκαιον εἶναι τὸν πόλεμον τόνδε, ἴσως δ' ὑμῶν οὐδεὶς λέξει ὡς ῥάδιον ἔσται τὸ τὸν στρατὸν τῶν Λακεδαιμονίων νῑκῆσαι.

_____

_____

_____

_____

19. μέγα κακὸν ἔφη ὁ Σωκράτης τὸ ἄνθρωπόν τινα ἀδικεῖν· καλὸν ἄρα τὸ μὴ ἀδικεῖν μηδὲ μῑκρὸν μηδένα.

_____

_____

20. ἀλλ' ἄττα πρὸς τοῖς ῥηθεῖσιν εἰπεῖν ἔτι βούλομαι· οὐδὲν ἐγώ εἰμι αἰτίᾱ τῶν τῇ πόλει συμφορῶν. πεπόνθᾱσι γὰρ πολλοὶ καὶ δὴ τεθνᾶσιν ὑπό τε τύχης καὶ διὰ γνώμᾱς κακάς.

_____

_____

_____

_____

21. περὶ μὲν τῶν ἄλλων οὐδὲν ὡς ἔπος εἰπεῖν ἐρῶ, ὠγαθοί, περὶ δὲ τοῦ πολεμεῖν χρὴ ὄντως καὶ ἀληθῶς τὴν ἐμὴν δόξαν εἰπεῖν. πολλοὶ γὰρ ὑμῶν τῇ τῶν ἐν τέλει γνώμῃ εἵποντο, νῦν δὲ βούλεσθε ἄλλως πως ἄγεσθαι.

_____

_____

_____

_____

22. πολλοί εἰσιν ἐν τῇ γῇ τῶν Λακεδαιμονίων οἳ τὰς πολέμου τέχνᾱς εὖ ἴσᾱσιν, ἀλλ' εἴ τις ἄρα τοῖς ἐκεῖ φρόνησίς ἐστιν, τοῖς γ' Ἀθηναίοις οὐδὲν βούλονται πολεμεῖν.

_____

_____

_____

_____

23. χρῆμα οὐ σμῑκρὸν ἡ καλὴ δόξα. αὐτὴν γὰρ λέγω σωτηρίᾱν τινὰ εἶναι καὶ δύναμιν.

_____

_____

_____

24. διὰ τέλους ἀκηκόατε, ὦ στρατιῶται, ἅπαντα. ὁρᾶτε τὰ ὅπλα. μένει ἡ μάχη ἄνδρας ἀγαθοὺς οἷς φόβος
οὐκ ἔστιν. ὑμᾶς ἐπὶ τοὺς πολεμίους ἄξω εἰ ἀνδρείᾱν ἕξετε. εἰ δὲ μή, πάνυ νῑκηθησόμεθα.

_____

_____

_____

_____

_____

25. δίκαιός εἰμι τούτους τοὺς ξένους εἰς τὴν πόλιν ἡμῶν δέξασθαι. εἰ γὰρ τὴν φύσιν μὲν ἐχθροί, ἀλλὰ τόν γε
νοῦν εἰσιν φίλοι.

_____

_____

_____

26. εἴ τις ὑπολαμβάνει ὡς σωφρόνως οἱ τῶν Ἀθηναίων στρατιῶται ἐκ τῆς μάχης ἔφυγον, μὰ τοὺς θεοὺς οὐκ
ὀρθῶς οἴεται.

_____

_____

_____

27. μόνος ἐγὼ ἁπάντων τῶν Ἑλλήνων ἠξιώθην τὸν στρατὸν ἀγαγεῖν. εἰ ἄρα ὑμεῖς, ὦ ἄνδρες στρατιῶται, ἐμοὶ μὴ ἐθελήσετε πείθεσθαι μηδὲ ἔπεσθαι, ἐγὼ σὺν ὑμῖν ἕψομαι καὶ ταὐτὰ οἴσω ὑμῖν.

28. περὶ ἀνδρείας ἐγώ ποτέ τινος τόδ᾽ ἤκουσα· οὐδέν ἐστιν εἰ μὴ ἀμαθία τις τῶν δεινῶν. οὐδεὶς γὰρ ἔρχεται ἐφ᾽ ἃ οἴεται κακὰ εἶναι οὐδ᾽ ἄρα ἐστὶ τοῦτ᾽ ἐν ἀνθρώπου φύσει.

29. οἱ ἐν τέλει νῦν ὄντες οὔτ᾽ ἴσασι τὰ τῆς δικαιοσύνης οὔτ᾽ ἔχουσι σωφροσύνην οὐδεμίαν. διὰ τί, ὦ πολῖται, αὐτοῖς χρὴ νοῦν προσέχειν;

30. εἴ τις τοὺς νόμους διαφθείρει δι᾽ ὧν ἔστιν μεγάλην εἶναι τὴν πόλιν, ἆρ᾽ ἐκεῖ χρὴ ἔτι ζῆν τοῦτον;

31. Α. τί σοι φόβος ἐστί; τί περὶ σοῦ οἱ ἄρχοντες διαλέγονται;
    Β. ἢ θανεῖν ἢ ζῆν· ὁ λόγος οὐ μακρὸς μακρῶν πέρι.
    Α. πόθεν σοι ἡ συμφορὰ ἥδε;
    Β. πόθεν; ἐκ τοὐρανοῦ. οὐδὲν γὰρ οἱ δαίμονές με φιλοῦσιν.

---

32. πρὸ τοῦ μὲν οἱ νόμοι τῶν παλαιῶν ὑφ' ἁπάντων ἐτῑμῶντο, νῦν δὲ οἱ νέοι οὐδενὶ νόμῳ πείθονται, οὐδὲ
    τοῖς τῶν πατέρων.

---

33. ὦ ἄνδρες στρατιῶται, ἴστε ὅτι οἱ μέλλοντες ἡμᾶς εἰς μάχην ἄξειν τῷ ὄντι πολέμιοί εἰσιν οἷσπερ καὶ ἡμᾶς
    ἀνάγκη. εἰ δὲ τοῦτο μαθήσεσθε, οὐ πεισθήσεσθέ τοῖς ψευδέσι λόγοις τοῖς τούτου τοῦ πονηροῦ ῥήτορος.

---

34. νῦν δεῖ ἐμὲ ἅπᾶσι τοῖς πολίταις τὴν ἀλήθειαν εἰπεῖν. εἰ γὰρ δὴ ἔγωγε τῶν νέων τοὺς μὲν διαφθείρω, τοὺς δὲ διέφθαρκα, χρὴ δή που αὐτοὺς κατ᾽ ἐμοῦ λέγειν καὶ παρ᾽ ἐμοῦ δίκην λαμβάνειν. εἰ δὲ μή, ἐλεύθερος ἔσομαι.

_____

_____

_____

_____

35. ἐγὼ μέν, ὦ ἄνδρες Ἀθηναῖοι, μὰ τοὺς θεοὺς οὔτε ἄδικον οὐδὲν οὔτ᾽ αἰσχρὸν εἴρηκα, ἀλλ᾽ ὀλίγ᾽ ἄττα ἃ οἶμαι τοὺς κινδύνους ὑμῖν δηλώσειν τοῦδε τοῦ πολέμου. οὔπω τοὺς ἐμοὺς λόγους μεμαθήκατε οὐδένας.

_____

_____

_____

_____

36. Α. τίνα ἔχει γνώμην ὁ διδάσκαλος περὶ τὸν σὸν λόγον;
    Β. φησί μ᾽ εὖ λέγειν πάνυ.
    Α. φησὶ τἀληθῆ.

_____

_____

_____

_____

37. τί, ὦ πολῖται, τῷ Δημοσθένει τῷδε πέπρᾱκται οὕτω κακόν; οὗτος ἐμός τε ἑταῖρος ἦν ἐκ παιδὸς καὶ ὑμῶν. τί νῦν ποτε τὸν αὐτὸν ἀποκτεῖναί φατε βούλεσθαι;

_____

_____

_____

_____

38. Α. τοὺς ποιητὰς πολλοῦ ποιοῦμαι οἳ παλαί᾽ ἄττα σοφὰ ἔλεγον.
    Β. οἱ μὲν παλαιοὶ λόγοι ἀλήθειαν ἔχουσί τινα, τῶν δὲ νῦν λεγομένων ψευδῆ τὰ πολλά.
    Α. ἆρ᾽ ὄντως σὺ φῂς οὐκ ἀληθῆ ἃ ὁ Γοργίᾱς ἡμᾶς διδάσκει καὶ οἱ ἄλλοι ῥήτορες;
    Β. φημί.

_____

_____

_____

_____

39. Α. ὁ φάσκων τὸ πλοῦτον ἔχειν ἀγαθὸν εἶναι, οὗτος ὡνὴρ ἴσως οὐδενὸς τήν γε σοφίᾱν ποιήσεται.
    Β. πλοῦτον δὴ ἄλλος ἔχει, ἄλλος οὐκ ἔχει, ἀλλ᾽ οὐδεὶς ἀνθρώπων, ὦ φίλ᾽ ἑταῖρε, σοφὸς οὐ βούλεται γενέσθαι.

_____

_____

_____

_____

40. A. ἆρ' οἴει δεῖν τοὺς ὑπὲρ τῶν νόμων μαχομένους τὸν νοῦν τοῖς μακροῖς καὶ ψευδέσι λόγοις προσχεῖν
ἐκείνου τοῦ αἰσχροῦ στρατηγοῦ;

   B. τί οὖν ἐχρῆν αὐτοὺς ποιεῖν; τότε γὰρ στρατηγὸς ἦν.

_____

_____

_____

_____

_____

41. οἶμαι δή τινας ὑμῶν, ὦ στρατιῶται, ἐθέλειν ἀκοῦσαι τὴν μάχην ἥπερ ἐγένετο τότε ἡμῖν πρὸς ἀλλήλους·
οἴεσθε γὰρ οὐδέν' ἀνθρώπων οὕτω κακῶς οὐδένα πολῑτῶν οὔποτε ποιεῖν. βούλομαι δὴ περὶ ταύτης ὑμῖν
ἐξ ἀρχῆς εἰπεῖν.

_____

_____

_____

_____

_____

42. τοὺς δόξαν ἔχοντας ἐπ' ἀνδρείᾳ χρὴ εἰς τὴν τῶν Λακεδαιμονίων γῆν ἀποπεμφθῆναι. οὐδεὶς γὰρ τούτων
οὔποθ' ὑπὸ φόβου οὐδενὸς φεύξεται. διὰ τέλους ἐκεῖ μενεῖ ἕκαστος.

_____

_____

_____

_____

43. τότε μὲν οἱ στρατηγοί τε καὶ στρατιῶται ἀπέθανον ἐκείνῳ ἐν τῷ πολέμῳ πολλοί τινες, νῦν δὲ ἡμεῖς τὴν
εἰρήνην ἄγομεν καὶ δὴ οἱ ἡμέτεροι πολέμιοι· οὐδεὶς ὑπ᾽ οὐδενὸς ἀποθνῄσκει.

_____

_____

_____

_____

44. ἀπέθνῃσκε κατὰ μοῖραν ὁ μέγας βασιλεύς. ἔλεγεν ὧδε πως· Παῖδες ἐμοὶ καὶ πάντες οἱ παρόντες
φίλοι, ἐμοὶ μὲν τοῦ βίου τὸ τέλος νῦν πάρεστιν· ἐκ πολλῶν τοῦτο σαφῶς οἶδα. ὑμᾶς δὲ χρή, μετὰ τὸν
θάνατόν μου, αἰεὶ λέγειν ὅτι βίον ἤγαγον εὐδαίμονα.

_____

_____

_____

_____

45. τίνι οὖν τὸ πλῆθος οἶμαι δεῖν πείθεσθαι; ἐγὼ μὲν ἅπαντα πεποίηκα ὑπὲρ τῶν πολιτῶν καὶ ἔτι καὶ νῦν
ποιῶ τὰ δέοντα. ἅπερ σύ, ὦ Δημόσθενες, φὴς ποιήσειν ποτέ, ἀλλὰ πᾶσι δῆλόν ἐστιν ὅτι βούλει σὺν
κακοῖς πράσσειν κακά.

_____

_____

_____

_____

46. Α. οὔτε ἑνὸς οὔτε τῶν πολλῶν ἐστι τὸ μὴ ὄν.

Β. πάνυ γε.

Α. τὸ δὲ ὄντως ὄν, ἆρ' ἐστὶν ἕν;

Β. ἐμοὶ γε, ὦ Σώκρατες, πολλὰ δὴ τὰ ὄντα.

Α. ἀλλ' ἡ δικαιοσύνη πρᾶγμά τι ἐστὶν ἢ οὐδὲν πρᾶγμα;

Β. πρᾶγμά τι, ὡς ἐγῷμαι.

Α. ἓν ἄρ' ἡ δικαιοσύνη τῶν ὄντων.

Β. πῶς γὰρ οὔ;

Α. καὶ δεῖ πολλὰ εἶναι τὰ ὄντα οὐδὲ ἕν.

---

47. Α. λέγομεν οὖν τὸ ἀγαθὸν εἶναι ὃ πάντες βούλονται. ἢ οὔ;

 Β. ὃ δὴ οἵ γ᾽ ἀγαθοί.

 Α. καὶ οἱ κακοὶ τοὐναντίον;

 Β. πάνυ γε.

 Α. ἀεὶ ταὐτὸν τὸ ἀγαθόν ἐστιν;

 Β. ἀλλὰ τί λέγεις, ὦ φίλε; οὐ γάρ πω ἕπομαι.

 Α. οἴει πολλὰ εἶναι ἀγαθὰ ἢ ἓν μόνον;

 Β. ἔμοιγ᾽ ἓν χρὴ εἶναι τὸ ἀγαθόν. σύ γ᾽ ἴσως δεῖν οἴει ταῦτα ἄλλως ἔχειν.

_____

_____

_____

_____

_____

_____

_____

48. Α. οἱ πολέμιοι ἡμῶν οὐκ ἴσασί πω τὴν ἡμετέρᾱν δύναμιν.

 Β. τίς δέ ποτ᾽ οὐκ οἶδεν ὅτι αἱ μεγάλαι πόλεις πρὸς τὰς σμῑκρὰς κατὰ τὸ φύσει δίκαιον πολεμοῦσιν;

_____

_____

_____

_____

49. Α. ἆρα ἀληθεῖς πάσᾱς τὰς λύπᾱς τε καὶ ἡδονὰς ἢ ψευδεῖς εἶναι λέγομεν; ἢ τὰς μὲν τινας ἀληθεῖς, τὰς δ' οὔ;

    Β. πῶς δ', ὦ ἑταῖρε, ψευδεῖς εἰσιν ἡδοναὶ ἢ λῦπαι;

    Α. πῶς δέ, ὦ φίλε, φόβοι ἀληθεῖς ἢ ψευδεῖς; ἢ δόξαι ἀληθεῖς ἢ ψευδεῖς;

50. χαλεπὰ δὴ τὰ παρόντα, ὦ ἄνδρες στρατιῶται, οὐδὲ πώποτε τῶν πολέμου πόνων πέπαυσθε. πολλαί εἰσιν καὶ μεγάλαι αἱ λῦπαι ἃς πεπόνθατε ὑπὸ τῶν πρὸς τὴν ἡμετέρᾱν πόλιν μαχομένων, ἀλλ' ὑμῖν ὁ στρατηγὸς ὁ φρένα δεινὸς εἴρηκε μηδένα ἔχειν θανάτου φόβον καὶ δὴ χαίρειν τῇ μελλούσῃ ἔσεσθαι μάχῃ. τίνι ἄρα γνώμῃ ταῦτ' ἀκηκόατε; τίνα τρόπον μαχεῖσθε; οὐδὲν φόβος ὑμῖν ἐστιν;

51. Α. τίνα εἶναι φὴς τὴν τῆς ψῡχῆς φύσιν;

    Β. ἀθάνατόν τι χρῆμα λέγω ταύτην.

    Α. οἴει, ὥσπερ οἱ πολλοί, ἐν Ἅιδου μετὰ τὸ σῶμα τεθνάναι ἔσεσθαι τὴν ψῡχήν;

    Β. οὐ πάνυ. παρὰ γὰρ Σωκράτους ἔμαθον ὡς ἔρχεταί τε ἡ παντὸς ἀνθρώπου ἀγαθοῦ ψῡχὴ παρὰ τοὺς θεοὺς καὶ τὴν δέχεται σοφίᾱν αὐτῶν.

    Α. ἄνευ οὖν τοῦ σώματος ἐς ἀεὶ ζῇ ἡ ψῡχὴ μετὰ τῶν δαιμόνων.

    Β. ὥς γ' ἔλεξεν ὁ Σωκράτης ὁ σοφός πρὸ τοῦ θανεῖν, καὶ οὐ πολλὰ ἄττα μετὰ ταῦτα διελέχθη.

_____

_____

_____

_____

_____

_____

_____

_____

52. Α. ἀνὴρ ὅς ἐστι φίλος, ἆρ' ἐστίν τῳ φίλος ἢ οὔ;

    Β. ἀνάγκη.

    Α. ἆρ' οὖν δι' οὐδὲν καὶ οὐδενὸς χάριν, ἢ διά τι καί του χάριν;

    Β. διά τι καί του χάριν.

    Α. ἆρ' ὅτι φίλος ἐστὶν ἐκεῖνο τὸ πρᾶγμα, οὗ χάριν φίλος ὁ φίλος τῷ φίλῳ ἢ οὔτε φίλος οὔτε ἐχθρός;

    Β. οὐ πάνυ ἐγὼ ἕπομαι.

    Α. ἀλλ' ὧδε ἴσως ἕψῃ καὶ σαφῶς εἴσῃ τὰ λεγόμενα.

    Β. πῶς;

_____

_____

_____

_____

_____

_____

_____

_____

_____

53. Α. δόξα, φαμέν, ἡμῖν ἔστι μὲν ψευδής, ἔστι δὲ καὶ ἀληθής;

    Β. ἔστιν.

    Α. ἕπεται δὲ ταύταις, ὃ πρὸ τούτου ἐλέγομεν, ἡδονὴ καὶ λύπη πολλάκις, ἀληθεῖ καὶ ψευδεῖ δόξῃ λέγω.

    Β. πάνυ γε.

    Α. ἀληθεῖς ἄρα καὶ ψευδεῖς εἰσιν αἱ ἡδοναὶ καὶ λῦπαι, ἢ πῶς οἴει τοῦτο ἔχειν;

    Β. οὕτως.

_____

_____

_____

_____

_____

_____

_____

C. Write these sentences in Greek.

1. After the victory few of the soldiers saw that they had been led by fortune or some divinity, but the foolish ones were rejoicing because of the things that they themselves had accomplished. The prudent ones, at least, were awaiting some new battle.

_____

_____

_____

2. If any man fled to that small island and was remaining there alone, he was not, I suppose, enduring the terrible experiences of war; but was he leading a happy life?

_____

_____

_____

3. Perhaps you suppose that the students of Gorgias are learning wisdom from him, but who truly of men are the ones learning, the wise or the ignorant? For if this man had (were having) any intelligence, he would not be accepting money from any young man.

_____

_____

_____

_____

4. If that fortunate general does not win in this battle, he will say, I suppose, that some misfortune happened on account of the bad character of the soldiers. For that wretched man does not know the work of a commander.

_____

_____

_____

_____

5. Very many of our soldiers would have died before the end of the battle if the good and moderate general had not led them out from great dangers. For the young ones of the army were ignorant of the art of war.

_____

_____

_____

_____

6. The enemies of Socrates said that this clever man had corrupted and was still corrupting the young men in Athens. They thought, after all, that the power of conversing was so great.

_____

_____

_____

_____

7. "Destroying our bodies is an easy thing, but never, mortals hateful to gods and men, will you destroy our great glory, which will always remain among the Greeks." So said the wretched soldiers of the Athenians (who had been) seized by the foreigners.

_____

_____

_____

_____

8. At that time, I was seeing that they were bearing labors and dangers well, but now I see that (they are bearing) good things moderately. How will these men not be honored because of (their) moderation?

_____

_____

_____

_____

9. No one ever yet have I seen in this city so foolish and without intelligence as Demosthenes. Not, after all, does leading soldiers in war teach either moderation or justice.

_____

_____

_____

_____

10. Where in the world are prudent men able to live (repeatedly) in peace? When will the men worthless in soul follow the road leading to justice? If they practice this virtue in the same manner as all just men, they will have a happy life.

_____

_____

_____

_____

11. A. How is this not ignorance, the (ignorance) of thinking that you know (things) that you do not know?

   B. Wisdom, then, is someone's knowing the things that he knows and (the things) that he does not know.

_____

_____

_____

_____

12. All Athenians, I suppose, have (their) sons taught courage and justice and moderation, but if any man considers these virtues of little value, what things in the world are his sons learning?

_____

_____

_____

_____

SUMMARIES AND SYNOPSES

Introduction

Introduction Summary: The Greek Alphabet

The Greek alphabet used in modern printed texts has twenty-four letters. The following chart presents them in their Greek order along with their conventional names and suggestions for pronunciation.

Uppercase	Lowercase	Name	Pronunciation
A	α	alpha	α (short) as the *first* **a** of a**w**ait (or as the **u** of **cu**p)
			ā (long) as the **a** of f**a**ther
B	β	beta	as **b**
Γ	γ	gamma	as the **g** of **g**et
			as the **n** of ba**n**k before γ, κ, ξ, or χ
Δ	δ	delta	as **d**
E	ε	epsilon	as the **e** of p**e**t
Z	ζ	zeta	as the **sd** of wi**sd**om
H	η	eta	as the **a** of l**a**te
Θ	θ	theta	as the **t** of **t**op or as the **th** of **th**eater
I	ι	iota	ι (short) as the **i** of b**i**t
			ī (long) as the **ee** of f**ee**t
K	κ	kappa	as **k**
Λ	λ	la(m)bda	as **l**
M	μ	mu	as **m**
N	ν	nu	as **n**
Ξ	ξ	xi	as the **x** of a**x**
O	ο	omicron	as the **o** of s**o**ft
Π	π	pi	as the **p** of to**p**
P	ρ	rho	as a rolled **r**
Σ, C	σ, ς, c	sigma	as the **s** of **s**oft
			as **z** before β, γ, or μ
T	τ	tau	as the **t** of **c**oat
Υ	υ	upsilon	υ (short) as the **u** of p**u**t
			ū (long) as the **oo** of f**oo**l
Φ	φ	phi	as the **p** of **p**eople or as the **f** of **f**eel
X	χ	chi	as the **c** of **c**at or as the **ch** of lo**ch**
Ψ	ψ	psi	as the **ps** of a**ps**e
Ω	ω	omega	as the **aw** of s**aw** or as the **o** of h**o**pe

Consonants

	Voiceless	Voiced	Aspirated	+ σ
Labials	π	β	φ	ψ
Dentals	τ	δ	θ	
Palatals	κ	γ	χ	ξ
Liquids	λ, ρ			
Nasals	μ, ν			
Sibilant	σ [ς, c]			

Vowels, Diphthongs, and Iota Subscripts and Adscripts

Vowels		Diphthongs
Short	Long	
α	ᾱ	αι as the **i** of **high**
ε	η	ει as the **a** of **late**
ι	ῑ	οι as the **oy** of b**oy**
ο	ω	υι as a combination of **u** and **i** (uwi) or as the **wi** of t**win**
υ	ῡ	αυ as the **ow** of h**ow**
		ευ as a combination of **e** and **u**
		ου as the **oo** of f**ool**
		ηυ hardly different from ευ

Iota Adscript	Iota Subscript	Iota Adscript with Capital Letters
ᾱι	ᾳ	Αι
ηι	ῃ	Ηι
ωι	ῳ	Ωι

Rough and Smooth Breathings

Rough Breathings	Smooth Breathings
ὁδός, Ὁδός	ἀγορά, Ἀγορά
αἱρέω, Αἱρέω	οἰκίᾱ, Οἰκίᾱ

Rules for the Possibilities of Accent

a = antepenult; **p** = penult; **u** = ultima

1.	a	p	ù	(if ultima is followed by another word)
2.	a	p	ú	(if ultima is followed by a punctuation mark that signals a pause)
3.	a	ṕ	u	(*not* possible if penult is long and ultima is short)
4.	á	p	ŭ	(ultima *must be short*)
5.	a	p	û	(ultima *must be long*)
6.	a	p̂	ŭ	(if penult is long and is accented and if ultima is short)

acute accent (´) raised tone
grave accent (`) no change in tone or tone raised less than for an acute
circumflex (ˆ, ̑, or ˜) raised and lowered tone

Chapter 1

Vocabulary

→ ἀγορά, ἀγορᾶς, ἡ agora, marketplace†
  οἰκίᾱ, οἰκίᾱς, ἡ house
→ σοφίᾱ, σοφίᾱς, ἡ wisdom
→ συμφορά, συμφορᾶς, ἡ circumstance; misfortune, disaster
  χώρᾱ, χώρᾱς, ἡ land; country

→ βουλή, βουλῆς, ἡ will; plan; council; advice
→ γνώμη, γνώμης, ἡ judgment; spirit, inclination; opinion
→ δίκη, δίκης, ἡ justice
  εἰρήνη, εἰρήνης, ἡ peace
→ Ἑλένη, Ἑλένης, ἡ Helen
  μάχη, μάχης, ἡ battle
→ ψῡχή, ψῡχῆς, ἡ soul; life force

→ Ἀλέξανδρος, Ἀλεξάνδρου, ὁ Alexander
  ἄνθρωπος, ἀνθρώπου, ὁ or ἡ human being, man
  ἑταῖρος, ἑταίρου, ὁ companion
  θεός, θεοῦ, ὁ or ἡ god; goddess
→ λόγος, λόγου, ὁ word; speech; argument
  νῆσος, νήσου, ἡ island
→ νόμος, νόμου, ὁ custom; law

→ ὁδός, ὁδοῦ, ἡ road, path; journey; way
  πόλεμος, πολέμου, ὁ war
→ Πρίαμος, Πριάμου, ὁ Priam

→ ἔργον, ἔργου, τό task, work; deed
  ζῷον, ζῴου, τό living being; animal
→ ὅπλον, ὅπλου, τό tool; *pl.*, arms, weapons
  τέκνον, τέκνου, τό child

→ εἰς, ἐς (prep. + acc.) to, toward; into; against; with a view to, regarding
→ ἐκ, ἐξ (prep. + gen.) (out) from, out of; resulting from, in accordance with
→ ἐν (prep. + dat.) in, on; among, in the presence of
→ καί (conj.) and; καί ... καί ... both ... and ...
      (adv.) even, also
  ὁ, ἡ, τό (article) the
→ περί (prep. + gen.) concerning, about
      (prep. + dat.) around
      (prep. + acc.) around; concerning, about
→ σύν/ξύν (prep. + dat.) (along) with; with the aid of; in accordance with
  ὦ (interj.) O

---

†An arrow next to a vocabulary word indicates that there is important additional information about the word in the vocabulary notes of the textbook.

Chapter 1 Summary: Noun Morphology and Syntax

Noun Morphology		First Declension				Second Declension			
		Long-Alpha		Eta		M./F.		N.	
		Sing.	*Pl.*	*Sing.*	*Pl.*	*Sing.*	*Pl.*	*Sing.*	*Pl.*
Nominative	1. subject	-ᾱ	-αι	-η	-αι	-ος	-οι	-ον	-α
	2. predicate nominative								
Genitive	1. "of"	-ᾱς	-ῶν	-ης	-ῶν	-ου	-ων	-ου	-ων
	2. "from"								
Dative	1. "to," "for"	-ᾳ	-αις†	-ῃ	-αις†	-ῳ	-οις†	ῳ	-οις†
	2. "with," "by (means of)"								
	3. "in," "on" (with preps.)								
Accusative	1. direct object	-ᾱν	-ᾱς	-ην	-ᾱς	-ον	-ους	-ον	-α
	2. "toward," "(in)to," "against" (with preps.)								
Vocative	direct address	-ᾱ	-αι	-η	-αι	-ε	-οι	-ον	-α

†The endings **-αις** and **-οις** have alternate forms: **-αισι(ν)** and **-οισι(ν)**.

REMEMBER: Long-alpha nouns have stems ending in **ε**, **ι**, or **ρ**. The *declension* of a noun is determined by looking at the genitive singular form of the full vocabulary entry. A genitive singular ending in **-ᾱς** or **-ης** indicates that the noun belongs to the first declension; a genitive singular ending in **-ου** indicates that the noun belongs to the second declension.

To decline a noun:
1. take the stem from the genitive singular form in the full vocabulary entry (e.g., **οἰκι-** from **οἰκίᾱ, οἰκίᾱς, ἡ** house; or **τεκν-** from **τέκνον, τέκνου, τό** child)
2. add the appropriate case endings to the stem.

Accent Rules for First- and Second-Declension Nouns

1. Nouns have *persistent* accent.
2. If the nominative singular has an acute on the ultima, the genitive and dative singular and plural have a circumflex on the ultima.
3. The nominative/vocative plural endings **-αι** and **-οι** (final **-αι** and final **-οι**) count as *short* for purposes of accent.
4. The genitive plural ending of *every* first-declension noun has a circumflex.

Noun Syntax

Nominative, Subject	a *subject* (that which is spoken about) of a verb
Predicate Nominative	an element that is *equivalent to* the subject and is joined to it by a *linking* or *copulative* verb
Genitive of Possession	a person or thing *owning* or *possessing* another noun
Genitive of Separation	1. a person or thing *from whom* or *which* something or someone else is *separated*
	2. sometimes accompanied by a preposition
Dative of Reference	a person *with reference to whom* the action of the verb occurs
Dative of Means or **Instrument**	a thing *by means of which* an action is performed
Accusative, Direct Object	a person or thing *receiving the action of the verb*
Vocative, Direct Address	a person or thing *addressed directly*

The Article

	Singular			*Plural*		
	M.	F.	N.	M.	F.	N.
Nom.	ὁ	ἡ	τό	οἱ	αἱ	τά
Gen.	τοῦ	τῆς	τοῦ	τῶν	τῶν	τῶν
Dat.	τῷ	τῇ	τῷ	τοῖς	ταῖς	τοῖς
Acc.	τόν	τήν	τό	τούς	τάς	τά

The article always agrees with its noun in *gender, number,* and *case.*

Uses of the Article

1. specific people/things: **οἱ νόμοι**, the (specific) customs (subj.)
2. names of famous or previously named people: **ὁ Πρίαμος**, Priam; **τῇ Ἑλένῃ**, for Helen
3. nouns *belonging* to someone: **τὰ τέκνα**, her (his, their) children
4. generic people/things: **οἱ ἄνθρωποι**, (the class of) human beings (subj.)
5. abstract nouns: **ἡ σοφίᾱ**, wisdom (subj.)

Attributive Position

When a word or phrase that limits a noun is placed directly after the article agreeing with the noun, it is in the attributive position.

τὰ ἐν τῇ χώρᾳ ζῷα	animals (subj. or d.o.) in the land (slight emphasis on *attributive*)
τὰ ζῷα τὰ ἐν τῇ χώρᾳ	animals (subj. or d.o.) in the land (slight emphasis on *noun*)
ζῷα τὰ ἐν τῇ χώρᾳ	animals (subj. or d.o.), the ones in the land (attributive added as afterthought)

Chapter 2

Vocabulary

→ **αἰτίᾱ, αἰτίᾱς, ἡ** cause; responsibility

→ **ἀρχή, ἀρχῆς, ἡ** beginning; (supreme) power, rule; empire

→ **δόξα, δόξης, ἡ** opinion, belief; reputation; glory; expectation

→ **θάλαττα, θαλάττης, ἡ** sea

→ **ἀλήθεια, ἀληθείᾱς, ἡ** truth

→ **μοῖρα, μοίρᾱς, ἡ** fate

→ **Γοργίᾱς, Γοργίου, ὁ** Gorgias

νεᾱνίᾱς, νεᾱνίου, ὁ young man

→ **Ἅιδης, Ἅιδου, ὁ** Hades

→ **Ἀτρείδης, Ἀτρείδου, ὁ** Atreides, son of Atreus

→ **Εὐρῑπίδης, Εὐρῑπίδου, ὁ** Euripides

ποιητής, ποιητοῦ, ὁ maker; poet

πολίτης, πολίτου, ὁ citizen

→ **δῆμος, δήμου, ὁ** (the) people

φόβος, φόβου, ὁ fear

οὗτος, αὕτη, τοῦτο (demonstr. adj./pron.) this; *pl.,* these (§20)

ἀγαθός, ἀγαθή, ἀγαθόν good

Ἀθηναῖος, Ἀθηναίᾱ, Ἀθηναῖον Athenian; *masc. pl. subst.,* Athenians

→ **δεινός, δεινή, δεινόν** fearsome, terrible; marvelous, strange; clever

δίκαιος, δικαίᾱ, δίκαιον right, just

→ **ἐχθρός, ἐχθρά, ἐχθρόν** hated, hateful; hostile; *masc. subst.,* enemy

κακός, κακή, κακόν bad, evil

καλός, καλή, καλόν beautiful; noble; fine

Λακεδαιμόνιος, Λακεδαιμονίᾱ, Λακεδαιμόνιον Lacedaemonian, Spartan; *masc. pl. subst.,* Lacedaemonians, Spartans

→ **μόνος, μόνη, μόνον** only, alone

σοφός, σοφή, σοφόν wise

→ **φίλος, φίλη, φίλον** (be)loved, dear; loving, friendly; *masc./fem. subst.,* friend; loved one

→ **ἄδικος, ἄδικον** unjust

→ **ἀθάνατος, ἀθάνατον** deathless, immortal

→ **ἀλλά** (conj.) but

→ **ἀπό** (prep. + gen.) (away) from

→ **διά** (prep. + gen.) through (prep. + acc.) on account of, because of

ἤ (conj.) or; **ἤ...ἤ...** either...or...

μή (adv.) not

μόνον (adv.) only

→ **οὐ, οὐκ, οὐχ** (adv.) not; **οὐ/μὴ μόνον... ἀλλὰ καί...** not only...but also...

Chapter 2 Summary: Noun and Adjective Morphology; Noun Syntax

Noun Morphology: First Declension (Concluded)

	Short-Alpha Nouns Stems ending in ε, ι, ρ		Masculine First-Declension Nouns	
Singular				
Nom.	-α	-α	-ᾱς	-ης
Gen.	-ᾱς	-ης	-ου	-ου
Dat.	-ᾳ	-ῃ	-ᾳ	-ῃ
Acc.	-αν	-αν	-ᾱν	-ην
Voc.	-α	-α	-ᾱ	-η/-α†

Plural	
Nom./Voc.	-αι
Gen.	-ῶν
Dat.	-αις
Acc.	-ᾱς

ἀλήθεια	δόξα	Γοργίᾱς	Ἅιδης	ποιητής
μοῖρα	θάλαττα	νεᾱνίᾱς	Ἀτρείδης	πολίτης
			Εὐρῑπίδης	

†If the nominative singular ends in -της, the vocative singular ending is -α. Otherwise, the vocative singular ending is -η.

First-Second Declension Adjectives

	With Three Endings						With Two Endings			
	Singular			*Plural*			*Singular*		*Plural*	
	M.	F.	N.	M.	F.	N.	M./F.	N.	M./F.	N.
Nom.	-ος	-η	-ον	-οι	-αι	-α	-ος	-ον	-οι	-α
Gen.	-ου	-ης	-ου	-ων	-ων	-ων	-ου	-ου	-ων	-ων
Dat.	-ῳ	-ῃ	-ῳ	-οις	-αις	-οις	-ῳ	-ῳ	-οις	-οις
Acc.	-ον	-ην	-ον	-ους	-ᾱς	-α	-ον	-ον	-ους	-α
Voc.	-ε	-η	-ον	-οι	-αι	-α	-ε	-ον	-οι	-α

Endings for Stems Ending in ε, ι, ρ (differ in feminine singular endings *only*)

	Singular		
	M.	F.	N.
Nom.	-ος	-ᾱ	-ον
Gen.	-ου	-ᾱς	-ου
Dat.	-ῳ	-ᾳ	-ῳ
Acc.	-ον	-ᾱν	-ον
Voc.	-ε	-ᾱ	-ον

1. Every adjective must agree with the noun it modifies in gender, number, and case.
2. Adjectives have *persistent* accents, and the accent is given by the *neuter* singular nominative form.
3. *Unlike* first-declension nouns, the accent on adjectives does *not* shift to the ultima in the feminine plural genitive form.

Demonstrative Adjective and Pronoun **οὗτος, αὕτη, τοῦτο** "this"; *pl.*, "these"

	Singular				*Plural*		
	M.	*F.*	*N.*		*M.*	*F.*	*N.*
Nom.	οὗτος	αὕτη	τοῦτο		οὗτοι	αὗται	ταῦτα
Gen.	τούτου	ταύτης	τούτου		τούτων	τούτων	τούτων
Dat.	τούτῳ	ταύτῃ	τούτῳ		τούτοις	ταύταις	τούτοις
Acc.	τοῦτον	ταύτην	τοῦτο		τούτους	ταύτᾱς	ταῦτα

There are *no* vocative forms for **οὗτος, αὕτη, τοῦτο**

Noun Syntax

Subjective Genitive

1. EXPRESSES THE PERSON OR THING *PERFORMING A VERBAL ACTION IMPLIED IN ANOTHER NOUN*
2. IN PROSE, OFTEN APPEARS IN THE *ATTRIBUTIVE POSITION*

τῇ τοῦ θεοῦ βουλῇ
by the will of the *god*

Objective Genitive

EXPRESSES THE PERSON OR THING *RECEIVING A VERBAL ACTION IMPLIED IN ANOTHER NOUN*

τὸν λόγων ποιητήν
the maker (d.o.) *of speeches*

Dative of Respect

1. LIMITS THE MEANING OF AN ADJECTIVE, VERB, CLAUSE, OR SENTENCE
2. SPECIFIES THE *RESPECT IN WHICH* AN ADJECTIVE, VERB, CLAUSE, OR SENTENCE IS TO BE UNDERSTOOD
3. MAY APPEAR WITH THE ARTICLE

ἄνθρωπον τῇ ἀληθείᾳ ἀγαθόν
a man (d.o.) good *in (respect to) truth*
a man (d.o.) *truly* good

Accusative of Respect

1. LIMITS THE MEANING OF AN ADJECTIVE, VERB, CLAUSE, OR SENTENCE
2. SPECIFIES THE *RESPECT IN WHICH* AN ADJECTIVE, VERB, CLAUSE, OR SENTENCE IS TO BE UNDERSTOOD
3. MAY APPEAR WITH THE ARTICLE

τῷ ψῡχὴν καλῷ
for the man noble *in (respect to) soul*

Apposition

1. THE PLACEMENT OF A NOUN (AN *APPOSITIVE*) NEXT TO ANOTHER NOUN IN ORDER TO DEFINE OR LIMIT IT
2. APPOSITIVE MUST BE IN THE SAME CASE AS THE WORD THAT IT DEFINES OR LIMITS.
3. MAY BE SET OFF BY COMMAS

τῷ Ἀλεξάνδρῳ, τέκνῳ Πριάμου
for Alexander, a *son* of Priam

Chapter 3

Vocabulary

→ γαῖα, γαίας, ἡ earth; land

→ γῆ, γῆς, ἡ earth; land

→ ξένος, ξένου, ὁ host, guest, guest-
friend; stranger, foreigner
οὐρανός, οὐρανοῦ, ὁ sky, heaven
πόνος, πόνου, ὁ labor, toil; distress,
suffering

→ σύμμαχος, συμμάχου, ὁ ally

→ ἄρχω, ἄρξω, ἦρξα, ἦρχα, ἦργμαι,
ἤρχθην rule (+ gen.); *middle*, begin
(+ gen.)

→ διδάσκω, διδάξω, ἐδίδαξα, δεδίδαχα,
δεδίδαγμαι, ἐδιδάχθην teach; explain;
middle, cause (someone) to be taught

→ ἐθέλω/θέλω, ἐθελήσω, ἠθέλησα,
ἠθέληκα, ——, —— be willing, wish

→ λέγω, λέξω, ἔλεξα/εἶπον, ——,
λέλεγμαι, ἐλέχθην say; speak (of), tell
(of), recount

→ μέλλω, μελλήσω, ἐμέλλησα, ——,
——, —— intend, be about, be likely
(+ inf.)

→ παύω, παύσω, ἔπαυσα, πέπαυκα,
πέπαυμαι, ἐπαύθην stop (trans.);
middle, stop (intrans.), cease

→ πείθω, πείσω, ἔπεισα, πέπεικα,
πέπεισμαι, ἐπείσθην persuade; *middle*,
obey; heed; believe (+ dat.)

→ πέμπω, πέμψω, ἔπεμψα, πέπομφα,
πέπεμμαι, ἐπέμφθην send

→ αἰσχρός, αἰσχρά, αἰσχρόν disgraceful,
shameful; ugly

→ κοινός, κοινή, κοινόν common (to),
shared (with); (+ gen. or dat.) public

→ ἆρα (interrog. particle) *introduces a
question*

→ γάρ (postpositive conj.)
explanatory, for
confirming, indeed, in fact

→ δέ (postpositive conj.)
adversative, but
connective, and
εὖ (adv.) well

→ μέν (postpositive particle) on the one
hand

→ μέν . . . , δέ . . . on the one hand . . . ,
on the other hand . . . ; . . . , but . . .
νῦν (adv.) now
πολλάκις (adv.) many times, often
πότε (interrog. adv.) when

→ πρός (prep. + gen.) from; by;
in the name of
(prep. + dat.) near; in addition to
(prep. + acc.) toward; against; in
reply to, in the face of, in relation to

→ πῶς (interrog. adv.) how

→ ὑπό (prep. + gen.) (from) under; by;
at the hands of
(prep. + dat.) under; under the
power of
(prep. + acc.) under; during

Chapter 3 Summary: New Verbs

	Active	*Middle*	*Passive*
ἄρχω	rule	begin	be ruled
διδάσκω	teach; explain	cause (someone) to be taught	be taught; be explained
ἐθέλω	be willing, wish		
λέγω	say; speak, tell (of), recount	R	be said; be spoken, be recounted; be called
μέλλω	intend, be about, be likely		
παύω	stop (trans.)	stop (intrans.); cease	be stopped
πείθω	persuade	obey; heed; believe	be persuaded
πέμπω	send	R	be sent

When no meanings are offered for a voice of a verb, the verb *never* appears in that voice. An R indicates that a verb *rarely* appears in that voice. Only commonly occurring forms should be included in a synopsis. See the vocabulary notes in the textbook for additional meanings.

Chapter 3 Summary: Tenses of the Indicative; Principal Parts; Properties of the Finite Verb

A **finite verb** is *defined* or *limited* by these five properties:

Person (1st, 2nd, or 3rd)
Number (Singular or Plural)
Tense (see below)
Voice (Active, Middle, Passive)
Mood (Indicative, Imperative, Subjunctive, Optative)

Tenses of the Indicative

Tense	*Time*	*Aspect*	*Sample Translation*
Present	present	simple (rare)	he persuades
		progressive	he is persuading
		repeated	he persuades (repeatedly)
Imperfect	past	progressive	he was persuading
		repeated	he persuaded (repeatedly)/
			he used to persuade
Future	future	simple	he will persuade
		progressive (rare)	he will be persuading
		repeated (rare)	he will persuade (repeatedly)
Aorist	past	simple	he persuaded
Perfect	present	completed	he has persuaded
Pluperfect	past	completed	he had persuaded
Future Perfect[†]	future	completed	he will have persuaded

[†]Forms of the future perfect appear in the morphology appendix *only*.

Principal Parts

παύω	παύσω	ἔπαυσα	πέπαυκα	πέπαυμαι	ἐπαύθην
1st sing.	1st sing.	1st sing.	1st sing.	1st sing.	1st sing.
present	future	aorist	perfect	perfect	aorist
active indic.	active indic.	active indic.	active indic.	middle/passive indic.	passive indic.
I am stopping	I shall stop	I stopped	I have stopped	I have stopped	I was stopped
(trans.)	(trans.)	(trans.)	(trans.)	(intrans.)/I have	
				been stopped	

Chapter 3 Summary: Omega Verb Morphology

	Present Active Indicative	Present Middle/Passive Indicative	Imperfect Active Indicative	Imperfect Middle/Passive Indicative	Future Active Indicative	Future Middle Indicative	Future Passive Indicative
	Present Stem +	Present Stem +	Augmented Present Stem +	Augmented Present Stem +	Future Stem +	Future Stem +	Unaugmented Aorist Passive Stem + -ησ- +
Singular							
1	-ω	-ομαι	-ον	-ομην	-ω	-ομαι	-ομαι
2	-εις	-ῃ/-ει	-ες	-ου	-εις	-ῃ/-ει	-ῃ/-ει
3	-ει	-εται	-ε(ν)	-ετο	-ει	-εται	-εται
Plural							
1	-ομεν	-ομεθα	-ομεν	-ομεθα	-ομεν	-ομεθα	-ομεθα
2	-ετε	-εσθε	-ετε	-εσθε	-ετε	-εσθε	-εσθε
3	-ουσι(ν)	-ονται	-ον	-οντο	-ουσι(ν)	-ονται	-ονται

Present Stem = Principal Part 1 without -ω
Augmented Present Stem (for verbs beginning with *consonants*) = ἐ + Present Stem (ἐ = Past Indicative Augment [P.I.A.])
(for verbs beginning with *vowels*) = Present Stem with *lengthened initial vowel* (initial α- is lengthened to η-.)

Future Stem = Principal Part 2 without -ω
Unaugmented Aorist Passive Stem (for verbs beginning with *consonants*) = Principal Part 6 without -ην and without P.I.A.
Unaugmented Aorist Passive Stem (for verbs beginning with *vowels*) = Principal Part. 6 without -ην and *shortened* initial vowel

Present Active Infinitive: Present Stem + -ειν
Present Middle/Passive Infinitive: Present Stem + -εσθαι
Future Active Infinitive: Future Stem + -ειν
Future Middle Infinitive: Future Stem + -εσθαι
Future Passive Infinitive: Unaugmented Aorist Passive Stem + -ησ- + -εσθαι
(All accents are *recessive*.)

Finite verb forms have *recessive accent*—an accent that *moves back* from the ultima as far as it can *while obeying the rules for the possibilities of accent*.

Subject-Verb Agreement: A finite verb agrees with its subject in person and number. (If the subject is *neuter plural*, the verb in Greek is regularly *singular*.)

Chapter 3 Summary: Noun Syntax

Retained Accusative

A NOUN IN THE ACCUSATIVE THAT APPEARS WITH A *PASSIVE* FORM OF A VERB (AS IF IT HAS BEEN *RETAINED* FROM A STATEMENT OF THE SAME IDEA IN THE ACTIVE VOICE)

τὸ τέκνον τὴν τῶν ποιητῶν σοφίᾱν διδάσκεται.
The child is being taught the *wisdom* of the poets.

Predicate Accusative

A NOUN IN THE ACCUSATIVE THAT IS *EQUIVALENT TO* OR *SAID ABOUT* ANOTHER NOUN IN THE ACCUSATIVE

τοὺς ξένους συμμάχους λέγομεν.
We call the strangers *allies.*

Cognate Accusative

AN *ACCUSATIVE, DIRECT OBJECT* THAT IS DERIVED FROM THE SAME ROOT AS THAT OF THE VERB

λόγον περὶ εἰρήνης ἔλεγον.
I was speaking a *speech* about peace.

Object Infinitive

1. AN INFINITIVE THAT IS THE *DIRECT OBJECT* OF ANOTHER VERB
2. IS NEGATED BY THE ADVERB **μή**

ὁ ποιητὴς ἐθέλει τοὺς νεᾱνίᾱς διδάσκειν.
The poet wishes *to teach* (repeatedly) the young men.

Genitive of Personal Agent

1. A NOUN IN THE GENITIVE CASE THAT EXPRESSES THE *AGENT* OR *PERSON BY WHOM* THE ACTION OF THE VERB IS DONE
2. MUST BE ACCOMPANIED BY A PREPOSITION (USUALLY **ὑπό**, SOMETIMES **πρός**)

ὑπὸ τοῦ Γοργίου ἐδιδάσκοντο.
They were being taught *by Gorgias.*

Dative of Indirect Object

1. A NOUN IN THE DATIVE CASE THAT EXPRESSES THE PERSON OR THING *INDIRECTLY AFFECTED BY OR INTERESTED IN* THE ACTION OF THE VERB
2. APPEARS WITH VERBS OF *GIVING, SHOWING, AND TELLING*
3. USES *NO* PREPOSITION

ἡ θεὸς ἀνθρώποις τὴν σοφίᾱν πέμπει.
The goddess is sending *men* wisdom.

Chapter 4

Vocabulary

→ ἀρετή, ἀρετῆς, ἡ excellence; valor; virtue
→ νίκη, νίκης, ἡ victory
→ τύχη, τύχης, ἡ chance, fortune

→ Ἑρμῆς, Ἑρμοῦ, ὁ Hermes

→ βίος, βίου, ὁ life; livelihood
→ βροτός, βροτοῦ, ὁ mortal
→ θάνατος, θανάτου, ὁ death
   υἱός, υἱοῦ, ὁ son

→ ἔχω, ἕξω/σχήσω, ἔσχον, ἔσχηκα,
   -έσχημαι, —— have, hold; inhabit,
   occupy; *intrans.*, be able (+ inf.); be
   (+ adv.); *middle,* hold on to, cling to
   (+ gen.)

→ ἀδικέω, ἀδικήσω, ἠδίκησα, ἠδίκηκα,
   ἠδίκημαι, ἠδικήθην (do) wrong (to);
   injure
→ ποιέω make; do; *middle,* make; do;
   deem, consider
→ πολεμέω, πολεμήσω, ἐπολέμησα,
   πεπολέμηκα, ——, ἐπολεμήθην make
   war (upon), be at war (with) (+ dat.);
   quarrel; fight; *passive,* be treated as an
   enemy, have war made upon (oneself)
→ φιλέω, φιλήσω, ἐφίλησα, πεφίληκα,
   πεφίλημαι, ἐφιλήθην love, like; be
   accustomed, be fond of (+ inf.)

→ νῑκάω conquer, defeat; prevail (over),
   win
→ τελευτάω, τελευτήσω, ἐτελεύτησα,
   τετελεύτηκα, ——, ἐτελευτήθην
   accomplish, end, finish; die
→ τῑμάω honor; *middle,* value, deem
   worthy

→ ἀξιόω, ἀξιώσω, ἠξίωσα, ἠξίωκα,
   ἠξίωμαι, ἠξιώθην think worthy; think
   (it) right; expect, require
→ δηλόω show, make clear, reveal

ἐκεῖνος, ἐκείνη, ἐκεῖνο (demonstr.
adj./pron.) that; *pl.,* those (§§44, 45)
ὅδε, ἥδε, τόδε (demonstr. adj./pron.)
this; *pl.,* these (§§43, 45)

μέγας, μεγάλη, μέγα great, big (§46)
νέος, νέᾱ, νέον new; young
ὀλίγος, ὀλίγη, ὀλίγον little, small;
pl., few
πολέμιος, πολεμίᾱ, πολέμιον of an
enemy, hostile; *masc. subst.,* enemy
→ πολύς, πολλή, πολύ much, many (§46)
πονηρός, πονηρά, πονηρόν worthless;
wicked
→ χαλεπός, χαλεπή, χαλεπόν severe,
harsh; difficult

→ δή (postpositive particle) certainly,
indeed, of course
→ ἐπί (prep. + gen.) in, on, upon
      (prep. + dat.) in, on; in addition to;
      for (i.e., because of); on condition of
      (prep. + acc.) to; against; for (the
      purpose of)
→ μετά (prep. + gen.) (along) with; with
      the aid of; in accordance with
      (prep. + acc.) after
→ οὕτω(ς) (adv.) in this way, thus, so
   ὧδε (adv.) in this way, so; in the
   following way

Chapter 4 Summary: New Verbs

	Active	Middle	Passive
ἀδικέω	(do) wrong; injure		be wronged; be injured
ποιέω	make; do	make; do; deem, consider	be made; be done
πολεμέω	make war (upon), be at war (with); quarrel, fight		have war made on, be treated as an enemy
φιλέω	love, like; be accustomed, be fond of	R	be loved, be liked
νῑκάω	conquer, defeat; prevail over, win	R	be conquered, be defeated
τελευτάω	accomplish, end, finish; die		R
τῑμάω	honor	value, deem worthy	be honored; be deemed worthy
ἀξιόω	think worthy; think it right; expect, require	R	be thought worthy
δηλόω	show, make clear, reveal		R
ἔχω	have, hold; inhabit, occupy; be able (+ inf.); be (+ adv.)	hold on to, cling to	be held; be inhabited, be occupied

When no meanings are offered for a voice of a verb, the verb *never* appears in that voice. An R indicates that a verb *rarely* appears in that voice. Only commonly occurring forms should be included in a synopsis. See the vocabulary notes in the textbook for additional meanings.

Chapter 4 Summary: Contracted Verbs

Accents

The accent on each contracted verb form is determined by where a *recessive* accent falls on the *uncontracted* form:

1. If the recessive accent on the uncontracted form falls on either of the syllables to be contracted (e.g., ποιέω, ποιέομεν), the contracted syllable receives the accent. If this accent falls on the *ultima*, it is a circumflex (e.g., ποιῶ). If this accent falls on the *penult* or *antepenult*, the accent is determined by the rules for the possibilities of accent (e.g., ποιοῦμεν).

2. If the recessive accent on the uncontracted form falls *before* the vowels that contract (e.g., ἐποίεον) the accent on the contracted form remains recessive according to the rules for the possibilities of accent (e.g., ἐποίουν).

Principal Parts

1. Principal parts of contracted verbs often follow regular patterns. When only the first principal part of an epsilon- or alpha-contracted verb is listed in the vocabulary, the remaining principal parts end in -ησω, -ησα, -ηκα, -ημαι, -ηθην and have regular reduplication in the fourth and fifth principal parts. When only the first principal part of an omicron-contracted verb is listed in the vocabulary, the remaining principal parts end in -ωσω, -ωσα, -ωκα, -ωμαι, -ωθην.

2. In the fourth and fifth principal parts of a verb that begins with an *aspirated consonant*, the first consonant becomes *unaspirated*: e.g., *φεφίληκα > πεφίληκα. This sound change is called the **dissimilation of aspirates**.

Rules of Contraction for Epsilon-Contracted Verbs

ε + ω = ω	ε + ε = ει
ε + ει = ει	ε + ο = ου
ε + η = η	
ε + ου = ου	

			Present Active Indicative		Present Middle/Passive Indicative	
Singular	1	ποιέω >	ποιῶ	ποιέομαι >	ποιοῦμαι
	2	ποιέεις >	ποιεῖς	ποιέη/ποιέει >	ποιῇ/ποιεῖ
	3	ποιέει >	ποιεῖ	ποιέεται >	ποιεῖται
Plural	1	ποιέομεν >	ποιοῦμεν	ποιεόμεθα >	ποιούμεθα
	2	ποιέετε >	ποιεῖτε	ποιέεσθε >	ποιεῖσθε
	3	ποιέουσι(ν) >	ποιοῦσι(ν)	ποιέονται >	ποιοῦνται

			Imperfect Active Indicative		Imperfect Middle/Passive Indicative	
Singular	1	ἐποίεον >	ἐποίουν	ἐποιεόμην >	ἐποιούμην
	2	ἐποίεες >	ἐποίεις	ἐποιέου >	ἐποιοῦ
	3	ἐποίεε >	ἐποίει	ἐποιέετο >	ἐποιεῖτο
Plural	1	ἐποιέομεν >	ἐποιοῦμεν	ἐποιεόμεθα >	ἐποιούμεθα
	2	ἐποιέετε >	ἐποιεῖτε	ἐποιέεσθε >	ἐποιεῖσθε
	3	ἐποίεον >	ἐποίουν	ἐποιέοντο >	ἐποιοῦντο

	Present Active Infinitive		Present Middle/Passive Infinitive	
	ποιέεεν >	ποιεῖν	ποιέεσθαι >	ποιεῖσθαι

Rules of Contraction for Alpha-Contracted Verbs

$\alpha + \omega = \omega$	$\alpha + \varepsilon = \bar{\alpha}$
$\alpha + o = \omega$	$\alpha + \varepsilon\iota = \alpha$
$\alpha + o\upsilon = \omega$	$\alpha + \eta = \alpha$

Present Active Indicative

Singular	1	νῑκάω >	**νῑκῶ**
	2	νῑκάεις >	**νῑκᾷς**
	3	νῑκάει >	**νῑκᾷ**
Plural	1	νῑκάομεν >	**νῑκῶμεν**
	2	νῑκάετε >	**νῑκᾶτε**
	3	νῑκάουσι(ν) >	**νῑκῶσι(ν)**

Present Middle/Passive Indicative

νῑκάομαι >	**νῑκῶμαι**
νῑκάῃ/νῑκάει >	**νῑκᾷ**
νῑκάεται >	**νῑκᾶται**
νῑκαόμεθα >	**νῑκώμεθα**
νῑκάεσθε >	**νῑκᾶσθε**
νῑκάονται >	**νῑκῶνται**

Imperfect Active Indicative

Singular	1	ἐνίκαον >	**ἐνίκων**
	2	ἐνίκαες >	**ἐνίκᾱς**
	3	ἐνίκαε >	**ἐνίκᾱ**
Plural	1	ἐνῑκάομεν >	**ἐνῑκῶμεν**
	2	ἐνῑκάετε >	**ἐνῑκᾶτε**
	3	ἐνίκαον >	**ἐνίκων**

Imperfect Middle/Passive Indicative

ἐνῑκαόμην >	**ἐνῑκώμην**
ἐνῑκάου >	**ἐνῑκῶ**
ἐνῑκάετο >	**ἐνῑκᾶτο**
ἐνῑκαόμεθα >	**ἐνῑκώμεθα**
ἐνῑκάεσθε >	**ἐνῑκᾶσθε**
ἐνῑκάοντο >	**ἐνῑκῶντο**

Present Active Infinitive

νῑκάεεν >	**νῑκᾶν**

Present Middle/Passive Infinitive

νῑκάεσθαι >	**νῑκᾶσθαι**

Rules of Contraction for Omicron-Contracted Verbs

$o + \omega = \omega$	$o + o = o\upsilon$
$o + \varepsilon\iota = o\iota$	$o + \varepsilon = o\upsilon$
$o + \eta = o\iota$	$o + o\upsilon = o\upsilon$

Present Active Indicative

Singular	1	δηλόω >	**δηλῶ**
	2	δηλόεις >	**δηλοῖς**
	3	δηλόει >	**δηλοῖ**
Plural	1	δηλόομεν >	**δηλοῦμεν**
	2	δηλόετε >	**δηλοῦτε**
	3	δηλόουσι(ν) >	**δηλοῦσι(ν)**

Present Middle/Passive Indicative

δηλόομαι >	**δηλοῦμαι**
δηλόῃ/δηλόει >	**δηλοῖ**
δηλόεται >	**δηλοῦται**
δηλοόμεθα >	**δηλούμεθα**
δηλόεσθε >	**δηλοῦσθε**
δηλόονται >	**δηλοῦνται**

Imperfect Active Indicative

Singular	1	ἐδήλοον >	**ἐδήλουν**
	2	ἐδήλοες >	**ἐδήλους**
	3	ἐδήλοε >	**ἐδήλου**
Plural	1	ἐδηλόομεν >	**ἐδηλοῦμεν**
	2	ἐδηλόετε >	**ἐδηλοῦτε**
	3	ἐδήλοον >	**ἐδήλουν**

Imperfect Middle/Passive Indicative

ἐδηλοόμην >	**ἐδηλούμην**
ἐδηλόου >	**ἐδηλοῦ**
ἐδηλόετο >	**ἐδηλοῦτο**
ἐδηλοόμεθα >	**ἐδηλούμεθα**
ἐδηλόεσθε >	**ἐδηλοῦσθε**
ἐδηλόοντο >	**ἐδηλοῦντο**

Present Active Infinitive

δηλόεεν >	**δηλοῦν**

Present Middle/Passive Infinitive

δηλόεσθαι >	**δηλοῦσθαι**

Chapter 4 Summary: New Morphology and Syntax

Demonstrative Adjectives and Pronouns

ὅδε, ἥδε, τόδε "this (here)," "these (here)"

	Singular				*Plural*		
	M.	F.	N.		M.	F.	N.
Nom.	ὅδε	ἥδε	τόδε		οἵδε	αἵδε	τάδε
Gen.	τοῦδε	τῆσδε	τοῦδε		τῶνδε	τῶνδε	τῶνδε
Dat.	τῷδε	τῆδε	τῷδε		τοῖσδε	ταῖσδε	τοῖσδε
Acc.	τόνδε	τήνδε	τόδε		τούσδε	τάσδε	τάδε

No vocative forms

ἐκεῖνος, ἐκείνη, ἐκεῖνο "that," "those"

	Singular				*Plural*		
	M.	F.	N.		M.	F.	N.
Nom.	ἐκεῖνος	ἐκείνη	ἐκεῖνο		ἐκεῖνοι	ἐκεῖναι	ἐκεῖνα
Gen.	ἐκείνου	ἐκείνης	ἐκείνου		ἐκείνων	ἐκείνων	ἐκείνων
Dat.	ἐκείνῳ	ἐκείνῃ	ἐκείνῳ		ἐκείνοις	ἐκείναις	ἐκείνοις
Acc.	ἐκεῖνον	ἐκείνην	ἐκεῖνο		ἐκείνους	ἐκείνᾱς	ἐκεῖνα

No vocative forms

Comparison of Demonstrative Adjectives and Pronouns

1. **ὅδε** points more emphatically to people or things close to the speaker or writer than **οὗτος**.
2. **ἐκεῖνος** points to people or things more remote from the speaker or writer.
3. **οὗτος** and **ἐκεῖνος** may point to well-known or notorious people or things.
4. **ὅδε** may refer to what *follows.*

    οὗτος may refer to what *precedes.*

    οὗτος may mean "the latter" and **ἐκεῖνος** "the former" when used in the same sentence and referring to two already mentioned elements.

The Irregular Adjectives **μέγας, μεγάλη, μέγα** and **πολύς, πολλή, πολύ**

μέγας, μεγάλη, μέγα
"great," "big"

πολύς, πολλή, πολύ
"much," "many"

| | *Singular* | | | | *Singular* | | |
	M.	F.	N.		M.	F.	N.
Nom.	μέγας	μεγάλη	μέγα		πολύς	πολλή	πολύ
Gen.	μεγάλου	μεγάλης	μεγάλου		πολλοῦ	πολλῆς	πολλοῦ
Dat.	μεγάλῳ	μεγάλη	μεγάλῳ		πολλῷ	πολλῇ	πολλῷ
Acc.	μέγαν	μεγάλην	μέγα		πολύν	πολλήν	πολύ
Voc.	μεγάλε	μεγάλη	μέγα		—	—	—

| | *Plural* | | | | *Plural* | | |
Nom.	μεγάλοι	μεγάλαι	μεγάλα		πολλοί	πολλαί	πολλά
Gen.	μεγάλων	μεγάλων	μεγάλων		πολλῶν	πολλῶν	πολλῶν
Dat.	μεγάλοις	μεγάλαις	μεγάλοις		πολλοῖς	πολλαῖς	πολλοῖς
Acc.	μεγάλους	μεγάλᾱς	μεγάλα		πολλούς	πολλάς	πολλά
Voc.	μεγάλοι	μεγάλαι	μεγάλα		—	—	—

Partitive Genitive

A noun representing the *whole* of which another noun is a *part*.

τῶν πολῑτῶν τοῖς ἀγαθοῖς ὅπλα πέμπομεν. We are sending weapons for the good ones *of the citizens.*

Genitive of Value

A noun *or* substantive expressing the price, worth, or value of something
Occurs with verbs that mean "value," "deem worthy," "consider"

πολλοῦ ποιοῦμαι ταύτην τὴν γνώμην. I consider this judgment *of much value.*

Substantive Use of the Article

An article joined with adverbs, prepositional phrases, or other words to create a substantive
Negated by **οὐ** for *specific* substantives and **μή** for *generic* substantives

Chapter 5

Vocabulary

→ **ἀνάγκη, ἀνάγκης, ἡ** necessity
→ **μαθητής, μαθητοῦ, ὁ** student
 τέχνη, τέχνης, ἡ skill, art

 διδάσκαλος, διδασκάλου, ὁ teacher

→ **ἄρχων, ἄρχοντος, ὁ** ruler, commander; archon, magistrate
→ **δαίμων, δαίμονος, ὁ or ἡ** divinity, divine power; spirit
→ **Ἕκτωρ, Ἕκτορος, ὁ** Hector
→ **Ἕλλην, Ἕλληνος, ὁ** Hellene, Greek
→ **ἐλπίς, ἐλπίδος, ἡ** hope; expectation
→ **ἔρως, ἔρωτος, ὁ** desire, passion, love
→ **Ζεύς, Διός, ὁ** Zeus
→ **παῖς, παιδός, ὁ or ἡ** child; slave
→ **ῥήτωρ, ῥήτορος, ὁ** public speaker, orator; rhetor
→ **φρήν, φρενός, ἡ** *sing. or pl.,* heart, mind, wits
→ **χάρις, χάριτος, ἡ** grace, favor, goodwill; delight; gratitude

→ **δῶμα, δώματος, τό** *sing. or pl.,* house, home
→ **σῶμα, σώματος, τό** body
→ **χρῆμα, χρήματος, τό** thing, matter, affair; *pl.,* goods, property, money

 ὅς, ἥ, ὅ (relative pron.), who, whose, whom; which, that (§53)

→ **ἄγω, ἄξω, ἤγαγον, ἦχα, ἦγμαι, ἤχθην** lead, bring; keep; *middle,* carry away with oneself; marry
→ **ἀκούω, ἀκούσομαι, ἤκουσα, ἀκήκοα, ——, ἠκούσθην** listen (to), hear (of)
→ **ἥκω, ἥξω, ——, ——, ——, ——** have come; be present
→ **μανθάνω, μαθήσομαι, ἔμαθον, μεμάθηκα, ——, ——** learn; understand

→ **δεῖ, δεήσει, ἐδέησε(ν), ——, ——, ——** (impersonal verb) it is necessary, must; there is need (+ gen.)
→ **εἰμί, ἔσομαι, ——, ——, ——, ——** be; exist; *impersonal,* it is possible (§55)

→ **ἄλλος, ἄλλη, ἄλλο** other, another
 βάρβαρος, βάρβαρον non-Greek, foreign; barbarous; *masc. pl. subst.,* foreigners; barbarians
 θνητός, θνητή, θνητόν mortal
 ῥάδιος, ῥαδίᾱ, ῥάδιον easy

→ **ἀεί/αἰεί** (adv.) always
→ **γε** (enclitic particle) *limiting,* at least, at any rate; *emphasizing,* indeed
→ **κατά** (prep. + gen.) down from, beneath; against
 (prep. + acc.) according to, in relation to; throughout
 μά (particle + acc.) *used in oaths,* by
 νή (particle + acc.) *expresses strong affirmation,* (yes,) by
→ **παρά** (prep. + gen.) from (the side of); by
 (prep. + dat.) near; at (the house of); among
 (prep. + acc.) to (the side of), beside; contrary to
 περ (enclitic particle) very, even
→ **ποτέ** (enclitic adv.) at some time, ever; **ποτέ ... ποτέ ...** at one time ..., at another time ...; sometimes ..., sometimes ...
 οὔποτε/μήποτε (adv.) never
 πως (enclitic adv.) somehow
→ **τε** (enclitic conj.) and
→ **τοι** (enclitic particle) surely, you know
→ **χάριν** (prep. + preceding gen.) for the sake of

Chapter 5 Summary: New Verbs

	Active	*Middle*	*Passive*
ἄγω	lead, bring; keep	carry away with oneself; marry	be led, be brought
ἀκούω	listen (to), hear (of)	(*future only*) listen (to), hear (of)	be listened (to), be heard
δεῖ	it is necessary, must; there is need		
εἰμί	be; exist; it is possible	(*future only*) be; exist; it is possible	
ἥκω	have come, be present		
μανθάνω	learn, understand	(*future only*) learn, understand	R

When no meanings are offered for a voice of a verb, the verb *never* appears in that voice. An R indicates that a verb *rarely* appears in that voice. Only commonly occurring forms should be included in a synopsis. See the vocabulary notes in the textbook for additional meanings.

Chapter 5 Summary: The Third Declension; Relative Pronoun

Case Endings of the Third Declension

| | Masculine/Feminine | | Neuter | |
	Singular	*Plural*	*Singular*	*Plural*
Nominative	—	**-ες**	—	**-α**
Genitive	**-ος**	**-ων**	**-ος**	**-ων**
Dative	**-ι**	**-σι(ν)**	**-ι**	**-σι(ν)**
Accusative	**-α/-ν**	**-ας**	—	**-α**
Vocative	—	**-ες**	—	**-α**

Special Morphology Rules for Third-Declension Nouns

Acc. Sing. **-ν** when stem ends in dental preceded by **-ι-** or **-υ-** *and* last syllable of stem is *not* accented (stem = **χάριτ-**; acc sing. = **χάριν**)

Voc. Sing. **stem** when stem ends in **-ρ, -λ,** or **-ν** and accent does *not* fall on last syllable of the stem
stem with final dental dropped when stem ends in dental
nom. sing. when stem ends in **-ρ, -λ,** or **-ν** and accent is on the ultima

Dat. Pl. *-νσι(ν) > **-σι(ν)** (drop **-ν**)
*-τσι(ν), -δσι(ν), -θσι(ν) > **-σι(ν)** (drop dental)
*-οντσι(ν) > **-ουσι(ν)** (assimilation, compensatory lengthening, spurious diphthong)

Relative Pronoun

| | Singular | | | Plural | | |
	M.	F.	N.	M.	F.	N.
Nom.	ὅς	ἥ	ὅ	οἵ	αἵ	ἅ
Gen.	οὗ	ἧς	οὗ	ὧν	ὧν	ὧν
Dat.	ᾧ	ᾗ	ᾧ	οἷς	αἷς	οἷς
Acc.	ὅν	ἥν	ὅ	οὕς	ἅς	ἅ

No vocative case forms.

The relative pronoun agrees with its antecedent in gender and number. Its case, however, is determined by its syntax within the relative clause.

Chapter 5 Summary: Enclitics and the Verb εἰμί

Enclitics

Monosyllabic	γε (enclitic particle) at least, at any rate (limits); indeed (emphasizes)
	περ (enclitic particle) very, even
	πως (enclitic adv.) somehow
	τε (enclitic conj.) and
	τοι (enclitic particle) surely, you know
Disyllabic	ποτέ (enclitic adv.) at some time, ever

Accent Rules for Enclitics

1.	a	p	ú	+ e or e-e (no change)
2.	a	p	û	+ e or e-e (no change)
3.	a	p̂	ú	+ e or e-e (acute added to ultima)
4.	á	p	ú	+ e or e-e (acute added to ultima)
5.	a	ṕ	u	+ e (no change)
6.	a	ṕ	u	+ e-é (acute added to ultima of enclitic)

1., 2.	ἀγαθός γε ποιητής	a *good*† poet (subj.)
	ἀδικεῖν τοι	to do wrong, you know
	ἀδικεῖν ποτε	to do wrong ever
3.	ταῦτά τοι	these things (subj. or d.o.), you know
	ταῦτά ποτε	these things (subj. or d.o.) at some time
4.	οὐ πείθεταί γε.	He is not obeying, at least.
	οὐ πείθεταί ποτε.	He does not obey ever.
5., 6.	ἑταίρους γε	*companions* (d.o.)
	τοῦτο οὐ λέγω ποτέ.	I do not say this thing ever.
	οὐ λέγω ποτὲ τοῦτο.	I do not say this thing ever.

When an enclitic follows a *proclitic*, the proclitic receives an acute accent.

οἵ γε πολῖται	the citizens, at least (subj.)
αἵ γ' ἀρεταί	the virtues, at least (subj.)
οὔτοι ἐθέλουσιν.	They are not, you know, willing.

When an enclitic follows *another* enclitic, the preceding enclitic receives an acute accent.

τοῦτό γέ τοι	*this thing* (subj. or d.o.), you know

A disyllabic enclitic sometimes begins a sentence or clause and in this position has an accent on the ultima.

ποτὲ διδάσκει, ποτὲ διδάσκεται.	Sometimes he is teaching, sometimes he is being taught.

†Italics indicate the emphasis placed on the adjective "good" by the enclitic γε.

The Verb εἰμί

εἰμί, ἔσομαι, —, —, —, — "be"; "exist"

	Present Active Indicative			Imperfect Active Indicative	
Singular					
1	**εἰμί**	I am		**ἦ** or **ἦν**	I was
2	**εἶ**	you are		**ἦσθα**	you were
3	**ἐστί(ν)**	he, she, it is		**ἦν**	he, she, it was
Plural					
1	**ἐσμέν**	we are		**ἦμεν**	we were
2	**ἐστέ**	you (pl.) are		**ἦτε**	you (pl.) were
3	**εἰσί(ν)**	they are		**ἦσαν**	they were

The third person singular form of the present active indicative of **εἰμί** is accented on the penult—**ἔστι(ν)**—when it is the first word in a sentence and when it signifies existence ("there is") or possibility ("it is possible").

ἔστι(ν) is also accented on the penult when it follows **οὐκ**, **μή**, **καί**, **ἀλλ'/ἀλλά**, or **τοῦτ'/τοῦτο**.

Future Middle Indicative
Future Stem: **ἐσ-**

Singular
1	**ἔσομαι**	I shall be
2	**ἔσῃ/ἔσει**	you will be
3	**ἔσται**	he, she, it will be

Plural
1	**ἐσόμεθα**	we shall be
2	**ἔσεσθε**	you (pl.) will be
3	**ἔσονται**	they will be

Present Active Infinitive: **εἶναι** to be
Future Middle Infinitive: **ἔσεσθαι** to be about to be

Chapter 6

Vocabulary

Ἀθῆναι, Ἀθηνῶν, αἱ Athens

→ δεσπότης, δεσπότου, ὁ master, lord; absolute ruler

→ ἐλευθερίᾱ, ἐλευθερίᾱς, ἡ freedom

δοῦλος, δούλου, ὁ slave

→ ἀγών, ἀγῶνος, ὁ contest; struggle

→ ἀνήρ, ἀνδρός, ὁ man; husband

ἐγώ, ἐμοῦ/μου I; me (§67)
ἡμεῖς, ἡμῶν we; us (§67)
σύ, σοῦ/σου you (§67)
ὑμεῖς, ὑμῶν you (pl.) (§67)
αὐτοῦ, αὐτῆς, αὐτοῦ him, her, it; them (§67)

→ βούλομαι, βουλήσομαι, ——, ——, βεβούλημαι, ἐβουλήθην want, wish

→ γίγνομαι, γενήσομαι, ἐγενόμην, γέγονα, γεγένημαι, —— become; happen; arise, be born

→ δέχομαι, δέξομαι, ἐδεξάμην, ——, δέδεγμαι, —— accept, receive; welcome

→ ἔρχομαι, ἐλεύσομαι, ἦλθον, ἐλήλυθα, ——, —— go, come

→ ὁράω, ὄψομαι, εἶδον, ἑώρᾱκα/ἑόρᾱκα, ἑώρᾱμαι/ὦμμαι, ὤφθην see

αὐτός, αὐτή, αὐτό -self, very; same (§66)
δῆλος, δήλη, δῆλον clear
ἄδηλος, ἄδηλον unclear

→ ἐλεύθερος, ἐλευθέρᾱ, ἐλεύθερον free
ἐμός, ἐμή, ἐμόν my (§67)
ἡμέτερος, ἡμετέρᾱ, ἡμέτερον our (§67)

→ ὀρθός, ὀρθή, ὀρθόν straight; correct
σός, σή, σόν your (§67)
ὑμέτερος, ὑμετέρᾱ, ὑμέτερον your (pl.) (§67)
χρηστός, χρηστή, χρηστόν useful; good

πᾶς, πᾶσα, πᾶν all, every; whole (§68)
ἅπᾱς, ἅπᾱσα, ἅπαν (quite) all, every; whole (§68)

ἄνευ (prep. + gen.) without

→ ὅτι (conj.) that; because

→ οὖν (postpositive conj.) then, therefore

→ οὔτε/μήτε ... οὔτε/μήτε ... (conj.) neither ... nor ...
πόθεν (interrog. adv.) from where
ποῖ (interrog. adv.) to where
ποῦ (interrog. adv.) where

→ ὑπέρ (prep. + gen.) over; on behalf of (prep. + acc.) beyond

→ ὡς (proclitic conj.) that; as

→ ὥσπερ (conj.) just as

Chapter 6 Summary: New Verbs

	Active	*Middle*	*Passive*
βούλομαι		want, wish	*(aorist only)* want, wish
γίγνομαι	*(perfect only)* become; happen; arise, be born	become; happen; arise, be born	
δέχομαι		accept, receive; welcome	
ἔρχομαι	*(aorist and perfect)* go, come	*(present, imperfect, and future)* go, come	
ὁράω	see	R *(except in future)* see	be seen

When no meanings are offered for a voice of a verb, the verb *never* appears in that voice. An R indicates that a verb *rarely* appears in that voice. Only commonly occurring forms should be included in a synopsis. See the vocabulary notes in the textbook for additional meanings.

Chapter 6 Summary: The Aorist Tense

Aorist Indicative

The aorist indicative has *past* time with *simple* aspect.

First Aorist (Prin. Part 3 ends in -**α**, -**αμην**)		**Second Aorist** (Prin. Part 3 ends in -**ον**, -**ομην**)		
First Aorist Active Indic.	*First Aorist Middle Indic.*	*Second Aorist Active Indic.*	*Second Aorist Middle Indic.*	*Aorist Passive Indic.*
Augmented Stem from Prin. Part 3 +	Augmented Stem from Prin. Part 3 +	Augmented Stem from Prin. Part 3 +	Augmented Stem from Prin. Part 3 +	Augmented Stem from Prin. Part 6 +

Singular

1 -**α**	-**αμην**	-**ον**	-**ομην**	-**ην**
2 -**ας**	-**ω**	-**ες**	-**ου**	-**ης**
3 -**ε(ν)**	-**ατο**	-**ε(ν)**	-**ετο**	-**η**

Plural

1 -**αμεν**	-**αμεθα**	-**ομεν**	-**ομεθα**	-**ημεν**
2 -**ατε**	-**ασθε**	-**ετε**	-**εσθε**	-**ητε**
3 -**αν**	-**αντο**	-**ον**	-**οντο**	-**ησαν**

Aorist Infinitives

(An aorist infinitive does *not always have past time* but *always has simple aspect*.)

First Aorist Active
Unaugmented Stem + -**αι**
  (-**αι** counts as *short*;
  accent *persistent* on penult)

Second Aorist Active
Unaugmented Stem + -**εῖν**
  (accent *persistent* on ultima)

Aorist Passive
Unaugmented Stem + -**ῆναι**
  (-**αι** counts as *short*;
  accent *persistent* on penult)

First Aorist Middle
Unaugmented Stem + -**ασθαι**
  (-**αι** counts as *short*; accent *recessive*)

Second Aorist Middle
Unaugmented Stem + -**έσθαι**
  (accent *persistent* on penult)

Ingressive Aorist

1. EXPRESSES THE *MOMENT* WHEN SOMETHING
   BECAME THE CASE OR OCCURRED
2. REQUIRES A SPECIAL TRANSLATION

ἦρξεν.
He *became ruler*.

Gnomic Aorist

1. EXPRESSES A TIMELESS GENERAL TRUTH
2. BEST TRANSLATED WITH THE ENGLISH PRESENT TENSE

ὁ πόλεμος ἀνθρώποις συμφορὰς ἐποίησεν.
War *makes* misfortunes for men.

"Aorist" (< ἀόριστος, "unlimited") refers to the fact that this tense reports a *simple occurrence* that is *not limited* as to continuance, repetition, or completion.

Chapter 6 Summary: αὐτός, Personal Pronouns, Possessive Adjectives

The Intensive Adjective αὐτός, αὐτή, αὐτό "-self," "very"; "same"

	Singular			*Plural*		
	M.	F.	N.	M.	F.	N.
Nom.	αὐτός	αὐτή	αὐτό	αὐτοί	αὐταί	αὐτά
Gen.	αὐτοῦ	αὐτῆς	αὐτοῦ	αὐτῶν	αὐτῶν	αὐτῶν
Dat.	αὐτῷ	αὐτῇ	αὐτῷ	αὐτοῖς	αὐταῖς	αὐτοῖς
Acc.	αὐτόν	αὐτήν	αὐτό	αὐτούς	αὐτάς	αὐτά

αὐτός intensifies ("-self," "very") in the *predicate* position ("**αὐτοὶ οἱ θεοί**, "the gods *themselves* [subj.]")
αὐτός means "same" in the attributive position (**οἱ αὐτοὶ πολῖται**, "the *same* citizens [subj.]")

Personal Pronouns

	First Person		**Second Person**	
Singular				
Nom.	ἐγώ	I	σύ	you
Gen.	ἐμοῦ, μου	of me	σοῦ, σου	of you
Dat.	ἐμοί, μοι	to/for me	σοί, σοι	to/for you
Acc.	ἐμέ, με	me (d.o.)	σέ, σε	you (d.o.)
Plural				
Nom.	ἡμεῖς	we	ὑμεῖς	you (pl.)
Gen.	ἡμῶν	of us	ὑμῶν	of you (pl.)
Dat.	ἡμῖν	to/for us	ὑμῖν	to/for you (pl.)
Acc.	ἡμᾶς	us (d.o.)	ὑμᾶς	you (pl.) (d.o.)

Possessive Adjectives

ἐμός, ἐμή, ἐμόν my
ἡμέτερος, ἡμετέρᾱ, ἡμέτερον our
σός, σή, σόν your
ὑμέτερος, ὑμετέρᾱ, ὑμέτερον your (pl.)

Appear in the *attributive* position

1. Alternate monosyllabic enclitics in gen., dat., and acc. sing.
2. Nom. forms used to add emphasis to the subject
3. **Appear in the *predicate* position when used as Gens. of Poss.**

Third Person

	Singular			*Plural*		
	M.	F.	N.	M.	F.	N.
Nom.†	—	—	—	—	—	—
Gen.	αὐτοῦ	αὐτῆς	αὐτοῦ	αὐτῶν	αὐτῶν	αὐτῶν
	of him	of her	of it	of them (m.)	of them (f.)	of them (n.)
Dat.	αὐτῷ	αὐτῇ	αὐτῷ	αὐτοῖς	αὐταῖς	αὐτοῖς
	to him	to her	to it	to them (m.)	to them (f.)	to them (n.)
Acc.	αὐτόν	αὐτήν	αὐτό	αὐτούς	αὐτάς	αὐτά
	him	her	it	them (m.)	them (f.)	them (n.)

Appear in the *predicate* position when used as Gens. of Poss.
†Nom. forms of third person personal pronoun are supplied by demonstrative pronouns.

Chapter 6 Summary: πᾶς, ἅπᾱς, and the Dative of the Possessor

πᾶς, πᾶσα, πᾶν
Stems: M./N., παντ-; F.: πᾱσ-

	M.	F.	N.
Singular			
Nom.	πᾶς	πᾶσα	πᾶν
Gen.	παντός	πάσης	παντός
Dat.	παντί	πάσῃ	παντί
Acc.	πάντα	πᾶσαν	πᾶν
Voc.	πᾶς	πᾶσα	πᾶν
Plural			
Nom./Voc.	πάντες	πᾶσαι	πάντα
Gen.	πάντων	πᾱσῶν	πάντων
Dat.	πᾶσι(ν)	πάσαις	πᾶσι(ν)
Acc.	πάντας	πάσᾱς	πάντα

ἅπᾱς, ἅπᾱσα, ἅπαν
Stems: M./N., ἁπαντ-; F., ἁπᾱσ-

	M.	F.	N.
Singular			
Nom.	ἅπᾱς	ἅπᾱσα	ἅπαν
Gen.	ἅπαντος	ἁπάσης	ἅπαντος
Dat.	ἅπαντι	ἁπάσῃ	ἅπαντι
Acc.	ἅπαντα	ἅπᾱσαν	ἅπαν
Voc.	ἅπᾱς	ἅπᾱσα	ἅπαν
Plural			
Nom./Voc.	ἅπαντες	ἅπᾱσαι	ἅπαντα
Gen.	ἁπάντων	ἁπᾱσῶν	ἁπάντων
Dat.	ἅπᾱσι(ν)	ἁπάσαις	ἅπᾱσι(ν)
Acc.	ἅπαντας	ἁπάσᾱς	ἅπαντα

πᾶς/ἅπᾱς

1. MOST OFTEN APPEARS IN THE *PREDICATE* POSITION: "EVERY" (SING.), "ALL" (PL. AND COLLECTIVE SING.)

   τὴν ὁδὸν ἅπᾱσαν
   every road (d.o.)

   πάντας τοὺς πολίτᾱς
   all the citizens (d.o.)

2. MAY APPEAR WITH A NOUN *WITHOUT* THE ARTICLE

   πᾶσιν ἄρχουσι
   for all rulers

3. IN *ATTRIBUTIVE* POSITION MEANS "WHOLE" (D.O.)

   τὸν πάντα λόγον
   the whole argument (d.o.)

Dative of the Possessor

1. INDICATES THE PERSON WHO POSSESSES SOMETHING
2. IS AN EXTENSION OF THE DATIVE OF REFERENCE
3. USUALLY OCCURS WITH THE VERB εἰμί, THE SUBJECT OF WHICH IS THE THING *POSSESSED*

τῷ δικαίῳ ἐστὶν ὁ βίος τῶν θεῶν.

To the just man is the life of the gods.

The just man has the life of the gods.

Chapter 6 Summary: Indirect Statement 1; Binary Construction

Indirect Statement

1. An Indirect Statement is a subordinate *noun clause* functioning as the object (sometimes the subject) of an introductory verb of saying, reporting, or answering. It is also introduced by other verbs and expressions of intellection: **λέγω, μανθάνω, πείθομαι, δῆλόν ἐστι(ν), δηλόω, ὁράω**.
2. A subordinating conjunction (**ὅτι** or **ὡς**, "that") is used.
3. The *tense* and *mood* of a verb in Indirect Statement *never change* when an introductory verb is in a *primary* tense.
4. The *tense* and *mood* of a verb in Indirect Statement *often* do not change when an introductory verb is in a *secondary* tense.[†]
5. Negations remain *unchanged* in an Indirect Statement.

Direct Statement	*Indirect Statements*
οἱ Ἀθηναῖοι τῶν νήσων ἄρχουσιν.	**λέγει ὅτι/ὡς οἱ Ἀθηναῖοι τῶν νήσων ἄρχουσιν.**
The Athenians are ruling the islands.	*He says* that the Athenians *are ruling* the islands.
	ἔλεγεν ὅτι/ὡς οἱ Ἀθηναῖοι τῶν νήσων ἄρχουσιν.
	He was saying that the Athenians *were ruling* the islands.
(Translations indicate that **ἄρχουσιν** is occurring *simultaneously* with the introductory verbs.)	**λέξει ὅτι/ὡς οἱ Ἀθηναῖοι τῶν νήσων ἄρχουσιν.**
	He will say that the Athenians *are ruling* the islands.
οἱ Ἀθηναῖοι τῶν νήσων ἄρξουσιν.	**λέγει ὅτι/ὡς οἱ Ἀθηναῖοι τῶν νήσων ἄρξουσιν.**
The Athenians will rule the islands.	*He says* that the Athenians *will rule* the islands.
	ἔλεγεν ὅτι/ὡς οἱ Ἀθηναῖοι τῶν νήσων ἄρξουσιν.
	He was saying that the Athenians *would rule* the islands.
(Translations indicate that **ἄρξουσιν** is occurring *after* the introductory verbs.)	**λέξει ὅτι/ὡς οἱ Ἀθηναῖοι τῶν νήσων ἄρξουσιν.**
	He will say that the Athenians *will rule* the islands.
οἱ Ἀθηναῖοι τῶν νήσων ἦρξαν.	**λέγει ὅτι/ὡς οἱ Ἀθηναῖοι τῶν νήσων ἦρξαν.**
The Athenians ruled the islands.	*He says* that the Athenians *ruled* the islands.
	ἔλεγεν ὅτι/ὡς οἱ Ἀθηναῖοι τῶν νήσων ἦρξαν.
	He was saying that the Athenians *had ruled* the islands.
(Translations indicate that **ἦρξαν** is occurring *prior to* the introductory verbs.)	**λέξει ὅτι/ὡς οἱ Ἀθηναῖοι τῶν νήσων ἦρξαν.**
	He will say that the Athenians *ruled* the islands.

[†]The mood of a verb in an Indirect Statement after a *secondary* tense introductory verb *may* change to the optative (Part 2, §142).

Binary Construction (Prolepsis)

A VERB WITH AN INDIRECT STATEMENT AS A DIRECT OBJECT AND A *SECOND* ACCUSATIVE, DIRECT OBJECT THAT	**ἆρ' ἐκεῖνον ὁρᾷς, ὅτι ἀδικεῖ;**
1. IS PLACED *BEFORE* THE INDIRECT STATEMENT	Do you see *that man*, that *he* is doing wrong?
2. IS SOMEONE OR SOMETHING THAT APPEARS IN OR IS REFERRED TO BY THE INDIRECT STATEMENT (USUALLY THE SUBJECT)	Do you see that that man is doing wrong?
3. *ANTICIPATES* THE SUBJECT OF THE INDIRECT STATEMENT	

About Meter Summary

A syllable counts as *long* if it contains:

1. a long vowel or diphthong (**long by nature**).

2. a short vowel followed by two or more consonants or the double consonants ζ, ξ, or ψ, *not necessarily in the same word* (**long by position**).

BUT REMEMBER:

   a. *all* diphthongs count as long for purposes of scansion.

   b. a syllable with a short vowel followed by a mute (γ, κ, χ, β, π, φ, δ, τ, θ) and a liquid (λ, ρ) or a nasal (μ, ν) may be long *or* short.

   c. word endings are *not* considered for determining length.

   d. the *last syllable* in every line of poetry *counts as long even if it is short.*

---

dactyl $-\cup\cup$	iambic metron x $-\cup-$
spondee $--$	anceps (long *or* short) x
iamb $\cup-$	foot division │
dactylic metron $-\cup\cup$	principal caesura ‖
spondaic metron $--$	hemiepes $-\overset{\smile}{\cup}\overset{\smile}{\cup}\vert-\overset{\smile}{\cup}\overset{\smile}{\cup}\vert-$

caesura	a word ending *within* a foot or metron
principal/main caesura	a key pausing point when a line of verse is recited
strong caesura	a principal caesura occurring after a long syllable
weak caesura	a principal caesura occurring after a short syllable
diaeresis	a pause when the end of a word and the end of a foot coincide
resolution	the replacement of a long or short syllable with two short syllables
synizesis	the pronunciation of two successive vowels or diphthongs in separate syllables as a single, long syllable
epic correption	a long vowel or diphthong at the end of a word counting as *short* when followed by a word beginning with a vowel

---

Iambic Trimeter (IT)

$$\text{x} \ -\cup- \ \vert \ \text{x} \ \Vert \ -\cup \ \Vert \ - \ \vert \ \text{x} \ -\cup \ \text{x}$$

σοὶ μὲν γᾰμεῖ |σθαι ‖ μόρσιμόν, │ γαμεῖν δ' ἐμοί.

Elegiac Couplet (EC)
Dactylic Hexameter (DH)

$$-\cup\cup \ \vert \ - \ \Vert \ \cup\cup \ \vert \ - \ \Vert \ \cup\cup \ \vert \ - \ \Vert \ \cup\cup \ \vert \ -\cup\cup \ \vert \ --$$

Dactylic Pentameter

$$-\cup\cup \ \vert \ -\cup\cup \ \vert \ - \ \Vert -\cup\cup \ \vert \ -\cup\cup \ \vert \ -$$

Ζεὺς κύκ │ νος, ταῦ │ ρος, ‖ σᾰτῠ │ ρος, χρῡ │ σὸς δι' ἔ │ ρωτα

Λήδης │ Εὐρώ │ πης, ‖ Ἀντιό │ πης Δᾰνᾰ │ ης

Chapter 7

Vocabulary

→ νοῦς, νοῦ, ὁ mind; sense; thought
πλοῦτος, πλούτου, ὁ wealth

→ γένος, γένους, τό race, descent; family;
sort, kind

→ γυνή, γυναικός, ἡ woman; wife

→ Δημοσθένης, Δημοσθένους, ὁ
Demosthenes

→ δύναμις, δυνάμεως, ἡ power; ability

→ Ἑλλάς, Ἑλλάδος, ἡ Hellas, Greece

→ ἔπος, ἔπους, τό word; pl., lines (of
verse), epic poetry; ὡς ἔπος εἰπεῖν,
so to speak; practically

→ μήτηρ, μητρός, ἡ mother

→ πάθος, πάθους, τό experience;
suffering; passion

→ πατήρ, πατρός, ὁ father

→ πόλις, πόλεως, ἡ city

→ πρᾶγμα, πράγματος, τό deed; matter,
thing; pl., affairs; troubles

→ Σωκράτης, Σωκράτους, ὁ Socrates

→ ὕβρις, ὕβρεως, ἡ insolence; (wanton)
violence

→ φύσις, φύσεως, ἡ nature

→ ἀποπέμπω, ἀποπέμψω, ἀπέπεμψα,
ἀποπέπομφα, ἀποπέπεμμαι,
ἀπεπέμφθην send away; middle, send
away from oneself

→ διαλέγομαι, διαλέξομαι, ——, ——,
διείλεγμαι, διελέχθην talk (with),
converse (with) (+ dat.); discuss (with)
(+ dat.)

→ ζηλόω, ζηλώσω, ἐζήλωσα, ἐζήλωκα,
——, —— emulate; envy; passive, be
deemed fortunate

→ πάρειμι, παρέσομαι, ——, ——, ——,
—— be present, be near; be ready

→ πάσχω, πείσομαι, ἔπαθον, πέπονθα,
——, —— suffer; experience

→ πράττω, πράξω, ἔπρᾱξα, πέπρᾱχα
(trans.)/πέπρᾱγα (intrans.), πέπρᾱγμαι,
ἐπρᾱχθην do; bring about; practice;
manage; intrans., fare

→ προσέχω, προσέξω, προσέσχον,
προσέσχηκα, ——, —— hold to; turn
to, apply; νοῦν/γνώμην προσέχειν,
to pay attention

→ χαίρω, χαιρήσω, ——, κεχάρηκα, ——
ἐχάρην rejoice (in), enjoy

→ ἕκαστος, ἑκάστη, ἕκαστον each (of
several)

→ ἀληθής, ἀληθές true, real; truthful
σαφής, σαφές clear, plain; certain, sure
ψευδής, ψευδές false

→ ὄντως (adv.) really, actually

→ οὐδέ/μηδέ (conj.) and not, nor;
(adv.) not even
οὐδέποτε/μηδέποτε (conj.) and not
ever, nor ever; (adv.) never

→ ποθέν (enclitic adv.) from somewhere

→ ποι (enclitic adv.) to somewhere

→ που (enclitic adv.) somewhere;
I suppose
τότε (adv.) then, at that time

Chapter 7 Summary: New Verbs

	Active	*Middle*	*Passive*
ἀποπέμπω	send away	send away from oneself	be sent away
διαλέγομαι		talk (with), converse (with); discuss (with)	(*aorist only*) talk (with), converse (with); discuss (with)
ζηλόω	emulate; envy		be deemed fortunate
πάρειμι	be present, be near; be ready	(*future only*) be present, be near; be ready	
πάσχω	suffer; experience	(*future only*) suffer; experience	
πράττω	do; bring about; practice; manage; fare	R	be done; be brought about; be practiced; be managed
προσέχω	hold to; turn to, apply	R	R
χαίρω	rejoice (in), enjoy		(*aorist only*) rejoice (in), enjoy

When no meanings are offered for a voice of a verb, the verb *never* appears in that voice. An R indicates that a verb *rarely* appears in that voice. Only commonly occurring forms should be included in a synopsis. See the vocabulary notes in the textbook for additional meanings.

Chapter 7 Summary: Participle Morphology

Summary of Present and Aorist Participle Endings

		M.	F.	N.
Present Active	Nom./Voc.	-ων	-ουσα	-ον
	Gen.	-οντος	-ουσης	-οντος
Present Middle/Passive	Nom.	-όμενος	-ομένη	-όμενον
	Gen.	-ομένου	-ομένης	-ομένου
First Aorist Active	Nom./Voc.	-ᾱς	-ᾱσα	-αν
	Gen.	-αντος	-ᾱσης	-αντος
First Aorist Middle	Nom.	-άμενος	-αμένη	-άμενον
	Gen.	-αμένου	-αμένης	-αμένου
Second Aorist Active	Nom./Voc.	-ών	-οῦσα	-όν
	Gen.	-όντος	-ούσης	-όντος
Second Aorist Middle	Nom.	-όμενος	-ομένη	-όμενον
	Gen.	-ομένου	-ομένης	-ομένου
Aorist Passive	Nom./Voc.	-είς	-εῖσα	-έν
	Gen.	-έντος	-είσης	-έντος

Notes on Accents

1. Accents on participles are *persistent*.

2. REMEMBER: A circumflex on the ultima occurs on the feminine plural genitive forms of the Present Active, First Aorist Active, Second Aorist Active, and Aorist Passive participles.

Summary of Dative Plural Endings for Present and Aorist Participles

Present Active	*-<u>οντ</u>σι(ν) > -ουσι(ν)
First Aorist Active	*-<u>αντ</u>σι(ν) > -ᾱσι(ν)
Second Aorist Active	*-<u>όντ</u>σι(ν) > -οῦσι(ν)
Aorist Passive	*-<u>έντ</u>σι(ν) > -εῖσι(ν)

Chapter 7 Summary: Participle Syntax

Participle as an Attributive Adjective

1. AGREES WITH THE NOUN IT MODIFIES IN GENDER, NUMBER, AND CASE
2. APPEARS IN THE ATTRIBUTIVE POSITION *OR* WITH A NOUN *WITHOUT* AN ARTICLE
3. MAY BE TRANSLATED INTO ENGLISH BY A RELATIVE CLAUSE

τὸν καλῶς λέγοντα ῥήτορα
the rhetor (d.o.) *speaking* well
the rhetor (d.o.) *who is speaking* well
πολῖται τοῖς νόμοις πειθόμενοι
citizens (subj.) *obeying* the laws
citizens (subj.) *who are obeying* the laws

Substantive Use of the Participle

1. APPEARS WITH OR WITHOUT AN ARTICLE
2. MAY BE TRANSLATED INTO ENGLISH BY A RELATIVE CLAUSE

τῷ θέλοντι
for the man *being willing*
for the man *who is willing*
λεγόμενα
things (subj. or d.o.) *being said*
things *that are being said*

The action of a present attributive or substantive participle is usually *simultaneous with* the action of the main verb of a sentence. The action of an aorist participle is usually *prior to* the action of the main verb of a sentence.

Common Substantives of Participles

τὸ ὄν, τὰ ὄντα	existence; reality (subj. or d.o.) ("the thing being"; "the things being")
τῷ ὄντι	in reality; really ("in respect to the thing being")
τὸ δέον, τὰ δέοντα	the necessary thing (subj. or d.o.); the necessary things (subj. or d.o.)
τὸ μέλλον, τὰ μέλλοντα	the future (subj. or d.o.) ("the thing about to be"; "the things about to be")
τὸ παρόν, τὰ παρόντα	the present (subj. or d.o.) ("the thing being present"; "the things being present")

Supplementary Participle

1. A PARTICIPLE *NOT* IN THE ATTRIBUTIVE POSITION THAT APPEARS WITH A VERB *TO EXTEND ITS MEANING*
2. AGREES WITH THE SUBJECT OF A VERB USED INTRANSITIVELY *OR* WITH THE OBJECT OF A VERB USED TRANSITIVELY
3. ENGLISH WORDS ("IN," "FROM") SOMETIMES ADDED FOR CLARITY
4. MAY OCCUR WITH παύω, ἀδικέω, ποιέω, νῑκάω, "PREVAIL (OVER)," OR ἄρχομαι, "BEGIN"

ἀδικεῖς τῑμᾶν τοὺς θεοὺς οὐκ ἐθέλουσα.
You do wrong *(in)* refusing to honor the gods.
τὸν Γοργίᾱν παύσω λέγοντα περὶ ἀρετῆς.
I shall stop Gorgias *(from)* speaking about virtue.

Chapter 7 Summary: Noun Morphology

Third Declension, σ-Stems

Σωκράτης, Σωκράτους, ὁ
Socrates
stem = **Σωκρατεσ-**

γένος, γένους, τό
race, descent; family; sort, kind
stem = **γενεσ-**

	Singular	Singular	Singular	Plural	Singular	Plural
Nom.	**-ης**	Σωκράτης	**-ος**	**-η**	γένος	γένη (<*γένεσα)
Gen.	**-ους**	Σωκράτους (<*Σωκράτεσος)	**-ους**	**-ῶν**	γένους (<*γένεσος)	γενῶν (<*γενέσων)
Dat.	**-ει**	Σωκράτει (<*Σωκράτεσι)	**-ει**	**-εσι(ν)**	γένει (<*γένεσι)	γένεσι(ν) (<*γένεσσι[ν])
Acc.	**-η**	Σωκράτη (<*Σωκράτεσα)	**-ος**	**-η**	γένος	γένη (<*γένεσα)
Voc.	**-ες**	Σώκρατες	**-ος**	**-η**	γένος	γένη (<*γένεσα)

1. No plural forms for nouns such as **Σωκράτης**.
2. **ε + α > η**.
3. *Recessive* accent on vocative singular for nouns such as **Σωκράτης**
4. Accusative singular **Σωκράτην** also occurs.

Third Declension, ι-Stems

πόλις, πόλεως, ἡ city

	Singular	Plural	Singular	Plural
Nom.	**-ις**	**-εις**	πόλις	πόλεις (< πόληες)
Gen.	**-εως**	**-εων**	πόλεως (< πόληος)	πόλεων (< πολίων)
Dat.	**-ει**	**-εσι(ν)**	πόλει (< *πόλιϊ)	πόλεσι(ν) (< πόλισι[ν])
Acc.	**-ιν**	**-εις**	πόλιν	πόλεις (< *πόλενς)
Voc.	**-ι**	**-εις**	πόλι	πόλεις (< πόληες)

1. Quantitative metathesis in genitive singular (**-ηο- > -εω-**) explains accent on **πόλεως**.
2. Accent on **πόλεων** arose by analogy with accent on **πόλεως**.

Chapter 7 Summary: Adjective Morphology, Noun Syntax

Third-Declension Adjectives Ending in -ης, -ες

ἀληθής, ἀληθές true, real
stem = **ἀληθεσ-**

Singular

	M./F.	N.		M./F.	N.	
Nom.	**-ης**	**-ες**		ἀληθής	ἀληθές	
Gen.	**-ους**	**-ους**		ἀληθοῦς	ἀληθοῦς	(< *ἀληθέσος)
Dat.	**-ει**	**-ει**		ἀληθεῖ	ἀληθεῖ	(< *ἀληθέσι)
Acc.	**-η**	**-ες**		ἀληθῆ	ἀληθές	(< *ἀληθέσα [m./f.])
Voc.	**-ες**	**-ες**		ἀληθές	ἀληθές	

Plural

	M./F.	N.		M./F.	N.	
Nom./Voc.	**-εις**	**-η**		ἀληθεῖς	ἀληθῆ	(< *ἀληθέσες [m./f.], *ἀληθέσα [n.])
Gen.	**-ων**	**-ων**		ἀληθῶν	ἀληθῶν	(< *ἀληθέσων)
Dat.	**-εσι(ν)**	**-εσι(ν)**		ἀληθέσι(ν)	ἀληθέσι(ν)	(< *ἀληθέσσι[ν])
Acc.	**-εις**	**-η**		ἀληθεῖς	ἀληθῆ	(< *ἀληθέσα [n.])

1. Masculine plural accusative (**ἀληθεῖς**) borrowed from masculine nominative/vocative plural.
2. Adverbs formed by adding **-ως** to the stem (e.g., *ἀληθέσως > **ἀληθῶς**)

Genitive of Cause

1. USES *NO PREPOSITION*
2. EXPRESSES THE CAUSE FOR THE ACTION OF A VERB

τῶν ὑμετέρων ἔργων χάριν ἔχομεν πάντες.
We all have gratitude *for/because of* your (pl.) *deeds.*

Dative of Cause

1. USES *NO PREPOSITION*
2. EXPRESSES THE CAUSE FOR THE ACTION OF A VERB

ἀπ' Ἀθηνῶν φόβῳ ἤλθομεν.
We went away from Athens *because of fear.*

Dative with a Compound Verb

1. APPEARS WITH A COMPOUND VERB
2. PREFIXES RELATED TO **ἐν, ἐπί, σύν, παρά, περί, πρός, ὑπό** USED TO FORM COMPOUND VERBS THAT *MAY* TAKE A DATIVE

αὐτῷ παρῆν.
I was near *him.*
τούτοις τοῖς λόγοις τὸν νοῦν οὐ προσέχω.
I am not paying attention *to these words.*

Chapter 8

Vocabulary

ἡδονή, ἡδονῆς, ἡ pleasure
λύπη, λύπης, ἡ pain
στρατιώτης, στρατιώτου, ὁ soldier
σωτηρίᾱ, σωτηρίᾱς, ἡ safety

κίνδῡνος, κινδύνου, ὁ danger
→ στρατηγός, στρατηγοῦ, ὁ general
στρατός, στρατοῦ, ὁ army

→ πλῆθος, πλήθους, τό great number,
multitude
→ τεῖχος, τείχους, τό wall

→ ——, ἀλλήλων (reciprocal pronoun)
one another, each other

→ ——, ἐρῶ, ——, εἴρηκα, εἴρημαι,
ἐρρήθην say, tell (of), speak (of)
→ ζάω, ζήσω, ——, ——, ——, —— be
alive, live
→ θνῄσκω, θανοῦμαι, ἔθανον, τέθνηκα,
——, —— die; *perfect,* be dead
→ ἀποθνῄσκω, ἀποθανοῦμαι,
ἀπέθανον, τέθνηκα, ——, ——
die; *perfect,* be dead
→ κτείνω, κτενῶ, ἔκτεινα, ——, ——,
—— kill
→ ἀποκτείνω, ἀποκτενῶ, ἀπέκτεινα,
ἀπέκτονα, ——, —— kill

→ μάχομαι, μαχοῦμαι, ἐμαχεσάμην, ——,
μεμάχημαι, —— fight (against) (+ dat.)
→ οἴομαι/οἶμαι, οἰήσομαι, ——, ——,
——, ᾠήθην think, suppose, believe
→ *φάσκω, ——, ——, ——, ——, ——
say, assert
→ φημί, φήσω, ἔφησα, ——, ——, ——
say, assert (§87)
→ χρή, χρῆσται, ——, ——, ——, ——
(impersonal verb) it is necessary, ought

→ ἐναντίος, ἐναντίᾱ, ἐναντίον facing,
opposite; opposing, contrary (to)
(+ gen. or dat.)
→ ἴσος, ἴση, ἴσον equal; fair
μακρός, μακρά, μακρόν large, great;
long, tall
→ (σ)μῑκρός, (σ)μῑκρά, (σ)μῑκρόν small
παλαιός, παλαιά, παλαιόν old, ancient

ἔτι (adv.) still, yet; οὐκέτι/μηκέτι (adv.)
no longer
→ ἴσως (adv.) equally; perhaps
→ πάνυ (adv.) altogether; very (much),
exceedingly; *in answers,* by all means,
certainly; οὐ πάνυ, not at all
→ πρό (prep. + gen.) before, in front of

Chapter 8 Summary: New Verbs

	Active	Middle	Passive
——, ἐρῶ	(*future and perfect*) say, tell (of), speak		be said, be spoken
ζάω	be alive, live		
θνῄσκω/ ἀποθνῄσκω	die	(*future only*) die	
κτείνω/ ἀποκτείνω	kill		
μάχομαι		fight (against)	
οἴομαι/οἶμαι		think, suppose, believe	(*aorist only*) think, suppose, believe
φάσκω	say, assert		R
φημί	say, assert	R	
χρή	it is necessary, ought		

When no meanings are offered for a voice of a verb, the verb *never* appears in that voice. An R indicates that a verb *rarely* appears in that voice. Only commonly occurring forms should be included in a synopsis. See the vocabulary notes in the textbook for additional meanings.

Chapter 8 Summary: Perfect and Pluperfect Morphology; Dative of Agent

Perfect Active Indicative
Stem from Principal Part 4
(drop **-α**) +

Perfect Middle/Passive Indicative
Stem from Principal Part 5
(drop **-μαι/-μμαι/-γμαι/-σμαι**) +

	Consonant Stems		
Regular	Labial	Palatal	Dental

Singular

			Regular	Labial	Palatal	Dental
1	**-α**		**-μαι**	**-μμαι**	**-γμαι**	**-σμαι**
2	**-ας**		**-σαι**	**-ψαι**	**-ξαι**	**-σαι**
3	**-ε(ν)**		**-ται**	**-πται**	**-κται**	**-σται**
Plural						
1	**-αμεν**		**-μεθα**	**-μμεθα**	**-γμεθα**	**-σμεθα**
2	**-ατε**		**-σθε**	**-φθε**	**-χθε**	**-σθε**
3	**-ᾱσι(ν)**		**-νται**	—	—	—

Pluperfect Active Indicative
Augmented Stem from Principal
Part 4 (drop **-α**) +

Pluperfect Middle/Passive Indicative
Augmented Stem from Principal Part 5
(drop **-μαι/-μμαι/-γμαι/-σμαι**) +

	Consonant Stems		
Regular	Labial	Palatal	Dental

Singular

			Regular	Labial	Palatal	Dental
1	**-η**		**-μην**	**-μμην**	**-γμην**	**-σμην**
2	**-ης**		**-σο**	**-ψο**	**-ξο**	**-σο**
3	**-ει(ν)**		**-το**	**-πτο**	**-κτο**	**-στο**
Plural						
1	**-εμεν**		**-μεθα**	**-μμεθα**	**-γμεθα**	**-σμεθα**
2	**-ετε**		**-σθε**	**-φθε**	**-χθε**	**-σθε**
3	**-εσαν**		**-ντο**	—	—	—

Perfect Active Infinitive
Stem from Principal Part 4
(drop **-α**)
Add:

Perfect Middle/Passive Infinitive
Stem from Principal Part 5
(drop **-μαι/-μμαι/-γμαι/-σμαι**)
Add:

	Consonant Stems		
Regular	Labial	Palatal	Dental
-σθαι	**-φθαι**	**-χθαι**	**-σθαι**

-έναι
(accent *fixed* on penult)

(accent *fixed* on penult)

1. The perfect indicative has *present* time with *completed* aspect.
2. The pluperfect indicative has *past* time with *completed* aspect.
REMEMBER: **πέπεμμαι** is an *irregular* consonant stem (ending in a labial) because it contains an additional **-μ-**, which it retains throughout its conjugation (e.g., **πέπεμψαι, ἐπέπεμπτο**).

Dative of Agent

1. IS A NOUN OR PRONOUN INDICATING THE PERSON
   BY WHOM AN ACTION REPORTED *IN THE PERFECT
   OR PLUPERFECT PASSIVE* HAS OR HAD BEEN DONE
2. USES *NO PREPOSITION*

ταῦτα τῷ ἄρχοντι ἐπέπρᾱκτο.
These things had been done *by the ruler*.

Chapter 8 Summary: φημί; Indirect Statement 2

φημί, φήσω, ἔφησα, —-, —-, —- say, assert

Long-vowel grade: φη- (*singular* forms); Short-vowel grade: φα- (other forms)

				Present Active Indicative	Imperfect Active Indicative
Singular					
1	-μι		-ν	φημί	ἔφην
2	-ς		-ς	φής	ἔφης/ἔφησθα
3	-σι(ν)		—	φησί(ν)	ἔφη
Plural					
1	-μεν		-μεν	φαμέν	ἔφαμεν
2	-τε		-τε	φατέ	ἔφατε
3	-ᾱσι(ν)		-σαν	φᾱσί(ν)	ἔφασαν

Present Active Infinitive: φάναι

REMEMBER: Present active participle supplied by **φάσκων, φάσκουσα, φάσκον**

Indirect Statement with a Subject Accusative and an Infinitive

1. There is no introductory conjunction.
2. The **Subject** is regularly in the **Accusative** case.
3. When the subject of the indirect statement is the same as the subject of the introductory verb, the subject of the indirect statement is not expressed, and any predicate is nominative.
4. The tense of the infinitive represents the tense (and often the aspect) of the verb in the original direct statement and has time relative to the introductory verb of saying:

> **present infinitive** = **time simultaneous**
> **future infinitive** = **time subsequent**
> **aorist infinitive** = **time prior**
> **perfect infinitive** = **time simultaneous + completed aspect**

5. Any negation in the original direct statement remains unchanged in the indirect statement.

Direct Statements	*Indirect Statements*
ἡ μάχη παύεται/ἐπαύθη/παυθήσεται/ πέπαυται.	**φῂς τὴν μάχην παύεσθαι/παυθῆναι/ παυθήσεσθαι/πεπαῦσθαι.**
The battle is being stopped/was stopped/ will be stopped/has been stopped.	You say that the battle is being stopped/was stopped/ will be stopped/has been stopped.
ἡ μάχη παύεται/ἐπαύθη/παυθήσεται/ πέπαυται.	**ἔφης τὴν μάχην παύεσθαι/παυθῆναι/ παυθήσεσθαι/πεπαῦσθαι.**
The battle is being stopped/was stopped/ will be stopped/has been stopped.	You were saying that the battle was being stopped/had been stopped/would be stopped/had been stopped.
ἡ μάχη οὐ παύεται/ἐπαύθη/παυθήσεται/ πέπαυται.	**φήσεις τὴν μάχην οὐ παύεσθαι/παυθῆναι/ παυθήσεσθαι/πεπαῦσθαι.**
The battle is not being stopped/was not stopped/will not be stopped/has not been stopped.	You will say that the battle is not being stopped/was not stopped/will not be stopped/has not been stopped.
δεινός εἰμι.	**Γοργίᾱς φησὶ δεινὸς εἶναι.**
I am clever.	Gorgias says that he is clever.

Chapter 8 Summary: Indirect Statement 3; Personal Construction; Verbs Introducing Indirect Statement; Articular Infinitive

Indirect Statement with a Subject Accusative and a Supplementary Participle

1. There is no introductory conjunction.
2. The **Subject** is regularly in the **Accusative** case, and the participle agrees with it.
3. When the subject of the indirect statement is the same as the subject of the introductory verb, the subject of the indirect statement is not expressed, and the participle is in the **nominative**.
4. The tense of the participle represents the tense (and often the aspect) of the verb in the original direct statement and has time relative to the introductory verb of saying:

present participle	=	**time simultaneous**
future participle	=	**time subsequent**
aorist participle	=	**time prior**
perfect participle	=	**time simultaneous + completed aspect**

5. Any negation in the original direct statement remains *unchanged* in the indirect statement.

Direct Statements

αἱ γυναῖκες εὖ πράττουσιν/εὖ ἔπρᾱξαν.
The women are faring well/fared well.

ἀκούω γυναῖκας εὖ πρᾱττούσᾱς/εὖ πρᾱξάσᾱς."
I hear that the women are faring well/fared well.

αἱ γυναῖκες εὖ πράττουσιν/εὖ ἔπρᾱξαν.
The women are faring well/fared well.

ἤκουσα γυναῖκας εὖ πρᾱττούσᾱς/εὖ πρᾱξάσᾱς.
I heard that the women were faring well/had fared well.

αἱ γυναῖκες εὖ πράττουσιν/εὖ ἔπρᾱξαν.
The women are faring well/fared well.

ἀκούσομαι γυναῖκας εὖ πρᾱττούσᾱς/εὖ πρᾱξάσᾱς."
I shall hear that the women are faring well/fared well.

αἱ γυναῖκες οὐκ εὖ πράττουσιν.
The women are not faring well.

ἤκουσα γυναῖκας οὐκ εὖ πρᾱττούσᾱς.
I heard that the women were not faring well.

ὁ δοῦλος εἰς μάχην πέμπεται.
The slave is being sent to battle.

ὁ δοῦλος ἔμαθεν εἰς μάχην πεμπόμενος.
The slave learned that he was being sent to battle.

Personal Constructions of Indirect Statement

1. SUBJECT OF INDIRECT STATEMENT IS SUBJECT OF MAIN VERB IN THE PASSIVE VOICE

   ὁ Πρίαμος λέγεται τοὺς υἱοὺς εἰς μάχην πέμψαι.
   Priam is said to have sent his sons into battle.

2. WITH CERTAIN ADJECTIVES AND

   A. SUPPLEMENTARY PARTICIPLE

   δῆλος εἶ ἐκεῖνο τὸ αἰσχρὸν ἔργον πρᾱξάς.
   You are clear having done (once) that shameful deed.
   It is clear that you did that shameful deed.

   B. A CLAUSE INTRODUCED BY **ὅτι/ὡς**

   δῆλός ἐστιν ὅτι ἐκεῖνο τὸ αἰσχρὸν ἔργον ἔπρᾱξεν.
   He is clear that he did that shameful deed.
   It is clear that he did that shameful deed.

   C. IN PLACE OF A SUBJECT ACCUSATIVE AND INFINITIVE

   δίκαιός εἰμι τόδε λέγειν.
   I am just (i.e., justified) to say (in saying) this thing.
   It is just that I say this thing.

Verbs Introducing Types of Indirect Statement

	ὅτι/ὡς with a Finite Verb	Subject Accusative with an Infinitive	Subject Accusative with a Supplementary Participle
ἀκούω	x	x	x
δῆλόν ἐστι(ν)	x		
δηλόω	x	x	x
——, ἐρῶ	x	x	
λέγω	x	x	
μανθάνω	x		x
οἴομαι/οἶμαι		x	
ὁράω	x		x
πείθω	x	x	x
φάσκω		x	
φημί		x	

Articular Infinitive

1. SUBSTANTIVE FORMED BY AN ARTICLE AND AN INFINITIVE (SINGULAR *ONLY*; *NO* VOCATIVE; TENSE INDICATES ASPECT *ONLY*)

   τὸ ἀδικεῖν
   (the) to do wrong; doing wrong

2. NEGATED WITH **μή**

   τὸ μὴ ἀδικεῖν
   not doing wrong

3. MAY HAVE SUBJECT ACCUSATIVE

   περὶ τοῦ τοὺς πολεμίους ὀφθῆναι
   concerning the enemies' being seen (once)

Chapter 9

Vocabulary

ἀμαθίᾱ, ἀμαθίᾱς, ἡ ignorance; stupidity
ἀνδρείᾱ, ἀνδρείᾱς, ἡ manliness;
courage
δικαιοσύνη, δικαιοσύνης, ἡ justice
σωφροσύνη, σωφροσύνης, ἡ
moderation

→ τρόπος, τρόπου, ὁ way, manner; habit;
pl., character

→ τέλος, τέλους, τό end, purpose; power
φρόνησις, φρονήσεως, ἡ intelligence,
understanding

τίς, τί (interrog. pron./adj.) who, what;
which (§93)
τις, τι (indef. pron./adj.) someone,
something; anyone, anything; some,
any (§94)

→ διαφθείρω, διαφθερῶ, διέφθειρα,
διέφθαρκα/διέφθορα, διέφθαρμαι,
διεφθάρην destroy (utterly); corrupt,
ruin
→ ἕπομαι, ἕψομαι, ἑσπόμην, ——, ——,
—— follow (+ dat.)
→ λαμβάνω, λήψομαι, ἔλαβον, εἴληφα,
εἴλημμαι, ἐλήφθην take, seize;
understand; receive; *middle,* take hold
(of)(+ gen.)
  → δίκην λαμβάνειν, to exact
      punishment

→ ὑπολαμβάνω, ὑπολήψομαι,
ὑπέλαβον, ὑπείληφα, ὑπείλημμαι,
ὑπελήφθην take up, reply; suppose
→ μένω, μενῶ, ἔμεινα, μεμένηκα, ——,
—— remain, stay; *trans.,* await
→ οἶδα, εἴσομαι, ——, ——, ——, ——
know (§92)
→ φέρω, οἴσω, ἤνεγκα/ἤνεγκον, ἐνήνοχα,
ἐνήνεγμαι, ἠνέχθην bear, bring, carry;
endure; *middle,* carry away with oneself;
win
→ φεύγω, φεύξομαι, ἔφυγον, πέφευγα,
——, —— flee, avoid, escape

ἄθλιος, ἀθλίᾱ, ἄθλιον wretched,
miserable

ἀμαθής, ἀμαθές ignorant, foolish
εὐδαίμων, εὔδαιμον fortunate, happy
σώφρων, σῶφρον moderate, prudent

εἷς, μία, ἕν (numerical adj.) one (§95)
οὐδείς, οὐδεμία, οὐδέν/ μηδείς,
μηδεμία, μηδέν (adj./substantive) no,
not any; no one, nothing (§95)

ἄν (particle) *used in the apodoses of some
conditional sentences* (§96)
→ ἄρα (postpositive particle) (so) then,
therefore; after all
εἰ (conj.) if
ἐκεῖ (adv.) there
→ πω (enclitic adv.) yet
  → πώποτε (adv.) ever yet

Chapter 9 Summary: New Verbs

	Active	Middle	Passive
διαφθείρω	destroy (utterly); corrupt, ruin		be destroyed (utterly); be corrupted, be ruined
ἕπομαι		follow	
λαμβάνω	take, seize; understand; receive	take hold of	be taken, be seized; be understood; be received
ὑπολαμβάνω	take up, reply; suppose	(*future only*) take up, reply; suppose	be taken up; be supposed
μένω	remain, stay; await		
οἶδα	know	(*future only*) know	
φέρω	bear, bring, carry; endure	carry away with oneself; win	be borne, be brought, be carried; be endured
φεύγω	flee, avoid, escape	(*future only*) flee, avoid, escape	

When no meanings are offered for a voice of a verb, the verb *never* appears in that voice. An R indicates that a verb *rarely* appears in that voice. Only commonly occurring forms should be included in a synopsis. See the vocabulary notes in the textbook for additional meanings.

Verbs Introducing Types of Indirect Statement

	ὅτι/ὡς with a Finite Verb	Subject Accusative with a Verb in the Infinitive	Subject Accusative with a Supplementary Participle
ὑπολαμβάνω	x	x	
οἶδα	x	x	x

Chapter 9 Summary: The Irregular Verb οἶδα

οἶδα, εἴσομαι, ——, ——, ——, —— know

	Perfect Active Indicative	Pluperfect Active Indicative
Singular		
1	οἶδα	ᾔδη/ᾔδειν
2	οἶσθα	ᾔδησθα/ᾔδεις
3	οἶδε(ν)	ᾔδει(ν)
Plural		
1	ἴσμεν	ᾖσμεν
2	ἴστε	ᾖστε
3	ἴσᾱσι(ν)	ᾖσαν/ᾔδεσαν

Perfect Active Infinitive: εἰδέναι

Chapter 9 Summary: Pronouns and Adjectives

Interrogative Pron./Adj. τίς, τί

	M./F.	N.
Singular		
Nom.	τίς	τί
Gen.	τίνος/τοῦ	τίνος/τοῦ
Dat.	τίνι/τῷ	τίνι/τῷ
Acc.	τίνα	τί
Plural		
Nom.	τίνες	τίνα
Gen.	τίνων	τίνων
Dat.	τίσι(ν)	τίσι(ν)
Acc.	τίνας	τίνα

Enclitic Indef. Pron./Adj. τις, τι

	M./F.	N.
Nom.	τις	τι
Gen.	τινός/του	τινός/του
Dat.	τινί/τῳ	τινί/τῳ
Acc.	τινά	τι
Nom.	τινές	τινά/ἄττα
Gen.	τινῶν	τινῶν
Dat.	τισί(ν)	τισί(ν)
Acc.	τινάς	τινά/ἄττα

REMEMBER: Acute accent on ultima *remains* even when followed by other words (but circumflex on alternate genitive/dative singular forms).

REMEMBER: All forms are *enclitic except* the alternate neuter plural nominative/accusative, ἄττα.

Translations (Interrogative)

	Beings	*Things*
As pronoun:		
Subject	who	what
Possessive	whose/of whom	whose/of what
Object of verbs and prepositions	whom	what
As adjective	what/which	what/which

Translations (Indefinite)

As pronoun	someone, anyone	something, anything
As adjective	some, any	some, any

When with a form of ἕκαστος, πᾶς, or ἅπᾶς, τις/τι may be translated "one": παντί τινι, "for every one." Sometimes τις/τι *cannot* be translated when used to emphasize indefiniteness.

The Adjectives **εἷς, μία, ἕν** and **οὐδείς, οὐδεμία, οὐδέν/μηδείς, μηδεμία, μηδέν**

	εἷς, μία, ἕν one			**οὐδείς, οὐδεμία, οὐδέν** not one, not any; no one, nothing			**μηδείς, μηδεμία, μηδέν** not one, not any; no one, nothing		
	M.	F.	N.	M.	F.	N.	M.	F.	N.
Nom.	εἷς	μία	ἕν	οὐδείς	οὐδεμία	οὐδέν	μηδείς	μηδεμία	μηδέν
Gen.	ἑνός	μιᾶς	ἑνός	οὐδενός	οὐδεμιᾶς	οὐδενός	μηδενός	μηδεμιᾶς	μηδενός
Dat.	ἑνί	μιᾷ	ἑνί	οὐδενί	οὐδεμιᾷ	οὐδενί	μηδενί	μηδεμιᾷ	μηδενί
Acc.	ἕνα	μίαν	ἕν	οὐδένα	οὐδεμίαν	οὐδέν	μηδένα	μηδεμίαν	μηδέν

REMEMBER: Both **εἷς** and **οὐδείς/μηδείς** may be used as adjectives *not* in the attributive position or, more commonly, as *substantives*.

When a *simple* negative (**οὐ** or **μή**) *follows* a *compound* negative (**οὐδείς, οὔτε, οὔποτε**), the meaning of a sentence is *positive*:

> **οὐδεὶς οὐκ ἤκουσεν.**   No one did not listen (i.e., Everyone listened).

When a *compound* negative (**οὐδείς, οὔτε, οὔποτε**) *follows* a *simple* negative or *another* compound negative, the negation is *strengthened*:

> **οὐκ ἤκουσεν οὐδείς.**   No one listened.
> **οὐδείς μοι οὐδὲν εἶπεν.**   No one said anything to me.

Chapter 9 Summary: Conditional Sentences; Adjective Morphology; Noun Syntax

Summary of Conditional Sentences

Name	Verbs in Greek	Verbs in English
Present Simple	Protasis: εἰ + Present Indicative	does[†]
	Apodosis: Present Indicative	does
Past Simple	Protasis: εἰ + Imperfect or Aorist Indicative	did
	Apodosis: Imperfect or Aorist Indicative	did
Future Most Vivid	Protasis: εἰ + Future Indicative	does
	Apodosis: Future Indicative	will do
Present Contrary-to-Fact	Protasis: εἰ + Imperfect Indicative	were doing
	Apodosis: Imperfect Indicative + ἄν	would be doing
Past Contrary-to-Fact	Protasis: εἰ + Aorist Indicative	had done
	Apodosis: Aorist Indicative + ἄν	would have done
Mixed Contrary-to-Fact	Protasis: εἰ + Aorist Indicative	had done
	Apodosis: Imperfect Indicative + ἄν	would be doing

[†]The model verb "to do" is used to indicate English translation formulas.

Third-Declension Adjectives: **-ων, -ον**

εὐδαίμων, εὔδαιμον fortunate, happy

stem = **εὐδαιμον-**

	Singular M./F.	N.	Plural M./F.	N.	Singular M./F.	N.	Plural M./F.	N.
Nom.	-ων	-ον	-ονες	-ονα	εὐδαίμων	εὔδαιμον	εὐδαίμονες	εὐδαίμονα
Gen.	-ονος	-ονος	-ονων	-ονων	εὐδαίμονος	εὐδαίμονος	εὐδαιμόνων	εὐδαιμόνων
Dat.	-ονι	-ονι	-οσι(ν)	-οσι(ν)	εὐδαίμονι	εὐδαίμονι	εὐδαίμοσι(ν)	εὐδαίμοσι(ν)
Acc.	-ονα	-ον	-ονας	-ονα	εὐδαίμονα	εὔδαιμον	εὐδαίμονας	εὐδαίμονα
Voc.	-ον	-ον	-ονες	-ονες	εὔδαιμον	εὔδαιμον	εὐδαίμονες	εὐδαίμονα

Dative of Manner

EXPRESSES THE *WAY IN WHICH* SOMETHING OCCURS OR IS DONE

USES *NO* PREPOSITION

IS SOMETIMES AN ADJECTIVE IN THE FEMININE SINGULAR
   THAT ASSUMES THE ELLIPSIS OF **ὁδῷ**

τούτῳ τῷ τρόπῳ αὐτοὺς πείσω.
I shall persuade them *in this way.*

πολλοὺς κοινῇ νόμους ἔχομεν.
We have many laws *in common.*

Adverbial Accusative

IS A WORD IN THE ACCUSATIVE CASE THAT FUNCTIONS
   AS AN ADVERB

IS AN EXTENSION OF THE CAPACITY OF THE ACCUSATIVE
   CASE TO EXPRESS EXTENT

USES *NO* PREPOSITION

τοῦτον τὸν τρόπον ἠδικήμεθα.
We have been wronged *in this way.*

Synopsis 1, Chapter 3

Principal Parts: _____

Person and Number: _____

	Active	Middle	Passive
Indicative			
Present	_____	_____	_____
Imperfect	_____	_____	_____
Future	_____	_____	_____
Infinitives			
Present	_____	_____	_____
Future	_____	_____	_____

Synopsis 2, Chapter 6

Principal Parts: _____

Person and Number: _____

	Active	Middle	Passive
Indicative			
Present	_____	_____	_____
Imperfect	_____	_____	_____
Future	_____	_____	_____
Aorist	_____	_____	_____
Infinitives			
Present	_____	_____	_____
Future	_____	_____	_____
Aorist	_____	_____	_____

Synopsis 3, Chapter 7

Principal Parts: _____

Person and Number: _____

Gender, Number, and Case: _____

	Active	*Middle*	*Passive*
Indicative			
Present	_____	_____	_____
Imperfect	_____	_____	_____
Future	_____	_____	_____
Aorist	_____	_____	_____
Infinitives			
Present	_____	_____	_____
Future	_____	_____	_____
Aorist	_____	_____	_____
Participles			
Present	_____	_____	_____
Aorist	_____	_____	_____

Name: _____

Synopsis 4, Chapter 8

Principal Parts: _____

Person and Number: _____

Gender, Number, and Case: _____

	Active	*Middle*	*Passive*
Indicative			
Present	_____	_____	_____
Imperfect	_____	_____	_____
Future	_____	_____	_____
Aorist	_____	_____	_____
Perfect	_____	_____	_____
Pluperfect	_____	_____	_____
Infinitives			
Present	_____	_____	_____
Future	_____	_____	_____
Aorist	_____	_____	_____
Perfect	_____	_____	_____
Participles			
Present	_____	_____	_____
Aorist	_____	_____	_____

Morphology Appendix

Many forms in this appendix are rare or nonexistent; they are presented as part of complete paradigms to serve as examples for analogous words.

Contents

Nouns

First-Declension Nouns

The chapter number in which the morphology is presented is given in parentheses following.

Long-Alpha (1)

οἰκίᾱ, οἰκίᾱς, ἡ
χώρᾱ, χώρᾱς, ἡ
ἀγορά, ἀγορᾶς, ἡ

Eta (1)

δίκη, δίκης, ἡ
βουλή, βουλῆς, ἡ

Singular

Nom.	**-ᾱ**	οἰκίᾱ	χώρᾱ	ἀγορά	**-η**	δίκη	βουλή
Gen.	**-ᾱς**	οἰκίᾱς	χώρᾱς	ἀγορᾶς	**-ης**	δίκης	βουλῆς
Dat.	**-ᾳ**	οἰκίᾳ	χώρᾳ	ἀγορᾷ	**-ῃ**	δίκῃ	βουλῇ
Acc.	**-ᾱν**	οἰκίᾱν	χώρᾱν	ἀγοράν	**-ην**	δίκην	βουλήν
Voc.	**-ᾱ**	οἰκίᾱ	χώρᾱ	ἀγορά	**-η**	δίκη	βουλή

Dual

Nom./Voc./Acc.	**-ᾱ**	οἰκίᾱ	χώρᾱ	ἀγορά	**-α**	δίκᾱ	βουλά
Gen./Dat.	**-αιν**	οἰκίαιν	χώραιν	ἀγοραῖν	**-αιν**	δίκαιν	βουλαῖν

Plural

Nom.	**-αι**	οἰκίαι	χῶραι	ἀγοραί	**-αι**	δίκαι	βουλαί
Gen.	**-ῶν**	οἰκιῶν	χωρῶν	ἀγορῶν	**-ῶν**	δικῶν	βουλῶν
Dat.	**-αις/**	οἰκίαις/	χώραις/	ἀγοραῖς/	**-αις/**	δίκαις/	βουλαῖς/
	-αισι(ν)	οἰκίαισι(ν)	χώραισι(ν)	ἀγοραῖσι(ν)	**-αισι(ν)**	δίκαισι(ν)	βουλαῖσι(ν)
Acc.	**-ᾱς**	οἰκίᾱς	χώρᾱς	ἀγοράς	**-ᾱς**	δίκᾱς	βουλάς
Voc.	**-αι**	οἰκίαι	χῶραι	ἀγοραί	**-αι**	δίκαι	βουλαί

Short-Alpha (2)

μοῖρα, μοίρᾱς, ἡ
δόξα, δόξης, ἡ

Masculine First-Declension (2)

νεᾱνίᾱς, νεᾱνίου, ὁ
Ἀτρείδης, Ἀτρείδου, ὁ
πολίτης, πολίτου, ὁ

Singular

Nom.	**-α**	μοῖρα	**-α**	δόξα	**-ᾱς**	νεᾱνίᾱς	
Gen.	**-ᾱς**	μοίρᾱς	**-ης**	δόξης	**-ου**	νεᾱνίου	
Dat.	**-ᾳ**	μοίρᾳ	**-ῃ**	δόξῃ	**-ᾳ**	νεᾱνίᾳ	
Acc.	**-αν**	μοῖραν	**-αν**	δόξαν	**-ᾱν**	νεᾱνίᾱν	
Voc.	**-ᾱ**	μοῖρα	**-α**	δόξαι	**-ᾱ**	νεᾱνίᾱ	

Dual

Nom./Voc./Acc.	**-ᾱ**	μοίρᾱ	**-ᾱ**	δόξᾱ	**-ᾱ**	νεᾱνίᾱ	
Gen./Dat.	**-αιν**	μοίραιν	**-αιν**	δόξαιν	**-αιν**	νεᾱνίαιν	

Plural

Nom.	**-αι**	μοῖραι		δόξαι	**-αι**	νεᾱνίαι	
Gen.	**-ῶν**	μοιρῶν		δοξῶν	**-ῶν**	νεᾱνιῶν	
Dat.	**-αις/**	μοίραις/		δόξαις/	**-αις/**	νεᾱνίαις/	
	-αισι(ν)	μοίραισι(ν)		δόξαισι(ν)	**-αισι(ν)**	νεᾱνίαισι(ν)	
Acc.	**-ᾱς**	μοίρᾱς		δόξᾱς	**-ᾱς**	νεᾱνίᾱς	
Voc.	**-αι**	μοῖραι		δόξαι	**-αι**	νεᾱνίαι	

Singular

Nom.	**-ης**	Ἀτρείδης	πολίτης
Gen.	**-ου**	Ἀτρείδου	πολίτου
Dat.	**-ῃ**	Ἀτρείδῃ	πολίτῃ
Acc.	**-ην**	Ἀτρείδην	πολίτην
Voc.	**-η/-α**	Ἀτρείδη	πολῖτα

Dual

Nom./Voc./Acc.	**-ᾱ**	Ἀτρείδᾱ	πολίτᾱ
Gen./Dat.	**-αιν**	Ἀτρείδαιν	πολίταιν

Plural

Nom.	**-αι**	Ἀτρεῖδαι	πολῖται
Gen.	**-ῶν**	Ἀτρειδῶν	πολῖτῶν
Dat.	**-αις/-αισι(ν)**	Ἀτρείδαις/	πολίταις/
		Ἀτρείδαισι(ν)	πολίταισι(ν)
Acc.	**-ᾱς**	Ἀτρείδᾱς	πολίτᾱς
Voc.	**-αι**	Ἀτρεῖδαι	πολῖται

Second-Declension Nouns

Masculine/Feminine (1)	Neuter (1)
νόμος, νόμου, ὁ	**τέκνον, τέκνου, τό**
θεός, θεοῦ, ὁ	

Singular

Nom.	**-ος**	νόμος	θεός	**-ον**	τέκνον
Gen.	**-ου**	νόμου	θεοῦ	**-ου**	τέκνου
Dat.	**-ῳ**	νόμῳ	θεῷ	**-ῳ**	τέκνῳ
Acc.	**-ον**	νόμον	θεόν	**-ον**	τέκνον
Voc.	**-ε**	νόμε	—	**-ον**	τέκνον

Dual

Nom./Voc./Acc.	**-ω**	νόμω	θεώ	**-ω**	τέκνω
Gen./Dat.	**-οιν**	νόμοιν	θεοῖν	**-οιν**	τέκνοιν

Plural

Nom.	**-οι**	νόμοι	θεοί	**-α**	τέκνα
Gen.	**-ων**	νόμων	θεῶν	**-ων**	τέκνων
Dat.	**-οις/-οισι(ν)**	νόμοις/νόμοισι(ν)	θεοῖς/θεοῖσι(ν)	**-οις/-οισι(ν)**	τέκνοις/τέκνοισι(ν)
Acc.	**-ους**	νόμους	θεούς	**-α**	τέκνα
Voc.	**-οι**	νόμοι	θεοί	**-α**	τέκνα

Contracted (7)

νοῦς, νοῦ, ὁ

Singular

Nom.	**-ος**	νοῦς
Gen.	**-ου**	νοῦ
Dat.	**-ῳ**	νῷ
Acc.	**-ον**	νοῦν
Voc.	**-ε**	νοῦ

Third-Declension Nouns

Masculine/Feminine Consonant Stems (5)

ῥήτωρ, ῥήτορος, ὁ
δαίμων, δαίμονος, ὁ
φρήν, φρενός, ἡ
ἐλπίς, ἐλπίδος, ἡ
ἄρχων, ἄρχοντος, ὁ
χάρις, χάριτος, ἡ

Singular

Nom.	—	ῥήτωρ	δαίμων	φρήν	ἐλπίς	ἄρχων	χάρις
Gen.	**-ος**	ῥήτορος	δαίμονος	φρενός	ἐλπίδος	ἄρχοντος	χάριτος
Dat.	**-ι**	ῥήτορι	δαίμονι	φρενί	ἐλπίδι	ἄρχοντι	χάριτι
Acc.	**-α/-ν**	ῥήτορα	δαίμονα	φρένα	ἐλπίδα	ἄρχοντα	χάριν
Voc.	—	ῥῆτορ	δαῖμον	φρήν	ἐλπί	ἄρχον	χάρι

Dual

Nom./Voc./Acc.	**-ε**	ῥήτορε	δαίμονε	φρένε	ἐλπίδε	ἄρχοντε	χάριτε
Gen./Dat.	**-οιν**	ῥητόροιν	δαιμόνοιν	φρενοῖν	ἐλπίδοιν	ἀρχόντοιν	χαρίτοιν

Plural

Nom.	**-ες**	ῥήτορες	δαίμονες	φρένες	ἐλπίδες	ἄρχοντες	χάριτες
Gen.	**-ων**	ῥητόρων	δαιμόνων	φρενῶν	ἐλπίδων	ἀρχόντων	χαρίτων
Dat.	**-σι(ν)**	ῥήτορσι(ν)	δαίμοσι(ν)	φρεσί(ν)	ἐλπίσι(ν)	ἄρχουσι(ν)	χάρισι(ν)
Acc.	**-ας**	ῥήτορας	δαίμονας	φρένας	ἐλπίδας	ἄρχοντας	χάριτας
Voc.	**-ες**	ῥήτορες	δαίμονες	φρένες	ἐλπίδες	ἄρχοντες	χάριτες

Neuter Consonant Stems (5)

σῶμα, σώματος, τό

Singular

Nom.	—	σῶμα
Gen.	**-ος**	σώματος
Dat.	**-ι**	σώματι
Acc.	—	σῶμα
Voc.	—	σῶμα

Dual

Nom./Voc./Acc.	**-ε**	σώματε
Gen./Dat.	**-οιν**	σωμάτοιν

Plural

Nom.	**-α**	σώματα
Gen.	**-ων**	σωμάτων
Dat.	**-σι(ν)**	σώμασι(ν)
Acc.	**-α**	σώματα
Voc.	**-α**	σώματα

Irregular Masculine/Feminine Consonant Stems

ἀνήρ, ἀνδρός, ὁ (6)
μήτηρ, μητρός, ἡ (7)
πατήρ, πατρός, ὁ (7)
γυνή, γυναικός, ἡ (7)

Singular

Nom.	—	ἀνήρ	μήτηρ	πατήρ	γυνή
Gen.	**-ος**	ἀνδρός	μητρός	πατρός	γυναικός
Dat.	**-ι**	ἀνδρί	μητρί	πατρί	γυναικί
Acc.	**-α**	ἄνδρα	μητέρα	πατέρα	γυναῖκα
Voc.	—	ἄνερ	μῆτερ	πάτερ	γύναι

Dual

Nom./Voc./.Acc.	**-ε**	ἄνδρε	μητέρε	πατέρε	γυναῖκε
Gen./Dat.	**-οιν**	ἀνδροῖν	μητέροιν	πατέροιν	γυναικοῖν

Plural

Nom.	**-ες**	ἄνδρες	μητέρες	πατέρες	γυναῖκες
Gen.	**-ων**	ἀνδρῶν	μητέρων	πατέρων	γυναικῶν
Dat.	**-σι(ν)**	ἀνδράσι(ν)	μητράσι(ν)	πατράσι(ν)	γυναιξί(ν)
Acc.	**-ας**	ἄνδρας	μητέρας	πατέρας	γυναῖκας
Voc.	**-ες**	ἄνδρες	μητέρες	πατέρες	γυναῖκες

Sigma Stems (7)

Σωκράτης, Σωκράτους, ὁ
γένος, γένους, τό

Singular

Nom.	**-ης**	Σωκράτης	**-ος**	γένος
Gen.	**-ους**	Σωκράτους	**-ους**	γένους
Dat.	**-ει**	Σωκράτει	**-ει**	γένει
Acc.	**-η**	Σωκράτη	**-ος**	γένος
Voc.	**-ες**	Σώκρατες	**-ος**	γένος

Dual

Nom./Voc./Acc.			**-ει**	γένει
Gen./Dat.			**-οιν**	γενοῖν

Plural

Nom.			**-η**	γένη
Gen.			**-ῶν**	γενῶν
Dat.			**-εσι(ν)**	γένεσι(ν)
Acc.			**-η**	γένη
Voc.			**-η**	γένη

Iota Stems (7)

πόλις, πόλεως, ἡ

Singular

Nom.	-ις	πόλις
Gen.	-εως	πόλεως
Dat.	-ει	πόλει
Acc.	-ιν	πόλιν
Voc.	-ι	πόλι

Dual

Nom.	-ει	πόλει
Gen.	-εοιν	πολέοιν

Plural

Nom.	-εις	πόλεις
Gen.	-εων	πόλεων
Dat.	-εσι(ν)	πόλεσι(ν)
Acc.	-εις	πόλεις
Voc.	-εις	πόλεις

Adjectives

First-Second-Declension Adjectives

With Three Nominative Singular Forms (2)
καλός, καλή, καλόν
Ἀθηναῖος, Ἀθηναίᾱ, Ἀθηναῖον

	M.	F.	N.	M.	F.	N.
Singular						
Nom.	-ος	-η	-ον	καλός	καλή	καλόν
Gen.	-ου	-ης	-ου	καλοῦ	καλῆς	καλοῦ
Dat.	-ῳ	-ῃ	-ῳ	καλῷ	καλῇ	καλῷ
Acc.	-ον	-ην	-ον	καλόν	καλήν	καλόν
Voc.	-ε	-η	-ον	καλέ	καλή	καλόν
Dual						
Nom./Voc./Acc.	-ω	-ω	-ω	καλώ	καλώ	καλώ
Gen./Dat.	-οιν	-αιν	-οιν	καλοῖν	καλαῖν	καλοῖν
Plural						
Nom.	-οι	-αι	-α	καλοί	καλαί	καλά
Gen.	-ων	-ων	-ων	καλῶν	καλῶν	καλῶν
Dat.	-οις/ -οισι(ν)	-αις/ -αισι(ν)	-οις/ -οισι(ν)	καλοῖς/ καλοῖσι(ν)	καλαῖς/ καλαῖσι(ν)	καλοῖς/ καλοῖσι(ν)
Acc.	-ους	-ᾱς	-α	καλούς	καλάς	καλά
Voc.	-οι	-αι	-α	καλοί	καλαί	καλά
Singular						
Nom.	-ος	-ᾱ	-ον	Ἀθηναῖος	Ἀθηναίᾱ	Ἀθηναῖον
Gen.	-ου	-ᾱς	-ου	Ἀθηναίου	Ἀθηναίᾱς	Ἀθηναίου
Dat.	-ῳ	-ᾳ	-ῳ	Ἀθηναίῳ	Ἀθηναίᾳ	Ἀθηναίῳ
Acc.	-ον	-ᾱν	-ον	Ἀθηναῖον	Ἀθηναίᾱν	Ἀθηναῖον
Voc.	-ε	-ᾱ	-ον	Ἀθηναῖε	Ἀθηναίᾱ	Ἀθηναῖον
Dual						
Nom./Voc./Acc.	-ω	-ω	-ω	Ἀθηναίω	Ἀθηναίω	Ἀθηναίω
Gen./Dat.	-οιν	-αιν	-οιν	Ἀθηναίοιν	Ἀθηναίαιν	Ἀθηναίοιν
Plural						
Nom.	-οι	-αι	-α	Ἀθηναῖοι	Ἀθηναῖαι	Ἀθηναῖα
Gen.	-ων	-ων	-ων	Ἀθηναίων	Ἀθηναίων	Ἀθηναίων
Dat.	-οις/ -οισι(ν)	-αις/ -αισι(ν)	-οις/ -οισι(ν)	Ἀθηναίοις/ Ἀθηναίοισι(ν)	Ἀθηναίαις/ Ἀθηναίαισι(ν)	Ἀθηναίοις/ Ἀθηναίοισι(ν)
Acc.	-ους	-ᾱς	-α	Ἀθηναίους	Ἀθηναίᾱς	Ἀθηναῖα
Voc.	-οι	-αι	-α	Ἀθηναῖοι	Ἀθηναῖαι	Ἀθηναῖα

With Two Nominative Singular Forms (2)

ἄδικος, ἄδικον

	M./F.	N.	M./F.	N.
Singular				
Nom.	**-ος**	**-ον**	ἄδικος	ἄδικον
Gen.	**-ου**	**-ου**	ἀδίκου	ἀδίκου
Dat.	**-ῳ**	**-ῳ**	ἀδίκῳ	ἀδίκῳ
Acc.	**-ον**	**-ον**	ἄδικον	ἄδικον
Voc.	**-ε**	**-ον**	ἄδικε	ἄδικον
Dual				
Nom./Voc./Acc.	**-ω**	**-ω**	ἀδίκω	ἀδίκω
Gen./Dat.	**-οιν**	**-οιν**	ἀδίκοιν	ἀδίκοιν
Plural				
Nom.	**-οι**	**-α**	ἄδικοι	ἄδικα
Gen.	**-ων**	**-ων**	ἀδίκων	ἀδίκων
Dat.	**-οις/** **-οισι(ν)**	**-οις/** **-οισι(ν)**	ἀδίκοις/ ἀδίκοισι(ν)	ἀδίκοις/ ἀδίκοισι(ν)
Acc.	**-ους**	**-α**	ἀδίκους	ἄδικα
Voc.	**-οι**	**-α**	ἄδικοι	ἄδικα

The Irregular Adjectives **μέγας, μεγάλη, μέγα** and **πολύς, πολλή, πολύ** (4)

	M.	F.	N.	M.	F.	N.
Singular						
Nom.	μέγας	μεγάλη	μέγα	πολύς	πολλή	πολύ
Gen.	μεγάλου	μεγάλης	μεγάλου	πολλοῦ	πολλῆς	πολλοῦ
Dat.	μεγάλῳ	μεγάλῃ	μεγάλῳ	πολλῷ	πολλῇ	πολλῷ
Acc.	μέγαν	μεγάλην	μέγα	πολύν	πολλήν	πολύ
Voc.	μεγάλε	μεγάλη	μέγα	—	—	—
Dual						
Nom./Voc./Acc.	μεγάλω	μεγάλᾱ	μεγάλω	—	—	—
Gen./Dat.	μεγάλοιν	μεγάλαιν	μεγάλοιν	—	—	—
Plural						
Nom.	μεγάλοι	μεγάλαι	μεγάλα	πολλοί	πολλαί	πολλά
Gen.	μεγάλων	μεγάλων	μεγάλων	πολλῶν	πολλῶν	πολλῶν
Dat.	μεγάλοις/ μεγάλοισι(ν)	μεγάλαις/ μεγάλαισι(ν)	μεγάλοις/ μεγάλοισι(ν)	πολλοῖς/ πολλοῖσι(ν)	πολλαῖς/ πολλαῖσι(ν)	πολλοῖς/ πολλοῖσι(ν)
Acc.	μεγάλους	μεγάλᾱς	μεγάλα	πολλούς	πολλάς	πολλά
Voc.	μεγάλοι	μεγάλαι	μεγάλα	—	—	—

The Intensive Adjective **αὐτός, αὐτή, αὐτό** (6)

	M.	F.	N.
Singular			
Nom.	αὐτός	αὐτή	αὐτό
Gen.	αὐτοῦ	αὐτῆς	αὐτοῦ
Dat.	αὐτῷ	αὐτῇ	αὐτῷ
Acc.	αὐτόν	αὐτήν	αὐτό
Dual			
Nom./Acc.	αὐτώ	αὐτά	αὐτώ
Gen./Dat.	αὐτοῖν	αὐταῖν	αὐτοῖν
Plural			
Nom.	αὐτοί	αὐταί	αὐτά
Gen.	αὐτῶν	αὐτῶν	αὐτῶν
Dat.	αὐτοῖς/	αὐταῖς/	αὐτοῖς/
	αὐτοῖσι(ν)	αὐταῖσι(ν)	αὐτοῖσι(ν)
Acc.	αὐτούς	αὐτάς	αὐτά

Third-Declension Adjectives

-ης, -ες (7)
ἀληθής, ἀληθές

	M./F.	N.	M./F.	N.
Singular				
Nom.	**-ης**	**-ες**	ἀληθής	ἀληθές
Gen.	**-ους**	**-ους**	ἀληθοῦς	ἀληθοῦς
Dat.	**-ει**	**-ει**	ἀληθεῖ	ἀληθεῖ
Acc.	**-η**	**-ες**	ἀληθῆ	ἀληθές
Voc.	**-ες**	**-ες**	ἀληθές	ἀληθές
Dual				
Nom./Voc./Acc.	**-ει**	**-ει**	ἀληθεῖ	ἀληθεῖ
Gen./Dat.	**-οιν**	**-οιν**	ἀληθοῖν	ἀληθοῖν
Plural				
Nom.	**-εις**	**-η**	ἀληθεῖς	ἀληθῆ
Gen.	**-ων**	**-ων**	ἀληθῶν	ἀληθῶν
Dat.	**-εσι(ν)**	**-εσι(ν)**	ἀληθέσι(ν)	ἀληθέσι(ν)
Acc.	**-εις**	**-η**	ἀληθεῖς	ἀληθῆ
Voc.	**-εις**	**-η**	ἀληθεῖς	ἀληθῆ

-ων, -ον (9)
εὐδαίμων, εὔδαιμον

	M./F.	N.	M./F.	N.
Singular				
Nom.	**-ων**	**-ον**	εὐδαίμων	εὔδαιμον
Gen.	**-ονος**	**-ονος**	εὐδαίμονος	εὐδαίμονος
Dat.	**-ονι**	**-ονι**	εὐδαίμονι	εὐδαίμονι
Acc.	**-ονα**	**-ον**	εὐδαίμονα	εὔδαιμον
Voc.	**-ον**	**-ον**	εὔδαιμον	εὔδαιμον
Dual				
Nom./Voc./Acc.	**-ε**	**-ε**	εὐδαίμονε	εὐδαίμονε
Gen./Dat.	**-οιν**	**-οιν**	εὐδαιμόνοιν	εὐδαιμόνοιν
Plural				
Nom.	**-ονες**	**-ονα**	εὐδαίμονες	εὐδαίμονα
Gen.	**-ονων**	**-ονων**	εὐδαιμόνων	εὐδαιμόνων
Dat.	**-οσι(ν)**	**-οσι(ν)**	εὐδαίμοσι(ν)	εὐδαίμοσι(ν)
Acc.	**-ονας**	**-ονα**	εὐδαίμονας	εὐδαίμονα
Voc.	**-ονες**	**-ονα**	εὐδαίμονες	εὐδαίμονα

The Irregular Adjectives **πᾶς, πᾶσα, πᾶν** and **ἅπᾱς, ἅπᾱσα, ἅπαν**

πᾶς, πᾶσα, πᾶν (6)   **ἅπᾱς, ἅπᾱσα, ἅπαν** (6)

	M.	F.	N.	M.	F.	N.
Singular						
Nom.	πᾶς	πᾶσα	πᾶν	ἅπᾱς	ἅπᾱσα	ἅπαν
Gen.	παντός	πάσης	παντός	ἅπαντος	ἁπάσης	ἅπαντος
Dat.	παντί	πάσῃ	παντί	ἅπαντι	ἁπάσῃ	ἅπαντι
Acc.	πάντα	πᾶσαν	πᾶν	ἅπαντα	ἅπᾱσαν	ἅπαν
Voc.	πᾶς	πᾶσα	πᾶν	ἅπᾱς	ἅπᾱσα	ἅπαν
Plural						
Nom.	πάντες	πᾶσαι	πάντα	ἅπαντες	ἅπᾱσαι	ἅπαντα
Gen.	πάντων	πᾱσῶν	πάντων	ἁπάντων	ἁπᾱσῶν	ἁπάντων
Dat.	πᾶσι(ν)	πάσαις	πᾶσι(ν)	ἅπᾱσι(ν)	ἁπάσαις	ἅπᾱσι(ν)
Acc.	πάντας	πάσᾱς	πάντα	ἅπαντας	ἁπάσᾱς	ἅπαντα
Voc.	πάντες	πᾶσαι	πάντα	ἅπαντες	ἅπᾱσαι	ἅπαντα

Numerical Adjectives

εἷς, μία, ἕν and **οὐδείς, οὐδεμία,
οὐδέν/μηδείς, μηδεμία, μηδέν** (9)

	εἷς, μία, ἕν			**οὐδείς, οὐδεμία, οὐδέν**			**μηδείς, μηδεμία, μηδέν**		
	M.	F.	N.	M.	F.	N.	M.	F.	N.
Nom.	εἷς	μία	ἕν	οὐδείς	οὐδεμία	οὐδέν	μηδείς	μηδεμία	μηδέν
Gen.	ἑνός	μιᾶς	ἑνός	οὐδενός	οὐδεμιᾶς	οὐδενός	μηδενός	μηδεμιᾶς	μηδενός
Dat.	ἑνί	μιᾷ	ἑνί	οὐδενί	οὐδεμιᾷ	οὐδενί	μηδενί	μηδεμιᾷ	μηδενί
Acc.	ἕνα	μίαν	ἕν	οὐδένα	οὐδεμίαν	οὐδέν	μηδένα	μηδεμίαν	μηδέν

The Article

ὁ, ἡ, τό (1)

	M.	F.	N.
Singular			
Nom.	ὁ	ἡ	τό
Gen.	τοῦ	τῆς	τοῦ
Dat.	τῷ	τῇ	τῷ
Acc.	τόν	τήν	τό
Dual			
Nom./Acc.	τώ	τώ	τώ
Gen./Dat.	τοῖν	ταῖν	τοῖν
Plural			
Nom.	οἱ	αἱ	τά
Gen.	τῶν	τῶν	τῶν
Dat.	τοῖς/ τοῖσι(ν)	ταῖς/ ταῖσι(ν)	τοῖς/ τοῖσι(ν)
Acc.	τούς	τάς	τά

Pronouns and Adjectives

The Demonstrative Pronouns and Adjectives **οὗτος, αὕτη, τοῦτο** (2), **ὅδε, ἥδε, τόδε** (4),
and **ἐκεῖνος, ἐκείνη, ἐκεῖνο** (4)

	οὗτος, αὕτη, τοῦτο			**ὅδε, ἥδε, τόδε**		
	M.	F.	N.	M.	F.	N.
Singular						
Nom.	οὗτος	αὕτη	τοῦτο	ὅδε	ἥδε	τόδε
Gen.	τούτου	ταύτης	τούτου	τοῦδε	τῆσδε	τοῦδε
Dat.	τούτῳ	ταύτῃ	τούτῳ	τῷδε	τῇδε	τῷδε
Acc.	τοῦτον	ταύτην	τοῦτο	τόνδε	τήνδε	τόδε
Dual						
Nom./Acc.	τούτω	τούτω	τούτω	τώδε	τώδε	τώδε
Gen./Dat.	τούτοιν	ταύταιν	τούτοιν	τοῖνδε	ταῖνδε	τοῖνδε
Plural						
Nom.	οὗτοι	αὗται	ταῦτα	οἵδε	αἵδε	τάδε
Gen.	τούτων	τούτων	τούτων	τῶνδε	τῶνδε	τῶνδε
Dat.	τούτοις/ τούτοισι(ν)	ταύταις/ ταύταισι(ν)	τούτοις/ τούτοισι(ν)	τοῖσδε	ταῖσδε	τοῖσδε
Acc.	τούτους	ταύτᾱς	τούτους	τούσδε	τάσδε	τάδε

	ἐκεῖνος, ἐκείνη, ἐκεῖνο		
	M.	F.	N.
Singular			
Nom.	ἐκεῖνος	ἐκείνη	ἐκεῖνο
Gen.	ἐκείνου	ἐκείνης	ἐκείνου
Dat.	ἐκείνῳ	ἐκείνῃ	ἐκείνῳ
Acc.	ἐκεῖνον	ἐκείνην	ἐκεῖνο
Dual			
Nom./Acc.	ἐκείνω	ἐκείνω	ἐκείνω
Gen./Dat.	ἐκείνοιν	ἐκείναιν	ἐκείνοιν
Plural			
Nom.	ἐκεῖνοι	ἐκεῖναι	ἐκεῖνα
Gen.	ἐκείνων	ἐκείνων	ἐκείνων
Dat.	ἐκείνοις/ ἐκείνοισι(ν)	ἐκείναις/ ἐκείναισι(ν)	ἐκείνοις/ ἐκείνοισι(ν)
Acc.	ἐκείνους	ἐκείνᾱς	ἐκείνους

The Reciprocal Pronoun ——, **ἀλλήλων** (8)

	M.	F.	N.
Dual			
Nom.	—	—	—
Gen./Dat.	ἀλλήλοιν	ἀλλήλαιν	ἀλλήλοιν
Acc.	ἀλλήλω	ἀλλήλᾱ	ἀλλήλω
Plural			
Nom.	—	—	—
Gen.	ἀλλήλων	ἀλλήλων	ἀλλήλων
Dat.	ἀλλήλοις/	ἀλλήλαις/	ἀλλήλοις/
	ἀλλήλοισι(ν)	ἀλλήλαισι(ν)	ἀλλήλοισι(ν)
Acc.	ἀλλήλους	ἀλλήλᾱς	ἀλλήλους

The Relative Pronoun **ὅς, ἥ, ὅ** (5)

	M.	F.	N.
Singular			
Nom.	ὅς	ἥ	ὅ
Gen.	οὗ	ἧς	οὗ
Dat.	ᾧ	ἧ	ᾧ
Acc.	ὅν	ἥν	ὅ
Dual			
Nom./Acc.	ὥ	ἅ	ὥ
Gen./Dat.	οἷν	αἷν	οἷν
Plural			
Nom.	οἵ	αἵ	ἅ
Gen.	ὧν	ὧν	ὧν
Dat.	οἷς/οἷσι(ν)	αἷς/αἷσι(ν)	οἷς/οἷσι(ν)
Acc.	οὕς	ἅς	ἅ

The Interrogative Pronoun and Adjective **τίς, τί** (9)   The Enclitic Indefinite Pronoun and Adjective **τις, τι** (9)

	M./F.	N.		M./F.	N.
Singular					
Nom.	τίς	τί		τις	τι
Gen.	τίνος/τοῦ	τίνος/τοῦ		τινός/του	τινός/του
Dat.	τίνι/τῷ	τίνι/τῷ		τινί/τῳ	τινί/τῳ
Acc.	τίνα	τί		τινά	τι
Dual					
Nom./Acc.	τίνε	τίνε		τινέ	τινέ
Gen./Dat.	τίνοιν	τίνοιν		τινοῖν	τινοῖν
Plural					
Nom.	τίνες	τίνα		τινές	τινά/ἄττα
Gen.	τίνων	τίνων		τινῶν	τινῶν
Dat.	τίσι(ν)	τίσι(ν)		τισί(ν)	τισί(ν)
Acc.	τίνας	τίνα		τινάς	τινά/ἄττα

Personal Pronouns (6)

	1st person **ἐγώ, ἐμοῦ** **ἡμεῖς, ἡμῶν**	2nd person **σύ, σοῦ** **ὑμεῖς, ὑμῶν**	3rd person **αὐτοῦ, αὐτῆς, αὐτοῦ**		
Singular			M.	F.	N.
Nom.	ἐγώ	σύ	—	—	—
Gen.	ἐμοῦ/μου	σοῦ/σου	αὐτοῦ	αὐτῆς	αὐτοῦ
Dat.	ἐμοί/μοι	σοί/σοι	αὐτῷ	αὐτῇ	αὐτῷ
Acc.	ἐμέ/με	σέ/σε	αὐτόν	αὐτήν	αὐτό
Dual					
Nom./Acc.	νώ	σφώ	αὐτώ	αὐτά	αὐτώ
Gen./Dat.	νῷν	σφῷν	αὐτοῖν	αὐταῖν	αὐτοῖν
Plural					
Nom.	ἡμεῖς	ὑμεῖς	—	—	—
Gen.	ἡμῶν	ὑμῶν	αὐτῶν	αὐτῶν	αὐτῶν
Dat.	ἡμῖν	ὑμῖν	αὐτοῖς/ αὐτοῖσι(ν)	αὐτοῖς/ αὐτοῖσι(ν)	αὐτοῖς/ αὐτοῖσι(ν)
Acc.	ἡμᾶς	ὑμᾶς	αὐτούς	αὐτάς	αὐτά

Omega (Thematic) Verbs

Present Indicative (3)

παύω, παύσω, ἔπαυσα, πέπαυκα, πέπαυμαι, ἐπαύθην
Present Stem: **παυ-**

	Active	Middle/Passive	Active	Middle	Passive
Singular					
1	**-ω**	**-ομαι**	παύω	παύομαι	παύομαι
2	**-εις**	**-η/-ει**	παύεις	παύει/παύῃ	παύει/παύῃ
3	**-ει**	**-εται**	παύει	παύεται	παύεται
Dual					
2	**-ετον**	**-εσθον**	παύετον	παύεσθον	παύεσθον
3	**-ετον**	**-εσθον**	παύετον	παύεσθον	παύεσθον
Plural					
1	**-ομεν**	**-ομεθα**	παύομεν	παυόμεθα	παυόμεθα
2	**-ετε**	**-εσθε**	παύετε	παύεσθε	παύεσθε
3	**-ουσι(ν)**	**-ονται**	παύουσι(ν)	παύονται	παύονται

Present Active Indicative of Contracted Verbs (4)

Epsilon-contracted verbs: ποιέω, ποιήσω, ἐποίησα, πεποίηκα, πεποίημαι, ἐποιήθην
Alpha-contracted verbs: τῑμάω, τῑμήσω, ἐτίμησα, τετίμηκα, τετίμημαι, ἐτῑμήθην
Omicron-contracted verbs: δηλόω, δηλώσω, ἐδήλωσα, δεδήλωκα, δεδήλωμαι, ἐδηλώθην
Present Stems: **ποιε-, τῑμα-, δηλο-**

		Epsilon		Alpha		Omicron	
Singular							
1	**-ω**	ποιέω >	ποιῶ	τῑμάω >	τῑμῶ	δηλόω >	δηλῶ
2	**-εις**	ποιέεις >	ποιεῖς	τῑμάεις >	τῑμᾷς	δηλόεις >	δηλοῖς
3	**-ει**	ποιέει >	ποιεῖ	τῑμάει >	τῑμᾷ	δηλόει >	δηλοῖ
Dual							
2	**-ετον**	ποιέετον >	ποιεῖτον	τῑμάετον >	τῑμᾶτον	δηλόετον >	δηλοῦτον
3	**-ετον**	ποιέετον >	ποιεῖτον	τῑμάετον >	τῑμᾶτον	δηλόετον >	δηλοῦτον
Plural							
1	**-ομεν**	ποιέομεν >	ποιοῦμεν	τῑμάομεν >	τῑμῶμεν	δηλόομεν >	δηλοῦμεν
2	**-ετε**	ποιέετε >	ποιεῖτε	τῑμάετε >	τῑμᾶτε	δηλόετε >	δηλοῦτε
3	**-ουσι(ν)**	ποιέουσι(ν) >	ποιοῦσι(ν)	τῑμάουσι(ν) >	τῑμῶσι(ν)	δηλόουσι(ν) >	δηλοῦσι(ν)

Present Middle/Passive Indicative of Contracted Verbs (4)

Epsilon-contracted verbs: ποιέω , ποιήσω, ἐποίησα, πεποίηκα, πεποίημαι, ἐποιήθην

Alpha-contracted verbs: τῑμάω , τῑμήσω, ἐτίμησα, τετίμηκα, τετίμημαι, ἐτῑμήθην

Omicron-contracted verbs: δηλόω , δηλώσω, ἐδήλωσα, δεδήλωκα, δεδήλωμαι, ἐδηλώθην

Present Stems: **ποιε-, τῑμα-, δηλο-**

Singular

1	**-ομαι**	ποιέομαι >	ποιοῦμαι	τῑμάομαι >	τῑμῶμαι	δηλόομαι >	δηλοῦμαι
2	**-η/-ει**	ποιέῃ >	ποιῇ	τῑμάῃ >	τῑμᾷ	δηλόῃ >	δηλοῖ
		ποιέει >	ποιεῖ	τῑμάει >	τῑμᾷ	δηλόει >	δηλοῖ
3	**-εται**	ποιέεται >	ποιεῖται	τῑμάεται >	τῑμᾶται	δηλόεται >	δηλοῦται

Dual

2	**-εσθον**	ποιέεσθον >	ποιεῖσθον	τῑμάεσθον >	τῑμᾶσθον	δηλόεσθον >	δηλοῦσθον
3	**-εσθον**	ποιέεσθον >	ποιεῖσθον	τῑμάεσθον >	τῑμᾶσθον	δηλόεσθον >	δηλοῦσθον

Plural

1	**-ομεθα**	ποιεόμεθα >	ποιούμεθα	τῑμαόμεθα >	τῑμώμεθα	δηλοόμεθα >	δηλούμεθα
2	**-εσθε**	ποιέεσθε >	ποιεῖσθε	τῑμάεσθε >	τῑμᾶσθε	δηλόεσθε >	δηλοῦσθε
3	**-ονται**	ποιέονται >	ποιοῦνται	τῑμάονται >	τῑμῶνται	δηλόονται >	δηλοῦνται

Imperfect Indicative (3)

παύω , παύσω, ἔπαυσα, πέπαυκα, πέπαυμαι, ἐπαύθην

Augmented Present Stem: **ἐπαυ-**

	Active	Middle/Passive	Active	Middle	Passive
Singular					
1	**-ον**	**-ομην**	ἔπαυον	ἐπαυόμην	ἐπαυόμην
2	**-ες**	**-ου**	ἔπαυες	ἐπαύου	ἐπαύου
3	**-ε(ν)**	**-ετο**	ἔπαυε(ν)	ἐπαύετο	ἐπαύετο
Dual					
2	**-ετον**	**-εσθον**	ἐπαύετον	ἐπαύεσθον	ἐπαύεσθον
3	**-ετην**	**-εσθην**	ἐπαυέτην	ἐπαυέσθην	ἐπαυέσθην
Plural					
1	**-ομεν**	**-ομεθα**	ἐπαύομεν	ἐπαυόμεθα	ἐπαυόμεθα
2	**-ετε**	**-εσθε**	ἐπαύετε	ἐπαύεσθε	ἐπαύεσθε
3	**-ον**	**-οντο**	ἔπαυον	ἐπαύοντο	ἐπαύοντο

Imperfect Active Indicative of Contracted Verbs (4)

Epsilon-contracted verbs: ποιέω, ποιήσω, ἐποίησα, πεποίηκα, πεποίημαι, ἐποιήθην
Alpha-contracted verbs: τῑμάω, τῑμήσω, ἐτίμησα, τετίμηκα, τετίμημαι, ἐτῑμήθην
Omicron-contracted verbs: δηλόω, δηλώσω, ἐδήλωσα, δεδήλωκα, δεδήλωμαι, ἐδηλώθην
Augmented Present Stems: **ἐποιε-, ἐτῑμα-, ἐδηλο-**

Singular

1	**-ον**	ἐποίεον >	ἐποίουν	ἐτίμαον >	ἐτίμων	ἐδήλοον >	ἐδήλουν
2	**-ες**	ἐποίεες >	ἐποίεις	ἐτίμαες >	ἐτίμᾱς	ἐδήλοες >	ἐδήλους
3	**-ε**	ἐποίεε >	ἐποίει	ἐτίμαε >	ἐτίμᾱ	ἐδήλοε >	ἐδήλου

Dual

2	**-ετον**	ἐποιέετον >	ἐποιεῖτον	ἐτῑμάετον >	ἐτῑμᾶτον	ἐδηλόετον >	ἐδηλοῦτον
3	**-ετην**	ἐποιεέτην >	ἐποιείτην	ἐτῑμαέτην >	ἐτῑμάτην	ἐδηλοέτην >	ἐδηλούτην

Plural

1	**-ομεν**	ἐποιέομεν >	ἐποιοῦμεν	ἐτῑμάομεν >	ἐτῑμῶμεν	ἐδηλόομεν >	ἐδηλοῦμεν
2	**-ετε**	ἐποιέετε >	ἐποιεῖτε	ἐτῑμάετε >	ἐτῑμᾶτε	ἐδηλόετε >	ἐδηλοῦτε
3	**-ον**	ἐποίεον >	ἐποίουν	ἐτίμαον >	ἐτίμων	ἐδήλοον >	ἐδήλουν

Imperfect Middle/Passive Indicative of Contracted Verbs (4)

Epsilon-contracted verbs: ποιέω, ποιήσω, ἐποίησα, πεποίηκα, πεποίημαι, ἐποιήθην
Alpha-contracted verbs: τῑμάω, τῑμήσω, ἐτίμησα, τετίμηκα, τετίμημαι, ἐτῑμήθην
Omicron-contracted verbs: δηλόω, δηλώσω, ἐδήλωσα, δεδήλωκα, δεδήλωμαι, ἐδηλώθην
Augmented Present Stems: **ἐποιε-, ἐτῑμα-, ἐδηλο-**

Singular

1	**-ομην**	ἐποιεόμην >	ἐποιούμην	ἐτῑμαόμην >	ἐτῑμώμην	ἐδηλοόμην >	ἐδηλούμην
2	**-ου**	ἐποιέου >	ἐποιοῦ	ἐτῑμάου >	ἐτῑμῶ	ἐδηλόου	ἐδηλοῦ
3	**-ετο**	ἐποιέετο >	ἐποιεῖτο	ἐτῑμάετο >	ἐτῑμᾶτο	ἐδηλόετο	ἐδηλοῦτο

Dual

2	**-εσθον**	ἐποιέεσθον >	ἐποιεῖσθον	ἐτῑμάεσθον >	ἐτῑμᾶσθον	ἐδηλόεσθον >	ἐδηλοῦσθον
3	**-εσθην**	ἐποιεέσθην >	ἐποιείσθην	ἐτῑμαέσθην >	ἐτῑμᾶσθην	ἐδηλοέσθην >	ἐδηλούσθην

Plural

1	**-ομεθα**	ἐποιεόμεθα >	ἐποιούμεθα	ἐτῑμαόμεθα >	ἐτῑμώμεθα	ἐδηλοόμεθα >	ἐδηλούμεθα
2	**-εσθε**	ἐποιέεσθε >	ἐποιεῖσθε	ἐτῑμάεσθε >	ἐτῑμᾶσθε	ἐδηλόεσθε >	ἐδηλοῦσθε
3	**-οντο**	ἐποιέοντο >	ἐποιοῦντο	ἐτῑμάοντο >	ἐτῑμῶντο	ἐδηλόοντο >	ἐδηλοῦντο

Future Indicative (3)

παύω, παύσω, ἔπαυσα, πέπαυκα, πέπαυμαι, ἐπαύθην
Future Active and Middle Stem: **παυσ-**
Unaugmented Aorist Passive Stem: **παυθ-** + **-ησ-** (passive)

	Active	Middle/Passive	Active	Middle	Passive
Singular					
1	**-ω**	**-ομαι**	παύσω	παύσομαι	παυθήσομαι
2	**-εις**	**-η/-ει**	παύσεις	παύσει/παύση	παυθήσει/παυθήση
3	**-ει**	**-εται**	παύσει	παύσεται	παυθήσεται
Dual					
2	**-ετον**	**-εσθον**	παύσετον	παύσεσθον	παυθήσεσθον
3	**-ετον**	**-εσθον**	παύσετον	παύσεσθον	παυθήσεσθον
Plural					
1	**-ομεν**	**-ομεθα**	παύσομεν	παυσόμεθα	παυθησόμεθα
2	**-ετε**	**-εσθε**	παύσετε	παύσεσθε	παυθήσεσθε
3	**-ουσι(ν)**	**-ονται**	παύσουσι(ν)	παύσονται	παυθήσονται

First Aorist Active and Middle Indicative and Aorist Passive Indicative (6)

παύω, παύσω, ἔπαυσα, πέπαυκα, πέπαυμαι, ἐπαύθην
Augmented Aorist Active and Middle Stem: **ἐπαυσ-**
Augmented Aorist Passive Stem: **ἐπαυθ-**

	Active	Middle	Passive	Active	Middle	Passive
Singular						
1	**-α**	**-αμην**	**-ην**	ἔπαυσα	ἐπαυσάμην	ἐπαύθην
2	**-ας**	**-ω**	**-ης**	ἔπαυσας	ἐπαύσω	ἐπαύθης
3	**-ε(ν)**	**-ατο**	**-η**	ἔπαυσε(ν)	ἐπαύσατο	ἐπαύθη
Dual						
2	**-ατον**	**-ασθον**	**-ητον**	ἐπαύσατον	ἐπαύσασθον	ἐπαύθητον
3	**-ατην**	**-ασθην**	**-ητην**	ἐπαυσάτην	ἐπαυσάσθην	ἐπαυθήτην
Plural						
1	**-αμεν**	**-αμεθα**	**-ημεν**	ἐπαύσαμεν	ἐπαυσάμεθα	ἐπαύθημεν
2	**-ατε**	**-ασθε**	**-ητε**	ἐπαύσατε	ἐπαύσασθε	ἐπαύθητε
3	**-αν**	**-αντο**	**-ησαν**	ἔπαυσαν	ἐπαύσαντο	ἐπαύθησαν

Second Aorist Active and Middle Indicative (6)

ἄγω, ἄξω, ἤγαγον, ἦχα, ἦγμαι, ἤχθην
Augmented Aorist Active and Middle Stem: **ἠγαγ-**

	Active	Middle	Active	Middle
Singular				
1	**-ον**	**-ομην**	ἤγαγον	ἠγαγόμην
2	**-ες**	**-ου**	ἤγαγες	ἠγάγου
3	**-ε(ν)**	**-ετο**	ἤγαγε(ν)	ἠγάγετο
Dual				
2	**-ετον**	**-εσθον**	ἠγάγετον	ἠγάγεσθον
3	**-ετην**	**-εσθην**	ἠγαγέτην	ἠγαγέσθην
Plural				
1	**-ομεν**	**-ομεθα**	ἠγάγομεν	ἠγαγόμεθα
2	**-ετε**	**-εσθε**	ἠγάγετε	ἠγάγεσθε
3	**-ον**	**-οντο**	ἤγαγον	ἠγάγοντο

Perfect Indicative (8)

παύω, παύσω, ἔπαυσα, πέπαυκα, πέπαυμαι, ἐπαύθην
Perfect Active Stem: **πεπαυκ-**
Perfect Middle/Passive Stem: **πεπαυ-**

	Active	Middle/Passive	Active	Middle	Passive
Singular					
1	**-α**	**-μαι**	πέπαυκα	πέπαυμαι	πέπαυμαι
2	**-ας**	**-σαι**	πέπαυκας	πέπαυσαι	πέπαυσαι
3	**-ε(ν)**	**-ται**	πέπαυκε(ν)	πέπαυται	πέπαυται
Dual					
2	**-ατον**	**-σθον**	πεπαύκατον	πέπαυσθον	πέπαυσθον
3	**-ατον**	**-σθον**	πεπαύκατον	πέπαυσθον	πέπαυσθον
Plural					
1	**-αμεν**	**-μεθα**	πεπαύκαμεν	πεπαύμεθα	πεπαύμεθα
2	**-ατε**	**-σθε**	πεπαύκατε	πέπαυσθε	πέπαυσθε
3	**-ᾱσι(ν)**	**-νται**	πεπαύκᾱσι(ν)	πέπαυνται	πέπαυνται

Pluperfect Indicative (8)

παύω, παύσω, ἔπαυσα, ⟦πέπαυκα⟧, ⟦πέπαυμαι⟧, ἐπαύθην
Augmented Perfect Active Stem: **ἐπεπαυκ-**
Augmented Perfect Middle/Passive Stem: **ἐπεπαυ-**

	Active	Middle/Passive	Active	Middle	Passive
Singular					
1	**-η**	**-μην**	ἐπεπαύκη	ἐπεπαύμην	ἐπεπαύμην
2	**-ης**	**-σο**	ἐπεπαύκης	ἐπέπαυσο	ἐπέπαυσο
3	**-ει(ν)**	**-το**	ἐπεπαύκει(ν)	ἐπέπαυτο	ἐπέπαυτο
Dual					
2	**-ετον**	**-σθον**	ἐπεπαύκετον	ἐπέπαυσθον	ἐπέπαυσθον
3	**-ετην**	**-σθην**	ἐπεπαυκέτην	ἐπεπαύσθην	ἐπεπαύσθην
Plural					
1	**-εμεν**	**-μεθα**	ἐπεπαύκεμεν	ἐπεπαύμεθα	ἐπεπαύμεθα
2	**-ετε**	**-σθε**	ἐπεπαύκετε	ἐπέπαυσθε	ἐπέπαυσθε
3	**-εσαν**	**-ντο**	ἐπεπαύκεσαν	ἐπέπαυντο	ἐπέπαυντο

Perfect and Pluperfect Middle/Passive Indicative: Consonant Stems (8)

ὁράω, ὄψομαι, εἶδον, ἑώρᾱκα/ἑόρᾱκα, ἑώρᾱμαι/ ὦμμαι , ὤφθην
πείθω, πείσω, ἔπεισα, πέπεικα, πέπεισμαι , ἐπείσθην
ἄρχω, ἄρξω, ἦρξα, ἦρχα, ἦργμαι , ἤρχθην

		Stem Ending in a Labial ὠπ-	Stem Ending in a Dental πεπειθ-	Stem Ending in a Palatal ἠρχ-
Perfect				
Singular				
1	**-μαι**	ὦμμαι	πέπεισμαι	ἦργμαι
2	**-σαι**	ὦψαι	πέπεισαι	ἦρξαι
3	**-ται**	ὦπται	πέπεισται	ἦρκται
Dual				
2	**-σθον**	ὦφθον	πέπεισθον	ἦρχθον
3	**-σθον**	ὦφθον	πέπεισθον	ἦρχθον
Plural				
1	**-μεθα**	ὤμμεθα	πεπείσμεθα	ἤργμεθα
2	**-σθε**	ὦφθε	πέπεισθε	ἦρχθε
3	—	—	—	—
Pluperfect				
Singular				
1	**-μην**	ὤμμην	ἐπεπείσμην	ἤργμην
2	**-σο**	ὦψο	ἐπέπεισο	ἦρξο
3	**-το**	ὦπτο	ἐπέπειστο	ἦρκτο
Dual				
2	**-σθον**	ὦφθον	ἐπέπεισθον	ἦρχθον
3	**-σθην**	ὤφθην	ἐπεπείσθην	ἦρχθην
Plural				
1	**-μεθα**	ὤμμεθα	ἐπεπείσμεθα	ἤργμεθα
2	**-σθε**	ὦφθε	ἐπέπεισθε	ἦρχθε
3	—	—	—	—

Infinitives

παύω, παύσω, ἔπαυσα, πέπαυκα, πέπαυμαι, ἐπαύθην
ἄγω, ἄξω, ἤγαγον, ἦχα, ἦγμαι, ἤχθην
Present Stem: **παυ-** (3)
Future Active and Middle Stem: **παυσ-** (3)
Unaugmented Aorist Passive Stem: **παυθ- + -ησ-** (3)
Unaugmented First Aorist Active and Middle Stem: **παυσ-** (6)
Unaugmented Second Aorist Active and Middle Stem: **ἀγαγ-** (6)
Unaugmented Aorist Passive Stem: **παυθ-** (6)
Perfect Active Stem: **πεπαυκ-** (8)
Perfect Middle/Passive Stem: **πεπαυ-** (8)

Tense	Active	Middle	Passive	Active	Middle	Passive
Present	**-ειν**	**-εσθαι**	**-εσθαι**	παύειν	παύεσθαι	παύεσθαι
Future	**-ειν**	**-εσθαι**	**-εσθαι**	παύσειν	παύσεσθαι	παυθήσεσθαι
1st Aorist	**-αι**	**-ασθαι**		παῦσαι[P]	παύσασθαι	
2nd Aorist	**-εῖν**	**-έσθαι**		ἀγαγεῖν	ἀγαγέσθαι[P]	
Aorist			**-ῆναι**			παυθῆναι[P]
Perfect	**-έναι**	**-σθαι**	**-σθαι**	πεπαυκέναι[P]	πεπαῦσθαι[P]	πεπαῦσθαι[P]

Forms marked with a [P] have persistent accents on their penults. The second aorist active infinitive has a persistent accent on its ultima. All other infinitives have recessive accents.

Present Infinitives of Contracted Verbs (4)

Epsilon-contracted verbs: ποιέω, ποιήσω, ἐποίησα, πεποίηκα, πεποίημαι, ἐποιήθην
Alpha-contracted verbs: τīμάω, τīμήσω, ἐτίμησα, τετίμηκα, τετίμημαι, ἐτīμήθην
Omicron-contracted verbs: δηλόω, δηλώσω, ἐδήλωσα, δεδήλωκα, δεδήλωμαι, ἐδηλώθην
Present Stems: **ποιε-, τīμα-, δηλο-**

Active			Middle/Passive		
-εεν	ποιέεεν >	ποιεῖν	**-εσθαι**	ποιέεσθαι >	ποιεῖσθαι
	τīμάεεν >	τīμᾶν		τīμάεσθαι >	τīμᾶσθαι
	δηλόεεν >	δηλοῦν		δηλόεσθαι >	δηλοῦσθαι

Participles, Overview (7)

παύω, παύσω, ἔπαυσα, πέπαυκα, πέπαυμαι, ἐπαύθην

ἄγω, ἄξω, ἤγαγον, ἦχα, ἦγμαι, ἤχθην

ποιέω, ποιήσω, ἐποίησα, πεποίηκα, πεποίημαι, ἐποιήθην
τιμάω, τιμήσω, ἐτίμησα, τετίμηκα, τετίμημαι, ἐτιμήθην
δηλόω, δηλώσω, ἐδήλωσα, δεδήλωκα, δεδήλωμαι, ἐδηλώθην

Present Stem: **παυ-**; Unaugmented First Aorist Active and Middle Stem: **παυσ-**;
Unaugmented Aorist Passive Stem: **παυθ-**;

Unaugmented Second Aorist Active and Middle Stem: **ἀγαγ-** (second aorist active and middle)

Present Stem: **ποιε-**
Present Stem: **τιμα-**
Present Stem: **δηλο-**

	Active	Middle	Passive
Present			
Nom.	παύων, παύουσα, παῦον	παυόμενος, παυομένη, παυόμενον	παυόμενος, παυομένη, παυόμενον
Gen.	παύοντος, παυούσης, παύοντος		
Nom.	ποιῶν, ποιοῦσα, ποιοῦν	ποιούμενος, ποιουμένη, ποιούμενον	ποιούμενος, ποιουμένη, ποιούμενον
Gen.	ποιοῦντος, ποιούσης, ποιοῦντος		
Nom.	τιμῶν, τιμῶσα, τιμῶν	τιμώμενος, τιμωμένη, τιμώμενον	τιμώμενος, τιμωμένη, τιμώμενον
Gen.	τιμῶντος, τιμώσης, τιμῶντος		
Nom.	δηλῶν, δηλοῦσα, δηλοῦν	δηλούμενος, δηλουμένη, δηλούμενον	δηλούμενος, δηλουμένη, δηλούμενον
Gen.	δηλοῦντος, δηλούσης, δηλοῦντος		
First Aorist Active and Middle and Aorist Passive			
Nom.	παύσας, παύσασα, παῦσαν	παυσάμενος, παυσαμένη, παυσάμενον	παυθείς, παυθεῖσα, παυθέν
Gen.	παύσαντος, παυσάσης, παύσαντος		παυθέντος, παυθείσης, παυθέντος
Second Aorist Active and Middle			
Nom.	ἀγαγών, ἀγαγοῦσα, ἀγαγόν	ἀγαγόμενος, ἀγαγομένη, ἀγαγόμενον	
Gen.	ἀγαγόντος, ἀγαγούσης, ἀγαγόντος		

Present Participle (7)
Present stem: **παυ-**

	Active M.	Active F.	Active N.	Middle M.	Middle F.	Middle N.	Passive M.	Passive F.	Passive N.
Singular									
Nom.	παύων	παύουσα	παῦον	παυόμενος	παυομένη	παυόμενον	παυόμενος	παυομένη	παυόμενον
Gen.	παύοντος	παυούσης	παύοντος	παυομένου	παυομένης	παυομένου	παυομένου	παυομένης	παυομένου
Dat.	παύοντι	παυούσῃ	παύοντι	παυομένῳ	παυομένῃ	παυομένῳ	παυομένῳ	παυομένῃ	παυομένῳ
Acc.	παύοντα	παύουσαν	παῦον	παυόμενον	παυομένην	παυόμενον	παυόμενον	παυομένην	παυόμενον
Voc.	παύων	παύουσα	παῦον	παυόμενε	παυομένη	παυόμενον	παυόμενε	παυομένη	παυόμενον
Dual									
Nom./Voc./Acc.	παύοντε	παυούσᾱ	παύοντε	παυομένω	παυομένᾱ	παυομένω	παυομένω	παυομένᾱ	παυομένω
Gen./Dat.	παυόντοιν	παυούσαιν	παυόντοιν	παυομένοιν	παυομέναιν	παυομένοιν	παυομένοιν	παυομέναιν	παυομένοιν
Plural									
Nom.	παύοντες	παύουσαι	παύοντα	παυόμενοι	παυόμεναι	παυόμενα	παυόμενοι	παυόμεναι	παυόμενα
Gen.	παυόντων	παυουσῶν	παυόντων	παυομένων	παυομένων	παυομένων	παυομένων	παυομένων	παυομένων
Dat.	παύουσι(ν)	παυούσαις	παύουσι(ν)	παυομένοις	παυομέναις	παυομένοις	παυομένοις	παυομέναις	παυομένοις
Acc.	παύοντας	παυούσᾱς	παύοντα	παυομένους	παυομένᾱς	παυόμενα	παυομένους	παυομένᾱς	παυόμενα
Voc.	παύοντες	παύουσαι	παύοντα	παυόμενοι	παυόμεναι	παυόμενα	παυόμενοι	παυόμεναι	παυόμενα

First Aorist Active and Middle Participles (7)
Unaugmented First Aorist Active and Middle Stem: **παυσ-**

	Active			Middle		
	M.	F.	N.	M.	F.	N.
Singular						
Nom.	παύσᾱς	παύσᾱσα	παῦσαν	παυσάμενος	παυσαμένη	παυσάμενον
Gen.	παύσαντος	παυσάσης	παύσαντος	παυσαμένου	παυσαμένης	παυσαμένου
Dat.	παύσαντι	παυσάσῃ	παύσαντι	παυσαμένῳ	παυσαμένῃ	παυσαμένῳ
Acc.	παύσαντα	παύσᾱσαν	παῦσαν	παυσάμενον	παυσαμένην	παυσάμενον
Voc.	παύσᾱς	παύσᾱσα	παῦσαν	παυσάμενε	παυσαμένη	παυσάμενον
Dual						
Nom./Voc./Acc.	παύσαντε	παυσάσᾱ	παύσαντε	παυσαμένω	παυσαμένᾱ	παυσαμένω
Gen./Dat.	παυσάντοιν	παυσάσαιν	παυσάντοιν	παυσαμένοιν	παυσαμέναιν	παυσαμένοιν
Plural						
Nom.	παύσαντες	παύσᾱσαι	παύσαντα	παυσάμενοι	παυσάμεναι	παυσάμενα
Gen.	παυσάντων	παυσᾱσῶν	παυσάντων	παυσαμένων	παυσαμένων	παυσαμένων
Dat.	παύσᾱσι(ν)	παυσάσαις	παύσᾱσι(ν)	παυσαμένοις	παυσαμέναις	παυσαμένοις
Acc.	παύσαντας	παυσάσᾱς	παύσαντα	παυσαμένους	παυσαμένᾱς	παυσάμενα
Voc.	παύσαντες	παύσᾱσαι	παύσαντα	παυσάμενοι	παυσάμεναι	παυσάμενα

Aorist Passive Participle (7)
Unaugmented Aorist Passive Stem: **παυθ-**

	Passive		
	M.	F.	N.
Singular			
Nom.	παυθείς	παυθεῖσα	παυθέν
Gen.	παυθέντος	παυθείσης	παυθέντος
Dat.	παυθέντι	παυθείσῃ	παυθέν
Acc.	παυθέντα	παυθεῖσαν	παυθέν
Voc.	παυθείς	παυθεῖσα	παυθέν
Dual			
Nom./Voc./Acc.	παυθέντε	παυθείσᾱ	παυθέντε
Gen./Dat.	παυθέντοιν	παυθείσαιν	παυθέντοιν
Plural			
Nom.	παυθέντες	παυθεῖσαι	παυθέντα
Gen.	παυθέντων	παυθεισῶν	παυθέντων
Dat.	παυθεῖσι(ν)	παυθείσαις	παυθεῖσι(ν)
Acc.	παυθέντας	παυθείσᾱς	παυθέντα
Voc.	παυθέντες	παυθεῖσαι	παυθέντα

Second Aorist Active and Middle Participles (7)
Unaugmented Second Aorist Active and Middle Stem: **ἀγαγ-**

	Active			Middle		
	M.	F.	N.	M.	F.	N.
Singular						
Nom.	ἀγαγών	ἀγαγοῦσα	ἀγαγόν	ἀγαγόμενος	ἀγαγομένη	ἀγαγόμενον
Gen.	ἀγαγόντος	ἀγαγούσης	ἀγαγόντος	ἀγαγομένου	ἀγαγομένης	ἀγαγομένου
Dat.	ἀγαγόντι	ἀγαγούσῃ	ἀγαγόντι	ἀγαγομένῳ	ἀγαγομένῃ	ἀγαγομένῳ
Acc.	ἀγαγόντα	ἀγαγοῦσαν	ἀγαγόν	ἀγαγόμενον	ἀγαγομένην	ἀγαγόμενον
Voc.	ἀγαγών	ἀγαγοῦσα	ἀγαγόν	ἀγαγόμενε	ἀγαγομένη	ἀγαγόμενον
Dual						
Nom./Voc./Acc.	ἀγαγόντε	ἀγαγούσᾱ	ἀγαγόντε	ἀγαγομένω	ἀγαγομένᾱ	ἀγαγομένω
Gen./Dat.	ἀγαγόντοιν	ἀγαγούσαιν	ἀγαγόντοιν	ἀγαγομένοιν	ἀγαγομέναιν	ἀγαγομένοιν
Plural						
Nom.	ἀγαγόντες	ἀγαγοῦσαι	ἀγαγόντα	ἀγαγόμενοι	ἀγαγόμεναι	ἀγαγόμενα
Gen.	ἀγαγόντων	ἀγαγουσῶν	ἀγαγόντων	ἀγαγομένων	παυσαμένων	ἀγαγομένων
Dat.	ἀγαγοῦσι(ν)	ἀγαγούσαις	ἀγαγοῦσι(ν)	ἀγαγομένοις	ἀγαγομέναις	ἀγαγομένοις
Acc.	ἀγαγόντας	ἀγαγούσᾱς	ἀγαγόντα	ἀγαγομένους	ἀγαγομένᾱς	ἀγαγόμενα
Voc.	ἀγαγόντες	ἀγαγοῦσαι	ἀγαγόντα	ἀγαγόμενοι	ἀγαγόμεναι	ἀγαγόμενα

Irregular Conjugations

ζάω, ζήσω, ——, ——, ——, —— (8)

Active

	Present Indicative	Imperfect Indicative
Singular		
1	ζῶ	ἔζων
2	ζῇς	ἔζης
3	ζῇ	ἔζη
Dual		
2	ζῆτον	ἐζῆτον
3	ζῆτον	ἐζήτην
Plural		
1	ζῶμεν	ἔζωμεν
2	ζῆτε	ἔζητε
3	ζῶσι(ν)	ἔζων

Present Active Infinitive: ζῆν
Present Active Participle: Nom. ζῶν, ζῶσα, ζῶν
                        Gen. ζῶντος, ζώσης, ζῶντος

οἶδα, εἴσομαι, ——, ——, ——, —— (9)
Active

	Perfect Indicative	Pluperfect Indicative
Singular		
1	οἶδα	ᾔδη/ᾔδειν
2	οἶσθα	ᾔδησθα/ᾔδεις
3	οἶδε(ν)	ᾔδει(ν)
Dual		
2	ἴστον	ᾖστον
3	ἴστον	ᾔστην
Plural		
1	ἴσμεν	ᾖσμεν
2	ἴστε	ᾖστε
3	ἴσᾱσι(ν)	ᾖσαν/ᾔδεσαν

Perfect Active Infinitive: εἰδέναι

-μι (Athematic) Verbs

Irregular Conjugations

εἰμί, ἔσομαι, ——, ——, ——, —— (5)

Active

	Present Indicative	Imperfect Indicative	Future Indicative
Singular			
1	εἰμί	ἦ/ἦν	ἔσομαι
2	εἶ	ἦσθα	ἔσῃ/ἔσει
3	ἐστί(ν)	ἦν	ἔσται
Dual			
2	ἐστόν	ἦστον	ἔσεσθον
3	ἐστόν	ἤστην	ἔσεσθον
Plural			
1	ἐσμέν	ἦμεν	ἐσόμεθα
2	ἐστέ	ἦτε	ἔσεσθε
3	εἰσί(ν)	ἦσαν	ἔσονται

Present Active Infinitive: εἶναι
Present Active Participle: Nom. ὤν, οὖσα, ὄν
                           Gen. ὄντος, οὔσης, ὄντος

φημί, φήσω, ἔφησα, ——, ——, —— (8)
Long-vowel grade stem: φη-
Short-vowel grade stem: φα-

Active

	Present Indicative	Imperfect Indicative
Singular		
1	φημί	ἔφην
2	φής	ἔφης/ἔφησθα
3	φησί(ν)	ἔφη
Dual		
2	φατόν	ἔφατον
3	φατόν	ἐφάτην
Plural		
1	φαμέν	ἔφαμεν
2	φατέ	ἔφατε
3	φᾱσί(ν)	ἔφασαν

Present Active Infinitive: φάναι
Present Active Participle: Nom. φάς, φᾶσα, φάν
                           Gen. φάντος, φάσης, φάντος

GREEK TO ENGLISH VOCABULARY

This Greek to English Vocabulary includes all the words from the vocabulary lists in Part 1 of *Learn to Read Greek*. Numbers in parentheses refer to chapter (e.g., 2) or section (e.g., §12) in which the vocabulary word is introduced. If only a chapter number is listed, the word or phrase appears in the chapter-opening vocabulary list; if the chapter number is followed by a dagger (†), the word or phrase appears in the vocabulary notes or in a section of the chapter.

ἀγαθός, ἀγαθή, ἀγαθόν good (2)

ἀγορά, ἀγορᾶς, ἡ agora, marketplace (1)

ἄγω, ἄξω, ἤγαγον, ἦχα, ἦγμαι, ἤχθην lead, bring; keep; *middle*, carry away with oneself; marry (5)

ἀγών, ἀγῶνος, ὁ contest; struggle (6)

ἄδηλος, ἄδηλον unclear (6)

ἀδικέω, ἀδικήσω, ἠδίκησα, ἠδίκηκα, ἠδίκημαι, ἠδικήθην (do) wrong (to); injure (4)

ἄδικος, ἄδικον unjust (2)

ἀεί (adv.) always (5)

ἀθάνατος, ἀθάνατον deathless, immortal (2)

Ἀθηνᾶ, Ἀθηνᾶς, ἡ Athena (§59)

Ἀθῆναι, Ἀθηνῶν, αἱ Athens (6)

Ἀθηναῖος, Ἀθηναίᾱ, Ἀθηναῖον Athenian; *masc. pl. subst.*, Athenians (2)

ἄθλιος, ἀθλίᾱ, ἄθλιον wretched, miserable (9)

Ἅιδης, Ἅιδου, ὁ Hades (2)

αἰεί (adv.) always (5)

αἰσχρός, αἰσχρά, αἰσχρόν disgraceful, shameful; ugly (3)

αἰτίᾱ, αἰτίᾱς, ἡ cause; responsibility (2)

ἀκούω, ἀκούσομαι, ἤκουσα, ἀκήκοα, ——, ἠκούσθην listen (to), hear (of) (5)

Ἀλέξανδρος, Ἀλεξάνδρου, ὁ Alexander (1)

ἀλήθεια, ἀληθείᾱς, ἡ truth (2)

ἀληθής, ἀληθές true, real; truthful (7)

ἀλλά (conj.) but; *in narrative transitions and responses in dialogue,* but yet; well . . . (2)

ἀλλὰ γάρ but as a matter of fact (3†)

ἀλλὰ δή but indeed, and in particular (4†)

——, ἀλλήλων (reciprocal pronoun) one another, each other (8)

ἄλλος, ἄλλη, ἄλλο other, another; *in the attributive position,* the rest (of) (5)

ἀμαθής, ἀμαθές ignorant, foolish (9)

ἀμαθίᾱ, ἀμαθίᾱς, ἡ ignorance; stupidity (9)

ἄν (particle) *used in the apodoses of some conditional sentences* (9)

ἀνάγκη, ἀνάγκης, ἡ necessity (5)

ἀνδρείᾱ, ἀνδρείᾱς, ἡ manliness; courage (9)

ἄνευ (prep. + gen.) without (6)

ἀνήρ, ἀνδρός, ὁ man; husband (6)

ἄνθρωπος, ἀνθρώπου, ὁ or ἡ human being, man (1)

ἀξιόω, ἀξιώσω, ἠξίωσα, ἠξίωκα, ἠξίωμαι, ἠξιώθην think worthy; think (it) right; expect, require (4)

ἅπᾱς, ἅπᾱσα, ἅπαν (quite) all, every; whole (6)

ἀπό (prep. + gen.) (away) from (2)

ἀπὸ κοινοῦ, at public expense (3†)

ἀποθνήσκω, ἀποθανοῦμαι, ἀπέθανον, τέθνηκα, ——, —— die; *perfect,* be dead (8)

ἀποκτείνω, ἀποκτενῶ, ἀπέκτεινα, ἀπέκτονα, ——, —— kill (8)

Ἀπόλλων, Ἀπόλλωνος, ὁ (voc. = Ἄπολλον) Apollo (§59)

ἀποπέμπω, ἀποπέμψω, ἀπέπεμψα,
  ἀποπέπομφα, ἀποπέπεμμαι,
  ἀπεπέμφθην send away; *middle,* send
  away from oneself (7)
ἆρα (interrog. particle) *introduces a question* (3)
ἄρα (postpositive particle) (so) then,
  therefore; after all (9)
ἀρετή, ἀρετῆς, ἡ excellence; valor;
  virtue (4)
Ἄρης, Ἄρεος/Ἄρεως, ὁ (voc. = Ἄρες) Ares
  (§59)
Ἄρτεμις, Ἀρτέμιδος, ἡ Artemis (§59)
ἀρχή, ἀρχῆς, ἡ beginning; (supreme) power,
  rule; empire (2)
  ἀρχὴν ποιεῖσθαι, to make a beginning,
  to begin (4†)
ἄρχω, ἄρξω, ἦρξα, ἦρχα, ἦργμαι, ἤρχθην
  rule (+ gen.); *middle,* begin (+ gen.) (3)
ἄρχων, ἄρχοντος, ὁ ruler, commander;
  archon, magistrate (5)
Ἀτρείδης, Ἀτρείδου, ὁ Atreides, son of
  Atreus (2)
αὐτός, αὐτή, αὐτό -self, very; same (6)
αὐτοῦ, αὐτῆς, αὐτοῦ him, her, it; them (6)
Ἀφροδίτη, Ἀφροδίτης, ἡ Aphrodite (§59)

βάρβαρος, βάρβαρον non-Greek, foreign;
  barbarous; *masc. pl. subst.,* foreigners;
  barbarians (5)
βίος, βίου, ὁ life; livelihood (4)
βουλή, βουλῆς, ἡ will; plan; council; advice (1)
  βουλὴν ποιεῖσθαι, to make a plan, to
  plan (4†)
βούλομαι, βουλήσομαι, ——, ——,
  βεβούλημαι, ἐβουλήθην want, wish (6)
βροτός, βροτοῦ, ὁ mortal (4)

γαῖα, γαίας, ἡ earth; land (3)
γάρ (postpositive conj.) *explanatory,* for;
  confirming, indeed, in fact (3)
γε (enclitic particle) *limiting,* at least, at any
  rate; *emphasizing,* indeed (5)

γένος, γένους, τό race, descent; family; sort,
  kind (7)
γῆ, γῆς, ἡ earth; land (3)
γίγνομαι, γενήσομαι, ἐγενόμην, γέγονα,
  γεγένημαι, —— become; happen;
  arise, be born (6)
γνώμη, γνώμης, ἡ judgment; spirit,
  inclination; opinion (1)
  γνώμην προσέχειν, to pay attention (7)
Γοργίας, Γοργίου, ὁ Gorgias (2)
γυνή, γυναικός, ἡ woman; wife (7)

δαίμων, δαίμονος, ὁ or ἡ divinity, divine
  power; spirit (5)
δέ (postpositive conj.) *adversative,* but;
  connective, and (3)
  μέν . . . , δέ . . . on the one hand . . . ,
  on the other hand . . . ; . . . , but . . . (3)
δεῖ, δεήσει, ἐδέησε(ν), ——, ——, ——
  (impersonal verb) it is necessary, must;
  there is need (+ gen.) (5)
δεινός, δεινή, δεινόν fearsome, terrible;
  marvelous, strange; clever (2)
δεσπότης, δεσπότου, ὁ master, lord; absolute
  ruler (6)
δέχομαι, δέξομαι, ἐδεξάμην, ——, δέδεγμαι,
  —— accept, receive; welcome (6)
δή (postpositive particle) certainly, indeed,
  of course (4)
δῆλος, δήλη, δῆλον clear (6)
δηλόω, δηλώσω, ἐδήλωσα, δεδήλωκα,
  δεδήλωμαι, ἐδηλώθην show, make
  clear, reveal (4)
Δημήτηρ, Δημητρός, ἡ (voc. = Δήμητερ)
  Demeter (§59)
δῆμος, δήμου, ὁ (the) people (2)
Δημοσθένης, Δημοσθένους, ὁ Demosthenes
  (7)
διά (prep. + gen.) through; (prep. + acc.) on
  account of, because of (2)
  διὰ τέλους, through to the end,
  completely (9†)

διαλέγομαι, διαλέξομαι, ——, ——,
    διείλεγμαι, διελέχθην talk (with),
    converse (with) (+ dat.); discuss (with)
    (+ dat.) (7)

διαφθείρω, διαφθερῶ, διέφθειρα,
    διέφθαρκα/διέφθορα, διέφθαρμαι,
    διεφθάρην destroy (utterly); corrupt,
    ruin (9)

διδάσκαλος, διδασκάλου, ὁ teacher (5)

διδάσκω, διδάξω, ἐδίδαξα, δεδίδαχα,
    δεδίδαγμαι, ἐδιδάχθην teach;
    explain; *middle,* cause to be taught (3)

δίκαιος, δικαίᾱ, δίκαιον right, just (2)

δικαιοσύνη, δικαιοσύνης, ἡ justice (9)

δίκη, δίκης, ἡ justice (1)
    δίκην λαμβάνειν, to exact punishment
    (9)

Διόνῡσος, Διονῡ́σου, ὁ Dionysus (§59)

δόξα, δόξης, ἡ opinion, belief; reputation;
    glory; expectation (2)

δοῦλος, δούλου, ὁ slave (6)

δύναμις, δυνάμεως, ἡ power; ability (7)

δῶμα, δώματος, τό *sing. or pl.,* house,
    home (5)

ἐγώ, ἐμοῦ/μου I; me (6)

ἐθέλω/θέλω, ἐθελήσω, ἠθέλησα, ἠθέληκα,
    ——, —— be willing, wish (3)

εἰ (conj.) if (9)

εἰμί, ἔσομαι, ——, ——, ——, —— be;
    exist; *impersonal,* it is possible (5)

εἰρήνη, εἰρήνης, ἡ peace (1)
    ἐπὶ εἰρήνης, in (time of) peace (4†)

εἰς (prep. + acc.) to, toward; into; against;
    with a view to, regarding (1)
    εἰς/ἐς κοινόν, openly, publicly (3†)
    ἐς/εἰς τέλος, to the end, in the long
    run (9†)

εἷς, μία, ἕν (numerical adj.) one (9)

ἐκ (prep. + gen.) (out) from, out of; resulting
    from, in accordance with (1)
    ἐκ κοινοῦ, at public expense (3†)

ἕκαστος, ἑκάστη, ἕκαστον each (of several) (7)

ἐκεῖ (adv.) there (9)

ἐκεῖνος, ἐκείνη, ἐκεῖνο (demonstr. adj./
    pron.) that; *pl.,* those (4)

Ἕκτωρ, Ἕκτορος, ὁ Hector (5)

Ἑλένη, Ἑλένης, ἡ Helen (1)

ἐλευθερίᾱ, ἐλευθερίᾱς, ἡ freedom (6)

ἐλεύθερος, ἐλευθέρᾱ, ἐλεύθερον free (6)

Ἑλλάς, Ἑλλάδος, ἡ Hellas, Greece (7)

Ἕλλην, Ἕλληνος, ὁ Hellene, Greek (5)

ἐλπίς, ἐλπίδος, ἡ hope; expectation (5)

ἐμός, ἐμή, ἐμόν my (6)

ἐν (prep. + dat.) in, on; among, in the
    presence of (1)

ἐναντίος, ἐναντίᾱ, ἐναντίον facing,
    opposite; opposing, contrary (to)
    (+ gen. or dat.) (8)
    (τὸ) ἐναντίον, in opposition, conversely
    (9†)

ἐναντίως (adv.) in opposition, conversely
    (8†)

ἐξ (prep. + gen.) (out) from, out of; resulting
    from, in accordance with (1)

ἐπί (prep. + gen.) in, on, upon; (prep. + dat.)
    in, on; in addition to; for (i.e., because
    of); on condition of; (prep. + acc.) to;
    against; for (the purpose of) (4)
    ἐπὶ εἰρήνης, in (time of) peace (4†)
    ἐπὶ (τὸ) πολύ to a great extent; for the
    most part (4†)

ἕπομαι, ἕψομαι, ἑσπόμην, ——, ——, ——
    (+ dat.) follow (9)

ἔπος, ἔπους, τό word; *pl.,* lines (of verse),
    epic poetry (7)

Ἐρατώ, Ἐρατοῦς, ἡ Erato (§59)

ἔργον, ἔργου, τό task, work; deed (1)

Ἑρμῆς, Ἑρμοῦ, ὁ Hermes (4)

ἔρχομαι, ἐλεύσομαι, ἦλθον, ἐλήλυθα, ——,
    —— go, come (6)

——, ἐρῶ, ——, εἴρηκα, εἴρημαι, ἐρρήθην
    say, tell (of), speak (of) (8)

ἔρως, ἔρωτος, ὁ desire, passion, love (5)

Ἔρως, Ἔρωτος, ὁ (voc. = Ἔρως)
    Eros (§59)

ἐς (prep. + acc.) to, toward; into; against; with a view to, regarding (1)

Ἑστίᾱ, Ἑστίᾱς, ἡ Hestia (§59)

ἑταῖρος, ἑταίρου, ὁ companion (1)

ἔτι (adv.) still, yet (8)

εὖ (adv.) well (3)

εὐδαίμων, εὔδαιμον fortunate, happy (9)

Εὐρῑπίδης, Εὐρῑπίδου, ὁ Euripides (2)

Εὐτέρπη, Εὐτέρπης, ἡ Euterpe (§59)

ἐχθρός, ἐχθρά, ἐχθρόν hated, hateful; hostile; *masc. subst.*, enemy (2)

ἔχω, ἕξω/σχήσω, ἔσχον, ἔσχηκα, -έσχημαι, —— have, hold; inhabit, occupy; *intrans.*, be able (+ inf.); be (+ adv.); *middle*, hold on to, cling to (+ gen.) (4)

ζάω, ζήσω, ——, ——, ——, —— be alive, live (8)

Ζεύς, Διός, ὁ Zeus (5)

ζηλόω, ζηλώσω, ἐζήλωσα, ἐζήλωκα, ——, —— emulate; envy; *passive*, be deemed fortunate (7)

ζῷον, ζῴου, τό living being; animal (1)

ἤ (conj.) or (2)
    ἤ . . . ἤ . . . either . . . or. . . (2)

ἡδονή, ἡδονῆς, ἡ pleasure (8)

ἥκω, ἥξω, ——, ——, ——, —— have come; be present (5)

ἡμεῖς, ἡμῶν we; us (6)

ἡμέτερος, ἡμετέρᾱ, ἡμέτερον our (6)

Ἥρᾱ, Ἥρᾱς, ἡ Hera (§59)

Ἥφαιστος, Ἡφαίστου, ὁ Hephaestus (§59)

θάλαττα, θαλάττης, ἡ sea (2)

Θάλεια, Θαλείᾱς, ἡ Thalia (§59)

θάνατος, θανάτου, ὁ death (4)

θέλω/ἐθέλω, ἐθελήσω, ἠθέλησα, ἠθέληκα, ——, —— be willing, wish (3)

θεός, θεοῦ, ὁ or ἡ god; goddess (1)

θνῄσκω, θανοῦμαι, ἔθανον, τέθνηκα, ——, —— die; *perfect*, be dead (8)

θνητός, θνητή, θνητόν mortal (5)

ἴσος, ἴση, ἴσον equal, even; flat; fair, impartial (8)

ἴσως (adv.) equally; perhaps (8)

καί (conj.) and (1); (adv.) even, also (1)
    καὶ γάρ, for in fact (3†)
    καὶ δή and indeed, and in particular (4†)
    καὶ δὴ καί and in particular (4†)
    καί . . . καί . . . both . . . and . . . (1)

κακός, κακή, κακόν bad, evil (2)

Καλλιόπη, Καλλιόπης, ἡ Calliope (§59)

καλός, καλή, καλόν beautiful; noble; fine (2)

κατά (prep. + gen.) down from, beneath; against; (prep. + acc.) according to, in relation to; throughout (5)

κίνδῡνος, κινδύνου, ὁ danger (8)

Κλειώ, Κλειοῦς, ἡ Clio (§59)

κοινά, κοινῶν, τά public treasury; public affairs (3†)

κοινόν, κοινοῦ, τό state, government (3†)

κοινός, κοινή, κοινόν common (to), shared (with) (+ gen. or dat.); public (3)
    ἀπὸ κοινοῦ, at public expense (3†)
    εἰς/ἐς κοινόν, openly, publicly (3†)
    ἐκ κοινοῦ, at public expense (3†)

κτείνω, κτενῶ, ἔκτεινα, ——, ——, —— kill (8)

Λακεδαιμόνιος, Λακεδαιμονίᾱ, Λακεδαιμόνιον Lacedaemonian, Spartan; *masc. pl. subst.*, Lacedaemonians, Spartans (2)

λαμβάνω, λήψομαι, ἔλαβον, εἴληφα, εἴλημμαι, ἐλήφθην take, seize; understand; receive; *middle*, take hold (of) (+ gen.) (9)
    δίκην λαμβάνειν, to exact punishment (9)

λέγω, λέξω, ἔλεξα/εἶπον, ——, λέλεγμαι, ἐλέχθην say, speak; tell (of), recount (3)

λόγος, λόγου, ὁ word; speech; argument (1)
  λόγους ποιεῖσθαι, to make words, to
  speak (4[†])
λύπη, λύπης, ἡ pain (8)

μά (particle + acc.) *used in oaths*, by (5)
μαθητής, μαθητοῦ, ὁ student (5)
μακρός, μακρά, μακρόν large, great; long,
  tall (8)
μανθάνω, μαθήσομαι, ἔμαθον, μεμάθηκα,
  ——, —— learn; understand (5)
μάχη, μάχης, ἡ battle (1)
μάχομαι, μαχοῦμαι, ἐμαχεσάμην, ——,
  μεμάχημαι, —— fight (against)
  (+ dat.) (8)
μέγας, μεγάλη, μέγα great, big (4)
  μέγα, greatly, to a great extent (9[†])
μέλλω, μελλήσω, ἐμέλλησα, ——, ——,
  —— intend, be about, be likely
  (+ inf.) (3)
Μελπομένη, Μελπομένης, ἡ Melpomene
  (§59)
μέν (postpositive particle) on the one
  hand (3)
  μέν . . . , δέ . . . on the one hand . . . ,
  on the other hand . . . ; . . . , but . . . (3)
  μὲν οὖν (particle combination) *in
  affirmations,* certainly, by all means;
  in corrections, no, on the contrary; *in
  transitions to a new subject,* so then,
  therefore (6)
μένω, μενῶ, ἔμεινα, μεμένηκα, ——,
  —— remain, stay; *trans.,* await (9)
μετά (prep. + gen.) (along) with; with the
  aid of; in accordance with; (prep. + acc.)
  after (4)
μή (adv.) not (2)
  μὴ μόνον . . . ἀλλὰ καὶ . . . not only . . .
  but also . . . (2)
μηδέ (conj.) and not, nor; (adv.) not even (7)
μηδείς, μηδεμία, μηδέν (adj./substantive) no,
  not any; no one, nothing (9)
  μηδέν, not at all (9[†])

μηδέποτε (conj.) and not ever, nor ever;
  (adv.) never (7)
μηδεπώποτε (adv.) not yet at any time,
  never yet (9[†])
μηκέτι (adv.) no longer (8)
μήποτε (adv.) never (5)
μήπω (adv.) not yet (9[†])
μηπώποτε (adv.) not yet at any time,
  never yet (9[†])
μήτε . . . μήτε . . . neither . . . nor . . . (6)
μήτηρ, μητρός, ἡ mother (7)
μῑκρός, μῑκρά, μῑκρόν small (8)
  μῑκρόν, a little (9[†])
μοῖρα, μοίρᾱς, ἡ fate (2)
μόνον (adv.) only (2)
μόνος, μόνη, μόνον only, alone (2)
Μοῦσα, Μούσης, ἡ Muse (§59)

νεᾱνίᾱς, νεᾱνίου, ὁ young man (2)
νέος, νέᾱ, νέον new; young (4)
νή (particle + acc.) *expresses strong
  affirmation,* (yes,) by (5)
νῆσος, νήσου, ἡ island (1)
νῑκάω, νῑκήσω, ἐνίκησα, νενίκηκα,
  νενίκημαι, ἐνῑκήθην conquer, defeat;
  prevail (over), win (4)
νίκη, νίκης, ἡ victory (4)
νόμος, νόμου, ὁ custom; law (1)
νοῦς, νοῦ, ὁ mind; sense; thought (7)
  νοῦν προσέχειν, to pay attention (7)
νῦν (adv.) now (3)
  (τὸ)(τὰ) νῦν, now; presently (9[†])

ξένος, ξένου, ὁ host, guest, guest-friend;
  stranger, foreigner (3)
ξύν (prep. + dat.) (along) with; with the
  aid of; in accordance with (1)

ὁ, ἡ, τό (article) the (1)
ὅδε, ἥδε, τόδε (demonstr. adj./pron.)
  this; *pl.,* these (4)
ὁδός, ὁδοῦ, ἡ road, path; journey;
  way (1)

οἶδα, εἴσομαι, ——, ——, ——, ——
     know (9)
οἰκίᾱ, οἰκίᾱς, ἡ house (1)
οἴομαι/οἶμαι, οἰήσομαι, ——, ——, ——,
     ᾠήθην think, suppose, believe (8)
ὀλίγος, ὀλίγη, ὀλίγον little, small; *pl.,* few (4)
ὄντως (adv.) really, actually (7)
ὅπλον, ὅπλου, τό tool; *pl.,* arms, weapons (1)
ὁράω, ὄψομαι, εἶδον, ἑώρᾱκα/ἑόρᾱκα,
     ἑώρᾱμαι/ὦμμαι, ὤφθην see (6)
ὀρθός, ὀρθή, ὀρθόν straight; correct (6)
ὅς, ἥ, ὅ (relative pron.) who, whose, whom;
     which, that (5)
ὅτι (conj.) that; because (6)
οὐ, οὐκ, οὐχ (adv.) not (2)
     οὐ μόνον . . . ἀλλὰ καί . . . not only . . .
     but also . . . (2)
     οὐ πάνυ, not at all (8)
οὐδέ (conj.) and not, nor; (adv.) not
     even (7)
οὐδείς, οὐδεμία, οὐδέν (adj./substantive)
     no, not any; no one, nothing (9)
     οὐδέν, not at all (9†)
οὐδέποτε (conj.) and not ever, nor ever;
     (adv.) never (7)
οὐδεπώποτε (adv.) not yet at any time,
     never yet (9†)
οὐκέτι (adv.) no longer (8)
οὖν (postpositive conj.) then, therefore (6)
οὔποτε (adv.) never (5)
οὔπω (adv.) not yet (9†)
οὐπώποτε (adv.) not yet at any time, never
     yet (9†)
Οὐρανίᾱ, Οὐρανίᾱς, ἡ Urania (§59)
οὐρανός, οὐρανοῦ, ὁ sky, heaven (3)
οὔτε . . . οὔτε . . . neither . . . nor . . . (6)
οὗτος, αὕτη, τοῦτο (demonstr. adj./pron.)
     this; *pl.,* these (2)
οὕτω(ς) (adv.) in this way, thus, so (4)

πάθος, πάθους, τό experience; suffering;
     passion (7)
παῖς, παιδός, ὁ or ἡ child; slave (5)

παλαιός, παλαιά, παλαιόν old, ancient (8)
πάνυ (adv.) altogether; very (much),
     exceedingly; *in answers,* by all means,
     certainly (8)
παρά (prep. + gen.) from (the side of); by;
     (prep. + dat.) near; at (the house of);
     among; (prep. + acc.) to (the side of),
     beside; contrary to (5)
πάρειμι, παρέσομαι, ——, ——, ——, ——
     be present, be near; be ready (7)
πᾶς, πᾶσα, πᾶν all, every; whole (6)
πάσχω, πείσομαι, ἔπαθον, πέπονθα, ——,
     —— suffer; experience (7)
πατήρ, πατρός, ὁ father (7)
παύω, παύσω, ἔπαυσα, πέπαυκα, πέπαυμαι,
     ἐπαύθην stop (trans.); *middle,* stop
     (intrans.), cease (3)
πείθω, πείσω, ἔπεισα, πέπεικα, πέπεισμαι,
     ἐπείσθην persuade; *middle,* obey;
     heed; believe (+ dat.) (3)
πέμπω, πέμψω, ἔπεμψα, πέπομφα, πέπεμμαι,
     ἐπέμφθην send (3)
περ (enclitic particle) very, even (5)
περί (prep. + gen.) concerning, about;
     (prep. + dat.) around; (prep.+ acc.)
     around; concerning, about (1)
     περὶ πολλοῦ of much value (4†)
πλῆθος, πλήθους, τό great number,
     multitude (8)
πλοῦτος, πλούτου, ὁ wealth (7)
πόθεν (interrog. adv.) from where (6)
ποθέν (enclitic adv.) from somewhere (7)
ποῖ (interrog. adv.) to where (6)
ποι (enclitic adv.) to somewhere (7)
ποιέω, ποιήσω, ἐποίησα, πεποίηκα,
     πεποίημαι, ἐποιήθην make; do; *middle,*
     make; do; deem, consider (4)
     ἀρχὴν ποιεῖσθαι, to make a beginning,
     to begin (4)
     βουλὴν ποιεῖσθαι, to make a plan,
     to plan (4)
     λόγους ποιεῖσθαι, to make words,
     to speak (4)

ποιητής, ποιητοῦ, ὁ maker; poet (2)

πολεμέω, πολεμήσω, ἐπολέμησα, πεπολέμηκα, ——, ἐπολεμήθην make war (upon), be at war (with) (+ dat.); quarrel; fight; *passive,* be treated as an enemy, have war made upon (oneself) (4)

πολέμιος, πολεμίᾱ, πολέμιον of an enemy, hostile; *masc. subst.,* enemy (4)

πόλεμος, πολέμου, ὁ war (1)
    ἐπὶ πολέμου (engaged) in war (4†)

πόλις, πόλεως, ἡ city (7)

πολίτης, πολίτου, ὁ citizen (2)

πολλάκις (adv.) many times, often (3)

Πολύμνια, Πολυμνίᾱς, ἡ Polymnia (§59)

πολύς, πολλή, πολύ much, many (4)
    ἐπὶ (τὸ) πολύ to a great extent; for the most part (4†)
    περὶ πολλοῦ of much value (4†)
    (τὰ) πολλά, many times, often; much, a lot (9†)
    (τὸ) πολύ, much, a lot (9†)

πονηρός, πονηρά, πονηρόν worthless; wicked (4)

πόνος, πόνου, ὁ labor, toil; distress, suffering (3)

Ποσειδῶν, Ποσειδῶνος, ὁ (voc. = Πόσειδον) Poseidon (§59)

πότε (interrog. adv.) when (3)

ποτέ (enclitic adv.) at some time, ever, in the world† (5)
    ποτέ . . . , ποτέ . . . at one time . . . , at another time . . . ; sometimes . . . , sometimes . . . (5)

ποῦ (interrog. adv.) where (6)

που (enclitic adv.) somewhere; I suppose (7)

πρᾶγμα, πράγματος, τό deed; matter, thing; *pl.,* affairs; troubles (7)

πράττω, πράξω, ἔπρᾶξα, πέπρᾶχα (trans.)/ πέπρᾱγα (intrans.), πέπρᾱγμαι, ἐπράχθην do; bring about; practice; manage; *intrans.,* fare (7)

Πρίαμος, Πριάμου, ὁ Priam (1)

πρό (prep. + gen.) before, in front of (8)
    πρὸ τοῦ before this (8†)
    πρὸ τούτου before this (8†)

πρός (prep. + gen.) from; by; in the name of; (prep. + dat.) near; in addition to; (prep. + acc.) toward; against; in reply to, in the face of, in relation to (3)

προσέχω, προσέξω, προσέσχον, προσέσχηκα, ——, —— hold to; turn to, apply (7)
    νοῦν/γνώμην προσέχειν, to pay attention (7)

πω (enclitic adv.) yet (9)

πώποτε (adv.) ever yet (9)

πῶς (interrog. adv.) how (3)

πως (enclitic adv.) somehow (5)

ῥᾴδιος, ῥᾳδίᾱ, ῥᾴδιον easy (5)

ῥήτωρ, ῥήτορος, ὁ public speaker, orator; rhetor (5)

σαφής, σαφές clear, plain; certain, sure (7)

σμῑκρός, σμῑκρά, σμῑκρόν small (8)
    σμῑκρόν, a little (9†)

σός, σή, σόν your (6)

σοφίᾱ, σοφίᾱς, ἡ wisdom (1)

σοφός, σοφή, σοφόν wise (2)

στρατηγός, στρατηγοῦ, ὁ general (8)

στρατιώτης, στρατιώτου, ὁ soldier (8)

στρατός, στρατοῦ, ὁ army (8)

σύ, σοῦ/σου you (6)

σύμμαχος, συμμάχου, ὁ ally (3)

συμφορά, συμφορᾶς, ἡ circumstance; misfortune, disaster (1)

σύν (prep. + dat.) (along) with; with the aid of; in accordance with (1)

Σωκράτης, Σωκράτους, ὁ Socrates (7)

σῶμα, σώματος, τό body (5)

σωτηρίᾱ, σωτηρίᾱς, ἡ safety (8)

σωφροσύνη, σωφροσύνης, ἡ moderation (9)

σώφρων, σῶφρον moderate, prudent (9)

τε (enclitic conj.) and (5)

τεῖχος, τείχους, τό wall (8)

τέκνον, τέκνου, τό child (1)

τελευτάω, τελευτήσω, ἐτελεύτησα,
   τετελεύτηκα, ——, ἐτελευτήθην
   accomplish, end, finish; die (4)

τέλος, τέλους, τό end, purpose; power (9)
   διὰ τέλους, through to the end,
   completely (9†)
   ἐν τέλει, in office, in power (9†)
   ἐς/εἰς τέλος, to the end, in the long
   run (9†)
   τέλος, finally (9†)

Τερψιχόρᾱ, Τερψιχόρᾱς, ἡ Terpsichore
   (§59)

τέχνη, τέχνης, ἡ skill, art (5)

τῑμάω, τῑμήσω, ἐτίμησα, τετίμηκα,
   τετίμημαι, ἐτῑμήθην honor; middle,
   value, deem worthy (4)

τίς, τί (interrog. pron./adj.) who, what;
   which (9)
   τί, why; how (9†)

τις, τι (indef. pron./adj.) someone,
   something; anyone, anything; some,
   any (9)
   τι, in any way; at all (9†)

τοι (enclitic particle) surely, you know (5)

τότε (adv.) then, at that time (7)

τρόπος, τρόπου, ὁ way, manner; habit; pl.,
   character (9)

τύχη, τύχης, ἡ chance, fortune (4)

ὕβρις, ὕβρεως, ἡ insolence; (wanton)
   violence (7)

υἱός, υἱοῦ, ὁ son (4)

ὑμεῖς, ὑμῶν you (pl.) (6)

ὑμέτερος, ὑμετέρᾱ, ὑμέτερον your (pl.) (6)

ὑπέρ (prep. + gen.) over; on behalf of; (prep.
   + acc.) beyond (6)

ὑπό (prep. + gen.) (from) under; by; at the
   hands of; (prep. + dat.) under; under
   the power of; (prep. + acc.) under;
   during (3)

ὑπολαμβάνω, ὑπολήψομαι, ὑπέλαβον,
   ὑπείληφα, ὑπείλημμαι, ὑπελήφθην
   take up, reply; suppose (9)

*φάσκω, ——, ——, ——, ——, ——
   say, assert (8)

φέρω, οἴσω, ἤνεγκα/ἤνεγκον, ἐνήνοχα,
   ἐνήνεγμαι, ἠνέχθην bear, bring, carry;
   endure; middle, carry away with oneself;
   win (9)

φεύγω, φεύξομαι, ἔφυγον, πέφευγα, ——,
   —— flee, avoid, escape (9)

φημί, φήσω, ἔφησα, ——, ——, —— say,
   assert (8)

φιλέω, φιλήσω, ἐφίλησα, πεφίληκα,
   πεφίλημαι, ἐφιλήθην love, like; regard
   with affection; approve of; kiss; be
   accustomed, be fond of (+ inf.) (4)

φίλος, φίλη, φίλον (be)loved, dear; loving,
   friendly; masc./fem. subst., friend; loved
   one (2)

φόβος, φόβου, ὁ fear (2)

Φοῖβος, Φοίβου, ὁ Phoebus (Apollo) (§59)

φρήν, φρενός, ἡ sing. or pl., heart, mind,
   wits (5)

φρόνησις, φρονήσεως, ἡ intelligence,
   understanding (9)

φύσις, φύσεως, ἡ nature (7)

χαίρω, χαιρήσω, ——, κεχάρηκα, ——,
   ἐχάρην rejoice (in), enjoy (7)

χαλεπός, χαλεπή, χαλεπόν severe, harsh;
   difficult (4)

χαλεπῶς (adv.) hardly, with difficulty (4†)

χάριν (prep. + preceding gen.) for the sake
   of (5)

χάρις, χάριτος, ἡ grace, favor, goodwill;
   delight; gratitude (5)

χρή, χρῆσται, ——, ——, ——, ——
   (impersonal verb) it is necessary, ought
   (8)

χρῆμα, χρήματος, τό thing, matter, affair; pl.,
   goods, property, money (5)

χρηστός, χρηστή, χρηστόν useful;
    good (6)
χώρᾱ, χώρᾱς, ἡ land; country (1)

ψευδής, ψευδές false (7)
ψῡχή, ψῡχῆς, ἡ soul; life force (1)

ὦ (interj.) O (1)
ὧδε (adv.) in this way, so; in the following
    way (4)
ὡς (proclitic conj.) that; as (6)
    ὡς ἀληθῶς, (so) truly, really (7[†])
    ὡς ἔπος εἰπεῖν, so to speak (7[†])
ὥσπερ (conj.) just as (6)

ENGLISH TO GREEK VOCABULARY

This English to Greek Vocabulary includes all the words from the vocabulary lists in Part 1 of *Learn to Read Greek*. Numbers in parentheses refer to chapter (e.g., 2) or section (e.g., §12) in which the vocabulary word is introduced. If only a chapter number is listed, the word or phrase appears in the chapter-opening vocabulary list; if the chapter number is followed by a dagger (†), the word or phrase appears in the vocabulary notes or in a section of the chapter.

ability δύναμις, δυνάμεως, ἡ (7)

be able *intrans.*, ἔχω, ἕξω/σχήσω, ἔσχον, ἔσχηκα, -έσχημαι, —— (+ inf.) (4)

about περί (prep. + gen.) (1); περί (prep. + acc.) (1)

be about μέλλω, μελλήσω, ἐμέλλησα, ——, ——, —— (+ inf.) (3)

absolute ruler δεσπότης, δεσπότου, ὁ (6)

accept δέχομαι, δέξομαι, ἐδεξάμην, ——, δέδεγμαι, —— (6)

accomplish τελευτάω, τελευτήσω, ἐτελεύτησα, τετελεύτηκα, ——, ἐτελευτήθην (4)

according to κατά (prep. + acc.) (5)

be accustomed φιλέω, φιλήσω, ἐφίλησα, πεφίληκα, πεφίλημαι, ἐφιλήθην (+ inf.) (4)

actually ὄντως (adv.) (7)

advice βουλή, βουλῆς, ἡ (1)

affair χρῆμα, χρήματος, τό (5)

affairs πράγματα, πρᾱγμάτων, τά (7)

after μετά (prep. + acc.) (4)

after all ἄρα (postpositive particle) (9)

against εἰς, ἐς (prep. + acc.) (1); πρός (prep. + acc.) (3); ἐπί (prep. + acc.) (4); κατά (prep. + gen.) (5);

agora ἀγορά, ἀγορᾶς, ἡ (1)

Alexander Ἀλέξανδρος, Ἀλεξάνδρου, ὁ (1)

be alive ζάω, ζήσω, ——, ——, ——, —— (8)

all πᾶς, πᾶσα, πᾶν (6); ἅπᾱς, ἅπᾱσα, ἅπαν (6)

ally σύμμαχος, συμμάχου, ὁ (3)

alone μόνος, μόνη, μόνον (2)

(along) with σύν/ξύν (prep. + dat.) (1); μετά (prep. + gen.) (4)

a lot (τὸ) πολύ (9†); τὰ πολλά (9†)

also καί (adv.) (1)

altogether πάνυ (adv.)(8)

always ἀεί/αἰεί (adv.) (5)

among ἐν (prep. + dat.) (1); παρά (prep. + dat.) (5)

ancient παλαιός, παλαιά, παλαιόν (8)

and καί (conj.) (1); δέ (postpositive conj.) (3); τε (enclitic conj.) (5)

and in particular καὶ δή (4†); καὶ δὴ καί (4†)

and not οὐδέ/μηδέ (conj.) (7)

and not ever οὐδέποτε/μηδέποτε (conj.) (7)

animal ζῷον, ζῴου, τό (1)

another ἄλλος, ἄλλη, ἄλλο (5)

any τις, τι (indef. adj.) (9)

anyone τις, τι (indef. pron.) (9)

anything τις, τι (indef. pron.) (9)

Aphrodite Ἀφροδίτη, Ἀφροδίτης, ἡ (§59)

Apollo Ἀπόλλων, Ἀπόλλωνος, ὁ (voc. = Ἄπολλον) (§59)

apply προσέχω, προσέξω, προσέσχον, προσέσχηκα, ——, —— (7)

archon ἄρχων, ἄρχοντος, ὁ (5)

Ares Ἄρης, Ἄρεος/Ἄρεως, ὁ (voc. = Ἄρες) (§59)

argument λόγος, λόγου, ὁ (1)

arise γίγνομαι, γενήσομαι, ἐγενόμην, γέγονα, γεγένημαι, —— (6)

armed σὺν ὅπλοις (1)

arms ὅπλα, ὅπλων, τά (1)

army στρατός, στρατοῦ, ὁ (8)

around περί (prep. + dat.) (1); περί (prep. + acc.) (1)

art τέχνη, τέχνης, ἡ (5)

Artemis Ἄρτεμις, Ἀρτέμιδος, ἡ (§59)

as ὡς (proclitic conj.) (6)

(but) as a matter of fact ἀλλὰ γάρ (3†)

assert *φάσκω, ——, ——, ——, ——, —— (8); φημί, φήσω, ἔφησα, ——, ——, —— (8)

at (the house of) παρά (prep. + dat.) (5)

at all τι (9†)

at any rate γε (enclitic particle) (5)

at least γε (enclitic particle) (5)

at one time . . . , at another time . . . ποτέ . . . , ποτέ . . . (5)

at public expense ἀπὸ/ἐκ κοινοῦ (3†)

at some time ποτέ (enclitic adv.) (5)

at that time τότε (adv.) (7)

at the hands of ὑπό (prep. + gen.) (3)

Athena Ἀθηνᾶ, Ἀθηνᾶς, ἡ (§59)

Athenian Ἀθηναῖος, Ἀθηναίᾱ, Ἀθηναῖον (2)

Athenians Ἀθηναῖοι, Ἀθηναίων, οἱ (2)

Athens Ἀθῆναι, Ἀθηνῶν, αἱ (6)

Atreides Ἀτρείδης, Ἀτρείδου, ὁ (2)

avoid φεύγω, φεύξομαι, ἔφυγον, πέφευγα, ——, —— (9)

await *trans.*, μένω, μενῶ, ἔμεινα, μεμένηκα, ——, —— (9)

(away) from ἀπό (prep. + gen.) (2)

bad κακός, κακή, κακόν (2)

barbarians βάρβαροι, βαρβάρων, οἱ (5)

barbarous βάρβαρος, βάρβαρον (5)

battle μάχη, μάχης, ἡ (1)

be *intrans.*, ἔχω, ἕξω/σχήσω, ἔσχον, ἔσχηκα, -έσχημαι, —— (+ adv.) (4); εἰμί, ἔσομαι, ——, ——, ——, —— (5)

be able *intrans.*, ἔχω, ἕξω/σχήσω, ἔσχον, ἔσχηκα, -έσχημαι, —— (+ inf.) (4)

be about μέλλω, μελλήσω, ἐμέλλησα, ——, ——, —— (+ inf.) (3)

be accustomed φιλέω, φιλήσω, ἐφίλησα, πεφίληκα, πεφίλημαι, ἐφιλήθην (+ inf.) (4)

be alive ζάω, ζήσω, ——, ——, ——, —— (8)

be at war (with) πολεμέω, πολεμήσω, ἐπολέμησα, πεπολέμηκα, ——, ἐπολεμήθην (+ dat.) (4)

be born γίγνομαι, γενήσομαι, ἐγενόμην, γέγονα, γεγένημαι, —— (6)

be dead *perfect*, θνήσκω, θανοῦμαι, ἔθανον, τέθνηκα, ——, —— (8); *perfect*, ἀποθνήσκω, ἀποθανοῦμαι, ἀπέθανον, τέθνηκα, ——, —— (8)

be deemed fortunate *passive*, ζηλόω, ζηλώσω, ἐζήλωσα, ἐζήλωκα, ——, —— (7)

be fond of φιλέω, φιλήσω, ἐφίλησα, πεφίληκα, πεφίλημαι, ἐφιλήθην (+ inf.) (4)

be likely μέλλω, μελλήσω, ἐμέλλησα, ——, ——, —— (+ inf.) (3)

be near πάρειμι, παρέσομαι, ——, ——, ——, —— (7)

be present ἥκω, ἥξω, ——, ——, ——, —— (5); πάρειμι, παρέσομαι, ——, ——, ——, —— (7)

be ready πάρειμι, παρέσομαι, ——, ——, ——, —— (7)

be treated as an enemy *passive*, πολεμέω, πολεμήσω, ἐπολέμησα, πεπολέμηκα, ——, ἐπολεμήθην (4)

be willing ἐθέλω/θέλω, ἐθελήσω, ἠθέλησα, ἠθέληκα, ——, —— (3)

bear φέρω, οἴσω, ἤνεγκα/ἤνεγκον, ἐνήνοχα, ἐνήνεγμαι, ἠνέχθην (9)

bearing arms σὺν ὅπλοις (1†)

beautiful καλός, καλή, καλόν (2)

because ὅτι (conj.) (6)

because of διά (prep. + acc.) (2)

become γίγνομαι, γενήσομαι, ἐγενόμην, γέγονα, γεγένημαι, —— (6)

before πρό (prep. + gen.) (8)

before this πρὸ τοῦ (8†); πρὸ τούτου (8†)

begin middle, ἄρχω, ἄρξω, ἦρξα, ἦρχα, ἦργμαι, ἤρχθην (+ gen.) (3)

    to begin ἀρχὴν ποιεῖσθαι (4†)

beginning ἀρχή, ἀρχῆς, ἡ (2)

belief δόξα, δόξης, ἡ (2)

believe middle, πείθω, πείσω, ἔπεισα, πέπεικα, πέπεισμαι, ἐπείσθην (+ dat.) (3); οἴομαι/οἶμαι, οἰήσομαι, ——, ——, ——, ᾠήθην (8)

beloved φίλος, φίλη, φίλον (2)

beneath κατά (prep. + gen.) (5)

beside παρά (prep. + acc.) (5)

beyond ὑπέρ (prep. + acc.) (6)

big μέγας, μεγάλη, μέγα (4)

body σῶμα, σώματος, τό (5)

both . . . and . . . καί . . . καί . . . (1)

bring ἄγω, ἄξω, ἤγαγον, ἦχα, ἦγμαι, ἤχθην (5); φέρω, οἴσω, ἤνεγκα/ἤνεγκον, ἐνήνοχα, ἐνήνεγμαι, ἠνέχθην (9)

bring about πράττω, πράξω, ἔπρᾱξα, πέπρᾱχα (trans.)/πέπρᾱγα (intrans.), πέπρᾱγμαι, ἐπράχθην (7)

but ἀλλά (conj.) (2); δέ (postpositive conj.) (3)

but as a matter of fact ἀλλὰ γάρ (3†)

but yet in narrative transitions and responses in dialogue, ἀλλά (conj.) (2†)

by πρός (prep. + gen.) (3); ὑπό (prep. + gen.) (3); παρά (prep. + gen.) (5); in oaths, μά (particle + acc.) (5); expressing strong affirmation, νή (particle + acc.) (5)

by all means in answers, πάνυ (adv.) (8); in affirmations, μὲν οὖν (particle combination) (6†)

call λέγω, λέξω, ἔλεξα/εἶπον, ——, λέλεγμαι, ἐλέχθην (3†)

Calliope Καλλιόπη, Καλλιόπης, ἡ (§59)

carry φέρω, οἴσω, ἤνεγκα/ἤνεγκον, ἐνήνοχα, ἐνήνεγμαι, ἠνέχθην (9)

carry away with oneself middle, ἄγω, ἄξω, ἤγαγον, ἦχα, ἦγμαι, ἤχθην (5); middle, φέρω, οἴσω, ἤνεγκα/ἤνεγκον, ἐνήνοχα, ἐνήνεγμαι, ἠνέχθην (9)

cause αἰτίᾱ, αἰτίᾱς, ἡ (2)

cause to be taught middle, διδάσκω, διδάξω, ἐδίδαξα, δεδίδαχα, δεδίδαγμαι, ἐδιδάχθην (3)

cease middle, παύω, παύσω, ἔπαυσα, πέπαυκα, πέπαυμαι, ἐπαύθην (3)

certain σαφής, σαφές (7)

certainly δή (postpositive particle) (4); in answers, πάνυ (adv.) (8); in affirmations, μὲν οὖν (particle combination) (6†)

chance τύχη, τύχης, ἡ (4)

character τρόποι, τρόπων, οἱ (9)

child τέκνον, τέκνου, τό (1); παῖς, παιδός, ὁ or ἡ (5)

circumstance συμφορά, συμφορᾶς, ἡ (1)

citizen πολίτης, πολίτου, ὁ (2)

city πόλις, πόλεως, ἡ (7)

clear δῆλος, δήλη, δῆλον (6); σαφής, σαφές (7)

clever δεινός, δεινή, δεινόν (2)

cling to middle, ἔχω, ἕξω/σχήσω, ἔσχον, ἔσχηκα, -έσχημαι, —— (+ gen.) (4)

Clio Κλειώ, Κλειοῦς, ἡ (§59)

come ἔρχομαι, ἐλεύσομαι, ἦλθον, ἐλήλυθα, ——, —— (6)

have come ἥκω, ἥξω, ——, ——, ——, —— (5)

common (to) κοινός, κοινή, κοινόν (+ gen. or dat.) (3)

companion ἑταῖρος, ἑταίρου, ὁ (1)

completely διὰ τέλους (9†)

concerning περί (prep. + gen.) (1); περί (prep. + acc.) (1)

conquer νῑκάω, νῑκήσω, ἐνίκησα, νενίκηκα, νενίκημαι, ἐνῑκήθην (4)

consider middle, ποιέω, ποιήσω, ἐποίησα, πεποίηκα, πεποίημαι, ἐποιήθην (4)

contest ἀγών, ἀγῶνος, ὁ (6)
contrary (to) ἐναντίος, ἐναντίᾱ, ἐναντίον (+ gen. or dat.) (8)
contrary to παρά (prep. + acc.) (5)
converse (with) διαλέγομαι, διαλέξομαι, ——, ——, διείλεγμαι, διελέχθην (+ dat.) (7)
conversely ἐναντίως (adv.) (8†); (τὸ) ἐναντίον (9†)
correct ὀρθός, ὀρθή, ὀρθόν (6)
corrupt διαφθείρω, διαφθερῶ, διέφθειρα, διέφθαρκα/διέφθορα, διέφθαρμαι, διεφθάρην (9)
council βουλή, βουλῆς, ἡ (1)
country χώρᾱ, χώρᾱς, ἡ (1)
courage ἀνδρείᾱ, ἀνδρείᾱς, ἡ (9)
custom νόμος, νόμου, ὁ (1)

danger κίνδῡνος, κινδύνου, ὁ (8)
dear φίλος, φίλη, φίλον (2)
death θάνατος, θανάτου, ὁ (4)
deathless ἀθάνατος, ἀθάνατον (2)
deed ἔργον, ἔργου, τό (1); πρᾶγμα, πρᾱ́γματος, τό (7)
deem *middle*, ποιέω, ποιήσω, ἐποίησα, πεποίηκα, πεποίημαι, ἐποιήθην (4)
deem worthy *middle*, τῑμάω, τῑμήσω, ἐτῑ́μησα, τετῑ́μηκα, τετῑ́μημαι, ἐτῑμήθην (4)
defeat νῑκάω, νῑκήσω, ἐνῑ́κησα, νενῑ́κηκα, νενῑ́κημαι, ἐνῑκήθην (4)
delight χάρις, χάριτος, ἡ (5)
Demeter Δημήτηρ, Δημητρός, ἡ (voc. = Δήμητερ) (§59)
Demosthenes Δημοσθένης, Δημοσθένους, ὁ (7)
descent γένος, γένους, τό (7)
desire ἔρως, ἔρωτος, ὁ (5)
destroy (utterly) διαφθείρω, διαφθερῶ, διέφθειρα, διέφθαρκα/διέφθορα, διέφθαρμαι, διεφθάρην (9)

die τελευτάω, τελευτήσω, ἐτελεύτησα, τετελεύτηκα, ——, ἐτελευτήθην (4); θνήσκω, θανοῦμαι, ἔθανον, τέθνηκα, ——, —— (8); ἀποθνήσκω, ἀποθανοῦμαι, ἀπέθανον, τέθνηκα, ——, —— (8)
   be dead *perfect*, θνήσκω, θανοῦμαι, ἔθανον, τέθηνκα, ——, —— (8); *perfect*, ἀποθνήσκω, ἀποθανοῦμαι, ἀπέθανον, τέθηνκα, ——, —— (8)
difficult χαλεπός, χαλεπή, χαλεπόν (4)
   with difficulty χαλεπῶς (adv.) (4†)
Dionysus Διόνῡσος, Διονύσου, ὁ (§59)
disaster συμφορά, συμφορᾶς, ἡ (1)
discuss (with) διαλέγομαι, διαλέξομαι, ——, ——, διείλεγμαι, διελέχθην (+ dat.) (7)
disgraceful αἰσχρός, αἰσχρά, αἰσχρόν (3)
distress πόνος, πόνου, ὁ (3)
divine power δαίμων, δαίμονος, ὁ or ἡ (5)
divinity δαίμων, δαίμονος, ὁ or ἡ (5)
do *active or middle*, ποιέω, ποιήσω, ἐποίησα, πεποίηκα, πεποίημαι, ἐποιήθην (4); πρᾱ́ττω, πρᾱ́ξω, ἔπρᾱξα, πέπρᾱχα (trans.)/πέπρᾱγα (intrans.), πέπρᾱγμαι, ἐπρᾱ́χθην (7)
(do) wrong (to) ἀδικέω, ἀδικήσω, ἠδίκησα, ἠδίκηκα, ἠδίκημαι, ἠδικήθην (4)
down from κατά (prep. + gen.) (5)
during ὑπό (prep. + acc.) (3)

each (of several) ἕκαστος, ἑκάστη, ἕκαστον (7)
each other ——, ἀλλήλων (reciprocal pronoun) (8)
earth γαῖα, γαίᾱς, ἡ (3); γῆ, γῆς, ἡ (3)
easy ῥᾴδιος, ῥᾳδίᾱ, ῥᾴδιον (5)
either ... or ... ἤ ... ἤ ... (2)
empire ἀρχή, ἀρχῆς, ἡ (2)
emulate ζηλόω, ζηλώσω, ἐζήλωσα, ἐζήλωκα, ——, —— (7)

end τελευτάω, τελευτήσω, ἐτελεύτησα, τετελεύτηκα, ——, ἐτελευτήθην (4); τέλος, τέλους, τό (9)

endure φέρω, οἴσω, ἤνεγκα/ἤνεγκον, ἐνήνοχα, ἐνήνεγμαι, ἠνέχθην (9)

enemy ἐχθρός, ἐχθροῦ, ὁ (2); πολέμιος, πολεμίου, ὁ (4)

of an enemy πολέμιος, πολεμίᾱ, πολέμιον (4)

be treated as an enemy passive, πολεμέω, πολεμήσω, ἐπολέμησα, πεπολέμηκα, ——, ἐπολεμήθην (4)

(engaged) in war ἐπὶ πολέμου (4†)

enjoy χαίρω, χαιρήσω, ——, κεχάρηκα, ——, ἐχάρην (7)

envy ζηλόω, ζηλώσω, ἐζήλωσα, ἐζήλωκα, ——, —— (7)

epic poetry ἔπη, ἐπῶν, τά (7)

equal ἴσος, ἴση, ἴσον (8)

equally ἴσως (adv.) (8)

Erato Ἐρατώ, Ἐρατοῦς, ἡ (§59)

Eros Ἔρως, Ἔρωτος, ὁ (voc. = Ἔρως) (§59)

escape φεύγω, φεύξομαι, ἔφυγον, πέφευγα, ——, —— (9)

Euripides Εὐρῑπίδης, Εὐρῑπίδου, ὁ (2)

Euterpe Εὐτέρπη, Εὐτέρπης, ἡ (§59)

even καί (adv.) (1); περ (enclitic particle) (5)

ever ποτέ (enclitic adv.) (5)

ever yet πώποτε (adv.) (9)

every πᾶς, πᾶσα, πᾶν (6); ἅπᾱς, ἅπᾱσα, ἅπαν (6)

evil κακός, κακή, κακόν (2)

to exact punishment δίκην λαμβάνειν (9)

exceedingly πάνυ (8)

excellence ἀρετή, ἀρετῆς, ἡ (4)

exist εἰμί, ἔσομαι, ——, ——, ——, —— (5)

expect ἀξιόω, ἀξιώσω, ἠξίωσα, ἠξίωκα, ἠξίωμαι, ἠξιώθην (4)

expectation δόξα, δόξης, ἡ (2); ἐλπίς, ἐλπίδος, ἡ (5)

experience πάθος, πάθους, τό (7); πάσχω, πείσομαι, ἔπαθον, πέπονθα, ——, —— (7)

explain διδάσκω, διδάξω, ἐδίδαξα, δεδίδαχα, δεδίδαγμαι, ἐδιδάχθην (3)

facing ἐναντίος, ἐναντίᾱ, ἐναντίον (+ gen. or dat.) (8)

fair ἴσος, ἴση, ἴσον (8)

false ψευδής, ψευδές (7)

family γένος, γένους, τό (7)

fare intrans., πρά̄ττω, πρά̄ξω, ἔπρᾱξα, πέπρᾱχα (trans.)/πέπρᾱγα (intrans.), πέπρᾱγμαι, ἐπρά̄χθην (7)

fate μοῖρα, μοίρᾱς, ἡ (2)

father πατήρ, πατρός, ὁ (7)

favor χάρις, χάριτος, ἡ (5)

fear φόβος, φόβου, ὁ (2)

fearsome δεινός, δεινή, δεινόν (2)

few ὀλίγοι, ὀλίγαι, ὀλίγα (4)

fight πολεμέω, πολεμήσω, ἐπολέμησα, πεπολέμηκα, ——, ἐπολεμήθην (4)

fight (against) μάχομαι, μαχοῦμαι, ἐμαχεσάμην, ——, μεμάχημαι, —— (+ dat.) (8)

finally τέλος (9†)

fine καλός, καλή, καλόν (2)

finish τελευτάω, τελευτήσω, ἐτελεύτησα, τετελεύτηκα, ——, ἐτελευτήθην (4)

flee φεύγω, φεύξομαι, ἔφυγον, πέφευγα, ——, —— (9)

follow ἕπομαι, ἕψομαι, ἑσπόμην, ——, ——, —— (+ dat.) (9)

be fond of φιλέω, φιλήσω, ἐφίλησα, πεφίληκα, πεφίλημαι, ἐφιλήθην (+ inf.) (4)

foolish ἀμαθής, ἀμαθές (9)

for explanatory, γάρ (postpositive conj.) (3); (i.e., because of) ἐπί (prep. + dat.) (4)

for (the purpose of) ἐπί (prep. + acc.) (4)

for in fact καὶ γάρ (3†)

for the most part ἐπὶ (τὸ) πολύ (4†)

for the sake of χάριν (prep. + preceding gen.) (5)

foreign βάρβαρος, βάρβαρον (5)

foreigner ξένος, ξένου, ὁ (3)

foreigners βάρβαροι, βαρβάρων, οἱ (5)
former ἐκεῖνος, ἐκείνη, ἐκεῖνο (4†)
fortunate εὐδαίμων, εὔδαιμον (9)
    be deemed fortunate *passive*, ζηλόω,
      ζηλώσω, ἐζήλωσα, ἐζήλωκα, ——, ——
      (7)
fortune τύχη, τύχης, ἡ (4)
free ἐλεύθερος, ἐλευθέρᾱ, ἐλεύθερον (6)
freedom ἐλευθερίᾱ, ἐλευθερίᾱς, ἡ (6)
friend φίλος, φίλου, ὁ (2); φίλη, φίλης, ἡ (2)
friendly φίλος, φίλη, φίλον (2)
from πρός (*prep.*) + *gen.* (3)
(away) from ἀπό (*prep.* + *gen.*) (2)
(out) from ἐκ, ἐξ (*prep.* + *gen.*) (1)
from (the side of) παρά (*prep.* + *gen.*) (5)
from somewhere ποθέν (*enclitic adv.*) (7)
from under ὑπό (*prep.* + *gen.*) (3)
from where πόθεν (*interrog. adv.*) (6)

general στρατηγός, στρατηγοῦ, ὁ (8)
get *simple aspect*, ἔχω, ἕξω/σχήσω, ἔσχον,
    ἔσχηκα, -ἔσχημαι, —— (4†)
glory δόξα, δόξης, ἡ (2)
go ἔρχομαι, ἐλεύσομαι, ἦλθον, ἐλήλυθα,
    ——, —— (6)
god θεός, θεοῦ, ὁ (1)
goddess θεός, θεοῦ, ἡ (1)
good ἀγαθός, ἀγαθή, ἀγαθόν (2); χρηστός,
    χρηστή, χρηστόν (6)
goods χρήματα, χρημάτων, τά (5)
goodwill χάρις, χάριτος, ἡ (5)
Gorgias Γοργίᾱς, Γοργίου, ὁ (2)
government κοινόν, κοινοῦ, τό (3†)
grace χάρις, χάριτος, ἡ (5)
gratitude χάρις, χάριτος, ἡ (5)
great μέγας, μεγάλη, μέγα (4); μακρός,
    μακρά, μακρόν (8)
great number πλῆθος, πλήθους, τό (8)
greatly μέγα (9†)
Greece Ἑλλάς, Ἑλλάδος, ἡ (7)
Greek Ἕλλην, Ἕλληνος, ὁ (5)
guest ξένος, ξένου, ὁ (3)
guest-friend ξένος, ξένου, ὁ (3)

habit τρόπος, τρόπου, ὁ (9)
Hades Ἅιδης, Ἅιδου, ὁ (2)
happen γίγνομαι, γενήσομαι, ἐγενόμην,
    γέγονα, γεγένημαι, —— (6)
happy εὐδαίμων, εὔδαιμον (9)
hardly χαλεπῶς (*adv.*) (4†)
harsh χαλεπός, χαλεπή, χαλεπόν (4)
hated ἐχθρός, ἐχθρά, ἐχθρόν (2)
hateful ἐχθρός, ἐχθρά, ἐχθρόν (2)
have ἔχω, ἕξω/σχήσω, ἔσχον, ἔσχηκα,
    -ἔσχημαι, —— (4)
have come ἥκω, ἥξω, ——, ——, ——, ——
    (5)
have war made upon one *passive*, πολεμέω,
    πολεμήσω, ἐπολέμησα, πεπολέμηκα,
    ——, ἐπολεμήθην (4)
hear (of) ἀκούω, ἀκούσομαι, ἤκουσα,
    ἀκήκοα, ——, ἠκούσθην (5)
heaven οὐρανός, οὐρανοῦ, ὁ (3)
Hector Ἕκτωρ, Ἕκτορος, ὁ (5)
heed *middle*, πείθω, πείσω, ἔπεισα, πέπεικα,
    πέπεισμαι, ἐπείσθην (+ *dat.*) (3)
Helen Ἑλένη, Ἑλένης, ἡ (1)
Hellas Ἑλλάς, Ἑλλάδος, ἡ (7)
Hellene Ἕλλην, Ἕλληνος, ὁ (5)
Hephaestus Ἥφαιστος, Ἡφαίστου, ὁ (§59)
her αὐτοῦ, αὐτῆς, αὐτοῦ (6)
Hera Ἥρᾱ, Ἥρᾱς, ἡ (§59)
Hermes Ἑρμῆς, Ἑρμοῦ, ὁ (4)
Hestia Ἑστίᾱ, Ἑστίᾱς, ἡ (§59)
him αὐτοῦ, αὐτῆς, αὐτοῦ (6)
hold ἔχω, ἕξω/σχήσω, ἔσχον, ἔσχηκα,
    -ἔσχημαι, —— (4)
hold on to *middle*, ἔχω, ἕξω/σχήσω, ἔσχον,
    ἔσχηκα, -ἔσχημαι, —— (+ *gen.*) (4)
hold to προσέχω, προσέξω, προσέσχον,
    προσέσχηκα, ——, —— (7)
home *sing. or pl.*, δῶμα, δώματος, τό (5)
honor τῑμάω, τῑμήσω, ἐτίμησα, τετίμηκα,
    τετίμημαι, ἐτῑμήθην (4)
hope ἐλπίς, ἐλπίδος, ἡ (5)
host ξένος, ξένου, ὁ (3)

hostile ἐχθρός, ἐχθρά, ἐχθρόν (2); πολέμιος, πολεμίᾱ, πολέμιον (4)

house οἰκίᾱ, οἰκίᾱς, ἡ (1); *sing. or pl.*, δῶμα, δώματος, τό (5)

how πῶς (interrog. adv.) (3); τί (9†)

how is it that πῶς (interrog. adv.) (3†)

human being ἄνθρωπος, ἀνθρώπου, ὁ or ἡ (1)

husband ἀνήρ, ἀνδρός, ὁ (6)

I ἐγώ, ἐμοῦ/μου (6)

I suppose που (enclitic adv.) (7)

if εἰ (conj.) (9)

ignorance ἀμαθίᾱ, ἀμαθίᾱς, ἡ (9)

ignorant ἀμαθής, ἀμαθές (9)

immortal ἀθάνατος, ἀθάνατον (2)

in ἐν (prep. + dat.) (1); ἐπί (prep. + gen.) (4); ἐπί (prep. + dat.) (4)

in accordance with ἐκ, ἐξ (prep. + gen.) (1); σύν/ξύν (prep. + dat.) (1); μετά (prep. + gen.) (4)

in addition to πρός (prep. + dat.) (3); ἐπί (prep. + dat.) (4)

in any way τι (9†)

in fact *confirming,* γάρ (postpositive conj.) (3)

in front of πρό (prep. + gen.) (8)

in office ἐν τέλει (9†)

in opposition ἐναντίως (adv.) (8†); (τὸ) ἐναντίον (9†)

and in particular καί δή (4†); καὶ δὴ καί (4†)

in power ἐν τέλει (9†)

in relation to πρός (prep. + acc.) (3); κατά (prep. + acc.) (5)

in reply to πρός (prep. + acc.) (3)

in the face of πρός (prep. + acc.) (3)

in the following way ὧδε (adv.) (4)

in the name of πρός (prep. + gen.) (3)

in the power of ἐν (prep. + dat.) (1†)

in the presence of ἐν (prep. + dat.) (1)

in the world ποτέ (enclitic adv.) (5†)

in this way οὕτω(ς) (adv.) (4); ὧδε (adv.) (4)

in (time of) peace ἐπὶ εἰρήνης (4†)

(engaged) in war ἐπὶ πολέμου (4†)

inclination γνώμη, γνώμης, ἡ (1)

indeed *confirming,* γάρ (postpositive conj.) (3); δή (postpositive particle) (4); *emphasizes,* γε (enclitic particle) (5)

injure ἀδικέω, ἀδικήσω, ἠδίκησα, ἠδίκηκα, ἠδίκημαι, ἠδικήθην (4)

insolence ὕβρις, ὕβρεως, ἡ (7)

intelligence φρόνησις, φρονήσεως, ἡ (9)

intend μέλλω, μελλήσω, ἐμέλλησα, ——, ——, —— (+ inf.) (3)

into εἰς, ἐς (prep. + acc.) (1)

island νῆσος, νήσου, ἡ (1)

it αὐτοῦ, αὐτῆς, αὐτοῦ (6)

it is necessary δεῖ, δεήσει, ἐδέησε(ν), ——, ——, —— (impersonal verb) (5); χρή, χρῆσται, ——, ——, ——, —— (impersonal verb) (8)

it is possible *used impersonally in 3rd person sing.,* εἰμί, ἔσομαι, ——, ——, ——, —— (5)

journey ὁδός, ὁδοῦ, ἡ (1)

judgment γνώμη, γνώμης, ἡ (1)

just δίκαιος, δικαίᾱ, δίκαιον (2)

just as ὥσπερ (conj.) (6)

justice δίκη, δίκης, ἡ (1); δικαιοσύνη, δικαιοσύνης, ἡ (9)

justly σὺν δίκη (1†)

keep ἄγω, ἄξω, ἤγαγον, ἦχα, ἦγμαι, ἤχθην (5)

kill κτείνω, κτενῶ, ἔκτεινα, ——, ——, —— (8); ἀποκτείνω, ἀποκτενῶ, ἀπέκτεινα, ἀπέκτονα, ——, —— (8)

kind γένος, γένους, τό (7)

know οἶδα, εἴσομαι, ——, ——, ——, —— (9)

labor πόνος, πόνου, ὁ (3)

Lacedaemonian Λακεδαιμόνιος, Λακεδαιμονίᾱ, Λακεδαιμόνιον (2)

Lacedaemonians Λακεδαιμόνιοι, Λακεδαιμονίων, οἱ (2)

land χώρᾱ, χώρᾱς, ἡ (1); γαῖα, γαίᾱς, ἡ (3); γῆ, γῆς, ἡ (3)

large μακρός, μακρά, μακρόν (8)

latter οὗτος, αὕτη, τοῦτο (4†)

law νόμος, νόμου, ὁ (1)

lead ἄγω, ἄξω, ἤγαγον, ἦχα, ἦγμαι, ἤχθην (5)

learn μανθάνω, μαθήσομαι, ἔμαθον, μεμάθηκα, ——, —— (5)

life βίος, βίου, ὁ (4)

life force ψῡχή, ψῡχῆς, ἡ (1)

like φιλέω, φιλήσω, ἐφίλησα, πεφίληκα, πεφίλημαι, ἐφιλήθην (4)

be likely μέλλω, μελλήσω, ἐμέλλησα, ——, ——, —— (+ inf.) (3)

lines (of verse) ἔπη, ἐπῶν, τά (7)

listen (to) ἀκούω, ἀκούσομαι, ἤκουσα, ἀκήκοα, ——, ἠκούσθην (5)

little ὀλίγος, ὀλίγη, ὀλίγον (4)

a little (σ)μῑκρόν (9†)

live ζάω, ζήσω, ——, ——, ——, —— (8)

livelihood βίος, βίου, ὁ (4)

living being ζῷον, ζῴου, τό (1)

long μακρός, μακρά, μακρόν (8)

lord δεσπότης, δεσπότου, ὁ (6)

love ἔρως, ἔρωτος, ὁ (5); φιλέω, φιλήσω, ἐφίλησα, πεφίληκα, πεφίλημαι, ἐφιλήθην (4)

loved φίλος, φίλη, φίλον (2)

loved one φίλος, φίλου, ὁ (2); φίλη, φίλης, ἡ (2)

loving φίλος, φίλη, φίλον (2)

magistrate ἄρχων, ἄρχοντος, ὁ (5)

majority *preceded by an article (whether modifying a noun or used substantively),* πολύς, πολλή, πολύ (4†)

make *active or middle,* ποιέω, ποιήσω, ἐποίησα, πεποίηκα, πεποίημαι, ἐποιήθην (4)

     to make a beginning ἀρχὴν ποιεῖσθαι (4†)

     to make a plan βουλὴν ποιεῖσθαι (4†)

     to make words λόγους ποιεῖσθαι (4†)

make clear δηλόω, δηλώσω, ἐδήλωσα, δεδήλωκα, δεδήλωμαι, ἐδηλώθην (4)

make war (upon) πολεμέω, πολεμήσω, ἐπολέμησα, πεπολέμηκα, ——, ἐπολεμήθην (+ dat.) (4)

maker ποιητής, ποιητοῦ, ὁ (2)

man ἄνθρωπος, ἀνθρώπου, ὁ (1); ἀνήρ, ἀνδρός, ὁ (6)

manage *trans.,* πράττω, πράξω, ἔπρᾱξα, πέπρᾱχα (trans.)/πέπρᾱγα (intrans.), πέπρᾱγμαι, ἐπράχθην (7)

manner τρόπος, τρόπου, ὁ (9)

many πολύς, πολλή, πολύ (4)

many times πολλάκις (adv.) (3); (τὰ) πολλά (9†)

marketplace ἀγορά, ἀγορᾶς, ἡ (1)

marry *middle,* ἄγω, ἄξω, ἤγαγον, ἦχα, ἦγμαι, ἤχθην (5)

marvelous δεινός, δεινή, δεινόν (2)

master δεσπότης, δεσπότου, ὁ (6)

matter χρῆμα, χρήματος, τό (5); πρᾶγμα, πράγματος, τό (7)

me ἐγώ, ἐμοῦ/μου (6)

Melpomene Μελπομένη, Μελπομένης, ἡ (§59)

mind *sing. or pl.,* φρήν, φρενός, ἡ (5); νοῦς, νοῦ, ὁ (7)

miserable ἄθλιος, ἀθλίᾱ, ἄθλιον (9)

misfortune συμφορά, συμφορᾶς, ἡ (1)

moderate σώφρων, σῶφρον (9)

moderation σωφροσύνη, σωφροσύνης, ἡ (9)

money χρήματα, χρημάτων, τά (5)

mortal βροτός, βροτοῦ, ὁ (4); θνητός, θνητή, θνητόν (5)

mother μήτηρ, μητρός, ἡ (7)

much πολύς, πολλή, πολύ (4); (adv.) (τὸ) πολύ (9†); (τὰ) πολλά (9†)

of much value περὶ πολλοῦ (4†)

multitude πλῆθος, πλήθους, τό (8)

Muse Μοῦσα, Μούσης, ἡ (§59)

must δεῖ, δεήσει, ἐδέησε(ν), ——, ——, —— (impersonal verb) (5)

my ἐμός, ἐμή, ἐμόν (6)

nature φύσις, φύσεως, ἡ (7)

near πρός (prep. + dat.) (3); παρά (prep. + dat.) (5)

be near πάρειμι, παρέσομαι, ——, ——, ——, —— (7)

necessity ἀνάγκη, ἀνάγκης, ἡ (5)

neither ... nor ... οὔτε/μήτε ... οὔτε/ μήτε ... (6)

never οὔ ποτε, οὔποτε/μή ποτε, μήποτε (5); οὐδέποτε/μηδέποτε (adv.) (7)

new νέος, νέα, νέον (4)

no οὐδείς, οὐδεμία, οὐδέν/μηδείς, μηδεμία, μηδέν (9)

no, on the contrary *in corrections,* μὲν οὖν (particle combination) (6)

no longer οὐκέτι/μηκέτι (adv.) (8)

no one οὐδείς, οὐδεμία, οὐδέν/μηδείς, μηδεμία, μηδέν (9)

noble καλός, καλή, καλόν (2)

non-Greek βάρβαρος, βάρβαρον (5)

nor οὐδέ/μηδέ (conj.) (7)

nor ever οὐδέποτε/μηδέποτε (conj.) (7)

not οὐ, οὐκ, οὐχ (adv.) (2); μή (adv.) (2)

not any οὐδείς, οὐδεμία, οὐδέν/μηδείς, μηδεμία, μηδέν (adj.) (9)

not at all οὐ πάνυ (8); οὐδέν/μηδέν (9⁺)

not even οὐδέ/μηδέ (adv.) (7)

not ever yet οὐπώποτε/μηπώποτε (9⁺); οὐδεπώποτε/μηδεπώποτε (9⁺)

not only ... but also ... οὐ/μὴ μόνον ... ἀλλὰ καὶ ... (2)

not yet οὔπω/μήπω (adv.) (9⁺)

not yet at any time οὐπώποτε/μηπώποτε (9⁺); οὐδεπώποτε/μηδεπώποτε (9⁺)

nothing οὐδείς, οὐδεμία, οὐδέν/μηδείς, μηδεμία, μηδέν (9)

now νῦν (adv.) (3); (τὸ)(τὰ) νῦν (9⁺)

O ὦ (interj.) (1)

obey *middle,* πείθω, πείσω, ἔπεισα, πέπεικα, πέπεισμαι, ἐπείσθην (+ dat.) (3)

occupy ἔχω, ἕξω/σχήσω, ἔσχον, ἔσχηκα, -έσχημαι, —— (4)

of an enemy πολέμιος, πολεμίᾱ, πολέμιον (4)

of course δή (postpositive particle) (4)

of much value περὶ πολλοῦ (4⁺)

(political) office ἀρχή, ἀρχῆς, ἡ (2⁺)

often πολλάκις (adv.) (3); (τὰ) πολλά (9⁺)

old παλαιός, παλαιά, παλαιόν (8)

on ἐν (prep. + dat.) (1); ἐπί (prep. + gen.) (4); ἐπί (prep. + dat.) (4)

on account of διά (prep. + acc.) (2)

on behalf of ὑπέρ (prep. + gen.) (6)

on condition of ἐπί (prep. + dat.) (4)

no, on the contrary *in corrections,* μὲν οὖν (particle combination) (6)

on the one hand μέν (postpositive particle) (3)
on the one hand ... , on the other hand ... μέν ... , δέ ... (3)

one εἷς, μία, ἕν (numerical adj.) (9)

one another ——, ἀλλήλων (reciprocal pronoun) (8)

only μόνος, μόνη, μόνον (2); μόνον (adv.) (2)

openly εἰς/ἐς κοινόν (3⁺)

opinion γνώμη, γνώμης, ἡ (1); δόξα, δόξης, ἡ (2)

opposing ἐναντίος, ἐναντίᾱ, ἐναντίον (+ gen. or dat.) (8)

opposite ἐναντίος, ἐναντίᾱ, ἐναντίον (+ gen. or dat.) (8)

or ἤ (conj.) (2)

orator ῥήτωρ, ῥήτορος, ὁ (5)

other ἄλλος, ἄλλη, ἄλλο (5)

ought χρή, χρῆσται, ——, ——, ——, —— (impersonal verb) (8)

our ἡμέτερος, ἡμετέρᾱ, ἡμέτερον (6)

(out) from ἐκ, ἐξ (prep. + gen.) (1)

out of ἐκ, ἐξ (prep. + gen.) (1)

over ὑπέρ (prep. + gen.) (6)

pain λύπη, λύπης, ἡ (8)

passion ἔρως, ἔρωτος, ὁ (5); πάθος, πάθους, τό (7)

path ὁδός, ὁδοῦ, ἡ (1)

to pay attention νοῦν/γνώμην προσέχειν (7)

peace εἰρήνη, εἰρήνης, ἡ (1)
    in (time of) peace ἐπὶ εἰρήνης (4†)

(the) people δῆμος, δήμου, ὁ (2)

perhaps ἴσως (adv.) (8)

persuade πείθω, πείσω, ἔπεισα, πέπεικα, πέπεισμαι, ἐπείσθην (3)

Phoebus Φοῖβος, Φοίβου, ὁ (§59)

plain σαφής, σαφές (7)

plan βουλή, βουλῆς, ἡ (1)
    to plan βουλὴν ποιεῖσθαι (4†)

pleasure ἡδονή, ἡδονῆς, ἡ (8)

poet ποιητής, ποιητοῦ, ὁ (2)

political office ἀρχή, ἀρχῆς, ἡ (2†)

Polymnia Πολύμνια, Πολυμνίας, ἡ (§59)

Poseidon Ποσειδῶν, Ποσειδῶνος, ὁ (voc. = Πόσειδον) (§59)

power δύναμις, δυνάμεως, ἡ (7); τέλος, τέλους, τό (9)

(supreme) power ἀρχή, ἀρχῆς, ἡ (2)

practically ὡς ἔπος εἰπεῖν (7)

practice trans., πράττω, πράξω, ἔπραξα, πέπρᾱχα (trans.)/πέπρᾱγα (intrans.), πέπρᾱγμαι, ἐπράχθην (7)

be present ἥκω, ἥξω, ——, ——, ——, —— (5); πάρειμι, παρέσομαι, ——, ——, ——, —— (7)

presently (τὸ)(τά) νῦν (9†)

prevail (over) νῑκάω, νῑκήσω, ἐνίκησα, νενίκηκα, νενίκημαι, ἐνῑκήθην (4)

Priam Πρίαμος, Πριάμου, ὁ (1)

property χρήματα, χρημάτων, τά (5)

prudent σώφρων, σῶφρον (9)

public κοινός, κοινή, κοινόν (3)

public affairs κοινά, κοινῶν, τά (3)

public speaker ῥήτωρ, ῥήτορος, ὁ (5)

public treasury κοινά, κοινῶν, τά (3)

publicly εἰς/ἐς κοινόν (3†)

to exact punishment δίκην λαμβάνειν (9)

purpose τέλος, τέλους, τό (9)

quarrel πολεμέω, πολεμήσω, ἐπολέμησα, πεπολέμηκα, ——, ἐπολεμήθην (4)

(quite) all ἅπᾱς, ἅπᾱσα, ἅπαν (6)

race γένος, γένους, τό (7)

be ready πάρειμι, παρέσομαι, ——, ——, ——, —— (7)

real ἀληθής, ἀληθές (7)

really ὄντως (adv.) (7); ὡς ἀληθῶς (7†)

receive δέχομαι, δέξομαι, ἐδεξάμην, ——, δέδεγμαι, —— (6); λαμβάνω, λήψομαι, ἔλαβον, εἴληφα, εἴλημμαι, ἐλήφθην (9)

recount λέγω, λέξω, ἔλεξα/εἶπον, ——, λέλεγμαι, ἐλέχθην (3)

regarding εἰς, ἐς (prep. + acc.) (1)

rejoice (in) χαίρω, χαιρήσω, ——, κεχάρηκα, ——, ἐχάρην (7)

remain μένω, μενῶ, ἔμεινα, μεμένηκα, ——, —— (9)

reply ὑπολαμβάνω, ὑπολήψομαι, ὑπέλαβον, ὑπείληφα, ὑπείλημμαι, ὑπελήφθην (9)

reputation δόξα, δόξης, ἡ (2)

require ἀξιόω, ἀξιώσω, ἠξίωσα, ἠξίωκα, ἠξίωμαι, ἠξιώθην (4)

responsibility αἰτίᾱ, αἰτίᾱς, ἡ (2)

(the) rest (of) in the attributive position, ἄλλος, ἄλλη, ἄλλο (5)

resulting from ἐκ, ἐξ (prep. + gen.) (1)

reveal δηλόω, δηλώσω, ἐδήλωσα, δεδήλωκα, δεδήλωμαι, ἐδηλώθην (4)

rhetor ῥήτωρ, ῥήτορος, ὁ (5)

right δίκαιος, δικαίᾱ, δίκαιον (2)

road ὁδός, ὁδοῦ, ἡ (1)

ruin διαφθείρω, διαφθερῶ, διέφθειρα, διέφθαρκα/διέφθορα, διέφθαρμαι, διεφθάρην (9)

rule ἀρχή, ἀρχῆς, ἡ (2); ἄρχω, ἄρξω, ἦρξα, ἦρχα, ἦργμαι, ἤρχθην (+ gen.) (3)

ruler ἄρχων, ἄρχοντος, ὁ (5)

safety σωτηρίᾱ, σωτηρίᾱς, ἡ (8)

same αὐτός, αὐτή, αὐτό (6)

say λέγω, λέξω, ἔλεξα/εἶπον, ——,
    λέλεγμαι, ἐλέχθην (3); ——, ἐρῶ,
    ——, εἴρηκα, εἴρημαι, ἐρρήθην (8);
    *φάσκω, ——, ——, ——, ——,
    —— (8); φημί, φήσω, ἔφησα, ——,
    ——, —— (8)

sea θάλαττα, θαλάττης, ἡ (2)

see ὁράω, ὄψομαι, εἶδον, ἑώρᾱκα/ἑόρᾱκα,
    ἑώρᾱμαι/ὦμμαι, ὤφθην (6)

seize λαμβάνω, λήψομαι, ἔλαβον, εἴληφα,
    εἴλημμαι, ἐλήφθην (9)

-self αὐτός, αὐτή, αὐτό (6)

send πέμπω, πέμψω, ἔπεμψα, πέπομφα,
    πέπεμμαι, ἐπέμφθην (3)

send away ἀποπέμπω, ἀποπέμψω, ἀπέπεμψα,
    ἀποπέπομφα, ἀποπέπεμμαι, ἀπεπέμφθην
    (7)

send away from oneself *middle,* ἀποπέμπω,
    ἀποπέμψω, ἀπέπεμψα, ἀποπέπομφα,
    ἀποπέπεμμαι, ἀπεπέμφθην (7)

sense νοῦς, νοῦ, ὁ (7)

severe χαλεπός, χαλεπή, χαλεπόν (4)

shameful αἰσχρός, αἰσχρά, αἰσχρόν (3)

shared (with) κοινός, κοινή, κοινόν (+ gen.
    or dat.) (3)

show δηλόω, δηλώσω, ἐδήλωσα, δεδήλωκα,
    δεδήλωμαι, ἐδηλώθην (4)

skill τέχνη, τέχνης, ἡ (5)

sky οὐρανός, οὐρανοῦ, ὁ (3)

slave παῖς, παιδός, ὁ or ἡ (5); δοῦλος,
    δούλου, ὁ (6)

small ὀλίγος, ὀλίγη, ὀλίγον (4); (σ)μῑκρός,
    (σ)μῑκρά, (σ)μῑκρόν (8)

so οὕτω(ς) (adv.) (4); ὧδε (adv.) (4)

so then *in transitions to a new subject,* μὲν
    οὖν (particle combination) (6†); ἄρα
    (postpositive particle) (9)

so to speak ὡς ἔπος εἰπεῖν (7)

Socrates Σωκράτης, Σωκράτους, ὁ (7)

soldier στρατιώτης, στρατιώτου, ὁ (8)

some τις, τι (indef. adj.) (9)

somehow πως (enclitic adv.) (5)

someone τις, τι (indef. pron.) (9)

something τις, τι (indef. pron.) (9)

sometimes . . . , sometimes . . . ποτέ . . . ,
    ποτέ . . . (5)

somewhere που (enclitic adv.) (7)

son υἱός, υἱοῦ, ὁ (4)

son of Atreus Ἀτρείδης, Ἀτρείδου, ὁ (2)

sort γένος, γένους, τό (7)

soul ψῡχή, ψῡχῆς, ἡ (1)

Spartan Λακεδαιμόνιος, Λακεδαιμονίᾱ,
    Λακεδαιμόνιον (2)

Spartans Λακεδαιμόνιοι, Λακεδαιμονίων,
    οἱ (2)

speak (of) λέγω, λέξω, ἔλεξα/εἶπον, ——,
    λέλεγμαι, ἐλέχθην (3); ——, ἐρῶ, ——,
    εἴρηκα, εἴρημαι, ἐρρήθην (8)
    to speak λόγους ποιεῖσθαι (4†)

speech λόγος, λόγου, ὁ (1)

spirit γνώμη, γνώμης, ἡ (1); δαίμων,
    δαίμονος, ὁ or ἡ (5)

state κοινόν, κοινοῦ, τό (3†)

stay μένω, μενῶ, ἔμεινα, μεμένηκα, ——,
    —— (9)

still ἔτι (adv.) (8)

stop (intrans.) *middle,* παύω, παύσω, ἔπαυσα,
    πέπαυκα, πέπαυμαι, ἐπαύθην (3)

stop (trans.) παύω, παύσω, ἔπαυσα, πέπαυκα,
    πέπαυμαι, ἐπαύθην (3)

straight ὀρθός, ὀρθή, ὀρθόν (6)

strange δεινός, δεινή, δεινόν (2)

stranger ξένος, ξένου, ὁ (3)

struggle ἀγών, ἀγῶνος, ὁ (6)

student μαθητής, μαθητοῦ, ὁ (5)

stupidity ἀμαθίᾱ, ἀμαθίᾱς, ἡ (9)

suffer πάσχω, πείσομαι, ἔπαθον, πέπονθα,
    ——, —— (7)

suffering πόνος, πόνου, ὁ (3); πάθος,
    πάθους, τό (7)

suppose οἴομαι/οἶμαι, οἰήσομαι, ——, ——,
    ——, ᾠήθην (8); ὑπολαμβάνω,
    ὑπολήψομαι, ὑπέλαβον, ὑπείληφα,
    ὑπείλημμαι, ὑπελήφθην (9)

supreme power ἀρχή, ἀρχῆς, ἡ (2)

sure σαφής, σαφές (7)

surely τοι (enclitic particle) (5)

take λαμβάνω, λήψομαι, ἔλαβον, εἴληφα, εἴλημμαι, ἐλήφθην (9)

take hold (of) *middle,* λαμβάνω, λήψομαι, ἔλαβον, εἴληφα, εἴλημμαι, ἐλήφθην (+ gen.) (9)

take up ὑπολαμβάνω, ὑπολήψομαι, ὑπέλαβον, ὑπείληφα, ὑπείλημμαι, ὑπελήφθην (9)

talk (with) διαλέγομαι, διαλέξομαι, ——, ——, διείλεγμαι, διελέχθην (+ dat.) (7)

tall μακρός, μακρά, μακρόν (8)

task ἔργον, ἔργου, τό (1)

teach διδάσκω, διδάξω, ἐδίδαξα, δεδίδαχα, δεδίδαγμαι, ἐδιδάχθην (3)

    cause to be taught *middle,* διδάσκω, διδάξω, ἐδίδαξα, δεδίδαχα, δεδίδαγμαι, ἐδιδάχθην (3)

teacher διδάσκαλος, διδασκάλου, ὁ (5)

tell (of) λέγω, λέξω, ἔλεξα/εἶπον, ——, λέλεγμαι, ἐλέχθην (3); ——, ἐρῶ, ——, εἴρηκα, εἴρημαι, ἐρρήθην (8)

Terpsichore Τερψιχόρᾱ, Τερψιχόρᾱς, ἡ (§59)

terrible δεινός, δεινή, δεινόν (2)

Thalia Θάλεια, Θαλείᾱς, ἡ (§59)

that ἐκεῖνος, ἐκείνη, ἐκεῖνο (demonstr. adj./pron.) (4); ὅς, ἥ, ὅ (rel. pron.) (5); ὅτι (conj.) (6); ὡς (proclitic conj.) (6)

the ὁ, ἡ, τό (article) (1)

them αὐτοῦ, αὐτῆς, αὐτοῦ (6)

then οὖν (postpositive conj.) (6); τότε (adv.) (7)

    (so) then ἄρα (postpositive particle) (9)

    so then *in transitions to a new subject,* μὲν οὖν (particle combination) (6[†])

there ἐκεῖ (adv.) (9)

there is need δεῖ, δεήσει, ἐδέησε(ν), ——, ——, —— (impersonal verb) (+ gen.) (5)

therefore οὖν (postpositive conj.) (6); *in transitions to a new subject,* μὲν οὖν (particle combination) (6); ἄρα (postpositive particle) (9)

these οὗτοι, αὗται, ταῦτα (demonstr. adj./pron.) (2); οἵδε, αἵδε, τάδε (demonstr. adj./pron.) (4)

thing χρῆμα, χρήματος, τό (5); πρᾶγμα, πράγματος, τό (7)

think οἴομαι/οἶμαι, οἰήσομαι, ——, ——, ——, ᾠήθην (8)

think (it) right ἀξιόω, ἀξιώσω, ἠξίωσα, ἠξίωκα, ἠξίωμαι, ἠξιώθην (4)

think worthy ἀξιόω, ἀξιώσω, ἠξίωσα, ἠξίωκα, ἠξίωμαι, ἠξιώθην (4)

this οὗτος, αὕτη, τοῦτο (demonstr. adj./pron.) (2); ὅδε, ἥδε, τόδε (demonstr. adj./pron.) (4)

those ἐκεῖνοι, ἐκεῖναι, ἐκεῖνα (demonstr. adj./pron.) (4)

thought νοῦς, νοῦ, ὁ (7)

through διά (prep. + gen.) (2)

through to the end, διὰ τέλους (9)

throughout κατά (prep. + acc.) (5)

thus οὕτω(ς) (adv.) (4)

in time of peace ἐπὶ εἰρήνης (4[†])

to εἰς, ἐς (prep. + acc.) (1); ἐπί (prep. + acc.) (4)

to (the side of) παρά (prep. + acc.) (5)

to a great extent ἐπὶ (τὸ) πολύ (4[†]); μέγα (9[†])

to somewhere ποι (enclitic adv.) (7)

to the end ἐς τέλος (9[†])

to where ποῖ (interrog. adv.) (6)

toil πόνος, πόνου, ὁ (3)

tool ὅπλον, ὅπλου, τό (1)

toward εἰς, ἐς (prep. + acc.) (1); πρός (prep. + acc.) (3)

treat ποιέω, ποιήσω, ἐποίησα, πεποίηκα, πεποίημαι, ἐποιήθην (+ adv.) (4†)

troubles πράγματα, πραγμάτων, τά (7)

true ἀληθής, ἀληθές (7)

truly ὡς ἀληθῶς (7†)

truth ἀλήθεια, ἀληθείᾱς, ἡ (2)

truthful ἀληθής, ἀληθές (7)

turn to προσέχω, προσέξω, προσέσχον, προσέσχηκα, ——, —— (7)

ugly αἰσχρός, αἰσχρά, αἰσχρόν (3)

unclear ἄδηλος, ἄδηλον (6)

under ὑπό (prep. + gen.) (3); ὑπό (prep. + dat.) (3); ὑπό (prep. + acc.) (3)

under the power of ὑπό (prep. + dat.) (3)

understand μανθάνω, μαθήσομαι, ἔμαθον, μεμάθηκα, ——, —— (5); λαμβάνω, λήψομαι, ἔλαβον, εἴληφα, εἴλημμαι, ἐλήφθην (9)

understanding φρόνησις, φρονήσεως, ἡ (9)

unjust ἄδικος, ἄδικον (2)

upon ἐπί (prep. + gen.) (4)

Urania Οὐρανίᾱ, Οὐρανίᾱς, ἡ (§59)

us ἡμεῖς, ἡμῶν (6)

valor ἀρετή, ἀρετῆς, ἡ (4)

value *middle,* τῑμάω, τῑμήσω, ἐτίμησα, τετίμηκα, τετίμημαι, ἐτῑμήθην (4)

very περ (enclitic particle) (5); αὐτός, αὐτή, αὐτό (6)

very (much) πάνυ (adv.) (8)

victory νίκη, νίκης, ἡ (4)

(wanton) violence ὕβρις, ὕβρεως, ἡ (7)

virtue ἀρετή, ἀρετῆς, ἡ (4)

wall τεῖχος, τείχους, τό (8)

want βούλομαι, βουλήσομαι, ——, ——, βεβούλημαι, ἐβουλήθην (6)

wanton violence ὕβρις, ὕβρεως, ἡ (7)

war πόλεμος, πολέμου, ὁ (1)

    be at war (with) πολεμέω, πολεμήσω, ἐπολέμησα, πεπολέμηκα, ——, ἐπολεμήθην (+ dat.) (4)

    (engaged) in war ἐπὶ πολέμου (4†)

    have war made upon one *passive,* πολεμέω, πολεμήσω, ἐπολέμησα, πεπολέμηκα, ——, ἐπολεμήθην (4)

    make war (upon) πολεμέω, πολεμήσω, ἐπολέμησα, πεπολέμηκα, ——, ἐπολεμήθην (+ dat.) (4)

way ὁδός, ὁδοῦ, ἡ (1); τρόπος, τρόπου, ὁ (9)

we ἡμεῖς, ἡμῶν (6)

wealth πλοῦτος, πλούτου, ὁ (7)

weapons ὅπλα, ὅπλων, τά (1)

welcome δέχομαι, δέξομαι, ἐδεξάμην, ——, δέδεγμαι, —— (6)

well εὖ (adv.) (3)

well, . . . *in narrative transitions and responses in dialogue,* ἀλλά (conj.) (2†)

what τίς, τί (interrog. pron./adj.) (9)

when πότε (interrog. adv.) (3)

where ποῦ (interrog. adv.) (6)

which ὅς, ἥ, ὅ (rel. pron.) (5); τίς, τί (interrog. adj.) (9)

who ὅς, ἥ, ὅ (rel. pron.) (5); τίς, τί (interrog. pron.) (9)

whole πᾶς, πᾶσα, πᾶν (6); ἅπᾱς, ἅπᾱσα, ἅπαν (6)

whom ὅς, ἥ, ὅ (rel. pron.) (5)

whose ὅς, ἥ, ὅ (rel. pron.) (5)

why τί (9†)

wicked πονηρός, πονηρά, πονηρόν (4)

wife γυνή, γυναικός, ἡ (7)

will βουλή, βουλῆς, ἡ (1)

be willing ἐθέλω/θέλω, ἐθελήσω, ἠθέλησα, ἠθέληκα, ——, —— (3)

win νῑκάω, νῑκήσω, ἐνίκησα, νενίκηκα, νενίκημαι, ἐνῑκήθην (4); *middle,* φέρω, οἴσω, ἤνεγκα/ἤνεγκον, ἐνήνοχα, ἐνήνεγμαι, ἠνέχθην (9)

wisdom σοφίᾱ, σοφίᾱς, ἡ (1)

wise σοφός, σοφή, σοφόν (2)

wish ἐθέλω/θέλω, ἐθελήσω, ἠθέλησα, ἠθέληκα, ——, —— (3); βούλομαι, βουλήσομαι, ——, ——, βεβούλημαι, ἐβουλήθην (6)

(along) with σύν/ξύν (prep. + dat.) (1); μετά (prep. + gen.) (4)

with a view to εἰς, ἐς (prep. + acc.) (1)

with difficulty χαλεπῶς (adv.) (4)

with the aid of σύν/ξύν (prep. + dat.) (1); μετά (prep. + gen.) (4)

without ἄνευ (prep. + gen.) (6)

wits *sing. or pl.*, φρήν, φρενός, ἡ (5)

woman γυνή, γυναικός, ἡ (7)

word λόγος, λόγου, ὁ (1); ἔπος, ἔπους, τό (7)

work ἔργον, ἔργου, τό (1)

worthless πονηρός, πονηρά, πονηρόν (4)

wretched ἄθλιος, ἀθλίᾱ, ἄθλιον (9)

wrong ἀδικέω, ἀδικήσω, ἠδίκησα, ἠδίκηκα, ἠδίκημαι, ἠδικήθην (4)

(yes,) by *expresses strong affirmation*, νή (particle + acc.) (5)

yet ἔτι (adv.) (8); πω (enclitic adv.) (9)

you (sing.) σύ, σοῦ/σου (6)

you (pl.) ὑμεῖς, ὑμῶν (6)

you know τοι (enclitic particle) (5)

young νέος, νέᾱ, νέον (4)

young man νεᾱνίᾱς, νεᾱνίου, ὁ (2)

your (sing.) σός, σή, σόν (6)

your (pl.) ὑμέτερος, ὑμετέρᾱ, ὑμέτερον (6)

Zeus Ζεύς, Διός, ὁ (5)

PRINCIPAL PARTS OF VERBS

When no meanings are offered for a voice of a verb, the verb *never* appears in that voice. An R indicates that a verb *rarely* appears in that voice. Only commonly occurring forms should be included in a synopsis.

Verb	Active	Middle	Passive
ἄγω, ἄξω, ἤγαγον, ἦχα, ἦγμαι, ἤχθην (5)	lead, bring; keep	carry away with oneself; marry	be led, be brought
ἀδικέω, ἀδικήσω, ἠδίκησα, ἠδίκηκα, ἠδίκημαι, ἠδικήθην (4)	(do) wrong (to); injure		be wronged; be injured
ἀκούω, ἀκούσομαι, ἤκουσα, ἀκήκοα, ——, ἠκούσθην (5)	listen (to), hear (of)	(*future only*) listen (to), hear (of)	be listened to, be heard
ἀξιόω, ἀξιώσω, ἠξίωσα, ἠξίωκα, ἠξίωμαι, ἠξιώθην (4)	think worthy; think (it) right; expect, require	R	be thought worthy
ἀποθνῄσκω, ἀποθανοῦμαι, ἀπέθανον, τέθνηκα, ——, —— (8)	die; *perfect*, be dead	(*future only*) die	
ἀποκτείνω, ἀποκτενῶ, ἀπέκτεινα, ἀπέκτονα, ——, —— (8)	kill		
ἀποπέμπω, ἀποπέμψω, ἀπέπεμψα, ἀποπέπομφα, ἀποπέπεμμαι, ἀπεπέμφθην (7)	send away	send away from oneself	be sent away
ἄρχω, ἄρξω, ἦρξα, ἦρχα, ἦργμαι, ἤρχθην (3)	rule (+ gen.)	begin (+ gen.)	be ruled
βούλομαι, βουλήσομαι, ——, ——, βεβούλημαι, ἐβουλήθην (6)		want, wish	(*aorist only*) want, wish
γίγνομαι, γενήσομαι, ἐγενόμην, γέγονα, γεγένημαι, —— (6)	(*perfect only*) become; happen; arise, be born	become; happen; arise, be born	
δεῖ, δεήσει, ἐδέησε(ν), ——, ——, —— (5)	it is necessary, must; there is a need (+ gen.)		

Verb	Active	Middle	Passive
δέχομαι, δέξομαι, ἐδεξάμην, —, δέδεγμαι, — (6)		accept, receive; welcome	R
δηλόω, δηλώσω, ἐδήλωσα, δεδήλωκα, δεδήλωμαι, ἐδηλώθην (4)	show, make clear, reveal		
διαλέγομαι, διαλέξομαι, —, —, διείλεγμαι, διελέχθην (7)		talk (with), converse (with), discuss (with) (+ dat.)	(aorist only) talk (with), converse (with), discuss (with) (+ dat.)
διαφθείρω, διαφθερῶ, διέφθειρα, διέφθορα/διέφθαρκα/διέφθορα, διέφθαρμαι, διεφθάρην (9)	destroy (utterly); corrupt, ruin		be destroyed (utterly); be corrupted, be ruined
διδάσκω, διδάξω, ἐδίδαξα, δεδίδαχα, δεδίδαγμαι, ἐδιδάχθην (3)	teach; explain	cause to be taught	be taught; be explained
ἐθέλω/θέλω, ἐθελήσω, ἠθέλησα, ἠθέληκα, —, — (3)	be willing, wish		
εἰμί, ἔσομαι, —, —, —, — (5)	be; exist; impers., it is possible	(future only) be; exist; impers., it is possible	
ἕπομαι, ἕψομαι, ἑσπόμην, —, —, — (9)		follow (+ dat.)	
ἔρχομαι, ἐλεύσομαι, ἦλθον, ἐλήλυθα, —, — (6)	go, come	go, come	
—, ἐρῶ, —, εἴρηκα, εἴρημαι, ἐρρήθην (8)	say, tell (of), speak (of)		be said, be spoken
ἔχω, ἕξω/σχήσω, ἔσχον, ἔσχηκα, -ἔσχημαι, — (4)	have, hold; inhabit, occupy; intrans., be able (+inf.); be (+ adv.)	hold on to, cling to	be held; be inhabited, be occupied
ζάω, ζήσω, —, —, —, — (8)	be alive, live		
ζηλόω, ζηλώσω, ἐζήλωσα, ἐζήλωκα, —, — (7)	emulate; envy		be deemed fortunate
ἥκω, ἥξω, —, —, —, — (5)	have come; be present		

Verb	Active	Middle (*future only*)	Passive
θνῄσκω, θανοῦμαι, ἔθανον, τέθνηκα, ——, —— (8)	die / *perfect*, be dead	die	
κτείνω, κτενῶ, ἔκτεινα, ——, ——, —— (8)	kill		
λαμβάνω, λήψομαι, ἔλαβον, εἴληφα, εἴλημμαι, ἐλήφθην (9)	take, seize; understand; receive	take hold (of) (+ gen.)	be taken, be seized; be understood; be received
λέγω, λέξω, ἔλεξα/εἶπον, ——, λέλεγμαι, ἐλέχθην (3)	say; speak (of), tell (of), recount; call	R	be said; be spoken, be recounted; be called
μανθάνω, μαθήσομαι, ἔμαθον, μεμάθηκα, ——, —— (5)	learn; understand	(*future only*) learn; understand	R
μάχομαι, μαχοῦμαι, ἐμαχεσάμην, ——, μεμάχημαι, —— (8)		fight (against) (+ dat.)	
μέλλω, μελλήσω, ἐμέλλησα, ——, ——, —— (3)	intend, be about, be likely		
μένω, μενῶ, ἔμεινα, μεμένηκα, ——, —— (9)	remain, stay; *trans.*, await		
νικάω, νικήσω, ἐνίκησα, νενίκηκα, νενίκημαι, ἐνικήθην (4)	conquer, defeat; prevail (over), win	R	be conquered, be defeated
οἶδα, εἴσομαι, ——, ——, ——, —— (9)	know	(*future only*) know	
οἴομαι/οἶμαι, οἰήσομαι, ——, ——, ——, ᾠήθην (8)		think, suppose, believe	(*aorist only*) think, suppose, believe
ὁράω, ὄψομαι, εἶδον, ἑώρακα/ἑόρακα, ἑώραμαι/ὦμμαι, ὤφθην (6)	see	R (*except in future*) see	be seen
πάρειμι, παρέσομαι, ——, ——, ——, —— (7)	be present, be near; be ready	(*future only*) be present, be near; be ready	

Verb	Active	Middle (*future only*)	Passive
πάσχω, πείσομαι, ἔπαθον, πέπονθα, —— (7)	suffer; experience	suffer; experience	
παύω, παύσω, ἔπαυσα, πέπαυκα, πέπαυμαι, ἐπαύθην (3)	stop (trans.)	stop (intrans.), cease	be stopped
πείθω, πείσω, ἔπεισα, πέπεικα, πέπεισμαι, ἐπείσθην (3)	persuade	obey; heed; believe (+ dat.)	be persuaded
πέμπω, πέμψω, ἔπεμψα, πέπομφα, πέπεμμαι, ἐπέμφθην (3)	send		be sent
ποιέω, ποιήσω, ἐποίησα, πεποίηκα, πεποίημαι, ἐποιήθην (4)	make; do	make; do; deem, consider	be made; be done
πολεμέω, πολεμήσω, ἐπολέμησα, πεπολέμηκα, ——, ἐπολεμήθην (4)	make war (upon), be at war (with) (+ dat.); quarrel; fight		have war made on (oneself), be treated as an enemy
πράττω, πράξω, ἔπραξα, πέπρᾱχα (trans.)/πέπρᾱγα (intrans.), πέπραγμαι, ἐπρᾱχθην (7)	do; bring about; practice; manage; *intrans, fare*	R	be done; be brought about; be practiced; be managed
προσέχω, προσέξω, προσέσχον, προσέσχηκα, ——, —— (7)	hold to; turn to, apply	R	R
τελευτάω, τελευτήσω, ἐτελεύτησα, τετελεύτηκα, ——, ἐτελευτήθην (4)	accomplish, end, finish; die		R
τιμάω, τιμήσω, ἐτίμησα, τετίμηκα, τετίμημαι, ἐτιμήθην (4)	honor	value, deem worthy	be honored; be deemed worthy
ὑπολαμβάνω, ὑπολήψομαι, ὑπέλαβον, ὑπείληφα, ὑπείλημμαι, ὑπελήφθην (9)	take up, reply; suppose	(*future only*) take up, reply; suppose	be taken up; be supposed
*φάσκω, ——, ——, ——, —— (8)	say, assert		
φέρω, οἴσω, ἤνεγκα/ἤνεγκον, ἐνήνοχα, ἐνήνεγμαι, ἠνέχθην (9)	bring, bear, carry; endure	carry away with oneself; win	be borne, be brought, be carried; be endured

Verb	Active	Middle (*future only*)	Passive
φεύγω, φεύξομαι, ἔφυγον, πέφευγα, ——, —— (9)	flee, avoid, escape	flee, avoid, escape	
φημί, φήσω, ἔφησα, ——, ——, —— (8)	say, assert	R	
φιλέω, φιλήσω, ἐφίλησα, πεφίληκα, πεφίλημαι, ἐφιλήθην (4)	love, like; be accustomed, be fond of (+ inf.)	R	be loved, be liked
χαίρω, χαιρήσω, ——, κεχάρηκα, ——, ἐχάρην (7)	rejoice (in), enjoy		(*aorist only*) rejoice (in), enjoy
χρή, χρῆσται, ——, ——, —— (8)	it is necessary, ought		

VERBS INTRODUCING
INDIRECT STATEMENT

	ὅτι/ὡς with a Finite Verb	Subject Accusative with an Infinitive	Subject Accusative with a Supplementary Participle
ἀκούω	x	x	x
δῆλόν ἐστι(ν)	x		
δηλόω	x	x	x
——, ἐρῶ	x	x	
λέγω	x	x	
μανθάνω	x		x
οἶδα	x	x	x
οἴομαι/οἶμαι		x	
ὁράω	x		x
πείθω	x	x	x
ὑπολαμβάνω	x	x	
φάσκω		x	
φημί		x	